Dynamics in Human and Primate Societies: Agent-Based Modeling of Social and Spatial Processes

DYNAMICS IN HUMAN AND PRIMATE SOCIETIES

Agent-Based Modeling of Social and Spatial Processes

Editors

Timothy A. Kohler

George J. Gumerman

Santa Fe Institute
Studies in the Sciences of Complexity

New York   Oxford
Oxford University Press
2000

Oxford University Press

Oxford   New York

Athens   Auckland   Bangkok   Bogotá   Buenos Aires   Calcutta
Cape Town   Chennai   Dar es Salaam   Delhi   Florence   Hong Kong   Istanbul
Karachi   Kuala Lumpur   Madrid   Melbourne   Mexico City   Mumbai
Nairobi   Paris   São Paulo   Singapore   Taipei   Tokyo   Toronto   Warsaw

and associated companies in
Berlin   Ibadan

Copyright © 2000 by Oxford University Press, Inc.

Published by Oxford University Press, Inc.
198 Madison Avenue, New York, New York 10016

Oxford is a registered trademark of Oxford University Press

Library of Congress Cataloging-in-Publication Data
Dynamics in human and primate societies : agent-based modeling of social
and spatial processes / [edited] by Timothy A. Kohler and George J. Gumerman.
p.   cm. — (Santa Fe Institute studies in the sciences of complexity)
Includes bibliographical references and index.
ISBN-13 978-0-19-513167-3; 978-0-19-513168-0 (pbk.)
ISBN 0-19-513167-3 (cloth); ISBN 0-19-513168-1 (pbk.)
1. Social evolution—Mathematical models.   2. Social evolution—Computer simulation
3. Social history—To 500—Mathematical models.   4. Social history—To 500—
Computer simulation.   5. Animal societies—Mathematical models.
6. Animal societies—Computer simulation.   7. Social behavior in animals—
Mathematical models.   8. Social behavior in animals—Computer simulation.
I. Kohler, Timothy A.   II. Gumerman, George J.   III. Series: Santa Fe Institute
studies in the sciences of complexity (Oxford University Press)
GN360.D89   2000
303.4'01'13—dc21   99-33379

5 7 9 8 6
Printed in the United States of America
on acid-free paper

About the Santa Fe Institute

The *Santa Fe Institute* (SFI) is a private, independent, multidisciplinary research and education center, founded in 1984. Since its founding, SFI has devoted itself to creating a new kind of scientific research community, pursuing emerging science. Operating as a small, visiting institution, SFI seeks to catalyze new collaborative, multidisciplinary projects that break down the barriers between the traditional disciplines, to spread its ideas and methodologies to other individuals, and to encourage the practical applications of its results.

All titles from the *Santa Fe Institute Studies in the Sciences of Complexity* series will carry this imprint which is based on a Mimbres pottery design (circa A.D. 950–1150), drawn by Betsy Jones. The design was selected because the radiating feathers are evocative of the out-reach of the Santa Fe Institute Program to many disciplines and institutions.

Contributors List

Robert L. Axtell, *Economic Studies, The Brookings Institution, 1775 Massachusetts Avenue, NW, Washington, DC 20036 and the Santa Fe Institute*

Irenaeus J. A. te Boekhorst, *University of Zurich, Department of Computer Science, Winterthurerstrasse 190, CH-8057 Zurich; e-mail: boekhors@ifi.unizh.ch*

Eric Carr, *Economic Systems and Operations Research, Department of Engineering, Stanford University, Palo Alto, CA 94305*

Jeffrey S. Dean, *Laboratory of Tree-Ring Research, P.O. Box 210058, University of Arizona, Tucson, AZ 85721-0058*

Jim Doran, *Department of Computer Science, University of Essex, Wivenhoe Park, Colchester, CO4 3SQ United Kingdom; e-mail: doraj@essex.ac.uk*

Joshua M. Epstein, *Economic Studies, The Brookings Institution, 1775 Massachusetts Avenue, NW, Washington, DC 20036 and the Santa Fe Institute*

Nigel Gilbert, *Department of Sociology, University of Surrey, Guildford, GU2 5XH, United Kingdom*

George J. Gumerman, *University of Arizona, Arizona State Museum, Building #26, Tucson, AZ 85721-0026*

Charlotte K. Hemelrijk, *University of Zurich, Department of Computer Science, Winterthurerstrasse 190, CH-8057 Zurich; e-mail: hemelrij@ifi.unizh.ch*

Timothy Kohler, *Washington State University, Department of Anthropology, College Hall, P.O. Box 644910, Pullman, WA 99164-4910 and the Santa Fe Institute; e-mail: tako@wsu.edu*

James Kresl, *Washington State University, Department of Anthropology, College Hall, P.O. Box 644910, Pullman, WA 99164-4910*

Mark Winter Lake, *Institute of Archaeology, University College London, 31-34 Gordon Square, London, WC1H 0PY*

J. Stephen Lansing, *University of Arizona, P.O. Box 210030, Tucson, AZ 85721*

Mark Lehner, *16 Hudson Street, Milton, MA 02186*

Stephen McCarroll, *University of California at San Francisco, 1350 Seventh Avenue, San Francisco, CA 94143*

Miles T. Parker, *The Brookings Institution, 1775 Massachusetts Avenue NW, Washington, DC 20036*

John W. Pepper, *University of Michigan, Museum of Zoology, Ann Arbor, MI 48109-1079*

Robert G. Reynolds, *Wayne State University, Department of Computer Science, 5143 Cass Avenue, Detroit, MI 48202*

Brian Skyrms, *University of California, Department of Philosophy, Irvine, CA 92697*

Cathy A. Small, *Northern Arizona University, Department of Anthropology, Box 15200, Flagstaff, AZ 86011*

Barbara Smuts, *University of Michigan, Museum of Zoology, Ann Arbor, MI 48109-1079*

Alan C. Swedlund, *University of Massachusetts at Amherst, Department of Anthropology, MA 01003*

Carla Van West, *Statistical Research Inc., 2500 N. Pantano, Suite 218, Tucson, AZ 31865*

Richard H. Wilshusen, *University of Colorado, Department of Anthropology, Boulder, CO 80309*

Henry T. Wright, *Museum of Anthropology, Ann Arbor, MI 48109-1079; e-mail: hwright@umich.edu*

Contents

Preface

The Santa Fe Institute (SFI) is interested in understanding evolving complex social, biological, and physical adaptive systems in a most general sense (see Cowan et al. 1994). Those of us at SFI interested in the evolution of social behavior have tended to focus on either small-scale societies or on specific aspects of more complex societies, such as the economy. The conference providing the genesis for this volume itself evolved from four previous efforts to understand and document the evolution of social and political complexity of the small-scale agricultural groups of the American Southwest.

The first of these was a workshop sponsored by the School of American Research, Santa Fe, held in 1983. The resulting volume (Cordell and Gumerman 1989) provided an overview of the Southwest by subareas. This volume emphasized periods of relative stasis that were punctuated by periods of rapid and similar changes area wide, which we called "hinge points." The second and third were sponsored jointly by the School and SFI and were a direct outgrowth of Murray Gell-Mann's interest in the prehistoric Southwest and his view that SFI's concepts and tools might be profitably used to understand evolving social complexity in the region. The second workshop, titled "The Organization and Evolution of Prehistoric Southwestern Society," emphasized evolutionary processes that crosscut locales and characterized the region (Gumerman 1994). Topics included environment and demography, land-use patterns, aggregation and abandonment, health and disease, and social and economic interaction. The third workshop followed a more typical SFI format (Gumerman and Gell-Mann 1994). The participants included not only archaeologists and ethnologists, but demographers, evolutionary biologists, computer modelers, and complexity theorists. Working groups focused, not only on the role of complexity theory and the prehistory of the Southwest, but also on the nature of archaeological explanation. The fourth workshop, held in 1992, proceeded logically from the others, focusing on "the way in which prehistoric Southwesterners made decisions and took steps to solve some of their everyday problems, and changed thereby the complexity of their economies, technologies, societies, and religious institutions" (Tainter and Tainter 1996:3).

The use of complexity theory has provided archaeologists with an expanded theoretical framework for understanding the past. Theoretical stances, such as classic systems theory, in some ways the precursor of complexity research (Miller 1965, Bertalanffy 1986), have provided productive ways of conceptualizing the evolutionary trajectory of preliterate societies, for example, by leading us to identify negative or positive feedback loops through which change is resisted or amplified.

Some of us at SFI felt, however, that there are aspects of the study of culture change as it is typically practiced that need to be modified. Narrative uses of theory, including concepts from complex adaptive system theory, have helped anthropologists understand how culture changes. But while such uses of these theories have helped in conceptualizing culture change in specific historical situations, they have not provided rigorous scientific explanations for cross-cultural processes of cultural evolution. New tools need to be developed and new structures for scholarly discourse need to be established to make significant advances in understanding social processes. Agent-based models are one of these tools, but there are certainly others, that have not as yet been used to address those questions that are our concern. SFI is a new and different structure for research that has provided an intellectual forum for making significant advances in understanding the essentials of human behavior. This structure needs to be reviewed, however, and perhaps modified to be more efficient in cross-disciplinary problem solving of these sorts. This volume reflects important changes in SFI's approach to understanding the human behavior. Contributors to the workshop and this volume include archaeologists who work with state-level societies, rather than only those focusing on the American Southwest. In addition, there are also ethnographers, primatologists, computer scientists, a sociologist, and a philosopher who as a group considerably expanded the range of our inquiry.

This volume grew out of a conference entitled "Understanding Small-Scale Societies Through Agent-Based Modeling" held at SFI in early December 1997. Funding was provided equally by grant CONF-217 to Tim Kohler and myself from the Wenner-Gren Foundation for Anthropological Research and from SFI. We precirculated a series of papers, including several by contributors to this volume, and asked all the authors to revise their papers in light of the often intense discussion that followed each presentation. We hope that the clarity of the cold winter sun of those December days shines through these chapters. We thank for their hard work each of the authors, Wenner-Gren and SFI for their support, and particularly Ellen Goldberg, President, SFI; Erica Jen, Vice President for Academic Affairs, SFI; and Andi Sutherland, Housing/Events Manager, SFI, for their enthusiasm and effectiveness in providing us with a constructive environment for research and discussion.

George J. Gumerman
Arizona State Museum, University of Arizona
and the Santa Fe Institute

REFERENCES

Bertalanffy, Ludwig von
1968 General Systems Theory. New York: George Brazillier.

Cowan, George A., David Pines, and David Meltzer
1994 Complexity: Metaphors, Models, and Reality. Santa Fe Institute Studies in the Sciences of Complexity, Proceedings Volume XIX. Reading, MA: Addison-Wesley.

Cordell, Linda S., and George J. Gumerman, eds.
1989 Dynamics of Southwest Prehistory. Washington, DC: Smithsonian Institution Press.

Gumerman, George J., ed.
1994 Themes in Southwest Prehistory. Santa Fe, NM: School of American Research Press.

Gumerman, George J., and Murray Gell-Mann, eds.
1994 Understanding Complexity in the Prehistoric Southwest. Santa Fe Institute Studies in the Sciences of Complexity, Proceedings Volume XVI. Reading, MA: Addison-Wesley.

Miller, James G.
1965 Living Systems: Basic Concepts. *Behav. Sci.* **10**:193–237.

Tainter, Joseph A., and Bonnie Bagley Tainter, eds.
1996 Evolving Complexity and Environmental Risk in the Prehistoric Southwest. Santa Fe Institute Studies in the Sciences of Complexity, Proceedings Volume XXIV. Reading, MA: Addison-Wesley.

Putting Social Sciences Together Again:
An Introduction to the Volume

Timothy A. Kohler

Whose game was empires and whose stakes were thrones,
Whose table earth—whose dice were human bones.

Lord Byron, *Age of Bronze*

We accept many definitions for games, most not so grandiose as those of Napoleon treated by Byron. Often when I demonstrate the simulation of Anasazi settlement discussed in chapter 7 of this volume someone will say, "This is just a game isn't it?" I'm happy to admit that it is, so long as our definition of games encompasses child's play—which teaches about and prepares for reality—and not just those frivolous pastimes of adults, which release them from it.

This volume is based on and made possible by recent developments in the field of agent-based simulation. More than some dry computer science technology or another corporate software gambit, this technology is in fact provoking great interest in the possibilities of simulating social, spatial, and evolutionary dynamics in human and primate societies in ways that have not previously been possible.

What is agent-based modeling? Models of this sort are sometimes also called individual-oriented, or distributed artificial intelligence-

Dynamics in Human and Primate Societies, edited by T. Kohler and
G. Gumerman, Oxford University Press, 1999. **1**

based. Action in such models takes place through agents, which are processes, however simple, that collect information about their environment, make decisions about actions based on that information, and act (Doran et al. 1994:200). Artificial societies composed of interacting collections of such agents allow controlled experiments (of the sort impossible in traditional social research) on the effects of tuning one behavioral or environmental parameter at a time (Epstein and Axtell 1996:1–20). Research using these models emphasizes dynamics rather than equilibria, distributed processes rather than systems-level phenomena, and patterns of relationships among agents rather than relationships among variables. As a result visualization is an important part of analysis, affording these approaches a sometimes gamelike and often immediately engaging quality. OK, I admit it—they're fun.

Despite our emphasis on agent-based modeling, we do not mean to imply that it should displace, or is always superior to, systems-level models based on, for example, differential equations. On the contrary: te Boekhorst and Hemelrijk (chapter 2) nicely demonstrate how these approaches may be complementary. Even more strongly, we do not argue that these activities should become, ahead of empirical research, the principal tool of social science. We do hope to demonstrate that these approaches deserve an important place in the social science toolkit.

All social simulation (whether of the agent-based type, or of whole systems in the tradition of Forrester [1968]; see also van der Leeuw and McGlade [1997]) is viewed with suspicion by many in the research community, even including some who accept the value of simulation for problems in the physical and biotic domains. I therefore begin this chapter with a perspective on why such doubts have arisen—and why the researchers whose work is assembled here think these approaches are useful nonetheless. I then continue with a discussion of some of the problems of anthropology—the social science I know best—that might be reduced by extended and rigorous application of the sorts of methods explored in this volume.

Interest in these models crosscuts the social sciences, humanities, and biological sciences. Recent important and strongly related contributions in the social sciences have issued, for example, from political scientists (Axelrod 1997) and from economists (Young 1998). In the final section of this chapter I suggest that these methods have great promise for re-integrating social sciences long isolated by artificial disciplinary boundaries.

1 PREDICAMENTS FOR SOCIAL SIMULATION

It is accepted by most historians and quite a few anthropologists that "the processes of events which constitute the world of nature are altogether different in kind from the processes of thought which constitute the world of [human] history" (Collingwood 1946:217). The key difference, according to Collingwood, is that historical processes involve the actions of self-aware individuals—actions based on understandings of history and of other actors, on self-criticism, and on internal valuations. In Collingwood's famous phrase, historical processes have both an outside *and* an inside; natural processes, only an outside. Of course the outsides (by which he meant "mere events": everything about an event "which can be described in terms of bodies and their movements" [1946:213]) are part of history. But *actions*, which are "the unity of the outside and inside of an event" are the true province of history, and to understand them we must enter into the thoughts of the agents.

One grand vision of the social world then, and likely the dominant one, holds that society and humanity are cut off from nature, at least to the extent that they participate in an additional ideational realm. This view, of course, resonates with intellectual understandings of the world that originate no later than the third-millennium normalfontB.C. milieu out of which arose the composition of Genesis. Aspects of this tradition were continued by the Sophists, who were attacked by Socrates for making man the measure of all things and judging truth and correct action to be determined only through the variable perception of individuals and communities. The work of Durkheim, much of Kroeber's (1917) thought and especially his concept of the superorganic, and the "thick description" of Clifford Geertz (1973) share a sympathy with the view that culture too is a thing that is both all-powerful and *sui generis*, neither reducible to another level for analysis, nor continuously connected with the biological realm from which it emerged. Many contributions to social research, beginning at least with the work of Peter Berger (e.g., 1963), add that the critical role of the researcher is to understand the subjectivities of individual experience and to chart how the sum of socially constructed meanings that constitute culture are continuously renegotiated through time.

1.1 WEAK ARTIFICIAL SOCIETIES

I have no illusions of being capable of disposing of a set of views of such venerable pedigree, and actually no wish to do so, but accepting such a perspective seems also to require accepting a view that simulation, at best, provides a set of tools that opens up only portions of human experience for examination. Most obviously, those portions would be Collingwood's "outsides" of social processes: issues of economy and subsistence, use of space, demography, and those aspects of kinship and sociopolitical structure that impinge on them. Indeed, all of the chapters in this volume deal with some combination of these outsides. These outsides are viewed as profitable domains for simulation because it can be argued, as do human behavioral ecologists, that the economic functions embedded within these suites of behaviors are the proximate tools of an ultimate causation springing from universal evolutionary demands. Therefore, although meaning would be ascribed by actors to their behavior in these arenas, actions should not depend solely (or perhaps even heavily) on those meanings for their consistency and pattern. It is, of course, also of considerable importance to those of us working with the archaeological record that behaviors in this arena have material outcomes.

By analogy with the "weak" and "strong" versions of artificial intelligence differentiated on the grandiosity of their claims, this position logically leads to a set of practices that could be called "weak social simulation." (Sober [1992] similarly extends this classification to artificial life.) Even social scientists who would question the extent of the rupture between historical and natural process (that is, those who wonder whether the "naturalistic fallacy" *is* a fallacy) agree that capabilities such as foresight, learning, creative thought, and memory that are emphasized in our species—though apparently not absent in our primate cousins (Byrne 1996)—impart a fluidity and tactical complexity to human affairs that taken together make social sciences the hard sciences. The claim of "weak social simulation" is simply that artificial societies are useful because without using the power of a computer and appropriate software the processes in question could not be studied effectively. This is because the systems of interest are composed of many agents interacting not only with each other but also with a possibly dynamic environment according to rulesets that may be complicated and may change over time. These problems are analytically intractable and, when studied through simulation, results often cannot be predicted with great accuracy even by the programmer.

Nevertheless, these are only toy worlds. These agents are shielded from most of the complexities of real life; as programmers we have done, in advance, the hard work of determining the possibly relevant features of the problem domain under investigation and endowing our agents with trial behaviors whose effects we wish to study. Readers will find these simulations useful to the extent that they agree that the programmers have indeed captured the relevant aspects of the problem domains in their worlds. These "worlds" are not themselves supposed to be societies. They are supposed to be like societies in some useful respects.

In a recent consideration of the limits of differential-equation models of social systems, Robert Rosen arrives (for related reasons) at a similarly modest conclusion concerning the appropriate targets for simulation:

> It must be emphasized that we can still make dynamical models of complex systems, just as we can formalize fragments of Number Theory. We can approximate, but only locally and temporarily, to inexact differential forms with exact ones under certain conditions. But we will have to keep shifting from model to model, as the causal structure in the complex system outstrips what is coded into any

particular dynamics. The situation is analogous to trying to use pieces of planar maps to navigate on a surface of a sphere (Rosen 1997:394).

The claim of weak social simulation, then, is emphatically not that the simulated processes as a whole constitute living societies within a computer that can be studied from any angle desired. These are not societies composed of individuals exhibiting common sense, who could learn, develop skills, classify, and generalize according to situationally appropriate criteria, imagine, and plan.

1.2 POSSIBLE PATHWAYS TO STRONG SOCIAL SIMULATION

Whether or not it is possible to effectively simulate the "insides" of human cognitive processes, and therefore (ultimately) human history à la Collingwood, is exactly the debate that has been raging within the cognitive sciences and particularly in the Artificial Intelligence (AI) community, and between the AI community and its detractors, for at least three decades (see Casti 1993; Dreyfus 1992; Searle 1980). It has appeared to most outside observers that the debate is being won by the detractors, and that both the top-down, symbol-and-rule-based representations of "good old fashioned AI" and the bottom-up, neural network approaches of the connectionistic school, were foundering on the possibly linked problems of the inability to build either expertise or broad common sense knowledge into computation. Opinions of philosophers such as Dreyfus that it *should* not be possible to endow machines with such capacities were underwritten by the inability of computer scientists to design such machines. Searle seems right when he argues that even though machines can be programmed to produce syntactically correct speech, these utterances are semantically empty in that they have no meaning for the computer.

The history of thought is full of useful *Gedankenexperimente*, and one of the most famous is due to William Paley, the late eighteenth century English archdeacon and author of *Natural Theology*. Were we to discover a watch on the ground and asked to explain its origin, we would judge (he suggests) from its complicated mechanism, and from the fact that when wound it kept time accurately, that it was the creation of an intelligent and skilled maker who had just this purpose in mind (see Cziko [1995:14–16] for a recent retelling). By this argument from design, and by analogy from technology to nature, it was clear to Paley that all the wonders of the natural world, too, had just such a Creator. In Darwinian hands, of course, goodness-of-fit between form and function in nature is regarded as due to selection, not Providence. Yet we have not carried the metaphorical lessons from this realization far enough in our thinking about human action and meaning; in effect, we have overcome our tendency to explain via a Creator, only to substitute ourselves as multiple creators. Because we see a fit between some of our actions and the understandings that we have built about the world, we are tempted to assume that all our actions, and those of others, are generated by those meanings and are (literally) meaningless without them.

There are other alternatives, and I hope the reader will tolerate a brief detour to explore one. John Tooby and Leda Cosmides, in an influential 1992 essay, identified a "Standard Social Science Model" (SSSM) of the world which by their analysis encompasses the following linked assertions:

1. Particular human groups are bounded by behavioral practices, beliefs, ideational systems, and symbols that are widely shared within groups but differ dramatically between groups;
2. These common elements are transmitted and maintained socially within each group;
3. Thus, all within-group similarities as well as all between-group differences are considered to be "cultural";
4. Culture is normally replicated without error from generation to generation;
5. This process is made possible by learning;
6. From the point-of-view of the group this process is considered socialization, and is imposed on the child by the group;
7. Individuals then are the more or less passive vessels for and products of their culture;
8. "What is organized and contentful in the minds of individuals comes from culture and is socially constructed";
9. "The features of a specific culture are the result of emergent group-level processes, whose determinants arise at the group level and whose outcome is not given specific shape or content by human biology, human nature, or any inherited psychological design. These emergent processes, operating at the sociocultural level, are the ultimate generator of the significant organization, both mental and social, that is found in human affairs";
10. In discussing culture, psychological factors other than a capacity for learning can be neglected, since learning by itself is sufficient to explain behavioral structure, within-group similarities, and between-group differences;
11. Evolved aspects of human behavior or psychological organization are negligible, and even if they exist have been imparted by culture with all significant form and direction (simplified from Tooby and Cosmides 1992: 31–32).

As an aside, it should be noted that the SSSM is very likely to yield predictions of human behavior at odds with the optimizing predictions of classical rationality. Although the extent to which the "behavioral practices, beliefs, ideational systems, and symbols that are widely shared within groups but differ dramatically between groups" are constrained by universal economies of selection could be an open question under the assumptions of the SSSM, in practice there is the widespread belief that these constraints are fairly unimportant.

To some extent the SSSM view of the world is of course correct. Speaking for the emerging field of evolutionary psychology, however, Tooby and Cosmides contend that even more is misleading. They see no reason that features of adult cognition not present at birth need be attributed only to culture; they contend that the SSSM requires a facile partitioning of nature and nurture that does not faithfully reflect the deep interaction over developmental and evolutionary time of biological and environmental factors; and they judge the tabula rasa concept implicit in the SSSM, which views the mind as a general-purpose learning (computing) device, to be an insufficient mechanism for many of the supposedly learned activities constituting culture.

In place of the SSSM, evolutionary psychologists propose that our cognitive and emotional apparatus is composed of many specialized "adaptations":

> an adaptation is (1) a system of inherited and reliably developing properties that recurs among members of a species that (2) became incorporated into the species' standard design because during the period of their incorporation, (3) they were coordinated with a set of statistically recurrent structural properties outside the adaptation (either in the environment or in the others parts of the organism), (4) in such a way that the causal interactions of the two (in the context of the rest of the properties of the organism) produced function outcomes that were ultimately tributary to propagation with sufficient frequency (i.e., it solved an adaptive problem for the organism) (Tooby and Cosmides 1992:61–62).

These adaptations were selected over millions of years in response to the most common conditions that as a group are referred to as the Environment of Evolutionary Adaptation (EEA), which is presumed to include small social groups, low overall population levels, simple technology, low impact of contagious diseases, and subsistence on naturally occurring resources. Our cognitive systems are seen as comprised of a large number of domain-specific adaptations that were critical in the EEA, including things like face-recognition modules, emotion-decoding modules, tool-use modules, sexual-attraction modules, grammar-acquisition modules, and so forth (Tooby and Cosmides 1992:113). Our famous human flexibility is attained on this view not through general-purpose computation, but by the interaction of sedimented layers of large numbers of domain-specific mechanisms, each of which has a reliable output given certain expected inputs.

Most radically, for our purposes, it has even been suggested that one such module may be a "theory of mind" that predisposes us to explain behavior as due to an internal dialogue that results in action when an appropriate "confluence of beliefs and desires" is reached (Tooby and Cosmides 1992:90; Leslie 1987). Children all over the world by three to five years of age, it appears, enunciate an interpretation of their own and other peoples' actions as due to beliefs and desires ("Why has Mary gone to the drinking fountain? Because she has a *desire* for water [i.e., she is thirsty] and she *believes* that water can be found at the water fountain" [Tooby and Cosmides 1992:90]). This "folk theory" that beliefs and desires actually exist and explain actions, provides the underpinning for interpretations of history (such as Collingwood's) that emphasize the history of thought. Of course, many scientifically oriented historians and anthropologists would think it condign punishment for Collingwood to have been the torchbearer for a mere "adaptation." They should rejoice not, however, since by this same logic this adaptation must have had selective value. This does not necessarily mean that this interpretation of actions was or is *true*; it may mean only that it allowed some exploitable predictions of others' actions.

The evolutionary psychological point of view has the compelling property that it helps us understand an apparent predicament in modeling human societies, which is as follows. It is felt by many anthropologists that although our ability to model societies is very primitive, that what we are able to do now, and what we can envision being able to do in the near future, approximates much more closely the operation of small-scale societies than it does modern industrial civilizations. This supposition, if true, could be explained by an evolutionary psychologist as a consequence of the fact that we can compose sets of rules that reasonably approximate adaptations (domain-specific cognitive functions). So long as we are modeling societies in their EEAs, these adaptations should specify most of the behaviors that might be expected. However, outputs from these mechanisms, given ranges of inputs for which they were not evolved, become increasingly unpredictable and perhaps more fully under the control of what general-purpose cognitive abilities or socially imparted norms we possess. As a result, as people depart from the conditions of their EEA, they might be expected to exhibit behaviors that are increasingly difficult to model, as they are less completely specified by their adaptations.

Unfortunately for this attractive point of view there are problems with the evolutionary psychology position that should prevent us from accepting it uncritically, without preventing us from entertaining its plausibility or attempting to evaluate its empirical claims. Robert Foley (1995/96) enumerates several such problems; why, for example, have selective forces over the last 10,000 years made so little headway in molding adaptations, and how does the presumably universal character of the EEA accommodate both regional diversity in the hunter-gatherer experience, and great diversity in adaptive traits and phylogenetic context over the 30 million or so years since the emergence of proto-hominoids?

Despite these problems, it appears that an evolutionary psychological view of the world would open up the possibility of "strong social simulation" by focusing simulation efforts on *evolving* adaptations and mechanisms for adjudicating among adaptations. The deep lesson from evolutionary psychology, whether or not its proponents turn out to be right about the particular adaptations they posit, is that we can not hope to understand how the mind works without taking into account its evolutionary development. Likewise, the sort of agents with very general capabilities that would be required for strong social simulation, if they can be produced at all, are much more likely to be achieved through evolution *in silico* than through explicit design.

Conveniently, for over a decade the emerging field of artificial life has been building tools that allow agents to learn (Holland et al. 1986) and evolve (Bäch 1996; Koza 1992). These techniques, however, remain to be effectively incorporated into most research in "artificial societies" thereby leaving in place one of the barriers that prevent our models from approaching the world with both realism and generality.

I believe, however, that most of the participants in the workshop from which this volume began see the goal of constructing "strong artificial societies" as either distant, or unattainable (of all of us, Doran [this volume] probably comes the closest to advocating the strong position). Although moving *toward* strong social simulation is a worthy goal, since it would enlarge the scope of the questions that could be asked, there is plenty of interesting work to do within a program that proposes only that our artificial societies are like real societies in some specific respects, which we wish to study. It is easy to see from Brian Skyrms' chapter how unrestrictive this position is, since he is able to use simulation techniques to study the evolution of systems of meaning and inference without, of course, having to impute understanding in any sense to the computer. We turn now to consider some of the ways in which this program may usefully augment traditional social science methods.

2   ROLES FOR A GENERATIVE SOCIAL SCIENCE

Social science is not primarily concerned with the behavior of isolated individuals. The critical questions are often of genesis of patterns and of processes: how do cooperative relations among unrelated individuals emerge and become stable? How do social institutions, norms, and values evolve? Or, we may be interested in questions that cannot be answered adequately without asking questions of genesis: why are some kinds of organizations common and others rare? Agent-based modeling holds out the promise of "growing" social phenomena as a way of understanding them (Epstein and Axtell 1996). The strengths of such a science are seemingly very different from the strengths of social science as traditionally practiced. Having spent some time above arguing for the plausibility of agent-based simulation in social research, let's examine some specific weaknesses in traditional social science that may be usefully augmented by a generative approach.

2.1   PROBLEM: ATTEMPTS TO UNDERSTAND SYSTEM BEHAVIOR THROUGH APPLICATION OF ANALYSES OF "VARIABLES" RATHER THAN THROUGH EXAMINATION OF AGENT INTERACTION AND COEVOLUTION

Although anthropology now shows healthy signs of moving in other directions, much analysis is conducted by conceptualizing and attempting to measure various "variables" of the social environment (say, degree of industrialization, degree of wealth, degree of intensification, population density, etc.) and then looking for relationships among these variables using statistical tools such as regression, path analysis, factor analysis, and so forth. Blalock (1982) offers a mature but traditional perspective on such analyses.

Consider, for example, analysis of a data set compiled by an archaeologist for some region in which a measure of economic intensification is regressed on population density through time, with the implicit causation that changes in population density caused changes in degree of intensification. From the perspective of agent-based modeling (that is, from our simulated version of what archaeologists often call the "systemic context" following Schiffer [1976]), these variables represent in part the high-level *outcomes*, probably averaged over a great deal of space and time, of a large number of agent decisions, actions, and practices. These outcomes are the things that we can measure, more or less, in the archaeological record. If there are regularities in the relationships of these outcomes, however, it will be because of behavioral and cognitive linkages between context and practice at the level of the agents. Therefore, these "variables" also operate as significant contexts within which agents make decisions and perform actions. So what we call "variables" in such analyses have the confusing dual status of outcomes of behavior and contexts for behavior, even though our usual analytic approaches require us to conceive of one variable as independent and the other as dependent.

What is the danger, you might say, of reifying these variables and pretending that one causes the other, so long as we understand that this is just a convenient shorthand for something that we would all agree to? The problem is the likelihood that there are *evolving coadaptational interactions* among the agents (and between the agents and their environments) in such settings, whereas the analysis of static variables as effective contexts for decisions assumes a fixed relationship among the agents and their environment. In modeling social systems, we shall be primarily concerned about changing strategies within and among social groups of various sizes, who are seeking advantage in competition, often through cooperation. Over long enough periods of time, we have to be concerned as well about changing relationships among trophic levels through genetic changes accompanying processes such as domestication. I think it is apparent that all the major transitions and processes that are of real interest to social scientists, from the domestication of plants and animals to the emergence of hierarchical relationships, the processes of ethnic emergence, selection by similarity, and so forth, all involve coadaptation or coevolution in fundamental ways. These are processes that for human societies have a complex time structure. As Nigel Gilbert points out in his contribution, uniquely in human societies do forecasts of performance have an ability to affect performances. The quote by Rousseau with which Brian Skyrms begins his chapter is a perfect illustration of why we have to consider coevolution (in this case, of mental capacity and speech delivery systems) in order to understand the paradox he poses.

Agent-based modeling is a way (the most practical and thorough way that I can see) for studying systems that are characterized by many coevolutionary interactions. Coevolutionary systems defy analysis in terms of traditional one-way cause-and-effect (Scott 1989), and we are still searching, I think, for satisfactory replacements for these concepts that will allow us to compare change in different systems and allow us to answer "why?" questions of perceived patterns. We will be aided and abetted in this search by scientists in other fields, particularly evolutionary ecology, who are facing similar problems (Thompson 1994), and by more general research in complex adaptive systems in which this problem presents itself in many guises. One possible response—that we should simply abandon explanation—seems to me to be unacceptable, if only on the grounds that evolution has shaped us as creatures that have for millennia used approximately correct, though crude, internal models of causation to great evolutionary advantage.

2.2 PROBLEM: TRADITIONAL METHODS OF ANALYSIS THAT ARE UNABLE TO COPE WITH A HIERARCHY OF EMERGENCE AND CIRCUMSTANCE

Charlotte Hemelrijk, one of the contributors to this volume, elsewhere (Hemelrijk 1996:191) cites with approval work by the ethologist Hinde (1982):

> Hinde distinguished four different levels of complexity, each with its own emergent properties: individual behavior, interactions, relationships, and social structure. Each level is described in terms of the level below it, and levels influence each other mutually. For instance, the nature of the participants' behavior influences their relationships, but these relationships also in turn affect the participants' behavior. A caution that follows from this view is that observed social structure can vary dramatically with circumstances, without any changes in the underlying motivational mechanisms or strategies.

This scheme decomposes social systems somewhat more than many. More generally, we might add genotypic systems at the bottom, and culture and ecosystems at the top (see also Holland 1995:10–12; Scott 1989:10). Regardless of how many layers are invoked, if it is true that behavior of agents at any given level of the hierarchy is partly an emergent result of behavior at the next lower level, and so on, we need a method that can use this information.

Traditional social science offers us a possibility here that is fundamentally different from the more usual analysis of the covariance of variables. Network analysis (e.g., Knoke and Kuklinski 1982) offers techniques for describing and analyzing the connectedness of individuals, objects, or events. It does not, however, provide us with a dynamic view of the emergence of those connections. We are brought back again to an awareness that our usual statistical approaches are, first of all, fundamentally descriptive, and secondly, incorporate temporal or evolutionary dimensions within their framework of r-mode (among variables) or q-mode (among actors) analyses only with great difficulty.

But Hinde's hierarchy is more behavioral than temporal. Perhaps traditional social science methods will perform better here; after all, we are adept at ways of discovering variable degrees of influence of a set of variables on some variable of interest. The problem, once again, is the distinction between a fundamentally descriptive analysis, and the generation of a phenomenon, which demonstrates at least one possible causal pathway for its development. Epstein and Axtell (1996:177) refer to such demonstrations as proofs of generative sufficiency. It is one thing to describe the structure of a house as seen from the street; it is quite another thing to build one.

It may be that there are many problems for which a single level of complexity (in Hinde's terms) is of such paramount importance that for practical purposes higher (and lower) levels can be ignored. Even in problems having this structure agent-based models can provide a useful demonstration of this fact if they are able to successfully reproduce the phenomena in question without reference to other levels in the hierarchy.

Finally, while we are discussing analytic difficulties in traditional approaches, we should consider that many social phenomena involve processes that are working at very different temporal and spatial scales. In their model of prehistoric Puebloan settlement in northeastern Arizona, for example, Jeff Dean et al. are able to take into account how some resource patches change in availability on cycles of years (at high frequency) while others change at time scales of many decades (low frequency). Integrating these different time scales would be extraordinarily difficult in some nongenerative approach to understanding this settlement system.

2.3 PROBLEM: TENDENCY TO BEGIN (AND END) ANALYSIS TOWARD THE UPPER END OF HINDE'S HIERARCHY

One important use of agent-based models to date has been in a spoiler role: to show, for example, that simple local rules might produce structures and processes thought to be governed by more complicated global rules, where global means at some higher level in a hierarchy such as that presented by Hinde. An early example of this is Schelling's "tipping" model to produce segregation (1978:101–110); we will see other examples here, as in René te Boekhorst and Charlotte Hemelrijk's chapter. In my view this use is entirely appropriate, as anthropology, for example, has almost certainly been guilty of attributing phenomena to culture that might well be explained in lower-level terms if we were willing to give this a serious try.

How simple might things be? The dynamics of the academic world appear to give points to those who are able to contrive the most ingeniously complicated explanations for social phenomena. Much too little effort has been expended to prospect for the simplest possible mechanisms that have sufficient explanatory power for the problem at hand. Anthropologists, for example, ought to examine seriously the possibility of explanations for phenomena that are not based on that variant of top-down modeling where culture explains everything. *Then* we will be in a better position to realize the long-term goals of understanding how at the same time agents interact with culture to change it, and how they are channeled by it (Giddens 1979).

A special (but very important) case of our failure to seriously consider simple explanations is the frequent disregard of the importance of space (referred to by one of our colloquy as "the final frontier") in interactive behavior. It is no coincidence that several contributors to this volume (see, for example, Mark Lake's chapter) are busy building bridges between geographic information systems and agent-based modeling. Within the context of multilevel selection theory, John Pepper and Barbara Smuts (chapter 3) examine the critical role of spatial distribution of plant resources in determining the success of two cooperative behaviors (alarm calling and feeding restraint).

3 MILES TO GO

In an introductory chapter one will be enthusiastic about one's subject. It is important to be fair as well. The conceptual work to be done before one even begins to build a model may in itself be prodigious, as Mark Lehner's detailed consideration of the parts and processes in ancient Egypt (chapter 12) wonderfully illustrates. Once constructed, agent-based models allow us to go from trial formulations of processes working on parts to a pattern, but how to move in the other direction is a fundamental problem; agent construction at this point is more art than science. Robert Reynolds (chapter 11) demonstrates a technique from machine learning that should prove useful for extracting trial agent rules for settlement from real settlement pattern data.

Even given some trial formulations of agent rules, models such as those presented here on Anasazi settlement represent mountains of effort distributed over several years and many individuals. Appropriate frameworks for building software, such as the Swarm system used in chapter 7 are in the public domain and are becoming easier to use, but still represent a challenge for almost any social scientist. Nor is there a single accepted platform for such work.

Let's also not confuse the promise of these approaches with what they have accomplished to date. As Jim Doran points out in chapter 5, agent-based approaches have the ability, in principle, to take into account rules, norms, differential learning contexts, and their changes. That they do not take advantage of these opportunities for the most part is perhaps a function of limited experience in representing cultural phenomena. Nevertheless, the contrast in attitudes with the early days of simulation when anthropologists explored the possibilities of systems theory for our field is evident. In 1972, for example, Michael Glassow told us that we would need to rid anthropology "of a plethora of terms and concepts which presently have questionable or unspecified analogs in the components and processes of real cultural systems. Abstractions such as "norms," "rules," "ideas," "goals," or "influences" are among the more obvious which fall into this category" (1972:292).

Complex adaptive systems theorists such as John Holland (1992) and Murray Gell-Mann (1992), on the other hand, consider schemata (of which rules, norms, etc. are "unfolded" examples) to be essential, defining features of complex adaptive systems that enable adaptation. Of course, this position brings with it the complicated challenge of representing these schemata. Fortunately these problems are also of interest to a new generation of researchers in artificial intelligence (see, for example, recent work on "learning in situated agents" [Lave and Wenger 1991]). Robert Reynolds, one of our participants, has elsewhere (e.g., 1994) discussed how the concept of culture, as something that shapes agents' behaviors and is in turn molded by the outcomes of those behaviors, can be implemented in a framework he calls *cultural algorithms*.

Also of interest is that—in principle at least—agent-based approaches admit an important role for history and contingency. We can examine, for example, the degree to which specific outcomes are dependent on specific initial or prior conditions, just as Lake (chapter 6) examines the different settlement patterns that might result in the Southern Hebrides given different initial points of colonization by Mesolithic foragers.

Agent-based simulation can also, in principle, accommodate models that invoke heterogeneity among agents, or which drive social change through shifting coalitions of agents, argued by many (e.g., Brumfiel 1992) to be a critical social dynamic.

4 CHALLENGES FOR AGENT-BASED MODELING: PUTTING SOCIAL SCIENCES TOGETHER AGAIN

Over the last several years, as an occasional participant in the Santa Fe Institute's activities, I have taken great pleasure in seeing how complex adaptive systems theory in general and agent-based models in particular provide a framework in which social scientists of diverse backgrounds can engage in productive discussion. The conference from which this book springs—which involved primatologists, archaeologists, cultural anthropologists, computer scientists, a sociologist, and a philosopher—is a handy example.

In this volume most of the contributors (Stephen Lansing and Mark Lehner being exceptions) draw relatively little on theory of complex adaptive systems but instead attempt to *apply* the spirit of complexity, through agent-based simulation, to real problems in the social sciences. Even in cases where we address a problem of limited scope, we find that these approaches require some consideration of those other processes that impinge importantly on the problems at hand, as Small points out in chapter 10. Simulation allows analysis within a complex environment. It forces archaeologists to think about the living societies they model. It forces primatologists to consider how spatial features and resource distributions affect interaction. It forces all of us to make explicit the many notions we have always vaguely held to be true. It allows us to visualize and analyze what we have not been able to even imagine: the organization generated through the parallel processes of many interacting entities. Finally, when undertaken within the framework of complex adaptive systems theory, it encourages us to think beyond our disciplinary boundaries, in a space where economists, for example, can be concerned with the evolution of social norms (see, for example, Bowles and Gintis 1998) or social structure (e.g., Young 1998), and physicists with the dynamics of social dilemmas (e.g., Glance and Huberman 1994). All of us in this volume hope our efforts propel us in some small way toward this space which really is the final frontier.

ACKNOWLEDGMENTS

I thank the Department of Archaeology where I was privileged to hold the Fulbright-Univeristy of Calgary Chair of North American Studies during the final phases of work on this chapter, and this volume; and Marilyn, Claire, and Sander for their patience and support.

REFERENCES

Axelrod, Robert
   1997 The Complexity of Cooperation: Agent-Based Models of Competition and Collaboration. Princeton, NJ: Princeton University Press.
Bäch, Thomas
   1996 Evolutionary Algorithms in Theory and Practice: Evolution Strategies, Evolutionary Programming, Genetic Algorithms. New York: Oxford University Press.
Berger, Peter
   1963 Invitation to Sociology. Garden City, NJ: Doubleday.
Blalock, Hubert M., Jr.
   1982 Conceptualization and Measurement in the Social Sciences. Beverly Hills, CA: Sage Publications.

Bowles, Samuel, and Herbert Gintis
1998 The Moral Economy of Communities: Structured Populations and the Evolution of Social Norms. Evolution and Human Behavior 19:2–25.

Brumfiel, Elizabeth M.
1992 Distinguished Lecture in Archeology: Breaking and Entering the Ecosystem—Gender, Class, and Faction Steal the Show. American Anthropologist 94:551–567.

Byrne, Richard W.
1996 Machiavellian Intelligence. Evolutionary Anthropology 5:172–180.

Byron, George Gordon, Lord
1823 [1993] The Age of Bronze; Or, Carmen Seculare et Annus Haud Mirabilis. In Lord Byron: The Complete Poetical Works. J. J. McGann, ed. Pp. 1–25, Vol. 7. Oxford: Clarendon Press.

Casti, John
1993 The Cognitive Revolution? Idealistic Studies 23:19–38.

Collingwood, R. G.
1946 The Idea of History. London: Oxford University Press.

Cziko, Gary
1995 Without Miracles: Universal Selection Theory and the Second Darwinian Revolution. Cambridge, MA: MIT Press.

Doran, Jim, Mike Palmer, Nigel Gilbert, and Paul Mellars
1994 The EOS Project: Modelling Upper Paleolithic Social Change. In Simulating Societies: The Computer Simulation of Social Phenomena. Nigel Gilbert and Jim Doran, eds. Pp. 195–221. London: UCL Press.

Dreyfus, Hubert L.
1992 What Computers Still Can't Do: A Critique of Artificial Reason. Cambridge, MA: MIT Press.

Epstein, Joshua M., and Robert Axtell
1996 Growing Artificial Societies: Social Science from the Bottom Up. Washington, DC: Brookings Institution Press and Cambridge, MA: MIT Press.

Foley, Robert
1995/96 The Adaptive Legacy in Human Evolution: A Search for the Environment of Evolutionary Adaptedness. Evolutionary Anthropology 4:194–203.

Forrester, J.
1968 Principles of Systems. Cambridge, UK: Wright-Allen Press.

Geertz, Clifford
1973 The Interpretation of Cultures. New York: Basic Books.

Gell-Mann, Murray
1992 Complexity and Complex Adaptive Systems. In The Evolution of Human Languages. John A. Hawkins and Murray Gell-Mann, eds. Pp. 1–

18. Santa Fe Institute Studies in the Sciences of Complexity, Proceedings Volume XI. Redwood City, CA: Addison-Wesley.

Giddens, Anthony
1979 Central Problems in Social Theory. London: Macmillan.

Glance, Natalie S., and Bernardo A. Huberman
1994 The Dynamics of Social Dilemmas. Scientific American 270(3):76–81.

Glassow, Michael A.
1972 Changes in the Adaptations of Southwestern Basketmakers: A Systems Perspective. *In* Contemporary Archaeology: A Guide to Theory and Contributions. Mark P. Leone, ed. Pp. 289–302. Carbondale and Edwardsville, IL: Southern Illinois University Press.

Hemelrijk, Charlotte K.
1996 Reciprocation in Apes: From Complex Cognition to Self-Structuring. *In* Great Ape Societies. W. C. McGrew, L. F. Merchant, and T. Nishida, eds. Pp. 185–195. New York: Cambridge University Press.

Hinde, R. A.
1982 Ethology: Its Nature and Relations with Other Sciences. Oxford: Oxford University Press.

Holland, John H.
1992 Adaptation in Natural and Artificial Systems: An Introductory Analysis with Applications to Biology, Control, and Artificial Intelligence. Cambridge, MA: MIT Press.
1995 Hidden Order: How Adaptation Builds Complexity. Reading, MA: Addison-Wesley.

Holland, John H., K. Holyoak, R. Nisbet, and P. Thagard
1986 Induction: Processes of Inference, Learning, and Discovery. Cambridge, MA: MIT Press.

Knoke, David, and James H. Kuklinski
1982 Network Analysis. Quantitative Applications in the Social Sciences 28. Beverly Hills, CA: Sage Publications.

Koza, John
1992 Genetic Programming: On the Programming of Computers By Means of Natural Selection. Cambridge, MA: MIT Press.

Kroeber, Alfred
1917 The Superorganic. American Anthropologist 19:163–213.

Lave, Jean, and Etienne Wenger
1991 Situated Learning: Legitimate Peripheral Participation. New York: Cambridge University Press.

van der Leeuw, Sander, and James McGlade
1997 Structural Change and Bifurcation in Urban Evolution: A Nonlinear Dynamical Perspective. *In* Time, Process, and Structured Transformation in Archaeology. Sander van der Leeuw and James McGlade, eds. Pp. 331–372. London: Routledge.

Leslie, A. M.
   1987 Pretense and Representation: The Origins of "Theory of Mind." Psychological Review 94:412–426.

Reynolds, Robert
   1994 Learning to Co-operate Using Cultural Algorithms. *In* Simulating Societies: The Computer Simulation of Social Phenomena. Nigel Gilbert and Jim Doran, eds. Pp. 223–244. London: University College London.

Rosen, Robert
   1997 Are Our Modelling Paradigms Non-Generic? *In* Time, Process and Structured Transformation in Archaeology. Sander van der Leeuw and James McGlade, eds. Pp. 383–395. London: Routledge.

Schelling, T. C.
   1978 Micromotives and Macrobehavior. New York: Norton.

Schiffer, Michael B.
   1976 Behavioral Archeology. New York: Academic Press.

Searle, John
   1980 Minds, Brains, and Programs. The Behavioral and Brain Sciences 3:417–457.

Scott, John Paul
   1989 The Evolution of Social Systems. New York: Gordon and Breach.

Sober, Elliott
   1992 Learning from Functionalism—Prospects for Strong Artificial Life. *In* Artificial Life II. Christopher G. Langton, Charles Taylor, J. Doyne Farmer, and Steen Rasmussen, eds. Pp. 749–765. Santa Fe Institute Studies in the Sciences of Complexity, Proceedings Volume XVII. Redwood City, CA: Addison-Wesley.

Thompson, John N.
   1994 The Coevolutionary Process. Chicago: University of Chicago Press.

Tooby, John, and Leda Cosmides
   1992 The Psychological Foundations of Culture. *In* The Adapted Mind: Evolutionary Psychology and the Generation of Culture. J. H. Barkow, L. Cosmides, and J. Tooby, eds. Pp. 19–136. New York: Oxford University Press.

Young, H. Peyton
   1998 Individual Strategy and Social Structure: An Evolutionary Theory of Institutions. Princeton, NJ: Princeton University Press.

Nonlinear and Synthetic Models for Primate Societies

Irenaeus J. A. te Boekhorst
Charlotte K. Hemelrijk

We explore some unorthodox models for studying primate societies as self-organized and, hence, nonlinear complex systems. The incentive is that the conventional rationalist-analytic approach often leads to superfluous and contrived explanations. This is due to the habit of seeking separate explanations for each observed phenomenon, the tendency to ascribe social patterns solely to cognitive or genetic qualities of individuals, and the use of a short-sighted logic that yields naïve predictions. These practices stem from the desire to produce testable predictions derived from a normative perspective, leading to a disregard of real world properties like nonlinear dynamics, the effects of numerous parallel interactions, and the importance of local spatial configurations. We illustrate how dynamical systems and individual-oriented models explicitly include these features by starting from a synthetic perspective. As a result, they generate versatile, and often counterintuitive, insights into primate social behavior. The hypotheses derived in this way are parsimonious in the sense that a multitude of patterns can be traced back to one and the same minimal set of interactive dynamics. This type of model therefore leads to more integrating and comprehensive explanations than the purely function-

Dynamics in Human and Primate Societies, edited by T. Kohler and G. Gumerman, Oxford University Press, 1999.   **19** alistic top-down approaches of cognitive science and neo-Darwinian evolutionary theory.

We suggest that building autonomous robots and studying their performance might yield additional understanding of self-organized collective behavior in the real world. As mechanistic implementations of principles discovered in silica, robots form an interesting extension to individual-oriented models because they confront us with important real world conditions and physical constraints that are hard to program or would go otherwise unnoticed.

1   INTRODUCTION

In this chapter we use examples from primatology to tackle problems in the study of (small-scale) human societies. In contrast to the usual rationale, our objective is not to learn about our own kind by regarding monkeys and apes as simplified versions of humans. Instead, we argue that certain features of both human and nonhuman social behavior rest on common principles of self-structuring and that studying these may shed light on general issues of social organization.

One of these issues is that many of the intricacies seen in interindividual relationships among human and nonhuman primates may come about for much simpler reasons than is mostly appreciated. On the other hand, current theories about the evolution of primate social systems grossly understate the complexity involved in such basic matters as group size and group composition. At first, these statements seem to contradict each other: if the organization of groups is complex, doesn't it follow that the same must logically hold for the social behavior of its members? In this chapter we show that this is not necessarily the case. These and other surprising explanations follow from models that deliberately include aspects that are normally circumvented: nonlinear dynamics, the effects of numerous parallel interactions, and the importance of local spatial configurations. Due to these features, the models aid in uncovering logical consequences that stretch further than the simple predictions derived from rationalistic considerations. The latter are typically founded on what are believed to be the "best" decisions (given certain constraints and in terms of a pay-off measurement such as profit or fitness) for an individual to take. Instead, the approach advocated here is "bottom-up" or synthetic, i.e., based on very simple premises about the direct realization of behavior and how these lead to the unfolding of complex interaction patterns. The aim is therefore not to find out what normative criteria are required for a close representation of observed facts or detailed predictions, but rather to learn how simple precepts can generate complex social structures. But before clarifying these matters in more detail, we first outline the conventional approach to the study of behavior.

2 EXPLAINING THE HOWS AND WHYS OF BEHAVIOR

2.1 THE PROXIMATE-ULTIMATE DICHOTOMY

As in other ethological studies, questions about primate behavior are commonly cast in Tinbergen's classification of levels of inquiry. These concern evolutionary history (phylogeny), evolutionary function as a result of natural selection ("ultimate" causation), direct or "proximate" causation (physiological and psychological mechanisms), and development. For short, ultimate questions are concerned with the "whys," whereas proximate analysis deals with the "hows" of behavior.

Ideally a researcher should address all these levels to arrive at an integrated picture of animal (primate) behavior. Such an understanding of behavior has, however, not yet been achieved (Bateson 1991). A major obstacle is the conviction that although both proximate and ultimate explanations should be studied, they also should be kept strictly separated. The consequent fragmented picture of a biological system built up from component mechanisms, each of them begging for its own adaptive explanation, prohibits a unified comprehension of behavior. Moreover, both ultimate and certain proximate explanations share a strong rationalist background and that may be an even greater source of troubles.

2.2 RATIONALIST THEORIES OF BEHAVIOR

Most proximate ethologists make a distinction between hard(wet)-ware explanations or physiological descriptions on the one hand, and the soft-ware analogy for understanding cognition and motivation on the other hand (Baerends 1976; Hinde 1982; Colgan 1989; Bateson 1991). The software descriptions are typically of an algorithmic nature and therefore are independent of the physical substrate. Dawkins (1976), for instance, states that for an understanding of the internal processes regulating behavior it is irrelevant whether these run on a computer or in an organism. What matters are the computational principles that guarantee an efficient performance of observed behavior. The force supposedly favoring this efficiency is natural selection (seen by Dennett [1995] as an algorithm itself, but see Ahouse [1998] for a critique on this interpretation).

In this way, natural selection is held responsible for the evolutionary reasons why an individual does something. Ultimate questions therefore try to explain the function of a particular behavioral trait. However, in a broader sense, "functionalism" refers to a complete reliance on algorithms (cf. Putnam 1975), and as such, software representations of proximate causation are as functionalist as ultimate explanations. Also note that the hardware/software distinction of behavior reflects the mind-body dualism of Cartesian rationalism, the mathematical ideology in which the functionalist stance is rooted.

The "programming description" approach of proximate ethology (Colgan 1989) fits in with the paradigm of classical Artificial Intelligence (AI) (Hendriks-Jansen 1996). These and other functionalist approaches (including neo-Darwinist interpretations of behavior) share a preoccupation with how a system *ought* to run (in accordance with the observers' norms) rather than with how it actually operates in a physical sense. Such a normative approach is fundamental to engineering and design, but also to economics as it deals with how humans should behave to maximize profits (Simon 1969). The decisions to attain this are called "rational," which is often equated with "intelligent." Many contemporary ethologists identify themselves with this view as they consider adaptations as economically engineered, and therefore intelligent, solutions optimally designed by natural selection.

How does a rational agent perform "intelligent" behavior? In line with the concepts of classical AI such an agent is an input-output device that performs formally defined tasks following the "sense-think-act cycle." After gathering information (the input), the agent processes it by linking the input to already stored information (the agents' internal representation of the world), and performs acts (the output) in accordance with decisions derived from the updated world model. The information processing is done centrally and consists of encoding and decoding symbols that are supposed to represent situations in the real world (Newell and Simon 1976). This "symbol-" or "information-processing approach" is the essence of the cognitive paradigm and has strongly influenced psychology (see, for instance, Pylyshyn 1984) and linguistics (e.g., Fodor 1976). Primate intelligence is almost unanimously viewed within this paradigm. Examples are the use of symbolic representation for studying language in apes (Savage-Rumbaugh 1986) and Matsuzawa's Chomskeyan tree-structure analysis of chimpanzee cognition (Matsuzawa 1996). A very straightforward connection with AI is the use of "production rules" to describe computation and mind reading in tactical deception by primates (Byrne and Whiten 1991). The impact on ethology can be recognized in the reliance of both ultimate explanations and the matching proximate "decisions" on the assumptions of neoclassical microeconomics (e.g., McFarland 1989) and methods of operations research (see, for instance, Cuthill and Houston 1997). Ethologists pursuing these analogies either ignore or are not aware of the growing dissent within the economist community about its own traditional preconceptions (Arthur 1989, 1990; Peters 1991; Epstein and Axtell 1996; Kirman 1997; Tamborini 1997).

For a rationalist understanding of a system, scientific questions are reduced to simple logical problems. This is done by conceptually decomposing the system in single units, studying these units in isolation, and evaluating the whole as a linear combination of the units' properties (Lewontin and Levins 1987). A homogeneous, decomposable, and deterministic (or mildly stochastic) world, made predictable by linearizing the dynamics or even by discarding them altogether, clearly eases a functionalist-rationalist approach. In neo-Darwinian evolutionary theory these simplifications take two forms. First of all, processes are reified as traits that are thought to be "coded" by genes. In turn, genes are seen as independent units that may change at random by mutation. Second, effects of history are neglected by adopting a peculiar kind of "actualism"; it is assumed that events currently experienced by individuals are the same as those that shaped behavior by natural selection on an evolutionary time scale. The inferred consequences of these events, framed within economic optimality models or game theory, are then put forward as evolutionary predictions (which are actually postdictions). This way of thinking permeates currently popular theories about primate social organization, which are briefly reviewed below.

3 FUNCTIONALIST THEORIES OF PRIMATE SOCIAL ORGANIZATION

3.1 INTELLIGENCE AND SOCIAL COMPLEXITY

An ambitious effort to bring together primate cognition, social behavior, and evolution is expressed in the "Social Intelligence Hypothesis" (SIH) (Byrne and Whiten 1988). According to its advocates, the ability to engage in elaborate social relationships is a cognitive capacity that has "evolved as an adaptation to the complexities of social living" (Humphrey 1976, quoted in Byrne and Whiten 1988). More specifically, it has been suggested that social intelligence is located in the brain or in parts thereof (the neocortex) (cf. Dunbar 1992). The complexity of social interactions is thus reduced to cognitive capacities seated inside individuals.

Studies of correlations between neocortex size and group size, after statistically controlling for ecological factors such as diet, home range size, and arboreality (e.g., Dunbar 1992; Sawaguchi 1992), are on a par with evolutionary theories on the behavioral ecology of primate sociality. The SIH would thus connect theories about the evolution of social structure and intelligence once the selective advantages of living in groups, the topic of the next section, are understood.

3.2 ULTIMATE EXPLANATIONS FOR PRIMATE SOCIAL SYSTEMS

From the observation that most primates live in groups, the rational deduction is that sociality must be a beneficial trait. The main advantage of group life is assumed to be protection, either against predators (van Schaik 1983) or against conspecific rival groups (Wrangham 1979). Competition plays an important but different role depending on the view. To van Schaik, competition for food *within groups* is an unavoidable *consequence* of group life that, together with its benefits, determines the optimal group size. In Figure 1, this trade-off (the "fitness function") is pictured as the maximum difference between a diminishing return curve of safety with increasing group size and a linear cost function due to competition. Wrangham (1980, 1987), in contrast, sees competition *between* groups as the ultimate *cause* of sociality, in the sense that large groups can displace smaller ones from vital resources. Following Trivers (1972), Wrangham assumes that these resources are different for the sexes: female reproductive success is enhanced more by food than by mates, while for males the opposite holds. When food occurs in large enough patches (e.g., large fruit trees), it pays females to stay in the group and build up social bonds with each other to defend these resources against rival groups. However, when food is widely dispersed, competition drives females apart. This in turn affects the social relationships among males, because now females become difficult to monopolize. Wrangham proposes that under these conditions males become the philopatric gender and evolve social bonding to cooperatively defend the females within their home range against raiding males of neighboring communities (the prototypical example of such a male-bonded primate species is the chimpanzee). In addition, social bonding is presumed to be facilitated by a high degree of relatedness, which is considered to be an unavoidable consequence of philopatry. Based on these suppositions, Wrangham's theory not only accounts for being in groups, but for the identity of the resident gender as well. In addition, it provides a coarse categorization of social relationships.

To arrive also at more detailed predictions of social relationships, van Schaik combines within- and between-group competition in an extended model (van Schaik 1989). Competition is decomposed into a scramble and a contest component, and both are further divided in weak and strong forms. From the resulting combinations, he draws up a classification of primate social systems into competitive regimes. The matching types of social organizations (in terms of "despotic" or "egalitarian" societies *sensu* Vehrencamp [1983]) are then interpreted as predictions. For example, if ecological conditions lead to contest competition between groups, alliance-formation will be important and therefore dominants must relax contest competition within the group. Otherwise subordinates might either refrain from taking any risks in between-group contests or even defect to another group (van Hooff and van Schaik 1992).

4   MODEL FORMALISMS BEYOND RATIONALISM

A test case for the functionalist-rationalist paradigm would be to see if mobile robots, designed according to the principles of classical AI, are able to perform meaningful behavior in the real world without human intervention. Such attempts failed (Brooks 1994). The lack of noise- and fault-tolerance, the want of generalization abilities, the sequential nature of operation, and the inability to catch up with the dynamics of the environment (Brooks 1994; Pfeifer and Scheier in press) are some well-known reasons for this failure. Apparently, properties of the real world set up difficulties that cannot be solved by a purely computational approach.

We focus on three of these real world properties: the nonlinear dynamics of processes, the simultaneous interaction of units, and the effects of local spatial configuration. These are responsible for context dependent, complex causalities, and therefore defy an overly rationalist approach. For example,

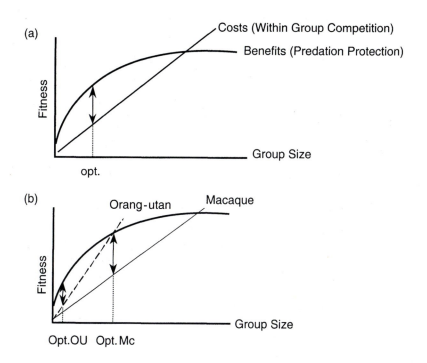

FIGURE 1 (a) van Schaik's model of optimal primate group size. (b) Hypothetical application of the model to explain species differences in optimal group size. Orang-utans are heavy arboreal frugivores that experience much stronger competition for food than the small, omnivorous macaques. Therefore the cost function of the orang-utans is steeper than the one of the macaques. Consequently, orang-utans experience a maximum net benefit at a smaller group size than macaques.

nonlinear systems can have more than one equilibrium, and these can be of different types (stable, unstable, and neutral). Slight changes in parameter values or initial values (for instance caused by noise) can cause the system to end up at another equilibrium than it would otherwise and in this way qualitatively change its behavior. In other words, a system can display multi-causality. A nonlinear dynamical systems model of between- and within-group competition (below) illustrates how this complicates setting up meaningful evolutionary hypotheses.

4.1 A DYNAMICAL SYSTEMS APPROACH TO COMPETITION WITHIN AND BETWEEN PRIMATE GROUPS

In a process-oriented view of primate societies, one deals with the interdependent *changes* of relevant variables in time. Accordingly, we propose a model of the form $dx_i/dt = x' = f(x_i)$, i.e., a set of coupled differential equations that describe how the change in a state variable is a function of itself and other state variables (this is the technical definition of a dynamical system).

As a starting point, the changes in group size are described by means of the logistic equation:

$$x' = rx - \frac{r}{k}x^2 = rx\left(1 - \frac{x}{k}\right). \tag{1}$$

The parameter r denotes the instantaneous rate of increase and is the sum of the net birthrate, $\rho =$ (births–deaths), and the net migration rate, $\mu =$ (emigrations–immigrations). For very small group sizes the effect of the damping term (rx^2/k) is negligible, leading to almost exponential growth. However, it quickly adopts inhibiting proportions for larger x and can therefore be interpreted as reflecting van Schaik's "within-group competition." A graph of $x' = f(x)$ against x (Figure 2(a)) is a parabola and identifies the system as nonlinear (otherwise the graph would be a straight line). The graph thus uncovers yet another property reserved for nonlinear systems: the possession of more than one equilibrium (or fixed point), i.e., that set of values of the state variables under which no change occurs and $x' = 0$. Here the fixed points are at $x = 0$ and at $x = k$. Inserting arrows along the x-axis (the "phase line") corresponding with growth (the region for which $x' = f(x) > 0$) or decay ($f(x) < 0$), reveals that the origin is unstable but that the fixed point at $x = k$ is stable. In other words, given $r > 0$, the group will always grow until it reaches a size of k. The parameter k therefore symbolizes the "carrying capacity" of the group's home range, i.e., the resources needed to sustain the group.

Between-group competition can be modeled by analogy to the Lotka-Volterra equations:

$$\begin{aligned}
x'_1 &= rx_1\left(1 - \tfrac{x_1}{k}\right) - sx_1x_2, \\
x'_2 &= Rx_2\left(1 - \tfrac{x_2}{K}\right) - Sx_1x_2.
\end{aligned} \tag{2}$$

The model now includes a mutual inhibition term that couples the logistic equations of group 1 and group 2. Points for which x'_1 or $x'_2 = 0$ are situated along lines (the isoclines) and visualized in a phase plot of x_2 against x_1 (Figure 2(b)). The equilibria of the complete system occur where the isoclines of x_2 intersect with those of x_1. Following the directions of the arrows representing the direction of change of x_1 and x_2, one sees that one of the groups grows until its size equals the carrying capacity, whereas simultaneously the other group becomes extinct. However, this scenario depends on the specific

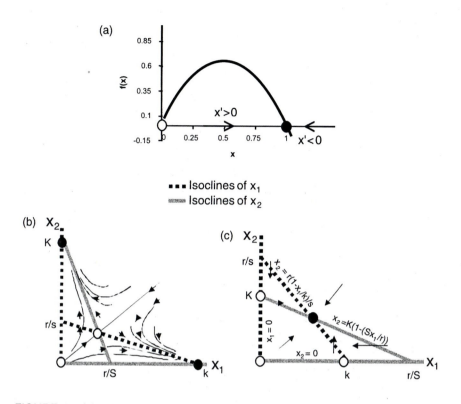

FIGURE 2 (a) Phase plot of the logistic equation $x' = f(x) = rx(1 - (x/K))$. (b)-(c) Phase space representations of the model for within-group competition and scramble competition between groups: (b) sloping isocline of x_2 is steeper than the one of x_1, implying $(r/S < k) \wedge (r/s < K)$ (or, equivalently, $(r/k < S) \wedge (r/K < s)$) and competitive exclusion. (c) the reversed case with $(r/k > S) \wedge (r/K > s)$, leading to coexistence. Open circles: unstable fixed points, black circles: stable fixed points. Equations for the isoclines are identical for both cases, but are only presented in (b). For further explanation, see text.

condition that the sloping isocline for x_2 is steeper than the one for x_1; if this situation is reversed and r is assumed to equal R,[1] coexistence results (Figure 2(c)). The reason for this is that now $\{(r/K > s) \wedge (r/k > S)\}$, i.e., each group inhibits itself more than it does the other.

Equation (2) can be interpreted as a model for between-group *scramble* competition because it formulates density effects irrespective of possible individual differences in dominance status or physical strength. Also, for the outcome of the between-group competition it is irrelevant which of the two groups is the larger one.

---

[1] For simplicity, the parameter values of the groups are henceforth set equal.

In the case of between-group contest competition *sensu* Wrangham, however, it is the smaller of the two groups that is displaced from vital resources by the larger one.

We infer that these evictions harm individuals in such a way that they reduce the size of their group. This is formulated by the function $\mu(x_{\text{ref}}, x_{\text{riv}}) = c \cdot \ln(x_{\text{ref}}/x_{\text{riv}})$, which implies a negative effect only when the reference group is smaller than a rival group (c is the coefficient for intergroup contest competition). This impact is modeled (somewhat loosely) after the expectation of van Hooff and van Schaik (1992) so that: (1) the smaller of the two groups experiences loss of members due to emigration (or death) following displacement by the larger group, (2) the larger ("winning") group attracts immigrants, and (3) nothing happens when the groups are of equal size. This is accomplished by replacing the net migration rate μ of r in the first model by the function $\mu(x_{\text{ref}}, x_{\text{riv}})$. The resulting model

$$x'_{\text{ref}} = r(x_{\text{ref}}, x_{\text{riv}}) \cdot x_{\text{ref}} \left(1 - \frac{x_{\text{ref}}}{k}\right), \tag{3}$$

where ref, riv = $\{1, 2\}$ and riv $\neq$ ref, with $r(x_{\text{ref}}, x_{\text{riv}}) = \rho + c \cdot \ln(x_{\text{ref}}/x_{\text{riv}})$, appears to have six isoclines and as many fixed points (Figure 3(a)). Inserting arrows that symbolize the direction of change reveals that half of the fixed points are stable. At $x_1 = k, x_2 = K$ resides a stable (attracting) equilibrium. It is flanked by two unstable fixed points that are located at the intersections of, respectively, the upper sloping isocline ($x_2 = x_1 e^{\rho/c}$) with $x_2 = K$ and the lower sloping isocline ($x_2 = x_1 e^{-\rho/c}$) with $x_1 = k$. These fixed points are "saddles"; they attract trajectories when far away but repel them when close by, either toward the central equilibrium or toward the "lateral" attractors at the coordinate axes. The trajectories that approach the saddle points at arbitrarily small distances are called separatrices because they divide the phase space in the basins of attraction of the central fixed point (shaded in Figure 3(a)) on the one hand and those of the lateral attractors on the other hand. The origin is a repellor.

The "standard expectation" of larger groups eliminating smaller ones holds for initial values outside the basin of attraction of the central fixed point, within it coexistence is guaranteed. The reference group can even grow in the presence of an initially larger rival group provided that $x_{\text{ref}} < k$ and $r(x_{\text{ref}}, x_{\text{riv}}) > 0$, i.e., its net rate of reproduction (ρ) surpasses losses due to emigration and death (induced by lost contests with the rival group). This holds as long as $x_{\text{riv}} > x_{\text{ref}} e^{-\rho/c}$ and therefore depends on the value of ρ/c. Changing ρ relative to c can be seen as pivoting the sloping isoclines around their origin (Figure 3(b)). When ρ increases to infinity (or c goes to zero), the upper isocline approaches the ordinate whereas the lower one goes into the direction of the abscissa. As a consequence, the upper and lower saddles are dragged, respectively, leftward and downward, thus enlarging the central basin of attraction and favoring coexistence. However, when ρ approaches zero, the isoclines turn toward each other until the saddles collide with the

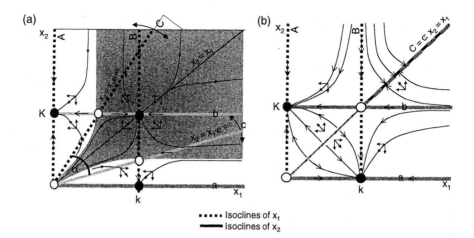

FIGURE 3   Phase space of the model for competition within groups and contest between groups. Open circles: unstable fixed points, black circles: stable fixed points. Fixed points are situated where isoclines of x_1 intersect those of x_2. Isoclines of x_1 (dotted lines, capital letters) are A: $x_1 = 0$, B: $x_1 = k$, C: $x_2 = x_1 \exp(\rho/c)$. Isoclines of x_2 (grey lines, small letters) are a: $x_2 = 0$, b: $x_2 = K$, c: $x_2 = x_1 \exp(-\rho/c)$. In (a) $\rho > 0$ and therefore the angle (α) between the sloping isoclines C and c is also larger than zero. This angle can be changed by pivoting C and c around their origin. (b) Bifurcation at $\rho = 0$ and hence $\alpha = 0$: the isoclines C and c coincide on the diagonal and the unstable collateral fixed points collapse with the central attractor to form an unstable equilibrium. Coexistence is now only possible above carrying capacity (the thick dotted line of fixed points).

central attractor. When this happens, the saddles are annihilated and what remains is an unstable equilibrium. Such a sudden alteration in the number of fixed points is called a bifurcation in dynamical systems jargon and implies an abrupt change in the behavior of the system. Coexistence is now only possible if both groups are above carrying capacity; when starting in that region of the phase space the size of both groups changes until their trajectories end up at the diagonal (i.e., when they are of equal size) which is actually a line of fixed points.

Between-group scramble competition can be included by replacing $\{r, R\}$ with $\{r(x_{\text{ref}}, x_{\text{riv}}), R(x_{\text{riv}}, x_{\text{ref}})\}$ in Eq. (2). As outlined above, coexistence in the presence of a between-group scramble competition requires both $r/k > S$ and $R/K > s$ given that the growth parameters (r, R) are equal. In the presence of a between-group contest, this condition becomes $\{(r(x_{\text{ref}}, x_{\text{riv}})/k > S) \wedge (R(x_{\text{ref}}, x_{\text{riv}})/K > s)\}$. But note that $r(x_{\text{ref}}, x_{\text{riv}})$ is a function that changes in time and increases at the expense of $R(x_{\text{riv}}, x_{\text{ref}})$. It follows that the parameters of growth are mostly unequal and that the simultaneous truth of both propositions will rarely be met. In other words, already small values of $\{s, S\}$ perturb the coexistence of contesting groups.

The essential difference between the traditional and the dynamical systems models is that in the latter competition within and between groups are not *additive components*, but *integrated dynamics* in the sense that they mutually affect each others' impact (a similar point was raised by Hemelrijk and Luteyn [1998]). Furthermore, the models show that introducing simple nonlinear dynamics leads to more diverse and subtle outcomes than those of the conventional approach. For instance, even if larger groups always negatively affect smaller ones by displacing them from vital resources, it is not necessarily true that in the long run an initially larger group eliminates a rival group. Instead, the eventual fate of a group depends critically on the strength of between-group competition relative to the net birth rate, the carrying capacity, and the initial group sizes. This suggests that for a range of parameter values the consequences of between-group contest selection do not necessarily favor the evolution of egalitarian behavior. On the other hand, between-group scramble competition—by sharpening between-group contest—may have a much stronger impact than that imposed by van Schaik (1989), who dismisses its effects on social relationships altogether.

4.2   INDIVIDUAL ORIENTED MODELS

It is generally acknowledged by primatologists that individual primates "decide" at the behavioral level which group size is optimal under a given set of ecological circumstances (e.g., Terborgh and Janson 1986). As a consequence, the dynamics at the group level are generally not considered in detail. However, as we have shown above, it is these dynamics that determine whether or not groups can coexist and thus set the conditions for the individuals' "options." But optimal individual decisions are hard to deduce under these circumstances because macropatterns generally have other properties than their constituent units. The role of between-group scramble might have been overlooked exactly because of this, as it is steered by the inequality $r(x_{\text{ref}}, x_{\text{riv}})/k > s$, which is not a trait of individuals.

Furthermore, it is generally unknown by what means individuals reach their optimal decisions. Although the "rules-of-the-thumb" type of explanations as proposed by optimization theorists (e.g., "giving-up" criteria by averaging experiences) may be easy problem-solving tricks from the viewpoint of the researcher, they still assume a global knowledge that escapes the mental powers of even the smartest ape.

There is yet another problem. By focusing exclusively on the possible benefits of being in an optimally sized group, the patterning potential of interindividual interactions is easily overlooked. These patterns develop on a behavioral time scale but can be robust enough to erroneously suggest a genetic basis.

More specifically, when a number of entities interact locally, their actions at first may occur at random. But once a critical small number of these units begin to behave in a coherent fashion, the pattern they create may influence the behavior of the others. If this causes the elicited units to join in the collective activity, the growing structure will "enslave" even more units (as Haken [1977] calls this synergetic principle). The feedback between the ongoing structuring of the macropattern and the behavior of the entities at the microlevel represents a kind of circular causality and is the hallmark of self-organization.

Spatial heterogeneity can have a dramatic impact on these processes, as it dictates which units are to interact and which are not. Depending on the dynamics, the history, and the states of the entities, this brings about patterns in the spatial distribution of the entities. In turn this may lead to the development of unexpected social relationships.

A sophisticated tool to study this type of spatial and temporal dynamics is individual-oriented modeling. In the form of MIRROR worlds, Hogeweg and Hesper (1983, 1985) have been using this model formalism for more than a decade to study various etho-ecological processes. In the simplest case, a MIRROR world is an artificial world consisting of a space that is subdivided in patches and in which a variety of DWELLERs roam. The DWELLERs' behavior depends on their local environment, i.e., the state of the PATCH and the presence and state of other DWELLERs nearby. DWELLERs are active "once in a while," i.e., asynchronously and not at every time step. If active, they perform simple TODO actions, which have the form: "if the local situation is such and such, do this." The actions change the state of the PATCH, the state of the currently active DWELLER, its spatial position, and the state of another DWELLER with which it interacts. These changes affect the subsequent TODOs of the DWELLER itself and of others.

It is important to realize that a MIRROR world is not meant to resemble a particular "real" world closely, but rather is designed to add an interesting world to our observational universe; it is a world with a life of its own. In other words, a MIRROR world is a paradigm system rather than a model in the strict sense. To emphasize the difference, MIRROR world entities are referred to in capitals.

Primatological applications are the implementations of "Artificial Apes" (CHIMPs and ORANGs, te Boekhorst and Hogeweg 1994a,b), "SKINNIES" (Hogeweg 1988), and the reciprocating agents "ESTIMATORS" and "PERCEIVERS" (Hemelrijk 1996a,b; 1997; 1998a,b). Because a detailed description of these studies can be found in the papers cited above, we confine ourselves to a summary of the CHIMP model and some results on the spatial structure of "ESTIMATORS" and "PERCEIVERS."

The rationale behind the CHIMP model was to find out whether chimpanzee-like social structure (a fission-fusion society in which the females are predominantly solitary and males group especially with each other, see Goodall [1986]) can emerge from simple rules about looking for food and

mates in a structured environment and without resorting to the usual sociobi-
ological cost/benefit assumptions about relatedness and neighboring communities (see section 3.2). This appeared indeed to be possible. As in chimpanzee
societies, male CHIMPs are more social than females. In the CHIMP world
this is a self-organized property that comes about because of the following
set of TODOs. Male CHIMPs approach others to see if they are cycling FE-
MALEs; if this is the case, the MALE stays with the FEMALE until she is no
longer in oestrus. However, if a MALE spots another which is also a MALE,
the consequence is that each approaches the other. When, in addition, they
happen to encounter each other in a small TREE, a reinforcing process sets
in: the TREE is depleted by the cofeeding CHIMPs before they are satiated,
and as a consequence they synchronously go to the nearest food TREE and
a travel band emerges. Being in a travel band speeds up the process because
the larger number of CHIMPs empties a TREE more quickly, which forces
them to travel further. In turn, this enhances encounter rate, a larger party
size, and therefore an even quicker depletion of food trees, further ranging etc.
FEMALEs are less social because they lack the partner-seeking TODO and
only look for food TREEs.

A nice spin-off of the model is that it immediately suggested an explanation for another puzzle: travel band formation in the presumed "solitary"
orang-utan. Because of their large body weight these animals are assumed to
suffer from severe feeding competition (Sugardjito et al. 1987). But if these
costs are the reason for solitariness, why then do orang-utans sometimes aggregate? The finding that they do so, especially during a period of the year
when many small trees simultaneously bear fruit (at least in the study area
where the first author collected data; see te Boekhorst et al. [1991]), points
to a CHIMP-like process. In agreement with this, te Boekhorst and Hogeweg
(1994b) found that a number of corollaries from the CHIMP world also held
in an ORANG world and could be confirmed with field data from wild orang-
utans. The most important one was that the probability to stay in a travel
band depended on the size of the previously visited food tree.

The worlds of the "Artificial Apes" focus on group composition rather
than on spatial structure of groups and social relationships between individuals within groups. The work of Hemelrijk shows how MIRROR worlds are
eminently suited to study these aspects as well. By reviewing some of her
results, we turn to some cognitive aspects of primate behavior.

4.3 SPATIAL STRUCTURE, SOCIAL RELATIONS, AND COGNITION

Primates are known for their high cognitive capacities, which are thought to
be especially manifest in their social behavior, particularly their dominance
interactions. These most often consist of threats and attacks and usually take
place between two individuals only. Sometimes, however, a third individual
intervenes by attacking one of the two combatants and in this way supports
the other. This is called coalition formation. Primates are generally assumed

to be highly strategic in their decisions as to when to form coalitions and with whom. For instance, they are thought to repay received support and presumed to keep records of the frequency of support received from every partner (de Waal and Luttrell 1988). Yet, in her individual-based computer simulations, Hemelrijk (1996a,b; 1997; 1998a,b) has made a first step toward showing how complex patterns of coalition formation may emerge in the absence of sophisticated cognitive reflections. Inspired by a simulation by Hogeweg (1988), she implemented a world in which entities perform dominance interactions when they perceive someone nearby; otherwise they follow straightforward rules of moving and turning (Figure 4). Entities have not been endowed with record keeping, rules to support others in fights or other strategic considerations. Dominance interactions in the model represent the so-called "winner-loser" effect." This effect has been established in many animal species, such as crustaceans, spiders, insects, amphibians, reptiles, birds, mammals, and humans. It implies that the effects of losing (and winning) are self-reinforcing, i.e., that losing a fight increases the probability of losing the next fight (even if the opponent is weak). By running the model, several forms of emergent social behavior have been noted. A dominance hierarchy arises (Figure 5(b)) and support is recorded; support even appears to be repaid, despite the absence of a motivation to aid or a mental mechanism to keep records of it. Reciprocation of

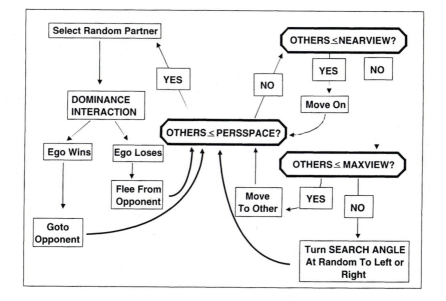

FIGURE 4   Behavioral rules of the enitities in Hemelrijk's models. Execution of acts depends on whether threshold values of three paramaters are surpassed that symbolize critical distances: "Personal Space" (PERSSPACE) < NEARVIEW < MAXVIEW.

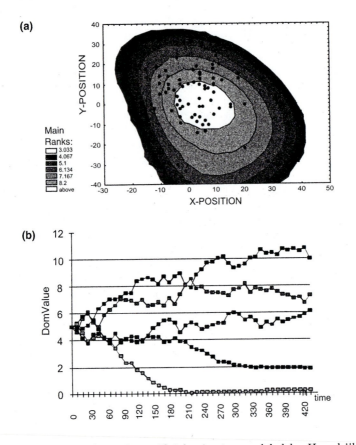

FIGURE 5 Some data from the artificial primates modeled by Hemelrijk. In the virtual worlds a social structure has emerged in which entities have developed a dominance status (b). Due to the interactions among the entities (see Figure 4), dominant entities especially occur at the center whereas subordinates mostly are at the periphery (a). In turn, this spatial structure reinforces the differentiation of the dominance hierarchy. In (a) the spatial positions of 8 entities are shown for every other time step. The surface contours in (a) are isoclines of identical mean rank and were obtained by cubic spline smoothing.

support appears to be a consequence of subsequent series of cooperative acts. These acts consist of two entities supporting each other in an alternating fashion by chasing away a third. Cooperation originates simply because by fleeing from the attack range of one opponent the victim ends up within that of the other opponent. This chain of events repeats itself until the spatial structure changes such that one of the two partners comes within attacking distance of the other. These series have been seen particularly in loose groups, because in such configurations entities are less disturbed and distracted by others. The consequences of different degrees of aggressiveness have been studied by varying the attack range of the entities. A striking result is that a wider attack range, leading to more aggression, increases the frequency of cooperation. Thus, the model points to some new questions that would not be asked when social behavior is merely approached from a cognitive perspective. For example, is cooperation (e.g., repayment of support) more general in loose than cohesive groups and more prevalent among animals that are more often aggressive? Furthermore, the outcomes clearly question the explanatory importance of game theoretical constructs such as the Prisoner's Dilemma. The observed uninterrupted series of immediate reciprocation of support conforms to the temporal structure of the Tit-for-Tat strategy (Axelrod and Hamilton 1981) and also other exhibitions of game theoretical parlance ("defection," "retaliation," "Tit-for-Two-Tats," and "Generous Tit-for-Tat") have been witnessed occasionally. However, these manifestations emanate without considering any particular costs or benefits associated with acts of cooperation and defection but are solely due to the intertwined effects of displaying dominance and social cohesion (Hemelrijk 1997). It is unlikely that a game theoretical analysis of this particular "world" would have led to the same conclusion.

Recent results (Hemelrijk 1998a,b) show that in addition to a dominance hierarchy and intricate social interactions, a social-spatial pattern arises with dominants in the center and subordinates at the periphery (Figure 5(a)). Remarkably, exactly the same social-spatial structure has been described for several primate species. In line with Hamilton's theory of the selfish herd (Hamilton 1971), it has been proposed that this configuration reflects competition for the safest place in the group. However, in the artificial primates it comes about without any positional preference and is nothing more than a consequence of dominants chasing away subordinates (Hemelrijk 1998a,b).

After varying the intensity of aggression, it appears that the social behavior of the artificial entities corresponds markedly with several characteristics (such as cohesiveness and degree of counter-attack) of certain fiercely and mildly aggressive primate species (such as, respectively, rhesus and Sulawesi monkeys, see Thierry [1985]). Apparently, this model captures essential characteristics of primates. It is therefore worthwhile to see if other patterns emerging in the model can be found in real primates. A candidate is the spatial centrality of dominants, which is more conspicuous in fierce than mild entities (Hemelrijk in press). Apart from these specific hypotheses, the model also yields general insight into how social-spatial structure forms an integral part of aggressive interactions and the development and maintenance of a dominance hierarchy. In this way, the model has shown how complex social interaction patterns are not exclusively controlled by genetically or cognitively predefined qualities of individuals but may arise also from local interactions.

5   EVALUATION

What is the epistemological status of the complex systems models discussed
so far? Although it could be argued that the behavioral rules in the individual-
oriented models reflect a kind of "costs" and "benefits," these are not explicitly
defined as such in order to evaluate optimization principles. In other words,
the starting point is not normative or ultimate. On the other hand, they are
also not specifically about mechanisms. The dynamical systems equations are
purely mathematical abstractions and too phenomenological to allow for a
mechanistic interpretation. The rule-based implementations underlying the
individual-oriented models are as disembodied and algorithmic as any computer program in the style of old fashioned AI. However, the crucial difference
with cognitive science (and a functionalist approach in general) is that here
the algorithms are not seen as explanations for behavior in themselves; they
only function to get the virtual entities to do what they have to do. The real
insight comes from the patterns that arise out of the interactions the entities are engaged in once they perform their basic behavior. A similar case
can be made for the dynamical systems approach; in both model formalisms
what matters is that they help us to discover logical consequences that, due
to nonlinearity and the multitude of interactions, our brains are unable to
foresee. To sum up, a complex systems approach is neither "ultimate" nor
"proximate" but "appropriate" in that it extends our insights and forestalls
naïve predictions.

Nevertheless, one may ask in what respects this view reflects reality. Does
self-organization only reside in equations and computer simulations or does
it also occur naturally? To establish this, building physical robots and doing
experiments with them is a promising approach for studying self-organized
behavior in the real world.

5.1   INSIGHTS FROM SITUATED ROBOTICS

As an example of insights gained from robotics, we briefly discuss the work
of Maris and te Boekhorst (1996) who have studied collective behavior in
groups of up to five "situated" robots. Situated robots operate on the basis
of their morphology, distributed control, and on interacting with the local
environment instead of computation, central planning, and global knowledge.
Because of this they suffer less from the computational overhead that comes
with the updating of internal representations and therefore adapt much more
quickly to changing environments than their classical predecessors. (For extensive argumentation in favor of this new paradigm in AI, see Brooks [1991];
Pfeifer and Verschure [1992]; Hendriks-Jansen [1996]; and Pfeifer and Scheier
[in press].)

The robots used by Maris and te Boekhorst (called Didabots, from "Di-
dactical Robot") are small, autonomous vehicles that together shift about half
of a set of randomly distributed polystyrene cubes in a central heap and line

up the remaining ones against the wall. From an engineering point of view this is a remarkable feat, given the complications when such a task has to be designed from scratch. The rationalist way to do this would be to include such faculties as object recognition and object handling, which ask for specific sensors, recognition schemata, and actuators. Furthermore, coordination in movement and timing and consensus about the decisions among the robots as to where and when to drop the objects demand quite complex cognitive capacities, so sophisticated software seems to be an unavoidable requirement.

However, none of these considerations is found back in the embarrassingly simple implementation used by Maris and te Boekhorst. Didabots are actually realized "Braitenberg vehicles," hypothetical, self-operating machines contrived by the neurobiologist Braitenberg (1984) as thought experiments. The basic mechanism is that the motors controlling the rotation speed of the wheels go faster the more there is of the quality to which the sensors (connected to the motors) are tuned. In this case the sensors detect infrared light that is reflected from objects after being radiated by IR transmitters on the robot. Four sensors are located laterally (two on each side) and one frontally. They are connected to the (two) motors in such a way that if the robot detects an obstacle on one side, the motors force forward movements on the wheel at the corresponding side and backward movement on the opposite wheel. As a consequence, the robot will turn away from the obstacle. For the experiments, the frontal IR-sensor is deactivated. This has the effect that the Didabot cannot "see" anything that is exactly in front of it and too small to be detected by any of the other sensors. Therefore, the Didabot collides with such an object and pushes it along until another obstacle (a wall, another object or another Didabot) is detected. Due to the subsequent avoidance movement, the shifted object is left behind. If the object is deposited close enough to another, they form a constellation that is large enough to be detected and avoided by the robots. In this way pairs are formed. The thusly increased patchiness of the environment improves the ability of the robots to bypass collisions. When only one robot is employed, the environment is soon structured sufficiently for the Didabot to maneuver almost without hitting cubes. In the numerous experiments that were performed, one single robot therefore never managed to form a single heap. Clusters grow by adding single blocks to existing "seeds" and seldom by shifting pairs or trios of cubes. Formation of large heaps thus depends critically on the availability of single cubes. These are supplied when using more than one robot: due to mutual avoidance movements, the robots now and then "erroneously" destroy pairs. However, when too many robots are around larger heaps are broken down. This explains why three robots appeared to be the "optimal" group size for forming one single, large cluster. Using smaller or larger numbers of robots results in less organized patterns of more than one heap and often some single cubes.

The Didabots, by interacting with each other and their surroundings, structure their environment. Because of this patterning their behavior changes: they interfere less often with objects and more with each other, and their travel paths appear to become less irregular in time. Because these behavioral changes in turn affect the clustering process, this is a typical example of the feedback between the pattern formation and the activities of entities responsible for that pattern. These experiments therefore demonstrate self-organization outside the computer that, more importantly, is amenable to experimentation.

The work of Maris and te Boekhorst was inspired by studies on ants (in particular by models of Deneubourg et al. [1990]) and indeed reflects certain aspects of the collective behavior of these insects. It is, however, unlikely that experiments with robots as simple as Didabots yield detailed models for the social behavior of (non)human primates. Nevertheless, building robots makes one aware of significant physical constraints that would go unnoticed when simulating artificial worlds in silica. But there is more that makes autonomous robots important as "tools for thought."

For one thing, the Didabots function as an important warning against the black-box character of proximate ethological models. To gauge the limits of the black-box approach, te Boekhorst and Maris (unpublished) have applied statistical tools commonly used by ethologists (such as factor analysis and the construction of Markov models, cf. van Hooff [1982]) to describe the behavior of Didabots. Although the analyses have revealed interesting and complex patterns, they did not lay bare anything about the internal mechanisms or "motivations" of the Didabots. This sobering fact becomes less discouraging when the focus of interest shifts from qualities of individuals to relations, because in that case a black box approach becomes less important. Likewise, statistics should concentrate on detecting patterns in relational dynamics. For this, nonlinear time series analysis seems a more appropriate tool than the linear techniques used by ethologists.

On the "ultimate" side, and imagining that Didabots are living creatures, one may come up with all kinds of amusing functional explanations of the heap-forming behavior. It might for instance be an energy-saving strategy, because the robots meander less after cleaning up the area. Or it increases opportunities for social interactions. Whatever the benefits, what exactly should be favored by natural selection when it operates on Didabots? Note that there is no "heap-building blue print" inside the Didabots, so there is no "gene for heap-building" to be promoted to the next generation. But also note that successful Didabots could be considered as "knock-out" mutants in which the gene representing the weight of the frontal sensor is missing. Just identifying the knocked-out gene and associating it with the observed behavior may then indeed lead to the erroneous conclusion that a "gene for cooperation" has been isolated. Unfortunately, instances of this misleading jargon from life-science industry and molecular biology increasingly show up in the media.

Finally, counter the idea that natural selection leads to ever more complicated "designs" by promoting increased capacities for information processing, here apparently complex social behavior is the consequence of constrained information in the form of physical short-sightedness. Abandoning short-sighted logic appears to be a prerequisite for forming this type of conclusion, which—in a nutshell—is the message of this chapter.

ACKNOWLEDGMENTS

The work of the second author was supported by a stipend from the Marie Heim Vögtlin Foundation and a grant from the "Kommision zur Förderung des akademischen Nachwuchses der Universität Zürich."

REFERENCES

Ahouse, J. C.
  1998 The Tragedy of A Priori Selectionism: Dennett and Gould on Adaptationism. Biology and Philosophy 13:359–391.

Arthur, W. Brian
  1989 Competing Technologies, Increasing Returns, and Lock-In by Historical Small Events: The Dynamics of Allocation Under Increasing Returns to Scale. Economic Journal 99:116–131.
  1990 Positive Feedbacks in the Economy. Scientific American 262(2):80–185.

Axelrod and Hamilton
  1981 The Evolution of Cooperation. Science 211:1390–1396.

Baerends, G. P.
  1976 The Functional Organisation of Behaviour. Animal Behaviour 24: 726–738.

Bateson, P.
  1991 Levels and Processes. In The Development and Integration of Behaviour. Essays in Honour of Robert Hinde. P. Bateson, ed. Pp. 3–16. Cambridge, UK: Cambridge University Press.

te Boekhorst, I. J. A., C. L. Schürmann, and J. Sugardjito
  1991 Residential Status and Seasonal Movements of Wild Orang-utans in the Gunung Leuser Reserve (Sumatera, Indonesia). Animal Behaviour 39:1098–1109.

te Boekhorst, I. J. A., and P. Hogeweg
  1994a Self-Structuring in Artificial "Chimps" Offers New Hypotheses for Male Grouping in Chimpanzees. Behaviour 130:3–4, 229–252.
  1994b Effects of Tree Size on Travelband Formation in Orang-utans: Data-Analysis Suggested By a Model Study. In Artificial Life IV. R. Brooks and P. Maes, eds. Pp. 119–129. Cambridge, MA: Bradford Books, MIT Press.

Braitenberg, V.
  1984 Vehicles. Experiments in Synthetic Psychology. Cambridge, MA:
       Bradford Books, MIT Press.

Brooks, R.
  1991 Intelligence Without Representations. Artificial Intelligence 47:
       139–159.
  1994 Intelligence Without Reason. *In* The "Artificial Life" Route to "Ar-
       tificial Intelligence." L. Steels and R. Brooks, eds. Pp. 25–81. Hillsdale,
       NJ: Erlbaum.

Byrne, R., and A. Whiten
  1988 Machiavellian Intelligence. Social Expertise and the Evolution of In-
       tellect in Monkeys, Apes, and Humans. Oxford: Clarendon Press.
  1991 Computation and Mindreading in Primate Tactical Deception. *In*
       Natural Theories of Mind. A. Whiten, ed. Pp. 127–141. Oxford: Black-
       well.

Colgan, P.
  1989 Animal Motivation. London: Chapman and Hall.

Cuthill, I. C., and A. I. Houston.
  1997 Managing Time and Energy. *In* Behavioural Ecology. An Evolution-
       ary Approach. J. R. Krebs and N. B. Davies, eds. Pp. 97–120. Oxford:
       Blackwell.

Dawkins, R.
  1976 Hierarchical Organization: A Candidate Principle for Ethology. *In*
       Growing Points in Ethology. P. P. G. Bateson and R. A. Hinde, eds.
       Pp. 7–54. Cambridge, UK: Cambridge University Press.

Deneubourg, J. L., S. Goss, N. R. Franks, A. Sendova-Franks, C. Detrain, and
L. Chretien.
  1990 The Dynamics of Collective Sorting: Robot-Like Ants and Ant-Like
       Robots. *In* Simulation of Adaptive Behaviour: From Animals to Ani-
       mats. J-A. Meyer and S. Wilson, eds. Pp. 356–363. Cambridge, MA:
       MIT Press.

Dennett, D. C.
  1995 Darwin's Dangerous Idea. Evolution and the Meanings of Life. New
       York: Simon and Schuster.

Dunbar, R. I. M.
  1992 Neocortex Size as a Constraint on Group Size in Primates. Journal
       of Human Evolution 20:469–493.

Epstein, J. M., and R. Axtell
  1996 Growing Artificial Societies: Social Science from the Bottom Up.
       Washington, DC: The Brookings Institution and Cambridge, MA: MIT
       Press.

Fodor, J. A.
  1976 The Language of Thought. New York: Cromwell.

Goodall, J.
  1986 The Chimpanzees of Gombe: Patterns of Behavior. Cambridge, MA: Belknapp Press, Harvard University Press.

Haken, H.
  1977 Synergetics: An Introduction. Heidelberg: Springer.

Hamilton, W. D.
  1971 Geometry for the Selfish Herd. Journal of Theoretical Biology 31: 295–311.

Hemelrijk, C. K.
  1996a Dominance Interactions, Spatial Dynamics and Emergent Reciprocity in a Virtual World. *In* From Animals to Animats IV. Fourth International Conference on Simulation of Adaptive Behavior. P. Maes, J-A. Meyer, J. Pollack, and S. W. Wilson, eds. Pp. 545–552. Cambridge, MA: Bradford Books, MIT Press.
  1996b Reciprocation in Primates: From Complex Cognition to Self-Structuring. *In* Great Ape Societies. W. C. McGrew, L. F. Marchant and T. Nishida, eds. Pp. 185–195. Cambridge, UK: Cambridge University Press.
  1997 Cooperation Without Genes, Games or Cognition. *In* Fourth European Conference on Artificial Life. P. Husbands and I. Harvey, eds. Pp. 511–520. Cambridge, MA: Bradford Books, MIT Press.
  1998a Spatial Centrality of Dominants Without Positional Preference. *In* Sixth International Conference on Artificial Life. C. Adami, R. K. Belew, H. Kitano, and C. Taylor, eds. Pp. 307–315. Cambridge, MA: Bradford Books, MIT Press.
  1998b Risk Sensitive and Ambiguity Reducing Dominance Interactions in a Virtual Laboratory. *In* From Animals to Animats V. Proceedings of the Fifth International Conference on Simulation of Adaptive Behavior. R. Pfeifer, B. Blumberg, J-A. Meyer, and S. W. Wilson, eds. Pp. 255–262. Cambridge, MA: Bradford Books, MIT Press.
  In press An Individual-Oriented Model on the Emergence of Despotic and Egalitarian Societies. Proceedings of the Royal Society London: Series B.

Hemelrijk, C. K., and M. Luteyn
  1998 Philopatry, Male Presence and Grooming Reciprocation Among Female Primates: A Comparative Perspective. Behavioral Ecology and Sociobiology 42:207–215.

Hendriks-Jansen, H.
  1996 Catching Ourselves in the Act. Situated Activity, Ineractive Emergence, Evolution and Human Thought. Cambridge, MA: Bradford Books, MIT Press.

Hinde, R. A.
  1982 Ethology: Its Nature and Relations with Other Sciences. Oxford: Oxford University Press.

Hogeweg, P., and B. Hesper
1983 The Ontogeny of Interaction Structure in Bumble Bee Colonies: A MIRROR World. Behavioral Ecology and Sociobiology 12:271–283.
1985 Socioinformatic Processes, a MIRROR Modelling Methodology. Journal of Theoretical Biology 113:311–330.

Hogeweg, P.
1988 MIRROR Beyond MIRROR, Puddles of LIFE. *In* Artificial Life II. Christopher G. Langton, Charles Taylor, J. Doyne Farmer, and Steen Rasmussen, eds. Pp. 297–316. Santa Fe Institute Studies in the Sciences of Complexity, Proceedings Volume XVII. Redwood City, CA: Addison-Wesley.

van Hooff, J. A. R. A. M.
1982 Categories and Sequences of Behavior: Methods of Description and Analysis. *In* Handbook of Methods in Nonverbal Behaviour. K. R. Scherer and P. Ekman, eds. Pp. 362–439. Cambridge, UK: Cambridge University Press.

van Hooff, J. A. R. A. M., and C. P. van Schaik
1992 Cooperation in Competition: The Ecology of Primate Bonds. *In* Coalitions and Alliances in Humans and Other Animals. A. H. Harcourt and F. B. M. de Waal, eds. Pp. 358–389. Oxford: Oxford University Press.

Humphrey, N.
1976 The Social Function of Intellect. *In* Growing Points in Ethology. P. G. Bateson and R. A. Hinde, eds. Pp. 303–317. Cambridge, UK: Cambridge University Press.

Kirman, A.
1997 The Economy as an Evolving Network. Journal of Evolutionary Economics 7:339–353.

Lewontin, R. C., and R. Levins
1987 Aspects of Wholes and Parts in Population Biology. *In* Evolution of Social Behavior and Integrated Levels. G. Greenberg and E. Tobach, eds. Pp. 31–52. Hillsdale, NJ: Erlbaum.

Maris, M., and I. J. A. te Boekhorst
1996 Exploiting Physical Constraints: Heap Formation Through Behavioral Error in a Group of Robots. *In* Intelligent Robots and Systems, Proceedings of the 1996 IEEE/RSJ International Conference on Intelligent Robots and Systems (IROS96) Part III. Pp. 1655–1661. Osaka.

Matsuzawa, T.
1996 Chimpanzee Intelligence in Nature and in Captivity: Isomorphisms of Symbol Use and Tool Use. *In* Great Ape Societies. W. C. McGrew, L. F. Marchant and T. Nishida, eds. Pp. 196–209. Cambridge, UK: Cambridge University Press.

McFarland, D.
   1989 Problems of Animal Behaviour. Harlow, UK: Longman House.

Newell, A., and H. A. Simon
   1976 Computer Science as Empirical Inquiry: Symbols and Search. Communications of the ACM 19, 3:113–126.

Peters, E. E.
   1991 Chaos and Order in the Capital Markets. A New View of Cycles, Prices and Market Volatility. New York: Wiley.

Pfeifer, R., and C. Scheier
   In press Understanding Intelligence. Cambridge, MA: MIT Press.

Pfeifer, R., and P. Verschure
   1992 Distributed Adaptive Control: A Paradigm for Designing Autonomous Agents. *In* Towards a Practice of Autonomous Systems: Proceedings of the First European Conference on Artificial Life. F. Varela and P. Bourgine, eds. Pp. 21–30. Cambridge, MA: MIT Press.

Putnam, H.
   1975 Philosophy and Our Mental Life. *In* Philosophical Papers 2: Mind, Language and Reality, Pp. 291–303. New York: Cambridge University Press.

Pylyshyn, Z.
   1984 Computation and Cognition. Cambridge, MA: MIT Press.

Savage-Rumbaugh, S. E.
   1986 Ape Language: From Conditioned Responses to Symbols. New York: Columbia University Press.

Sawaguchi, T.
   1992 The Size of the Neocortex in Relation to Ecology and Social Structure in Monkeys and Apes. Folia Primatologica 58:131–145.

Simon, H. A.
   1969 The Sciences of the Artificial. Cambridge, MA: MIT Press.

Sugardjito, J., I. J. A. te Boekhorst, and J. A. R. A. M. van Hooff
   1987 Ecological Constraints on the Grouping of Wild Orang-utans (*Pongo pygmaeus*) in the Gunung Leuser National Park, Sumatera, Indonesia. International Journal of Primatology 8:17–41.

Tamborini, R.
   1997 Knowledge and Economic Behavior. A Constructivist Approach. Journal of Evolutionary Economics 7:49–72.

Terborgh, J., and C. H. Janson
   1986 The Socioecology of Primate Groups. Annual Review of Ecology and Systematics 17:111–135.

Thierry, B.
  1985 Patterns of Agonistic Interactions in Three Species of Macaque (*Macaca mulatta, M. fasciculatis, M. tonkeana*). Aggressive Behavior 11: 223–233.

Trivers, R. L.
  1972 Parental Investment and Sexual Selection. *In* Sexual Selection and the Descent of Man 1871–1971. B. Campbell, ed. Pp. 136–179. Chicago, IL: Aldine.

van Schaik, C. P.
  1983 Why are Diurnal Primates Living in Groups? Behaviour 87:120–144.
  1989 The Ecology of Social Relationships Amongst Female Primates. *In* Comparative Socioecology. V. Standen and R. A. Foley, eds. Pp. 195–218. Oxford: Blackwell.

Vehrencamp, S. L.
  1983 A Model for the Evolution of Despotic Versus Egalitarian Societies. Animal Behavior 31:667–682.

de Waal, F., and L. Luttrell
  1988 Mechanisms of Social Reciprocity in Three Primate Species: Symmetrical Relationship Characteristics or Cognition? Ethology and Sociobiology 9:101–118.

Wrangham, R. W.
  1979 On the Evolution of Ape Social Systems. Social Science Information 18:335–368.
  1980 An Ecological Model of Female-Bonded Primate Groups. Behaviour 75:262–300.
  1987 Evolution of Social Structure. *In* Primate Societies. B. B. Smuts, D. L. Cheney, R. M. Seyfarth, R. W. Wrangham, and T. T. Struhsaker, eds. Pp. 282–296. Chicago, IL: Chicago University Press.

The Evolution of Cooperation in an Ecological Context: An Agent-Based Model

John W. Pepper
Barbara B. Smuts

1 INTRODUCTION

The social and behavioral sciences have a long-standing interest in the factors that foster selfish (or individualistic) versus altruistic (or cooperative) behavior. Since the 1960s, evolutionary biologists have also devoted considerable attention to this issue. In the last 25 years, mathematical models (reviewed in Wilson and Sober 1994) have shown that, under particular demographic conditions, natural selection can favor traits that benefit group members as a whole, even when the bearers of those traits experience reduced reproductive success relative to other members of their group. This process, often referred to as "trait group selection" (D. S. Wilson 1975) can occur when the population consists of numerous, relatively small "trait groups," defined as collections of individuals who influence one another's fitness as a result of the trait in question. For example, consider a cooperative trait such as alarm calling, which benefits only individuals near the alarm caller.[1] A trait group would include all individuals whose fitness depends on whether or not a given individual

---

[1]For this chapter, we define "cooperation" to include any behavior that raises the fitness, or average reproductive success, of the group in which it occurs, but decreases the actor's fitness relative to other group members. Within evolutionary biology, such

gives an alarm call. If the cooperative trait confers sufficiently large reproductive benefits on the average group member, it can spread. This is because trait groups that happen to include a large proportion of cooperators will send out many more offspring into the population as a whole than will groups containing few, or no cooperators. Thus, even though noncooperators out reproduce cooperators *within* trait groups (because they experience the benefits of the presence of cooperators without incurring the costs), this advantage can be offset by differences in rates of reproduction *between* trait groups. Numerous models of group selection (Wilson and Sober 1994) show that whether cooperative traits (as defined in footnote 1) can spread depends on the relative magnitude of fitness effects at these two levels of selection (within and between trait groups). In addition, there is a growing body of empirical evidence for the operation of group selection in nature (e.g., Colwell 1981; Breden and Wade 1989; Bourke and Franks 1995; Stevens et al. 1995; Seeley 1996; Miralles et al. 1997; Brookfield 1998) and under experimental conditions (reviewed in Goodnight and Stevens 1997).

These developments have highlighted two critical factors that combined determine the strength of between-group selection. The first of these is the structuring of fitness effects, i.e., which individuals are affected by the expression of the trait, to what extent, and in which direction. The second important factor is the genetic structure of trait groups, i.e., the extent to which individuals who influence one another's fitness through a particular trait are more likely to share the alleles underlying that trait than members of the population at large. Kin-directed behavior is the most biologically important source of genetic structure, and it has received the most attention from evolutionary biologists (Hamilton 1964). Because kin-directed behavior facilitates between-group selection by decreasing genetic variance within trait groups and increasing it between trait groups, some evolutionary biologists, including W. D. Hamilton, the formulator of kin selection theory, have regarded kin selection as a special case of group selection (Hamilton 1975:337; Futuyma 1986:264; Breden 1990; Queller 1991). Others have argued that kin selection is an alternative to group selection. According to this view, although group selection can occur without kin selection in theory, the necessary conditions are so stringent as to make it unimportant in nature (e.g., Maynard Smith 1964, 1976; Williams 1966; Grafen 1984; Alexander 1989). Over the last 30 years, the debates about group versus individual selection and kin selection have played a central role among those interested in social evolution and the functioning of small-scale societies (e.g., E. O. Wilson 1975; Trivers 1985; Alexander 1987; Cronin 1991;, Wilson and Sober 1994; Sober and Wilson 1998).

---

behaviors are often referred to as "altruistic." We avoid this term because it has been used in different ways by different authors, generating considerable confusion (Wilson and Dugatkin 1992). Ours is a very specific definition of the term cooperation that does not necessarily correspond to the way it is used by other researchers. For example, "cooperation" is sometimes employed to refer to joint actions (e.g., cooperative hunting) that *raise* the fitness of cooperators relative to other group members.

Formal mathematical models have clarified the role of local fitness effects and population genetic structure as causal factors in group selection but have almost completely failed to address how they can arise within an ecological context. Fitness effects and population structure are often represented in ways that have more to do with the exigencies of equation-based modeling than with how organisms behave in nature. Such models demonstrate that cooperation can evolve under the specified conditions, but they leave unexplored the critical question of whether the kinds of local fitness effects and genetic population structure they assume are realistic, and how they might come about. Here we describe a model in which both local fitness effects and population genetic structure emerge through the actions of individuals following simple yet plausible rules of behavior in spatially varying environments. We use the model to explore three interrelated questions raised by approaching multilevel selection from an ecological perspective:

1. How easily can ecological variation alone generate local fitness effects and genetic structure sufficient to drive the evolution of cooperation through trait group selection?
2. Given reasonable ecological assumptions, does between-group selection require association among kin in order to be effective, or can cooperation spread even in the absence of kin selection?
3. Do the answers to questions 1 and 2 vary depending on the nature of the cooperative trait in question?

To address the third question, we investigate the evolution of two different cooperative traits with long histories in the literature on the evolution of cooperation: alarm calling and feeding restraint. Alarm calling is perhaps the classic example of altruistic behavior among nonhumans and was one of the first to be extensively studied in the field (e.g., Sherman 1977; Hoogland 1983). Feeding restraint was proposed by Wynne-Edwards (1962) as a widespread behavior that evolved through group selection, but his arguments were not well supported either theoretically or empirically. More recently the issue of feeding restraint or "prudent predation" has been revisited for specific cases (e.g., Hart et al. 1991; Frank 1996; Hemptinne and Dixon 1997; Miralles et al. 1997).

Virtually all published quantitative models of group selection are based on systems of equations. However, such models have several critical limitations for modeling multilevel selection. First, they require simplifying assumptions, such as homogeneous randomly mixed populations and infinite population sizes, that can limit the possible outcomes in important ways. Second, in equation-based models, population structure (the division of a population into more or less discrete groups, or the absence of such divisions), must be assumed a priori. Many authors have argued that unlike those found in mathematical models, groups in the real world do not act as vehicles of selection strongly enough to affect evolutionary outcomes because they are too few in number, too long in generation time, or too amorphous and ephemeral (e.g., Williams 1966; Dawkins 1982:100, 1989:297).

In an effort to overcome these problems, researchers in a growing number of fields are turning to an approach called "agent-based" or "individual-based" modeling. The essence of this approach is that instead of using equations that apply uniformly to the entire system, the model consists of individuals or "agents" that interact according to an explicit set of rules of behavior. Advantages include the ability to represent the behaviors and interactions of individuals in a more direct and natural way, to incorporate variation over space and time, and to incorporate nonlinear dynamics (Huston et al. 1988; Judson 1994; Belew et al. 1996). In addition, agent-based models require no starting assumptions about the nature of groups or nonrandom interactions among individuals; instead, population structure can be generated by simple rules of interaction. Moreover, recent advances in object-oriented programming techniques have greatly facilitated the use of agent-based models of biological processes (Judson 1994; Reynolds and Acock 1997; Sequeira et al. 1997). Despite their success in other areas, agent-based models have been used surprisingly little in evolutionary biology. This chapter is a first step in applying the tools of agent-based modeling to the long-standing problem of multilevel selection.

Our goal in this preliminary study was not to produce a realistic representation of any specific system, but rather to construct a "minimal model" of multilevel selection in an ecological context, one which leaves out as much as possible while still capturing the essential properties of interest (Roughgarden et al. 1996). Our hope is that understanding the dynamics of a simple (and relatively manageable) model will help generate useful new hypotheses about when and how group-beneficial traits can evolve in nature.

2   THE MODEL

The computer model included resources (plants) growing in two-dimensional space, and agents (foragers) moving about, eating food, interacting, reproducing, and dying. We assumed only that individuals showed some very simple behaviors, such as a tendency to move toward food. We then explored the question of whether individuals, by pursuing unevenly distributed resources, would generate sufficient population structure to drive significant levels of between-group selection. Like those in the real world, the groups that formed in this model did not have discrete boundaries, either in space or time. Instead these "trait groups" were characterized by shared fitness effects that varied continuously in strength over both space and time.

2.1   THE MODEL WORLD

The model world was a two-dimensional grid, wrapped around in both axes to avoid edge effects. It contained two kinds of agents: plants and foragers.

TABLE 1   Standard parameter settings.

Parameter	Value
All experiments	
Minimum number of plants	500
Plant maximum size (energy units)	10
Starting number of foragers	40
Forager starting energy (energy units)	50
Forager metabolic rate (energy units)	2
Forager fertility threshold (energy units)	100
Alarm-calling experiments	
Plant linear growth rate (energy units)	1
Forager feeding restraint (% left uneaten)	1%
Probability of predator attack	0.02
Alarm-calling range (# of cells)	5
Feeding restraint experiments	
Plant logistic growth rate r	0.2
Forager feeding restraint (% left uneaten)	1% or 50%
Probability of predator attack	0

Because we wished to control the distribution of plants as an experimental variable, plants were created only at the start of a run, and did not move, die, or reproduce. A plant's only "behaviors" were to grow and be eaten, while foragers moved about seeking and eating plants, reproducing, and dying. In each run, all plants were identical except for the amount of energy they started with (see Table 1 and below), but foragers could include two types differing in their tendency to cooperate. During each time step each agent (plant or forager) was activated once in random order.

A plant's energy store represented the amount of food energy potentially available to foragers. At the start of a run each plant's initial energy was set to a uniform random number between zero and a fixed maximum. During each time step a plant's energy could increase through growth, and decrease if a forager fed on it. For simplicity we assumed that feeding transferred energy from plants to foragers with 100% efficiency.

Runs that included both cooperative and noncooperative foragers began with equal numbers of each.[2] At the start of a run each initial forager was endowed with an energy level chosen as a uniform random number between zero

---

[2]Because our experiments started with equal numbers of selfish and cooperative foragers, they did not address what has been termed the "problem of origination": that some cooperative traits cannot spread through selection unless they first reach a minimum threshold frequency. Wilson and Dugatkin (1997) have argued that this apparent obstacle is an artifact of the simplifying assumption of discrete traits. When traits are modeled instead as varying along a continuous spectrum (like most real traits), the problem of origination disappears. We plan to investigate this question in future studies.

and the fertility threshold, and placed on a randomly chosen cell containing a plant. At each time step, foragers could gain energy by eating plants, increasing their own energy store by the same amount they reduced the plant's. They also lost energy each time step as a fixed metabolic cost, regardless of whether or not they moved. If their energy store reached zero they died, but they did not have maximum life spans. If a forager's energy level reached an upper fertility threshold it reproduced asexually, creating an offspring with the same heritable traits as itself (e.g., tendency to cooperate). At the same time the parent's energy store was reduced by the offspring's initial energy. Newborn offspring occupied the cell nearest to their parent that was not already occupied by a forager. (Ties between equally close cells were broken randomly.) Newborn foragers were not activated (did not move or eat) until the time step after their birth.

Foragers moved according to the following rules: They examined their current cell and the eight adjacent cells, and from those not occupied by another forager chose the cell containing the largest plant (with ties broken randomly). If the chosen cell offered enough food to meet their metabolic costs for one time step they moved there; otherwise they moved to a randomly chosen adjacent cell if any were unoccupied. These rules simulated the behavior of individuals exploiting locally available resources as long as they can sustain themselves, but seeking a new food source instead when they cannot meet their minimum nutritional requirements.

We examined two forms of cooperation, alarm calling and feeding restraint. Each trait was controlled by a single haploid locus with two alleles that did not mutate, so that offspring always inherited their parent's trait. In each experiment, we allowed cooperative foragers to differ from selfish foragers in just one trait. The standard parameter settings shown in Table 1 were used in each run unless otherwise noted.

2.2 RESOURCE DISTRIBUTION

To examine the effects of resource distribution on the evolution of cooperation, we systematically varied the spatial distribution of plants using two parameters. At the start of a run, the program placed plants into evenly spaced square patches with one plant population (hereafter simply referred to as a "plant") in each cell. The "patch width" parameter controlled how many cells wide each patch was in each axis, and "gap width" controlled the distance between patches in each axis. The program first placed the specified minimum number of plants into patches, and then added any additional plants and empty cells required to create a uniform square world without any partially filled or unevenly spaced patches. Figure 1 illustrates the patchy plant distribution pattern resulting from one setting of these parameters.

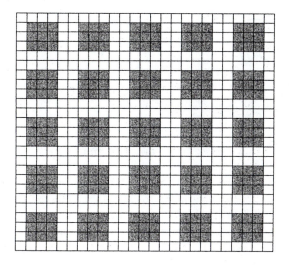

FIGURE 1   A representative resource distribution pattern. Filled squares represent cells occupied by a plant, and unfilled squares represent empty cells. This world was generated by setting the minimum number of plants to 200, the patch width to 3, and the gap width to 2. To create a uniform square world, the program increased the actual number of plants to 225 to create 25 patches, each consisting of 9 plants.

2.3   ALARM CALLING

For experiments on alarm calling we added predation to the model. With each time step, each forager experienced a 2% chance of being targeted by a predator. When a currently active forager was targeted other nearby foragers could give an alarm call, depending on their genotype. Alarm callers always called when a "neighbor" (any individual within the calling range of five cells) was targeted. (Targeted individuals themselves never called.) Calling had two effects: it reduced the chance that the predator would make a kill, and also exposed the caller to the risk of death. Noncallers never called, but benefited from having alarm callers nearby when they were targeted. Once a forager had been targeted, the probability of a kill was $1/(n+1)$, where $n = $ the number of alarm calls. (One was added to the denominator to avoid a denominator of zero when no callers were present.) If the predator did make a kill, its victim was chosen with equal probability from among its original target and any neighbors that called. Note that under these rules, as the local density of callers increased, the benefit to the group increased and the cost to each caller (in terms of risk of death) decreased. For these experiments we employed a simple food growth rule of the type used in previous agent-based models (e.g., Epstein and Axtell 1996). Plants grew at the constant rate of 1 energy unit per time step, up to the maximum of 10 energy units.

2.4 FEEDING RESTRAINT

For experiments on feeding restraint, we removed predation from the model so that foragers never gave alarm calls. Instead, the two types differed only in their feeding behavior. When unrestrained foragers ate, they took 99% of the plant's energy. (We set this parameter at less than 100% so that plants could continue to grow after being fed on, rather than being permanently destroyed.) In contrast, restrained foragers ate only half of the plant they fed on.[3]

To create a group benefit of feeding restraint, we altered the pattern of plant growth for these experiments. Instead of the linear growth pattern used in the alarm-calling experiments, plants followed a logistic growth pattern, with the logistic rate of growth set to 0.2 (Figure 2); as before, maximum plant size was limited to 10 units. The S-shaped logistic growth curve is typical of populations with growth limited by the environment's carrying capacity (Ricklefs 1990). Unlike resources that grow linearly, food sources with logistic growth can be over-exploited, leading to a sharply reduced growth rate or even the destruction of the resource. This situation, and the conflict between individual and group interests that drives it, has been referred to as the "tragedy of the commons" (Hardin 1968, 1998; Feeny et al. 1990).

2.5 IMPLEMENTATION

The program was written in the Objective-C language, using the Swarm library for agent-based modeling developed at the Sante Fe Institute (Minar et al. 1996). The program includes both an interactive graphical user interface and a batch mode. Multiple batch runs on a distributed network were controlled using the Drone program written by T. Belding at the University of Michigan's Program for the Study of Complex Systems. The program was run under Unix on Hewlett-Packard 9000 series workstations, but is also portable to Swarm environments on Windows platforms, and is available on request.

---

[3]Note that this difference in feeding behavior affects the minimum size plant that will meet a forager's maintenance energy requirement, and thus that will be attractive. All foragers have the same metabolic rate of 2 energy units per time step. To gain this much energy unrestrained foragers must feed on a plant containing at least 2.02 units of energy ($2.02 \times 99\% = 2$), whereas restrained foragers require a larger plant containing at least 4 units of energy ($4 \times 50\% = 2$). Recall that in choosing a cell to move to, foragers find the accessible cell with the highest food yield, but if that yield falls below the starvation level they move randomly instead. Thus if the largest available plant contained between 2.02 and 4 energy units, an unrestrained forager would feed on it and grow, while a restrained forager would begin to starve and to wander randomly.

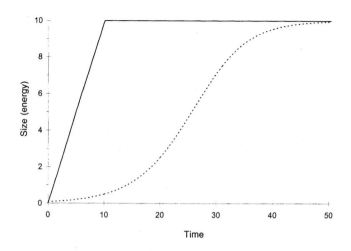

FIGURE 2 A comparison of linear growth (solid line) with logistic growth (dashed line). Under linear growth a plant increases its energy by a fixed amount each time step up to the maximum size. Under logistic growth, the increase per time step $= r * N * (K - N)/K$, where r = logistic growth rate, N = current size, and K = maximum size. The line shown represents a starting size of $N = 0.1$. In this model size corresponded to energy content, and the parameters r and K were set per Table 1.

3   THE EXPERIMENTS

3.1   PART 1: COOPERATION VS. SELFISHNESS IN UNIFORM ENVIRONMENTS

Our first set of experiments was designed to validate the model and to demonstrate that it successfully captured the tension between conflicting levels of selection. For these runs plants were not clumped into patches, but were instead distributed uniformly, one in every cell. For each form of cooperation, we compared the performance of cooperative and selfish foragers in both pure and mixed populations.

In experiments on alarm calling, pure populations of alarm callers experienced much less predation than noncallers, and as a result maintained larger populations (Figure 3). This showed that the increased death rate caused by alarm calling was more than offset by the protection afforded by neighboring foragers. However, when we included both alarm callers and noncallers in the same population, both callers and noncallers benefited from the presence of alarm-calling neighbors, while noncallers avoided the risks associated with calling. As a result, they survived better and consistently out-competed alarm callers, leading to fixation of the noncalling trait (Figure 4). The loss of alarm

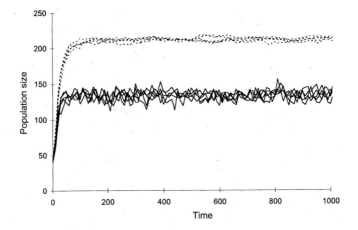

FIGURE 3 Population size as a function of time for pure populations of alarm callers (dotted lines) and noncallers (solid lines) in a uniform environment (single patch width = 529, gap width = 0). The five runs shown for each forager type used the same parameter settings (see Table 1) but different random number seeds.

callers from the population resulted in the same high predation rate and reduced population size shown by the initially pure population of noncallers (Figure 3).

In the experiments on feeding restraint, plants followed a logistic growth curve; consequently their growth was severely reduced by unrestrained feeding. Pure populations of unrestrained feeders first went through a phase of near-exponential growth as they moved quickly from one plant to the next, consuming them almost entirely. However, this population explosion soon resulted in the over-exploitation of all available plants, causing a collapse in food productivity followed by a crash in the forager population. This crash usually resulted in extinction, but in some runs foragers survived the initial population crash to enter a stable oscillation in population size (Figure 5). In contrast, pure populations of restrained feeders did not over-exploit plants to the point of being effectively unproductive. As a result, pure populations of restrained foragers persisted indefinitely, and at a dramatically higher carrying capacity than pure populations of unrestrained foragers (Figure 5).

Combining restrained and unrestrained feeders in the same population resulted in the same initial boom and bust seen in pure populations of unrestrained foragers. Because restrained foragers extracted less energy from plants of the same size, they were unable to compete and disappeared from the population in every run. Unrestrained feeders either died out as well, or recovered to establish a relatively small population that oscillated in size indefinitely (Figure 6).

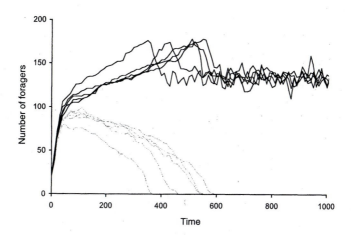

FIGURE 4   Number of alarm callers (dotted lines) and noncallers (solid lines) over time in mixed populations in a uniform environment (single patch width = 529, gap width = 0). Five runs are shown, each using the same parameter settings (see Table 1) but different random number seeds. The drop in the number of noncallers in each run immediately follows the loss of alarm callers from the population in the same run.

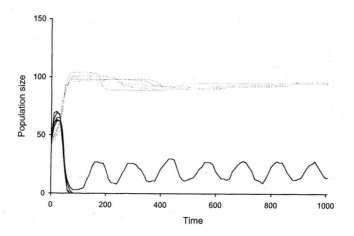

FIGURE 5   Population size as a function of time for pure populations of restrained (dotted lines) and unrestrained (solid lines) feeders in a uniform environment (single patch width = 529, gap width = 0). The five runs shown for each forager type used the same parameter settings (see Table 1) but different random number seeds. Populations of unrestrained feeders usually crashed to extinction, but occasionally survived the initial crash to establish a stable size oscillation caused by time-lagged negative feedback. In this cycle high population density reduced the producitivity of plants, leading to starvation and a reduced population size. Reduced feeding then led to increased food population and higher birth rates, repeating the cycle. Such oscillations are typical of some natural populations (Ricklefs 1990).

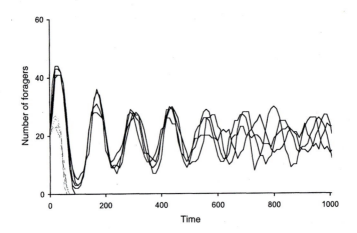

FIGURE 6 Number of restrained (dotted lines) and unrestrained (solid lines) foragers over time in mixed populations in a uniform environment (single patch width = 529, gap width = 0). Five runs are shown, each using the same parameter settings (see Table 1) but different random number seeds. The restraint allele was always lost, leading either to the population's extinction (in one of the five runs) or to a pure population of unrestrained foragers that oscillated in size, as in Figure 5.

To summarize, in uniform environments a similar pattern emerged for both forms of cooperation. In each case, cooperation benefited the populations in which it occurred. However, within mixed populations cooperation of either form was inevitably out-competed and replaced by its selfish counterpart, to the detriment of the population as a whole. The rest of our experiments concern the effects of nonuniform environments on evolution in mixed populations.

3.2 PART 2: RESOURCE DISTRIBUTION AND THE EVOLUTION OF ALARM CALLING

To investigate ecological influences on the evolution of alarm calling, we examined mixed populations of callers and noncallers in patchy environments. We varied patch width from 1 to 10, and gap width from 1 to 10, for a total of 100 different parameter settings. None of these plant distribution patterns completely precluded migration between patches, as even newborn foragers could traverse up to 25 cells without eating before starving to death (50 energy units at birth/2 units metabolic cost per time step, Table 1).

When plants were concentrated into discrete patches, foragers spent most of their time within patches, typically leaving them only after most plants were consumed to below the minimum yield for forager subsistence (see footnote 3). Moreover, when patches were widely separated, foragers leaving a patch were more likely to either return to it or starve while wandering randomly than

TABLE 2 Final frequency of alarm callers as a function of patch and gap width. One run of 10,000 time steps was performed at each parameter setting. Averages over the last 1,000 time steps are shown. Boldface indicates frequencies > 0.5. There was no evidence of stable equilibria, so that all of these runs would presumably have gone to fixation given sufficient time. *Population went extinct.

Patch width	Gap width									
	1	2	3	4	5	6	7	8	9	10
1	0	*	*	*	*	*	*	*	*	*
2	0	*	*	*	*	*	*	*	*	*
3	0	0	0	0.3	**1**	**1**	**1**	**1**	**1**	**1**
4	0	0	0	0	0	0	0	**0.6**	**0.6**	**0.8**
5	0	0	0	0	0	0	0	0	0.1	0.2
6	0	0	0	0	0	0	0	0	0.1	0
7	0	0	0	0	0	0	0	0	0	0
8	0	0	0	0	0	0	0	0	0	0
9	0	0	0	0	0	0	0	0	0	0
10	0	0	0	0	0	0	0	0	0	0

they were to successfully disperse to a new patch. Within a given patch, non-callers had higher survival rates than alarm callers for two reasons. First, they avoided the increased risk of death associated with calling, and secondly, they also paradoxically received more protection through alarm calls. To illustrate this latter effect, assume that all occupants of a patch are within calling range of each other and that no other foragers are. Then if the patch holds N callers, each caller is protected by $N - 1$ calls when targeted by a predator, whereas each noncaller is protected by N calls. Because of their survival advantage, noncallers tended to quickly take over mixed patches. However, patches with a lower frequency of callers were more vulnerable to predation, and those occupied only by noncallers were often emptied by predation, leaving an opportunity for later colonization by either type. In contrast, patches occupied only by callers were rarely emptied by predation unless they were very small.

Both the size of patches and the distance between them affected the evolution of cooperation. If food patches were too small and widely separated they could not support any foragers for long, and the population went extinct. Subject to this constraint however, the evolution of alarm calling was promoted by small and widely spaced patches (Table 2).[4]

---

[4]In the implementation described here, alarm calling was very costly because it put the caller at as much risk as the original target. As a result, alarm calling evolved only within a narrow range of plant distribution patterns (Table 2). In another version of the model in which the cost of calling was energetic rather than through risk of death, alarm calling was favored under a much wider range of ecological conditions. We suspect that reducing the risk of calling to a more realistic level would similarly broaden the range of conditions under which calling would evolve.

3.3   PART 3: RESOURCE DISTRIBUTION AND THE EVOLUTION OF FEEDING RESTRAINT

To investigate ecological effects on the evolution of feeding restraint, we performed a second sweep of the 10×10 parameter space for plant distribution patterns, this time starting with equal numbers of restrained and unrestrained feeders. There was no predation, and plant growth was logistic.

In a patchy environment, an unrestrained forager first colonizing a new patch accumulated energy rapidly and, unless the patch was quite small, quickly began reproducing. The resulting local population explosion typically exhausted all plants in the patch before any of them had time to regenerate. This resulted in the dispersal of hungry descendants in all directions, leaving behind an abandoned and unproductive patch of plants that did not regenerate for many time steps.

In contrast, patches inhabited only by restrained feeders were not over-exploited to the point of becoming unproductive, but instead established a pattern of sustainable harvest. After plants were reduced to below the forager maintenance requirement, making them unattractive, they recovered enough to sustain foragers again within only a few time steps. As a result, patches larger than a single cell that were occupied only by restrained feeders did not become exhausted and were not abandoned. Instead, birth and immigration into the patch was approximately balanced by dispersal as foragers occasionally failed to find sufficient food and wandered out of the patch. This pattern continued until an unrestrained forager invaded the patch and consumed the plants at a much higher rate, reproducing along the way if the patch was large enough. The patch then became unprofitable first for restrained foragers, then for unrestrained foragers, and was typically abandoned by both.

In patches containing both restrained and unrestrained foragers, unrestrained foragers gained more energy because they ate almost twice as much from plants of the same size ($99\%/50\% = 1.98$). Feeding rate was an accurate proxy for fitness because it was the only factor determining both survival and reproduction. Thus within patches occupied by both forager types, unrestrained foragers always had higher average fitness. The fact that restraint could spread to fixation under some conditions (Table 3) therefore demonstrated that it was favored by the greater productivity of patches occupied by restrained foragers. As with the alarm-calling trait, both the size and spacing of patches affected the outcome of selection. Restrained feeding spread to fixation only when food patches were small and widely separated (Table 3).

3.4   PART 4: KIN SELECTION AS A COMPONENT OF BETWEEN-GROUP SELECTION

Although it is sometimes contrasted with group selection (e.g., Maynard Smith 1976; Dawkins 1982:288; Frank 1988:37; Alexander 1989), kin selection is now generally recognized as fitting within the framework of group selection theory (Hamilton 1975; Wade 1985; Futuyma 1986; Breden 1990; Queller 1991;

TABLE 3   Final frequency of restrained feeders as a function of patch and gap width. One run of 10,000 time steps was performed at each parameter setting. Averages over the last 1,000 time steps are shown. Boldface indicates frequencies > 0.5. *Population went extinct.

Patch width	Gap width 1	2	3	4	5	6	7	8	9	10
1	0	*	*	*	*	*	*	*	*	*
2	0	0	0	*	*	*	*	*	*	*
3	0	0	**1**	**1**	**1**	**1**	**1**	**1**	**1**	**1**
4	0	0	0	**1**	**1**	**1**	**1**	**1**	**1**	**1**
5	0	0	0	0	0	**1**	**1**	**1**	**1**	**1**
6	0	0	0	0	0	0	0	**1**	**1**	**1**
7	0	0	0	0	0	0	0	0	0	0
8	0	0	0	0	0	0	0	0	0	0
9	0	0	0	0	0	0	0	0	0	0
10	0	0	0	0	0	0	0	0	0	0

Frank 1995; Sober and Wilson 1998). Groups composed of genetic relatives facilitate group selection because genetic variance within groups is lower and genetic variance between groups is higher compared with populations containing groups of random composition. Was association among kin an important component of group selection in our model?

Although the model did not include any mechanism for discriminating kin from nonkin, it nonetheless held the potential for significant levels of kin selection. Offspring were born next to their parents, and tended to remain so for some time after birth, especially when food patches were small and isolated. Both forms of cooperation affected only nearby individuals, and so could be directed disproportionately toward relatives bearing the same gene for cooperation. Spatial association among relatives could thus be a key element of selection for cooperation in this model.

To examine whether cooperation could evolve without any spatial association between kin, we repeated the experiments in Parts 2 and 3 above with one modification: instead of newborn foragers being placed in the nearest open cell to their parents, their birth location was chosen randomly from all unoccupied cells in the grid. When we repeated the experiment on alarm calling (Table 2) with birth locations randomized, alarm calling never spread. Instead the noncalling trait went to fixation under every resource distribution pattern. In contrast, when we repeated the experiment on feeding restraint with randomized birth locations, restraint did spread to fixation under some resource distribution conditions. However, the conditions for the evolution of restraint were more restricted without parent-offspring association than when offspring were born next to their parents (Tables 3 and 4).

TABLE 4   Final frequency of restrained feeders with offspring dispersing randomly. All parameters were set as in Table 3, but newborn offspring were placed at random locations. One run of 10,000 time steps was performed at each parameter setting. Averages over the last 1000 time steps are shown. Boldface indicates frequencies > 0.5. *Population went extinct.

Patch width	Gap width 1	2	3	4	5	6	7	8	9	10
1	0	*	*	*	*	*	*	*	*	*
2	0	0	0	*	*	*	*	*	*	*
3	0	0	**1**	**1**	**1**	**1**	**1**	**1**	**1**	**1**
4	0	0	0	**1**	**1**	**1**	**1**	**1**	**1**	**1**
5	0	0	0	0	0	0	0	0	0.1	**1**
6	0	0	0	0	0	0	0	**1**	**1**	**1**
7	0	0	0	0	0	0	0	0	0	0
8	0	0	0	0	0	0	0	0	0	0
9	0	0	0	0	0	0	0	0	0	0
10	0	0	0	0	0	0	0	0	0	0

3.5   PART 5: QUANTIFYING MULTILEVEL SELECTION

To move beyond verbal descriptions and arguments about levels of selection, it is necessary to actually quantify selection at each relevant level. Of course this requires that we explicitly define the groups involved, but that was not a simple task for trait groups in our model. Because trait group membership was not imposed as an assumption of the model, the boundaries of fitness effects between individuals shifted with each interaction. Moreover, in the case of feeding restraint it was not clear, even in principle, how to determine trait group boundaries, because an individual's current fitness depended on the actions of other individuals many time steps in the past.

Given these difficulties, we chose to measure selection within and among patches as a proxy for selection within and among actual trait groups. Patches corresponded well to trait groups when they were well separated, and in the case of alarm calling, when they were small enough to be entirely within the calling range of any patch occupant. Foragers not currently located in a patch were considered to be members of the last patch they had occupied. Foragers born outside of any patch were assigned at birth to the patch their parent currently belonged to.

To measure selection within and between patches, we used a powerful approach that underlies much of modern multilevel selection theory (Frank 1995). This is Price's (1970, 1972) covariance formula for partitioning change in the frequency of an allele[5]:

$$\Delta p = \frac{\text{cov}_n(w_g, p_g)}{w} + \frac{\text{ave}_n, [\text{cov}(w_{gi}, p_{gi})]}{w}. \tag{1}$$

The first term on the right side of this equation represents the change in allele frequency caused by between-patch selection, and the second term represents the change due to within-patch selection. Definitions are as follows: Δp = total change in allele frequency in population; w_g = group fitness (mean progeny per member of the gth group); p_g = allele frequency within the gth group; cov_n = covariance among groups, weighted by group size in the parental generation; w = average population fitness (mean progeny per individual); w_{gi} = fitness of the ith individual in the gth group; p_{gi} = allele frequency within the ith individual in the gth group (either 0 or 1); cov = covariance among individuals within the gth group; and ave_n = average of the within-group covariances, weighted by progeny per group. Because life spans overlapped in our model, we defined a "generation" as a single time step of the model, and an individual's "progeny" as any offspring it produced, plus itself if it survived the time step.

Figures 7 and 8 illustrate the application of this formula to one run of the model for alarm calling and feeding restraint, respectively, under the same plant distribution pattern. The allele for each type of cooperation increased in frequency through between-patch selection and decreased through within-patch selection. The overall change in allele frequency was the sum of these two effects, and thus the evolutionary outcome depended on their relative strengths. We repeated the experiments in Parts 2 through 4 using this analysis, and found that for both forms of cooperation under all resource distribution patterns, within-patch selection decreased the frequency of cooperation. Thus cooperation spread to fixation only when positive between-patch selection was of greater magnitude than negative within-patch selection.

4 DISCUSSION

The model captured the essential properties of opposing levels of selection, in that each form of cooperation was favored by between-group selection but diminished in frequency through within-group selection. Thus the evolutionary outcome in a given run depended not on which form of selection was operating but on their relative strengths.

The varying outcomes we observed as we modified plant distribution patterns provided interesting answers to the three questions posed in the intro-

---

[5]Our notation follows Grafen (1985), but we have added Price's (1972) explicit notation for weighted statistical functions. Hamilton (1975) left the weighting of covariance out of his notation, mentioning it only in the text, and some later authors dropped it entirely (Grafen 1985; Bourke and Franks 1995). As a result their formulas are not strictly correct unless all groups are assumed to be the same size

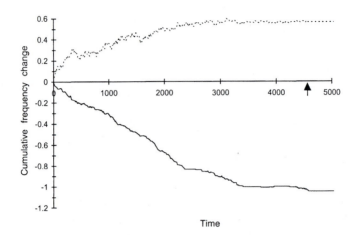

FIGURE 7   Cumulative change in the frequency of the alarm-calling allele during one run due to within-patch selection (solid line) and between-patch selection (dotted line). Because the allele began at a frequency of 0.5, the total frequency change represented by the sum of the two lines equaled −0.5 when noncalling reached fixation (at arrow). Note that substantial between-group selection for alarm calling was outweighted by stronger within-group selection against calling. Patch width = 4, gap width = 5, and all other parameters were set as per Table 1. Calculations were based on Eq. (1).

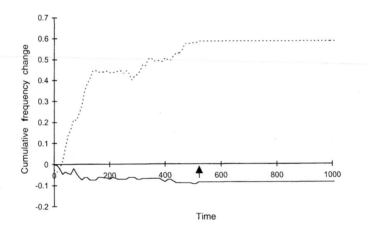

FIGURE 8   Cumulative change in the frequency of the feeding restraint allele due to within-patch selection (solid line) and between-patch selection (dotted line). Because the allele began at a frequency of 0.5, the total frequecy change represented by the sum of the two lines equaled 0.5 when restraint reached fixation (at arrow). Note that within-group selection against feeding restraint was outweighed by stronger between-group selection for restraint. Patch width = 4, gap width = 5, and all other parameters were set as per Table 1. Calculations were based on Eq. (1).

duction. First, they showed that variation in an ecological factor—the patchiness of food distribution—can by itself create sufficient population structure to generate significant between-group selection, leading to the spread of group-beneficial cooperative traits. Second, we found that between-group selection could lead to the spread of the cooperative trait of feeding restraint even without positive assortment among kin. Third, the dynamics of selection on the two traits we examined showed both similarities and differences. Both cooperative traits were more likely to spread under similar ecological conditions (small patches separated by large gaps), but the mechanisms differed to some extent for the two traits.

Changing the distribution pattern of plants affected whether cooperation evolved through two different causal mechanisms—by changing the size of trait groups, and by changing their temporal stability. In the following sections we discuss each of these mechanisms in turn, and then explore similarities and differences in how they affected the evolution of each trait.

4.1 RESOURCE DISTRIBUTION AFFECTED TRAIT GROUP SIZE

It is important to keep in mind that trait groups are defined not in terms of geographical clustering, but in terms of fitness effects—specifically whether the fitness of some individuals is affected by the genotypes of others. Thus even if individuals do not form spatial clusters, trait groups come into existence whenever a trait expressed by one individual affects the fitness of a subset of other individuals in the population. In those runs in which foragers clustered within discrete food patches, the resulting spatial groups corresponded more or less closely with trait groups, but did not exactly coincide with them. The fitness effects of the trait could either extend beyond the patch, or apply to only a subset of the patch's inhabitants. Indeed, even when resources (and thus foragers) were evenly distributed, trait groups existed with respect to alarm calling or feeding restraint because these traits affected the fitness of a set of nearby individuals.

Although resource distribution did not define trait groups, it did influence them. Patch size affected the average number of foragers within a given radius, so that smaller patches led to smaller trait groups. Distance between patches was important in limiting trait groups to only those foragers within a single patch. When patches were close together the occupants of different patches affected one another's fitness, so that trait groups could encompass the occupants of multiple patches. Thus small patches and large gaps both decreased average trait group size.

Smaller trait groups in turn increased the strength of between-group selection relative to within-group selection by changing the partitioning of genetic variance. Selection at any level requires that the units being selected vary genetically, and all else being equal, the strength of selection increases with the genetic variance among units. In a subdivided population, all variance among individuals can be partitioned into within- and between-group components, and the proportion of the total variance found at each level strongly affects the relative strength of within- versus between-group selection (Price 1972; Hamilton 1975; D. S. Wilson 1975). The smaller groups are, the more variance is shifted from within to between groups, and thus the stronger the between-group component of selection becomes relative to the within-group component. Because small isolated patches reduced trait group size, both small patches and large gaps facilitated the evolution of both forms of cooperation.[6]

4.2 RESOURCE DISTRIBUTION AFFECTED POPULATION MIXING

Food distribution influenced not only how clustered or dispersed foragers were at any given moment, but also how freely the population mixed over time. Patchy environments effectively restricted foragers' movement patterns, causing them to repeatedly interact with the same individuals. Both environmental parameters played a role: larger gaps inhibited migration between patches and kept foragers in the same patch longer, while larger patches let some patch inhabitants escape the influence of others, permitting trait group membership to shift as individuals moved within the patch. Thus small patches and large gaps both stabilized trait group membership by reducing mixing. This facilitated the evolution of cooperation through two different mechanisms, one involving the genetic make-up of trait groups, and the other involving the distribution of the benefits of cooperation. Each mechanism had important effects on only one of the two forms of cooperation we examined.

4.2.1 Population Mixing Reduced the Genetic Variance Between Trait Groups.
One effect of population mixing in our model was that it reduced the tendency for kin (individuals with the same allele for cooperation due to common descent) to be together more often than nonkin, and thus to interact more. Positive assortment of kin into trait groups (termed "kin selection") (Maynard Smith 1964) is important for the same reasons outlined above; it increases genetic variance between groups and reduces it within groups. In nature, kin selection often involves organisms recognizing their kin and actively directing cooperative behaviors toward them, but it need not. In all our experiments except part 4, offspring were born near their parents, creating spatial association and thus higher rates of interaction among kin than non-kin. However, in the absence of kin recognition, foragers tended to wander away from kin over time. The extent to which kin assorted positively within trait groups thus depended on the balance between births and population mixing. When patchy food distribution restricted movements largely to within patches, clusters of

---

[6]Note that trait groups have a fixed size in some models of cooperation, such as the "Prisoner's Dilemma," in which all groups are of size two (Axelrod 1984). In such models resource distribution would not affect trait group size, but could still influence the evolution of cooperation through its effects on population mixing (see below).

kin could arise and persist. In contrast, when food was distributed more uniformly, movements were less restricted and the population mixed constantly, removing the positive assortment of kin as fast as it was produced by new births.[7]

Eliminating positive assortment among kin affected the two cooperative traits differently. Kin-based interaction was necessary for the evolution of alarm calling, as consistent with considerable empirical evidence (e.g., Sherman 1977; Hoogland 1983). However, it was not necessary for the evolution of feeding restraint (section 4 above). This result is particularly significant given that some workers view group selection as an alternative formulation of kin selection (Bell 1997:530; Maynard Smith 1998). To understand the difference between these two forms of cooperation, we must distinguish group-beneficial traits that reduce their bearer's fitness relative to the population as a whole from those that reduce individual fitness only relative to the rest of the trait group. To distinguish between these alternatives, Wilson (1979, 1980) coined the terms "strong altruism" and "weak altruism," respectively. For strongly altruistic traits, the net effect of dispensing group benefits is to lower the bearer's reproduction relative to the population as a whole. Therefore such traits can spread only if their bearers more than offset this disadvantage by receiving more than their share of the benefits dispensed by other cooperators (usually kin). Such inclusive fitness effects arise only if there is positive assortment, meaning that altruists are more likely than nonaltruists to interact with other altruists. In other words, the genetic variance between groups must be higher than expected if groups were random samples of the population (Bell 1997:526). In contrast, weakly altruistic traits lower the bearer's fitness relative to the trait group, but not relative to the population as a whole. As a result, they can spread without positive assortment (Hamilton 1975; D. S. Wilson 1975, 1979, 1990).

In this model, alarm calling was "strongly altruistic" because it conferred only costs and no benefits on its bearer. Thus it could not spread without positive assortment, and in our model, spatial proximity between parents and their offspring was the only way this could come about. In contrast, feeding restraint conferred benefits as well as costs on its bearer, by increasing plant productivity and thus later food availability. Thus feeding restraint was not necessarily strongly altruistic—if the benefits of restraint exceeded the costs for the individual expressing it, that individual's fitness increased. (Whether this actually occurred depended on the frequency of restraint among the patch's inhabitants.) Thus the spread of alarm calling depended on kin selection because it was always strongly altruistic, while this was not true of

---

[7] Our model would be a more realistic representation of social behavior in humans and other primates if we added kin recognition, and the tendency both to preferentially associate with kin and to direct cooperative acts toward them. These features would greatly facilitate the evolution of cooperation, and in this sense our model was conservative in leaving them out.

feeding restraint. Note, however, that feeding restraint was always at least "weakly altruistic"—i.e., it reduced individual fitness relative to the rest of the trait group—because neighbors (other trait group members) reaped the benefits of another's restraint without paying the cost.

Given the importance of genetic structure for between-group selection, it may seem surprising that feeding restraint could evolve so readily when offspring dispersed to random locations, preventing positive assortment of kin among patches (Table 4). The explanation lies in the difference between cooperative traits that benefit the entire trait group including the actor (those with "whole-group effects"), versus traits that benefit only other group members (those with "other-only group effects"). In a large randomly assorting population, the average genotype of the "recipients" of an act (those individuals included in its group-level effect) is uncorrelated with that of the actor if the trait has other-only-group effects. In contrast, if the trait has whole-group effects, then as trait groups become smaller the actor itself constitutes an increasing proportion of the act's recipients, causing an increasingly positive correlation between the genotype of the actor and the average genotype of the recipients (Figure 9). This is another mechanism, in addition to positive assortment, by which the benefits of cooperation can be directed disproportionately to cooperators. Cooperative traits with other-only-group effects (such as alarm calling) are necessarily strongly altruistic, and thus cannot evolve without positive assortment. Those traits with whole-group effects (such as feeding restraint) will be only weakly altruistic if the actor's share of the group benefit exceeds the individual cost of the act. Under these conditions positive assortment is not necessary for the trait to spread.

4.2.2 Population Mixing Reduced the Acquisition of Delayed Benefits.

For feeding restraint specifically, population mixing tended to prevent the evolution of cooperation for a second reason unrelated to genetic structure. The cost of feeding restraint was immediate, but the potential benefits of improved food supply were deferred for at least one time step and potentially many more. This delay affected which individual received the benefit from an act of restraint, and also how much benefit accrued.

In freely mixing populations, the individual paying the cost of an act of restraint was rarely among those reaping the benefits. A forager that showed restraint was likely to move away before its restraint paid off in an improved local food supply. As a result restraint became strongly altruistic, and could not evolve without the positive assortment of kin that was absent from freely mixing populations. In contrast, when patches were isolated foragers tended to stay within them, and when patches were small they contained few competitors. Under these conditions the restrained individual was usually among those benefiting from its behavior, so that restraint was only weakly altruistic and could evolve without positive assortment of kin.

A second consequence of the delayed benefit of restraint was that the size of its ultimate payoff depended on the social environment. Refraining from

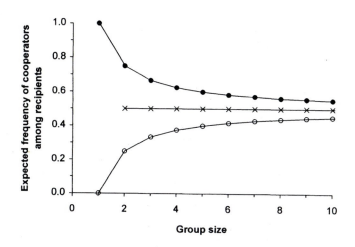

FIGURE 9   Effect of actor's genotype on the average genotype of a social act's recipients in a randomly assorting population. If a cooperative trait has a group effect that excludes the actor (cross marks), the frequency of cooperators among recipients is uncorrelated with the genotype of the actor. In contrast, if the trait's group-level effect includes the actor, the frequency of cooperators among recipients depends increasingly on the genotype of the actor as group size falls. In small groups the recipients of cooperative acts (filled circles) are biased toward cooperators, while the recipients of selfish acts (open circles) are biased toward selfish individuals. This figure assumes haploid single-locus control of the trait, with cooperative and selfish alleles at frequencies of 0.5, and infinite population size.

destroying a plant's productivity could potentially yield benefits for many time steps into the future. However, if the same plant was over-exploited two time steps later, the benefits would have little time to accumulate. Thus the full benefits of restraint were only realized in small isolated patches where clusters of restrained feeders could persist for some time without invasion by unrestrained feeders. In freely mixing populations, even if a restrained feeder stayed nearby to reap the delayed benefits of sustainable harvesting, the chances were high that an unrestrained feeder would soon arrive and terminate those benefits by over-exploiting the plant and destroying its productivity. Thus it was an important feature of the model that the benefits of restraint were not fixed as they typically are in equation-based models, but varied with the social environment in a realistic way.

Small, isolated patches were more favorable to restraint through their effects on selection at both levels. At the between-group level, patchy environments increased the total payoff of restraint to all trait group members, increasing between-group selection for cooperation. At the within-group level, patchy environments allowed restrained foragers to collect a larger share of the payoff from their own restraint, thus reducing within-group selection against them. A variant of our model showed that the combined effect of these two factors was decisive. We gave foragers exclusive access to a floating "territory" consisting of the cells they had visited during the last several time steps. As a result population mixing was greatly reduced, and the benefits of restraint were both larger and directed primarily to the restrained individual. Under these conditions, feeding restraint spread rapidly even in uniform environments.

4.2.3 Cooperation Evolved Without a Discrete Mixing Phase.

Because of its within-group disadvantage, cooperation can only spread through an advantage in founding new groups. Successful groups must be able to export their productivity from the local area, so that their reproductive success is not suppressed by local population regulation (Wilson et al. 1992). This creates a tension between the need for mobility in order to found new groups and the need for isolation to prevent selfish immigrants from invading cooperative groups. In some models of "viscous" (nonmixing) populations, cooperation cannot easily evolve because groups that are sufficiently isolated for altruists to prosper are also too isolated to export their productivity. This is apparently true of Wright's (1945) early model of group selection (Sober and Wilson 1998:61), and also of models of plant-like organisms that do not move during their lifetimes, so that mixing is restricted to local dispersal of offspring (Wilson et al. 1992; Queller 1994).

In many group selection models this problem is overcome by alternating between an interaction phase, during which the population is structured into trait groups and fitnesses are determined, and a mixing phase, during which individuals or propagules are randomly recombined to create new groups (Wilson 1975, 1980). Indeed some authors have suggested that a discrete mixing phase is necessary for group selection to be effective (Dugatkin and Reeve 1994). Obviously, this would significantly limit the role of group selection in nature.

In the current model there was no discrete mixing phase, yet local subpopulations of cooperators were able to export their productivity and thereby escape local population regulation. This occurred because a patch approaching its carrying capacity became less attractive to its occupants as their feeding rates fell, leading some to disperse and eventually colonize new patches. As a result, cooperative groups continued to reproduce faster and send out more dispersers than selfish groups, giving them an advantage in colonizing empty patches. Instead of the migration rate between patches being a uniform parameter, as it typically is in equation-based models, the rate of emigration from a patch increased with its frequency of cooperators. This pattern, which increased the strength of between-group relative to within-group selection, emerged as a natural consequence of the foragers' movement rules.

Our results show that increasing mobility tends to reduce the effect of between-group selection through several mechanisms. However, some degree of population mixing is also necessary for between-group selection to occur. This suggests that if gaps were too large, cooperative groups would become too isolated to export their productivity, and between-group selection would become ineffective. Further experiments with larger gap sizes have confirmed this. When gap width was increased to 30 cells, successful migration was almost impossible and each patch was effectively isolated. Under these conditions the overall frequency of cooperators in the population never rose significantly regardless of patch size. Instead it fell until all mixed patches had been taken over by selfish foragers. If mutation was added to the model, cooperation continued to decline in frequency until it disappeared.

4.3 CONCLUDING REMARKS

Many of the issues we examine in this chapter have been studied previously using equation-based approaches (reviewed in Wilson and Sober 1994). What can we gain by revisiting them using a new methodological paradigm? The agent-based approach offers several important advantages, all stemming from the fact that necessary assumptions concern the traits and behaviors of individuals rather than the global patterns that arise through their interactions. This makes it easier to evaluate the appropriateness of the assumptions and to adjust them to reflect the real world. It also means that the simplifying assumptions necessary to make the model tractable are less likely to inadvertently bias the results. In particular, in equation-based models parameters critical to the outcome of multilevel selection, such as the benefits and costs of cooperative acts and the rates of migration between groups, are uniform and fixed. In this agent-based model the values of these parameters emerge through the interactions of individuals, and can thus vary over both space and time in realistic ways. Our results suggest that this local spatial and temporal variation can have important effects. Moreover, these critical parameters can interact with one another in complex ways impossible to incorporate into equation-based models. For example, ecological conditions can affect population genetic structure, which in turn can affect the magnitudes of costs and benefits, which in turn can affect reproductive rates and thereby change emigration rates, which in turn feed back onto population structure. Such interactions may explain some of the differences between our conclusions and those of previous modeling studies.

Gilpin (1975) developed a model of predators and prey based on differential equations that is similar in spirit to our model of feeding restraint. Predators that hunted more efficiently out-competed less efficient hunters within the same patch, but were prone to over-exploiting local prey populations, leading to the local extinction of both predators and prey. Under some parameter settings between-group selection overwhelmed within-group selection, leading to the evolution of less efficient hunting (analogous to our feeding restraint). In particular, less efficient hunting was favored by small population size per patch, low migration between patches, and rapid extinction of a patch once invaded. These parameters correspond to small patch width, large gap width, and low intrinsic rate of plant growth, respectively, in our model.

In an influential review, Maynard Smith (1976) re-analyzed Gilpin's rather complex model in simpler terms that apply in general to group selection models based on the differential extinction and colonization of patches. He concluded that whether altruism evolves depends on a single variable, $M =$ the average number of selfish dispersers to leave a patch before it goes extinct and successfully colonize a patch not already containing selfish individuals. When $M > 1$ selfishness spreads, and when $M < 1$ altruism is favored. With a few adjustments (e.g., treating the abandonment of a patch as a local extinction), this analysis also describes the dynamics of our model.

Maynard Smith (1976:281) was cautious in evaluating the implications of these results for nature, commenting only that, "It is hard to say how often the condition $M < 1$ will hold in nature." Other authors have been less circumspect, however. According to Grafen (1984), "The final consensus on these models was that the conditions for A1 [altruism] to be successful were too stringent to be realistic." Dugatkin and Reeve (1994) express the same opinion regarding patch extinction-recolonization models. In his recent textbook, Ridley (1996) echoes this sentiment and extends his conclusion to all models of group selection. Regarding the condition $M < 1$, he asserts that, "This number is so small that we can expect selfish individual adaptations to prevail in nature. Group selection, we conclude, is a weak force." Surprisingly, none of these authors provide or cite evidence to support their conclusions. Our results suggest they may be premature even if limited to patch extinction-recolonization models. In a plausible ecological and behavioral setting, the requirements for the evolution of cooperation through between-group selection did not appear to be unrealistically stringent in any obvious way.

Other agent-based studies have concluded that even without an imposed group structure, including a spatial dimension can strongly affect the outcome of various forms of social and ecological interaction (e.g., Nowak et al. 1994; Colegrave 1997; Wilson 1998). In particular, localized interactions can facilitate the evolution of cooperation through reciprocal altruism (Ferriere and Michod 1996; Nakamura et al. 1997). However, we are not aware of previous studies showing that food distribution alone can generate sufficient population structure to permit group-beneficial traits to evolve, even in the absence of reciprocal altruism and kin selection. Interestingly, D. S. Wilson (1975:145) anticipated this result in an early formulation of trait group selection, in which he concluded that "...spatial heterogeneity, by partitioning the deme [population] spatially, may be expected to enforce trait-groups and enhance group selection."

Our preliminary work with this model has shown that groups emerging through the behavior of individual agents in patchy environments are sufficient to drive the evolution of group-beneficial traits, even in the absence of kin selection. This demonstrates that effective between-group selection does not depend on the kind of discrete and stable groups that are typical of equation-based models, but may not be typical in nature. In future studies we plan to explore the sensitivity of our results to various parameters and assumptions, as well as to extend the model in new directions.

The agent-based approach to modeling multilevel selection may prove useful for modeling real systems as well as exploring general principles. In particular, our model of feeding restraint may have applications in ecology, because patchy resource distribution and logistic growth of food resources are both ubiquitous in nature (Ricklefs 1990). These factors could conceivably generate strong enough between-group selection to produce observable levels of feeding restraint in real organisms. Recent empirical studies provide some support for this suggestion (e.g., Frank 1996; Hemptinne and Dixon 1997; Miralles et al. 1997). Further use of agent-based models may help to both guide and interpret the results of such empirical research. Similar models may also prove useful in helping us to understand the ecological and demographic conditions leading to sustainable resource management in small-scale human societies (e.g., Lansing and Kremer 1993; Lansing this volume) and the failures of sustainability that plague our planet today. Indeed, the global collapse of food resources in our model is closely analogous to the current global crash in fish populations as a result of unrestrained "feeding" by competing fishing fleets (Roberts 1997; McGinn 1998). Agent-based models may prove useful in both the research and public education needed to avert such tragedies of the commons in the future.

ACKNOWLEDGMENTS

We thank the University of Michigan's Program for the Study of Complex Systems for providing the computer resources and software used in this study. We are also grateful to Rick Riolo for providing invaluable technical support and advice, as well as software for collating and summarizing program output. Parts of the program were based on code generously provided by David Groom and Nelson Minar. We are grateful to Tim Kohler for encouraging us to participate in this volume. For valuable feedback on earlier drafts we thank Keith Hunley, Tim Kohler, Steve Lansing, Rick Riolo, Robert Smuts, Beverly Strassman, David Sloan Wilson, and the members of our fall 1989 graduate seminar on multilevel selection. This research was funded in part by the University of Michigan's Information Technology Division/College of Literature, Science and Arts joint grant program.

REFERENCES

Alexander, Richard D.
    1987 The Biology of Moral Systems. Hawthorne, NY: Aldine de Gruyter.

1989 Evolution of the Human Psyche. *In* The Human Revolution: Behavioural and Biological Perspectives on the Origins of Modern Humans. P. Mellars and C. Stringer, eds. Pp. 455–513. Princeton, NJ: Princeton University Press.

Axelrod, Robert
1984 The Evolution of Cooperation. New York: Basic Books.

Belew, Richard K., Melanie Mitchell, and David H. Ackley
1996 Computation in the Natural Sciences. *In* Adaptive Individuals in Evolving Populations. Richard K. Belew and Melanie Mitchell, eds. Pp. 431–440. Santa Fe Institute Studies in the Sciences of Complexity, Proceedings Volume XXVI. Reading, MA: Addison-Wesley.

Bell, Graham
1997 Selection: The Mechanism of Evolution. New York: Chapman and Hall.

Bourke, Andrew F. G., and Nigel R. Franks
1995 Social Evolution in Ants. Princeton, NJ: Princeton University Press.

Breden, F. J.
1990 Partitioning of Covariance as a Method of Studying Kin Selection. Trends in Ecology and Evolution 5:224–228.

Breden, F. J., and Michael J. Wade
1989 Selection Within and Between Kin Groups of the Imported Willow Leaf Beetle. American Naturalist 134:35–50.

Brookfield, J. F. Y.
1998 Quorum Sensing and Group Selection. Evolution 52:1263–1269.

Colegrave, Nick
1997 Can a Patchy Population Structure Affect the Evolution of Competition Strategies? Evolution 51:483–492.

Colwell, R. K.
1981 Group Selection Is Implicated in the Evolution of Female-Biased Sex Ratios. Nature 290:401–404.

Cronin, Helena
1991 The Ant and the Peacock: Altruism and Sexual Selection from Darwin to Today. Cambridge, UK: Cambridge University Press.

Dawkins, Richard
1982 The Extended Phenotype. Oxford: Oxford University Press.
1989 The Selfish Gene. 2nd edition. Oxford: Oxford University Press.

Dugatkin, Lee A., and H. Kern Reeve
1994 Behavioral Ecology and Levels of Selection: Dissolving the Group Selection Controversy. Advances in the Study of Behavior 23:101–133.

Epstein, Joshua. M., and Robert Axtell

1996 Growing Artificial Societies: Social Science from the Bottom Up. Washington, DC: Brookings Institution Press and Cambridge, MA: MIT Press.

Feeney, D., F. Berkes, B. McCay, and J. M. Acheson
1990 The Tragedy of the Commons: Twenty-Two Years Later. Human Ecology 18:1–19.

Ferriere, Regis, and Richard E. Michod
1996 The Evolution of Cooperation in Spatially Heterogeneous Populations. American Naturalist 147:692–717.

Frank, Robert H.
1988 Passions Within Reason: The Strategic Role of the Emotions. New York: W. W. Norton.

Frank, Steven A.
1995 George Price's Contributions to Evolutionary Genetics. Journal of Theoretical Biology 175:373–388.
1996 Models of Parasite Virulence. Quarterly Review of Biology 71:37–78.

Futuyma, Douglas J.
1986 Evolutionary Biology. 2nd edition. Sunderland, MA: Sinauer Associates.

Gilpin, Michael E.
1975 Group Selection in Predator-Prey Communities. Princeton, NJ: Princeton University Press.

Grafen, Alan
1984 Natural Selection, Kin Selection and Group Selection. In Behavioural Ecology: An Evolutionary Approach. J. R. Krebs and N. B. Davies, eds. Pp. 62–84. Sunderland, MA: Sinauer Associates.

Hamilton, William D.
1964 The Genetical Evolution of Social Behavior, I and II. Journal of Theoretical Biology 7:1–52.
1975 Innate Social Aptitudes of Man: An Approach from Evolutionary Genetics. In ASA Studies 4: Biosocial Anthropology. R. Fox, ed. Pp. 133–53. London: Malaby Press.

Hardin, Garrett
1968 The Tragedy of the Commons. Science 162:1243–1248.
1998 Extensions of "The Tragedy of the Commons." Science 280:682–683.

Hart, D. D., S. L. Kohler, and R. G. Carlton
1991 Harvesting of Benthic Algae By Territorial Grazers: The Potential for Prudent Predation. Oikos 60:329–335.

Hemptinne, J. L., and A. F. G. Dixon
1997 Are Aphidophagous Ladybirds (Cocinellidae) Prudent Predators? Biological Agriculture and Horticulture 15:151–159.

Hoogland, John L.

1983 Nepotism and Alarm Calling in the Black-Tailed Prairie Dog, *Cynomys ludovicianus*. Animal Behaviour 31:472–479.

Huston, Michael, Donald DeAngelis, and Wilfred Post
1988 New Computer Models Unify Ecological Theory. Bioscience 38:682–691.

Judson, Olivia P.
1994 The Rise of the Individual-Based Model in Ecology. Trends in Ecology and Evolution 9:9–14.

Lansing, J. Stephen, and James N. Kremer
1993 Emergent Properties of Balinese Water Temple Networks: Coadaptation on a Rugged Fitness Landscape. *In* Artificial Life III. Christopher Langton, ed. Pp. 201–224. Santa Fe Institute Studies in the Sciences of Complexity, Proceedings Volume XVII. Reading, MA: Addison-Wesley.

Maynard Smith, John
1964 Group Selection and Kin Selection. Nature 201:1145–1147.
1976 Group Selection. Quarterly Review of Biology 51:277–283.
1998 The Origin of Altruism. Nature 393:639–640.

McGinn, A. P.
1998 Rocking the Boat: Conserving Fisheries and Protecting Jobs. Worldwatch Paper #142 (June). Washington, DC: Worldwatch Institute.

Minar, Nelson, Roger Burkhart, Christopher Langton, and Manor Askenazi
1996 The Swarm Simulation System: A Toolkit for Building Multi-Agent Systems. Working Paper 96-06-042, Santa Fe Institute, Santa Fe, NM.

Miralles, R., A. Moya, and S. F. Elena
1997 Is Group Selection a Factor in Modulating the Virulence of RNA Viruses? Genetical Research 69:165–172.

Nakamura, M., H. Matsuda, and Y. Iwasa
1997 The Evolution of Cooperation in a Lattice-Structured Population. Journal of Theoretical Biology 184:65–81.

Nowak, Andrzej, Bibb Latane, and Maciej Lewenstein
1994 Social Dilemmas Exist in Space. *In* Social Dilemmas and Cooperation. U. Schultz, W. Albers, and U. Mueller, eds. Pp. 269–289. New York: Springer-Verlag.

Price, George R.
1970 Selection and Covariance. Nature 227:520–521.
1972 Extension of Covariance Selection Mathematics. Annals of Human Genetics 35:485–490.

Queller, David C.
1991 Group Selection and Kin Selection. Trends in Ecology and Evolution 6:64.
1994 Genetic Relatedness in Viscous Populations. Evolutionary Ecology 8:70–73.

Reynolds, J. F., and B. Acock
1997 Modularity and Genericness in Plant and Ecosystem Models. Ecological Modelling 94:7–16.

Ricklefs, Robert E.
1990 Ecology. 3rd edition. New York: W. H. Freeman.

Ridley, Mark
1996 Evolution. 2nd edition. Cambridge, MA: Blackwell Science.

Roberts, C. M.
1997 Ecological Advice for the Global Fisheries Crisis. Trends in Ecology and Evolution 12:35–38.

Roughgarden, Jonathan, Aviv Bergman, Sharoni Shafir, and Charles Taylor
1996 Adaptive Computation in Ecology and Evolution: A Guide for Future Research. *In* Adaptive Individuals in Evolving Populations. Richard K. Belew and Melanie Mitchell, eds. Pp. 25–30. Santa Fe Institute Studies in the Sciences of Complexity, Proceedings Volume XXVI. Reading, MA: Addison-Wesley.

Seeley, Thomas
1996 The Wisdom of the Hive: The Social Physiology of Honeybee Colonies. Cambridge, MA: Harvard University Press.

Sequeira, R. A., R. L. Olson, and J. M. McKinion
1997 Implementing Generic, Object-Oriented Models in Biology. Ecological Modelling 94:17–31.

Sherman, Paul W.
1977 Nepotism and the Evolution of Alarm Calling. Science 197:1246–1253.

Sober, Elliott, and David Sloan Wilson
1998 Unto Others: The Evolution and Psychology of Unselfish Behavior. Cambridge, MA: Harvard University Press.

Stevens, L., C. J. Goodnight, and S. Kalisz
1995 Multilevel Selection in Natural Populations of *Impatiens capensis*. American Naturalist 145:513–526.

Trivers, Robert L.
1985 Social Evolution. Menlo Park, CA: Benjamin/Cummings.

Wade, Michael J.
1985 Soft Selection, Hard Selection, Kin Selection, and Group Selection. American Naturalist 125:61–73.

Williams, George C.
1966 Adaptation and Natural Selection. Princeton, NJ: Princeton University Press.

Wilson, David Sloan
1975 A Theory of Group Selection. Proceedings of the National Academy of Science 72:143–146.

1979 Structured Demes and Trait-Group Variation. American Naturalist 113:606–610.

1980 The Natural Selection of Populations and Communities. Menlo Park, CA: Bemjamin/Cummings.

1990 Weak Altruism, Strong Group Selection. Oikos 59:135–140.

1997 Human Groups as Units of Selection. Science 276:1816–17.

Wilson, David Sloan, and Lee A. Dugatkin
1992 Altruism: Contemporary Debates. *In* Keywords in Evolutionary Biology. E. F. Keller and E. A. Lloyd, eds. Pp. 29–33. Cambridge, MA: Harvard University Press.

1997 Group Selection and Assortative Interactions. American Naturalist 149:336–351.

Wilson, David Sloan, and Elliott Sober
1994 Reintroducing Group Selection to the Human Behavioral Sciences. Behavioral and Brain Sciences 17:585–654.

Wilson, David Sloan, G. B. Pollock, and Lee A. Dugatkin
1992 Can Altruism Evolve in Purely Viscous Populations? Evolutionary Ecology 6:331–341.

Wilson, Edward O.
1975 Sociobiology. Cambridge, MA: Harvard University Press.

Wilson, William G.
1998 Resolving Discrepancies Between Deterministic Population Models and Individual-Based Simulations. American Naturalist 151:116–134.

Wright, Sewall
1945 Tempo and Mode in Evolution: A Critical Review. Ecology 26:415–419.

Wynne-Edwards, V. C.
1962 Animal Dispersion in Relation to Social Behaviour. Edinburgh: Oliver and Boyd.

Evolution of Inference

Brian Skyrms

... a substitution of voice for gesture can only have been made by common consent, something rather difficult to put into effect by men whose crude organs had not yet been exercised; something indeed, even more difficult to conceive of having happened in the first place, for such a unanimous agreement would need to be proposed, which means that speech seems to be absolutely necessary to establish the use of speech.

> Jean-Jacques Rousseau
> *A Discourse on Inequality*
> Part I

1 INTRODUCTION

Rousseau began his discussion of the origin of language with a paradox that echoes through modern philosophy of language. How can we explain the genesis of speech without presupposing speech, reference without presupposing reference, meaning without presupposing meaning? A version of this paradox forms the basis of Quine's attack on the logical empiricist doctrine that logic

Dynamics in Human and Primate Societies, edited by T. Kohler and G. Gumerman, Oxford University Press, 1999.

derives its warrant from conventions of meaning—that logical truths are true and logical inferences are valid by virtue of such conventions. Quine raised the general skeptical question of how conventions of language could be established without preexisting language, as well as calling attention to more specific skeptical circularities. If conventions of logic are to be set up by explicit definition, or by axioms, must we not presuppose logic to unpack those conventions?

2 LEWIS' THEORY OF CONVENTION

David Lewis (1969) sought to answer these skeptical doubts within a game theoretical framework in his book, *Convention*. This account contains fundamental new insights, and I regard it as a major advance in the theory of meaning. Lewis sees a convention as being a special kind of strict Nash equilibrium in a game that models the relevant social interaction. To say that a convention is a Nash equilibrium is to say that if an individual deviates from a convention which others observe, he is no better off for that. To say that it is a *strict* Nash equilibrium is to say that he is actually worse off. To this, Lewis adds the additional requirement that an individual unilateral deviation makes *everyone* involved in the social interaction worse off, so that it is in the common interest to avoid such deviations.

A theory of convention must answer two fundamental questions: how do we arrive at conventions?, and by virtue of what considerations do conventions remain in force? Within Lewis' game-theoretic setting, these questions become, respectively, the problems of *equilibrium selection* and *equilibrium maintenance*.

On the face of it, the second problem may seem to have a trivial solution—the equilibrium is maintained because it is an equilibrium! No one has an incentive to deviate. In fact, since it is a strict equilibrium, everyone has an incentive not to deviate. This is part of the answer, but Lewis shows that this is not the whole answer.

There is an incentive to avoid unilateral deviation, but, for example, if you expect me to deviate you might believe you would be better off deviating as well. And if I believe that you have such beliefs, I may expect you to deviate and by virtue of such expectations deviate myself. It is when I believe that others will not deviate that I must judge deviation to be against my own interest. The self-reinforcing character of strict Nash equilibrium must be backed by a hierarchy of appropriate interacting expectations.

These considerations lead to Lewis' introduction of the concept of common knowledge. A proposition, P, is common knowledge among a group of agents if each of them knows that P, and each of them knows that each of them knows that P, and so forth for all finite levels. To the requirement that a convention must be the appropriate kind of strict Nash equilibrium, he adds the additional requirement that it be backed by the appropriate kind of common knowledge.

The game must be common knowledge to the players along with the fact that their actions are jointly at that equilibrium of the game that constitutes the convention.

Considerations of common knowledge are thus at the center of Lewis' theory of equilibrium maintenance. What about equilibrium selection? A convention is typically an equilibrium in an interaction, which admits many different equilibria. That is what makes conventions conventional. An alternative equilibrium might have done as well. How, then, do the agents involved come to coordinate on one of the many possible equilibria involved? Lewis, following Schelling, identifies three factors, which may affect equilibrium selection: prior agreement, precedent, and salience. A *salient* equilibrium (Schelling's focal equilibrium) is one which "stands out" to the agents involved for some reason or another. Salience is a psychological property, and the causes of salience are not restricted in any way. Prior agreement and precedent can be viewed as special sources of salience.

3   SIGNALING GAMES IN *CONVENTION*

Lewis discusses the conventionality of meaning in the context of signaling games.[1] We suppose that one player, the Sender, comes into possession of some private knowledge about the world, and wishes to share it with another player, the Receiver—who could use that knowledge to make a more informed decision. The decision has payoff implications for both Sender and Receiver, and their interests in this decision are common, which is why both wish the decision to be an informed one.

The Sender has a number of potential messages or signals that he can send to the Receiver to convey that information, the only hitch being that the "messages" have no preexisting meaning. The model that Lewis considers has an equal number of states of the world, S, messages, M, and acts, A. The payoffs for both players make the game a game of common interest—for example, where the number of states, messages, and acts is three, we might have payoffs:

	Act 1	Act 2	Act 3
State 1	1,1	0,0	0,0
State 2	0,0	1,1	0,0
State 3	0,0	0,0	1,1

(where payoffs are entered as: sender payoff, receiver payoff). We will assume in this example that states are equiprobable.

A *Sender's strategy* in this game is a rule which associates each state with a message to be sent in that state; a *Receiver's strategy* associates each

---

[1] A more general model of sender-receiver games was introduced and analyzed by Crawford and Sobel (1982).

message with an act to be taken if that message is received. Sender's strategy and Receiver's strategy taken together associate an act taken by the Receiver with each state of the world. If, for every state, the act taken is optimal for that state, the combination of Sender's strategy and Receiver's strategy is called a *Signaling System*. For example, for three states, messages, and acts, the following is an example of a signaling system:

<table>
<tr><td>**Sender's Strategy**</td><td>**Receiver's strategy**</td></tr>
<tr><td>$S_1 \rightarrow M_1$</td><td>$M_1 \rightarrow A_1$</td></tr>
<tr><td>$S_2 \rightarrow M_2$</td><td>$M_2 \rightarrow A_2$</td></tr>
<tr><td>$S_3 \rightarrow M_3$</td><td>$M_3 \rightarrow A_3$</td></tr>
</table>

It is evident, however, that this is not the only signaling system for this game. If we take it, and permute the messages in any way, we get another equally good signaling system—for example:

<table>
<tr><td>**Sender's Strategy**</td><td>**Receiver's strategy**</td></tr>
<tr><td>$S_1 \rightarrow M_3$</td><td>$M_3 \rightarrow A_1$</td></tr>
<tr><td>$S_2 \rightarrow M_1$</td><td>$M_1 \rightarrow A_2$</td></tr>
<tr><td>$S_3 \rightarrow M_2$</td><td>$M_2 \rightarrow A_3$</td></tr>
</table>

Thus the meaning of a message is a function of which signaling system is operative—meaning emerges from social interaction.

Signaling systems are clearly Nash equilibria of the Sender-Receiver game. They are not the only Nash equilibria of the game. There are totally noncommunicative equilibria, where the Sender always sends the same message and the Receiver performs the same action regardless of the message received, such as:

<table>
<tr><td>**Sender's Strategy**</td><td>**Receiver's strategy**</td></tr>
<tr><td>$S_1 \rightarrow M_1$</td><td>$M_3 \rightarrow A_2$</td></tr>
<tr><td>$S_2 \rightarrow M_1$</td><td>$M_1 \rightarrow A_2$</td></tr>
<tr><td>$S_3 \rightarrow M_1$</td><td>$M_2 \rightarrow A_2$</td></tr>
</table>

This *is* an equilibrium, no matter how inefficient it is, since neither player can improve his payoff by unilaterally switching strategies. There are equilibria in which partial information is transmitted, such as:

<table>
<tr><td>**Sender's Strategy**</td><td>**Receiver's strategy**</td></tr>
<tr><td>$S_1 \rightarrow M_1$</td><td>$M_1 \rightarrow A_1$</td></tr>
<tr><td>$S_2 \rightarrow M_1$</td><td>$M_2 \rightarrow A_1$</td></tr>
<tr><td>$S_3 \rightarrow M_3$</td><td>$M_3 \rightarrow A_3$</td></tr>
</table>

In addition to signaling systems, there is a whole range of other equilibria in these signaling games.

But signaling systems are special. They are not only Nash equilibria, but also strict Nash equilibria. And they are the kind of strict Nash equilibria that are *conventions* in Lewis' general theory of convention. The other nonsignaling system equilibria do not come up to these standards. Unilaterally changing a potential response to an unsent message or unilaterally changing the circumstance in which you send a message, which will be ignored, is of no consequence. It does not make one better off, but it does not make one worse off either. So signaling systems are conventions, and the only conventions, in the kind of Sender-Receiver game that has been described.

(This striking result depends to a certain extent on the modeling decision to make the number of states, messages, and actions equal. Suppose that we add a fourth message to our three-state, three-act game—and extend a signaling system equilibrium of the original game by extending the receiver's strategy to take act one if message four were received. According to the sender's strategy message four is never sent, so what the receiver would do if she received that message is of no consequence. Thus we do not have a strict equilibrium, and we do not have a Lewis convention of the game with the enlarged message space. This is perhaps not as serious a difficulty as it may at first seem. Let us bracket these concerns for now. We will return to this matter later in a different context.)

Lewis' account is a fundamental advance in the philosophy of meaning. It focuses attention on social interaction and information transmission. And it provides an account of how conventions of meaning can be maintained.

Still, it does not appear that Lewis' account has completely answered the skeptical doubts with which we began. The skeptic will ask for the origin of all the common knowledge invoked by the account of equilibrium maintenance for conventions. And he will ask for a noncircular account of equilibrium selection for equilibria that constitute conventions of meaning. Prior agreement and precedent can hardly be invoked to explain the genesis of meaningful signals. And where is the salience in Lewis' models of signaling games? All signaling system equilibria are equally good. None seems especially salient. Perhaps some sort of salience extrinsic to the model might get us off the ground, but we lack any explicit theory of such salience.

4   BIRDS DO IT, BEES DO IT

Lewis' theory of convention is framed within a theory of interactive rational choice, and the heavy requirements of that theory are exploited by the skeptic. As an antidote to skeptical doubts we might do well to remind ourselves that all sorts of organisms have developed effective signaling systems presumably without the benefit of extensive common knowledge or even explicit rational choice.

The lowly bee has somehow developed and maintains a signaling system, which successfully encodes and transmits information regarding the location and quality of a food source. Bird brains are adequate for using signals for warning, indicating territory, and mating. Several different animals have species-specific alarm calls. Perhaps the best studied are the vervet monkeys who are the focus of Cheney and Seyfarth's (1990) delightful book, *How Monkeys See the World*. Vervets are prey to three main kinds of predator: leopards, snakes, and eagles. For each there is a different alarm call, and each alarm call elicits a different action, appropriate to the type of predator that triggers the call. The situation is remarkably close to that modeled in a Lewis Sender-Receiver game.[2] What account can we give of animal communication?

5   EVOLUTION

Maynard Smith and Price (1973) have introduced a notion of equilibrium maintenance into evolutionary theory, that of an *evolutionarily stable strategy*. The leading idea is that an evolutionarily stable strategy must be able to resist invasion by a small number of mutants. Given certain idealizing assumptions, this yields the definition of Maynard Smith and Parker (1976)—in a population playing the strategy, either the natives do better against themselves than a mutant, or both do equally well against the natives, but the natives do better against the mutant.

Suppose we have a species in which an individual sometimes finds herself in the role of sender, sometimes in the role of receiver. Individuals have "strategies" (or rules or routines) that determine how they play the game in each role. Suppose that a population consists of individuals who all have the same strategy, which is a signaling system in a Lewis signaling game. If you consider potential mutations to other strategies in the game, you will see that a signaling system is here an evolutionarily stable strategy.

If we look for evolutionarily stable strategies of the signaling game other than signaling systems, we find that they do not exist. The other Nash equilibria of the game correspond to strategies that fail the test of evolutionary stability. For example, consider a population with the noninformative strategy of always sending the same signal, regardless of the state observed and always taking the same act, regardless of the signal received. That population can be invaded by a mutant playing a signaling system. When playing against natives, both natives do equally badly. But when playing against mutants, mutants rather than natives do the best.

This striking conclusion, like Lewis' result that signaling systems are conventions, depends on our modeling assumption that the number of states, messages, and acts are equal. If we add some extra messages to the model, then signaling systems will not be evolutionarily stable strategies in the sense

---

[2]Some differences are discussed in chapter 5 of Skyrms' (1996) *Evolution of the Social Contract*. Especially see the section on "Signals for Altruists."

of Maynard Smith and Parker. The reason, as before, is that we can consider a mutant whose strategy specifies a different response to a message that is never sent. Such a mutant will not be eliminated. The difficulty, however, does not seem so serious, since the mutant *behaves* just like the native, in sending signals and in reacting to signals actually sent. We can shift our attention to a class of behaviorally equivalent strategies and consider evolutionarily stable classes as ones such that in a population using members of the class, any mutant strategy outside the class will be eliminated. Then the connection between evolutionary stability and signaling systems can be recaptured. The interested reader can find this worked out in Wärneryd (1993).

Evolutionary stability gives a qualitative account of equilibrium maintenance, but how do we get to a particular equilibrium in the first place? We find one attractive suggestion in a remarkable passage from Darwin's (1898) *Descent of Man*:

> Since monkeys certainly understand much that is said to them by man, and when wild, utter signal cries of danger to their fellows; and since fowls give distinct warnings for danger on the ground, or in the sky from hawks (both, as well as a third cry, intelligible to dogs), may not an unusually wise ape-like animal have imitated the growl of a beast of prey, and thus have told his fellow-monkeys the nature of the expected danger? This would have been the first step in the formation of language.

Darwin knows of species-specific alarm calls. Modern studies support his remarks about the alarm calls of fowl (Evans et al. 1994). He knows that one species may be able to use the information in another species' alarm call. Cheney and Seyfarth found that vervets use the information in the alarm calls of the superb starling. Darwin also has a hypothesis about the genesis of animal signaling.

The hypothesis is that the crucial determinant of the signaling system selected is *natural salience*. The prey imitate the natural sounds of the predator to communicate the presence of the predator to their fellows. The only problem with this suggestion is that there seems to be no empirical evidence in support of it. For other kinds of animal signals, such as threat displays, natural salience provides a plausible explanation for the origin of the signal. Baring of teeth in dogs retains its natural salience. But species-specific alarm calls do not resemble the sounds made by the type of predator that they indicate. Of course it is still possible that they began in the way suggested by Darwin, and that the course of evolution so modified them that their origins are no longer discernible. But in the absence of evidence to this effect we are led to ask whether signaling systems could evolve without benefit of natural salience.

We can approach this question by applying a simple model of differential reproduction, *replicator dynamics* (Taylor and Jonker 1978; Schuster and

Sigmund 1983), to a Lewis sender-receiver game. We can let all kinds of combinations of sender and receiver strategies arise in the population. Start with some population proportions picked at random, and examine the results of differential reproduction on that population over time. Then choose new population proportions at random and repeat the process. I ran such a computer simulation, with the result that signaling systems *always* evolved. The signaling system which evolved was not always the same. Each possible signaling system evolved in some of the trials. The equilibria that are not signaling systems never evolved. The reason for this is that they are dynamically unstable. Only signaling systems are attractors in the evolutionary dynamics.

If natural salience had been present at the start of the process, it could have had the effect of constraining initial conditions so as to fall within the basin of attraction of a "natural signaling system." In the absence of natural salience, where meaning is purely conventional, signaling systems arise spontaneously, but which signaling system is selected depends on the vagaries of the initial stages of the evolutionary process.

Evolutionary dynamics has provided an answer to the skeptical doubts with which we ended section 3. We have an account of the spontaneous emergence of signaling systems, which does not require preexisting common knowledge, agreement, precedent, or salience.

6 LEARNING

Is the point confined to strictly evolutionary settings? Adam Smith (1849), in *Considerations Concerning the First Formation of Languages* (quoted in Blume et al. [1996]), suggested a different approach:

> Two savages, who had never been taught to speak, but had been bred up remote from the societies of men, would naturally begin to form that language by which they would endeavor to make their mutual wants intelligible to each other, by uttering certain sounds, whenever they meant to denote certain objects.

Smith is suggesting that, given the proper incentives, signaling systems can arise naturally from the dynamics of *learning*.

It is not feasible to carry out Smith's thought experiment, but Blume et al. saw whether undergraduates at the University of Iowa would spontaneously learn to play some signaling system in a sender-receiver game of the kind discussed by Lewis. They take extraordinary precautions to exclude natural salience from the experimental setting. Sender and receiver communicate to each other over a computer network. The messages available to the sender are the asterisk and the pound sign, {∗,#}. These are identified to the players as possible messages on their computer screens. The order in which they appear on a given player's screen is chosen at random to control for the possibility that order of presentation might function as the operative salience cue. Then players repeatedly play a Lewis signaling game. Players are kept informed of the history of play of the group.[3] Under these conditions the players rapidly[4] learn to coordinate on one signaling system or another.

The result might be expected, because the qualitative dynamical behavior of the replicator dynamics that explain evolutionary emergence of signaling systems are shared by a wide range of adaptive dynamics. In Lewis signaling games, which are games of common interest, evolutionary dynamics, learning dynamics, and almost any reasonable sort of adaptive dynamics leads to successful coordination on a signaling system equilibrium. In the absence of natural salience, which signaling system emerges depends on the vicissitudes of initial conditions and chance aspects of the process. But some signaling system does evolve because signaling systems are powerful attractors in the dynamics, and other Nash equilibria of the game are dynamically unstable.

7   UNANSWERED QUESTIONS

The dynamics of evolution and learning show us how signaling systems can emerge spontaneously. The skeptical doubts concerning equilibrium selection and equilibrium maintenance raised at the end of section 3 are completely answered by the dynamical approach. But we began with skeptical doubts about the status of *logic*. And although our account of the dynamics of Lewis signaling games has given us an account of the emergence of a kind of meaning, it has not given us an account of logical truth or logical inference based on that meaning.

We are still very far from an account of the evolution of logic. I do not have a general account to offer here, but I would like to indicate a few steps that we can take in the desired direction.

8   PROTO-TRUTH FUNCTIONS

As a first step, I propose that we modify Lewis signaling games to allow for the possibility that the sender's observation gives him less than perfect information about the relevant state of the world. For example, suppose that a vervet sender could sometimes determine the exact kind of predator, but sometimes only tell that it is a leopard or a snake.

It may well be that the optimal evasive action, given that a leopard or snake is present, is different from either the optimal act for leopard or the optimal act for snake. One would not want to stumble on the snake while running for the nearest tree to escape the leopard. One would not want to

---

[3] The group consists of 6 senders and 6 receivers. After each play of the signaling game, the players are updated on what happened.

[4] In 15 or 20 periods.

draw a leopard's attention by standing up straight and scanning the ground for snakes. A new message should not be hard to come by. (In fact vervets that have migrated to new localities where they are faced with new predators that call for new evasive action have developed new messages and the appropriate signaling system [Kavanaugh 1980; Cheney and Seyfarth 1990].)

So we have now a model with four types of knowledge that senders may have, four messages, and four states with a common interest payoff structure as before. Then the evolutionary (or learning) dynamics is no different than the one we would have if we had four predators, four messages, and four appropriate evasive actions in the original story. The story is the same. A signaling system will emerge with signals for eagle, snake, leopard, and *leopard or snake*. The last signal I call a *proto-truth function*. The truth function "or" is a sentence connective which forms a compound sentence that is true just in case at least one of its constituent simple sentences is true. The last signal need not be a complex sentence with meaningful parts, one of which is the truth function "or," but one way of giving its meaning is as a truth function.[5]

More generally, we can modify the Lewis model by letting nature decide randomly the specificity with which the sender can identify the state of nature.[6] Then, given the appropriate common interest structure, we have the conditions for the emergence of a rich signaling system with lots of proto-truth functional signals.

We are now well out of the vervets' league, and perhaps into the province of "an unusually wise ape-like animal," but I will continue to frame my example in terms of the vervets for the sake of narrational continuity. Our sender may now have proto-truth functional signals for both "snake or leopard" and for "not-leopard."

9   INFERENCE

Now I would like to complicate the model a little more. Most of the time, one member of the troop detects a predator, gives the alarm call appropriate to her state of knowledge, and everything goes as in the last section. This predominant scenario is sufficiently frequent to fix a signaling system, which includes proto-truth functions.

Occasionally, two members of the troop detect a predator at the same time, and both give alarm calls. Sometimes they both have maximally specific information, and both give the alarm call for the specific predator. Sometimes, however, they will have complementary imprecise information as, for example, when one signals *snake or leopard* and the other signals *not-leopard*.

Since the senders detect the presence of a predator independently and at approximately the same time, they just use their strategies in the signaling

---

[5]There are, of course, other ways of giving its meaning, such as terrestrial predator.

[6]Nature chooses a random information partition, and the sender is informed only of the cell that contains the actual situation.

game of the last section. What do the receivers do? Initially some will do one thing and some will do another. Those who take the evasive action appropriate to snakes will, on average, fare better than those who don't. Over time, evolution, learning, or any reasonable adaptive dynamics will fix this behavior. Here we have a kind of evolution of inference, where the inference is based on the kind of meaning explicated by Lewis signaling games.

The setting need not be the Amboseli forest preserve and the signaling game need not involve alarm calls. The essential points are that a signaling system evolves for communicating partial information, that the receiver may get multiple signals encoding various pieces of information, and that it is in the common interest of sender and receiver that the latter takes the action that is optimal in light of all the information received. When these conditions are realized, adaptive dynamics favors the emergence of inference.

10 CONCLUSION

We have an account of the formation of rudimentary conventions of meaning, and of rudimentary inference based on that meaning. Evolution of a correct rule of inference naturally depends on the repeated occurrence of situations where there is a positive payoff for acting on the right conclusion. There are a number of major steps that remain to be taken before we could talk about the evolution of *logic*—even the simplest system of logic[7]—but the task does not seem insuperable, and it invites further investigation.

REFERENCES

Blume, A., D. W. DeJong, Y-G. Kim, and G. B. Sprinkle
    1996 Evolution of the Meaning of Messages in Sender-Receiver Games. Working Paper, University of Iowa.

Cheney, D., and R. M. Seyfarth
    1990 How Monkeys See the World: Inside the Mind of Another Species. Chicago, IL: University Chicago Press.

Crawford, V. P., and J. Sobel
    1982 Strategic Information Transmission. Econometrica 50:1431–1451.

Darwin, Charles
    1898 The Descent of Man and Selection in Relation to Sex. 2d ed. London: J. Murray.

---

[7] We would have to account for the evolution of the truth functional connectives, as parts of language used to form compound sentences, and for the evolution of general formal rules of inference such as disjunctive syllogism. The vervets have no use for such machinery, and this projected account would have to be framed in a much richer context of information processing than that of alarm calls.

Evans, C. S., C. L. Evans, and P. Marler
1994 On the Meaning of Alarm Calls: Functional Reference in an Avian Vocal System. Animal Behavior 45:23–38.

Kavanaugh, M.
1980 Invasion of the Forest By an African Savannah Monkey: Behavioral Adaptations. Behavior 73:238–260.

Lewis, D.
1969 Convention. Cambridge, MA: Harvard University Press.

Maynard Smith, John, and G. Parker
1976 The Logic of Asymmetric Contests. Animal Behavior 24:159–179.

Maynard Smith, John, and G. Price
1973 The Logic of Animal Conflicts. Nature 246:15–18.

Rousseau, J.
1984 A Discourse on Inequality. M. Cranston, trans. New York: Penguin Books.

Schuster, P., and K. Sigmund
1983 Replicator Dynamics. Journal of Theoretical Biology 100:535–538.

Smith, A.
1849 Considerations Concerning the First Formation of Languages. *In* The Theory of Moral Sentiments: or, An Essay Towards an Analysis of the Principles By Which Men Naturally Judge Concerning the Conduct and Character, First of Their Neighbours, and Afterwards of Themselves. To Which Is Added, a Dissertation on the Origin of Languages. Edinburgh: John D. Lowe.

Skyrms, Brian
1996 Evolution of the Social Contract. New York: Cambridge University Press.

Taylor, P., and L. Jonker
1978 Evolutionarily Stable Strategies and Game Dynamics. Mathematical Biosciences 40:145–156.

Wärneryd, K.
1993 Cheap Talk, Coordination and Evolutionary Stability. Games and Economic Behavior 5:532–546.

Trajectories to Complexity in Artificial Societies: Rationality, Belief, and Emotions

Jim E. Doran

This chapter illustrates and discusses the use of agent-based artificial societies to explore possible trajectories into social complexity through the integration of ideas from both anthropology and agent technology. Particular attention is paid to the role of rational cooperation, collective belief, and emotional dynamics in these trajectories. Some methodological problems associated with the use of artificial societies to build social theory are also discussed, especially how best to reduce the impact of our own cultural preconceptions.

1 INTRODUCTION

Computer simulation work in archaeology and anthropology is more than 25 years old (see Doran and Hodson 1975, chapter 11; Doran 1990; and compare Halpin to appear). After a period of enthusiasm in the early 1980s interest waned, but recently there have been a number of important computer-based studies of (human) social phenomena using so-called *agent-based modeling* (e.g., Kohler et al. this volume) and *agent-based artificial societies* (e.g., Epstein and Axtell 1996), and more are in progress. Both types of study involve (software) agents, that is, according to a standard textbook definition, *entities which perceive and act in an environment* (Russell and Norvig 1995:49).

Dynamics in Human and Primate Societies, edited by T. Kohler and G. Gumerman, Oxford University Press, 1999.

Reactive agents are typically built around a small number of relatively simple situation-to-action rules. Deliberative agents are more complex, typically posting goals and then forming and executing plans to achieve them. It is this rapidly developing "agent technology," largely based upon artificial intelligence studies, that is the driving force behind the new work.

The methodology associated with both agent-based modeling and agent-based artificial societies emphasizes the ability to address explicitly processes of cognition, and hence phenomena that previous models could not tackle, and also the ability to explore what could happen rather than what has happened or is happening. However, unlike agent-based modeling, artificial societies are, in essence, models without a specific target system, and it has been argued that this type of modeling permits the study of societies and their processes in the abstract (Epstein and Axtell 1996; Doran 1997). An underlying assumption is that it is possible and useful for social scientists to explore wide-ranging and abstract social theories and that these theories can be expressed in terms of computational processes.

2 TRAJECTORIES TO SOCIAL COMPLEXITY

For a number of years, research at the University of Essex in agent-based artificial societies has particularly concerned the "emergence" trajectories by which a small-scale society, in its environment, may move autonomously from relatively simple (distributed, no ranking or centralized decision making) to complex (ranking/hierarchy, with centralized decision making and a degree of specialization). The aim is to explore causes, triggers, key processes, and "bottlenecks."

2.1 RELEVANT ANTHROPOLOGICAL STUDIES

The emergence of social complexity in human societies has, of course, been very extensively discussed by archaeologists, anthropologists, and others. There are a number of particular studies that have influenced our thinking at Essex. In an early but influential paper, Flannery (1972) presented a cybernetic model of society and its dynamics, centering on the concept of a control hierarchy and mechanisms that can modify the hierarchy such as promotion and linearization. At about the same time, Rappaport (1971, 1984) examined the processes by which a society may come to be structured and controlled by ritual and ideology and how these processes fit into the emergence of centralized decision making. Wright and Zeder (1977), in experiments with a simulation of a linear exchange system, showed how the properties of the system (what would now probably be called a multiagent system) could usefully be established irrespective of any sociocultural instance. An important but largely unexplored question is just how the cybernetic conceptual repertoire deployed by these and many other studies of that period connects to the agent repertoire used throughout this chapter.

In a major review, Johnson and Earle (1987) put forward a general model for the emergence of complexity. They argued that population growth is the key trigger. Brumfiel and Earle (1987) considered, in particular, the role played by specialization and exchange in the formation of complex societies. In both studies (and many others) the idea of redistribution was important—bringing products to the center and then reallocating them.

Sanders and Webster (1978) proposed that the emergence process should be seen as multicausal, multistage, and multitrajectory with conditions at trajectory branch points. This notion is easily taken up in a computational context.

Boehm (1993) emphasized the overriding of the checks which restrain aspiring leaders. He portrayed centralized decision making as the outcome of a failure of the social mechanisms that normally keep leadership in check. In cybernetic terms it is a "failure" of negative feedback. This suggests that members of the society are relatively aware of what is happening, and that this awareness is significant. It implies that they are able to formulate internal representations of their situation and the options open to them, and that these are causally significant at a group level. It is closely relevant that Renfrew (1987) discussed the notion of a collective representation, or "collective mappa" in his phrase.

Many of these ideas will be prominent, if somewhat reshaped, in what follows even though, from the perspective of computer-based modeling, the concepts and processes in the different theories mentioned are often ill-defined and ambiguous. There is a tendency to ignore the detail of microlevel processes, especially cognitive processes. No doubt this partly stems from the conviction that such matters are irrelevant to the understanding of societies, but also because they tend to lie outside the competence and interests of the authors. The EOS project to be discussed below illustrates just how much detail must be added to an existing anthropological theory to formulate it for computer work. Agent-based artificial societies at least enable us to examine the coherence of the various theories of the origins of social complexity that have been proposed, while including details of cognitive processing. It may even be possible to gain original insights. But just how can the "emergence of complexity" be translated into the terms of an agent-based artificial society?

3 TRAJECTORIES TO SOCIAL COMPLEXITY IN COMPUTATIONAL TERMS

The requirement of a trajectory to social complexity may be posed in simple or complex forms, depending upon whether it is limited to centralized decision making, or also includes such matters as specialization and territory. Minimally there is a computational interpretation of agents in a spatial environment. Initially there are no interagent relationships in existence (other, perhaps, than some interpretation of "family" relationships), but there comes into being an objectively discernible decision-making hierarchy. It is apparent that there are many different ways in which this requirement may be made precise. The EOS project, which is described briefly below, chose one of them.

3.1 THE EOS PROJECT

Mellars (1985) has examined in detail the particular environmental circumstances in the Upper Palaeolithic period in southwestern France which seem to have triggered a first flowering of complex human society. Following Mellars, the EOS Project (Doran et al. 1994; Doran and Palmer 1995) has used an artificial society to explore how, in circumstances of population concentration, the way in which a social hierarchy and centralized decision making (subordination tree) could develop from certain basic assumptions about the cognitive properties of the deliberative agents involved, notably their self-interested rational decision making, planning, and cooperation in the context of resource gathering. The agents in this study have a relatively complex internal structure, making use of quite advanced artificial intelligence techniques.

Detailed results have been obtained and have confirmed that Mellars' theories linking population concentration to the development of centralized decision making could indeed be given a coherent interpretation in computational terms. However, the complexity of the system as a whole has made it very difficult to achieve a comprehensive understanding of its behavior by systematic experimentation.

3.1.1 Hunter-Gatherer Decision Making.

A current project, related to though simpler than the EOS project, is directed to the strategic decision making of hunter-gatherer groups and its impact upon the archaeological record (Manologlou forthcoming). The objective is to integrate Binford's classic study of group hunter-gatherer strategies (Binford 1980) with Mithen's computer simulation study linking individual hunting strategy to faunal deposition (Mithen 1990) and with Renfrew's notion of a "collective mappa," and so be able to relate a pseudo-archaeological record—ultimately, of course, a real archaeological record—to both micro and macro aspects of group hunting strategy.

We have implemented (within the object-oriented programming language C++) a created landscape over which hunters and prey move on a minute by minute basis. Each day the hunters can choose between resting at their base camp, hunting individually following one of several possible strategies, hunting a previously detected herd of prey in a group, or selecting some of their number to form a party to move to a field camp with the intention of hunting from the field camp the following day(s). Following Mithen (1990), these choices are determined primarily by the experiences of and information collected individually by hunters on the previous day, which the hunters "pool" in the evening when they, in effect, form a collective view (a "collective mappa") and decide what is to happen on the following day. The hunters' collective decision making is determined by 12 heuristic situation-action rules.

In the creation of this scenario many detailed design decisions have been made and parameters set. These determine, for example, the features of the "landscape" including the difficulty of crossing certain types of terrain, route-finding by the hunters, and the heuristic rules that determine collective decision making, including the precise criteria for moving to a field camp (selected from a set of possible camps). We have attempted to be realistic in our design choices, but there is no question of this being a specific simulation of a specific hunting group or locality.

Many factors can be varied in particular experiments, for example, the numbers of hunters and prey (following Binford, the latter is linked to a notion of mean annual temperature), the number of days the scenario is to last, the activity level of the hunters, and the probability with which a particular pursuit of a prey will prove successful. As the scenario is executed, the faunal debris at each camp is recorded and cumulated, and the various decisions made by the hunters are logged.

Experimentation is under way, and as it proceeds, we hope to find non-trivial relationships between "archaeologically recoverable" patterns of faunal remains and the "unobservable" daily hunting strategies selected by the hunters. In due course we hope also to demonstrate some of the special circumstances in which hunter-gatherers can become semisedentary as conjectured by Mellars.

3.2 BEYOND RATIONALITY

In the EOS and hunter-gatherer projects just described, the agents are "rational" in the sense that they use their beliefs to select actions to best achieve their goals (Binmore et al. in press)—and their beliefs are generally taken to be sound or nearly so. But there are problems with designing the agents in our created multiagent societies to be rational in this sense. Leaving aside the issue of our limited ability actually to construct such agents, it is counterintuitive. Observation of the dynamics of actual human societies, especially at times of crisis, strongly suggests that rationality based on sound beliefs is at best part of the story. Everything suggests there is at work a mixture of rational calculation, group emotions, and collective belief or ideology that may range far from objective reality (see, for example, the classic study of Tsembagañ society by Rappaport [1984]).

At Essex in recent years we have therefore begun to study agent-based emergence trajectories involving:

- substantial collective *misbelief* within a (sub)society of agents, and
- the *dynamics of collective emotions* within a (sub)society of agents.

These topics and our associated experimentation are discussed below.

3.3 COLLECTIVE (MIS)BELIEFS

It is a commonplace that all human societies construct collective belief systems (e.g., religious or political), which greatly influence their behavior (Renfrew 1994). As indicated earlier, Rappaport (1971) has put forward a view of the origins of belief systems in terms of their social function in controlling a society of complex and intelligent individuals. How do these ideas and theories translate into the computational world of artificial societies? Remarkably, experiments with computer-based multiagent systems show that for a variety of reasons (for example, localization in time and space, faulty generalization, and communication) computational deliberative agents also cannot avoid partial belief and misbelief.

3.3.1 Agents and (Mis)Beliefs.   The notion of "belief" is a difficult one. Here, a belief is taken merely to be a proposition which an agent holds (at some time) to be true of the world (at some time) or of a hypothetical world. The issue of degrees of belief is ignored. A concept then is a related set of beliefs about some conceived entity or class of entities.

The typical agent architecture incorporates a changing set of beliefs and concepts, which may be either explicitly represented or implicitly encoded. It follows that there is a wider set of beliefs, distributed over the agents, which determines their collective actions. Agents may or may not tend to have beliefs in common.

Let us assume that the beliefs are explicitly stored and communicable. They are necessarily stored in some specific internal (computational) language, however simple, which will normally be quite different from the communication language.

In human societies beliefs change and evolve in important ways. For example, Mithen (1996) and Sperber (1994) have discussed the origins of anthropomorphic beliefs and their significance, and Read (1987) has suggested that generalization of beliefs about family relationships played an important part in the development of human society. Similarly, beliefs can be made to mutate and evolve within artificial societies by specific processes of modification in the context of observation, adaptation, and interagent communication all of which are subject to error.

Since collective beliefs determine collective action, different patterns of beliefs necessarily have different survival potential (depending upon environmental characteristics) for the agents that carry them. Effective patterns of belief tend to "win out" and become dominant. Of course, "winning" patterns are not necessarily "true"—misbelief may be functional (Doran 1998).

The impact of beliefs may be summed up as follows:

Beliefs + Situation-Action Rules $\Longrightarrow$ Behavior

Beliefs + Goals + "Rational" Planning $\Longrightarrow$ Behavior

corresponding to reactive and deliberative agents, respectively.

3.3.2 The SCENARIO-3 Experiments and "Cults." In a series of experiments with agent populations in the SCENARIO-3 multiagent testbed we have explored how specific misbeliefs in the existence of unreal agents, and believed relationships with them, may inhibit groups of agents from attempting to "kill" one another—which they would otherwise do—to their mutual benefit (Doran 1998).

In these experiments, agents have beliefs about the existence (and location etc.) of other individual agents and of immobile resources that may be "harvested." An agent may, with very low probability at any moment, wrongly come to believe that a particular resource is, in fact, an agent and react to it accordingly. We call such a pseudo-agent a *resource agent*. A misbelief in a resource agent may then be passed to the believing agent's spatial neighbors and descendants. In consequence there may emerge sets of agents, which we call cults, which have in common their collective belief in a particular resource agent. Set within a suitable (and limited) pattern of possible SCENARIO-3 interagent relationships, the agents within a cult treat one another a little differently. They pass information among themselves and do not kill one another. All other things being equal, the effect of a cult is a substantially larger average population size.

The key to the formation of cults is the effective "immortality" of the resource agents. In the testbed, resources are harvested but never deleted. It is this immortality which holds the cult together for many generations.

It is tempting to relate such notions of collective misbelief to theories of "ideology." Indeed we are currently investigating the notion of a *biased ideology*, as may be captured within an artificial society. By a biased ideology we mean a collective belief system which, objectively viewed, systematically favors a subset of the population to the detriment of the remainder. Notice that this definition leaves open whether the bias is in any sense recognized or intended by all or any of the members of the population.

3.3.3 Cults and the Emergence of Centralized Decision Making. The two sets of experiments just described are targeted at the same naturally occurring phenomenon: the emergence of centralized and hierarchically organized decision making. The EOS experiments have emphasized rational cooperation among agents. The SCENARIO-3 experiments have addressed the functional impact of collective belief. But intuitively, rational calculation and collective belief are part and parcel of the same emergence process. But exactly how? The key seems to lie in the formation and stabilization of collective (mis)beliefs about a leadership role by way of the processes of belief modification mentioned earlier. These at least reinforce, perhaps typically replace, rational judgment.

3.4   THE ROLE OF EMOTIONS IN SOCIAL DYNAMICS

It is relatively easy to accept that belief and collective (mis)belief must play a part in our theories of the emergence of social complexity. But bringing in group emotions and dynamics is potentially much more controversial. Not only might emotions (anger, joy, guilt, shame, fear) seem largely irrelevant to the emergence of social complexity, they might well seem impossible to address on a computer. In fact, the modeling of emotions is an active topic in artificial intelligence and cognitive science, and there is an emerging repertoire of ideas and techniques that we are drawing upon in our work at Essex.

What *are* "emotions"? There are, of course, competing views. Here, emotions are considered as essentially corresponding to internal processes (laid down early in human evolution) that determine certain "simple" types of behavior, which can quickly and easily be triggered without necessary recourse to high-level cognition, and which can easily be passed from one agent to another in the sense that if the process is active in one agent, it can easily trigger the same process in another neighboring agent. To translate this idea into more computational terms, we need the idea of an agent's *control parameters*—those adjustable settings that determine an agent's activity in detail. Such parameters could include, for example, the size of the agent's working memory, the frequency with which the agent creates plans and their precise structure, the number of goals the agents can consider at the same time, the speed with which the agent can move, the intensity with which the agent typically sends signals, and many more. Every nontrivial agent architecture must include many such parameters.

Hence we come to the following definition:

(Pseudo-)emotions are certain distinctive patterns of cognitive and physical behavior in an agent. These patterns of behavior derive from particular and frequently occurring combinations of settings of the agent's control parameters, which are triggered (a) in particular types of environmental, including social, situations and (b) by the reactivation of emotionally charged memories.[1] Further, (pseudo-) emotions (that is, patterns of control parameter settings) may directly "spread" from one agent to another via, for example, processes analogous to the observation of "body language," and without the intervention of symbolic communication.

This view of pseudo-emotions involves nothing mysterious. In particular, it does not seek to address the subjective experience of emotion. And it is a natural generalization of the rather too simple notion of emotionally determined behavior as merely rule selection mediated by ad hoc "emotional variables." It also emphasizes the ability of emotions to spread throughout a population of agents.

3.4.1 Emotional Energy and the Emergence of Centralized Decision Making.

What is the impact of individual and collective emotions on the emergence of central

---

[1]For example, the loading into the agents working memory of a structure representing an emotionally charged episode from the past.

decision making and coordination? It seems helpful to follow Randall Collins by distinguishing between particular emotions, for example those mentioned above, and the concept of *emotional energy* (Collins 1990), which is intended to capture the idea of those types of emotional states that particularly impact an individual's intellectual and physical performance in social contexts. Collins has suggested that:

> An accurate view of the macrostructure, stripped down to its skeleton of microsimulations linked together in time and space, would reveal waves of emotion, attached to cognitions and motivating physical behavior, flowing across social space. We would then be in a position to test theories of how emotional energies operate both to stably reproduce social structure, and to energize the dynamics of conflict and change (Collins 1990:52).

Following Collins, Hoe (1997) has studied how in a society of agents social behavior, notably an interpretation of rituals, may drive the dynamics of emotional energy and interact with patterns of resource gathering. In Hoe's work, agents that find themselves in spatial proximity may engage in a "ritual" the important effect of which is to enhance the participants' emotional energy. Agents who miss out on the ritual suffer a decline in emotional energy. Hoe has conducted simple experiments linking the frequency of rituals in the artificial society to its average emotional "tone" and, hence, its effectiveness at resource acquisition.

This approach may easily be taken further. Consider, for example, the emergence of a *collective emotional profile* among the agents, perhaps in association with a particular system of collective beliefs. The emergence of a particular profile might well favor fast and flexible goal-directed action and be interpretable as the initialization and stabilization in the society of a "wave of enthusiasm" which raises collective performance and hence, perhaps, enables hierarchy formation.

A collective emotional profile seems more likely to appear in the context of population concentration, echoing a central element of Mellars' model and the EOS work discussed earlier. Alternatively, we might speculate that a collective emotional profile favoring "energetic" cognition might tend to have effects similar to that of population concentration.

3.4.2 How Important Are Pseudo-Emotions for Social Modeling?

That collective emotion plays a role in the emergence of complex society is immediately plausible. The idea agrees with our intuitive understanding of revolutionaries swept along on a wave of feeling and the often sudden rise of great empires driven by an all-consuming ideology. More generally, it is natural to conjecture that wherever and whenever human social behavior is hemmed in by rules, procedures, and norms that go unchallenged, then rational calculation is the key. But when the rules, procedures, and norms are absent or surmountable, then the roles of collective misbelief and collective emotion become important—too important to ignore if the social dynamics are to be understood and predicted.

4 METHODOLOGICAL PROBLEMS WITH ARTIFICIAL SOCIETIES

Recall that, in the foregoing, a distinction has been made between *agent-based modeling*, which is akin to traditional computer simulation but utilizing agent technology, and *agent-based artificial societies* where there is no specific society (or organization) which is to be modeled. In the latter, the aim is to discover more about the properties, in the abstract, of important social processes and their interaction. The recognized advantages of agent-based artificial societies include: that they avoid problems of validation (since there is no specific target system to be validated against), that they can ask what *could be* as well as address what is or has been, and that agents may be cognitively quite complex and hence offer insight into the relationship between microlevel cognition and macrolevel social behavior. But there are major methodological problems that the experiments described above have encountered, and which therefore are discussed below.

4.1 THE TECHNICAL REQUIREMENT AND ITS BIAS

Implementing agents with nontrivial cognitive or "intelligent" abilities requires artificial intelligence (AI) techniques. This is not a technology easily available to social scientists. Worse, AI has traditionally been first and foremost an engineering discipline. Its goal has been to design and build devices that have useful functions (often from a rationalist or mathematical logic perspective). This is somewhat, if not entirely, skewed to modeling or bottom-up theory building from artificial societies. So that even when the relevant expertise is available, it may well come with the wrong conceptual slant. This is a pervasive problem that will not easily be overcome.

4.2 THE PROBLEM OF EXPERIMENTAL COMPLEXITY

Experimenting with artificial societies is not easy. The detailed logs of experimental trials are typically extremely extensive. Assessing them is not only laborious, but risks the introduction of a preconceived conceptual repertoire to judge what is important amid a mass of detail. Furthermore, artificial societies are typically heavily parameterized, with explicit parameters merely the "tip of the iceberg" of implicit assumptions. The more complex the agent cognition, the more adjustable parameters there are. Thoroughly "mapping" the parameter space of an artificial society may well be prohibitively time consuming, and, in practice, is usually replaced by an unreliable combination of limited experimentation that holds most parameters constant and ad hoc insight.

4.3   THE PROBLEM OF OUR OWN CULTURAL PRECONCEPTIONS

The methodological difficulties identified in the preceding sections involve the problem of avoiding building our own cultural preconceptions into our conclusions. This issue, discussed below, is seen as a major problem with using artificial societies to build social theory, and one which is often not adequately recognized. Both in building artificial societies and interpreting their behavior, we are likely merely to create images of our own preconceptions.

It is not easy to identify our own cultural preconceptions, but a glance at how cultural beliefs vary from one human society to another and in one human society through time, makes clear that at any time and place such preconceptions do exist. For example, even within the narrow domain of enquiry considered here, the contrast between the cybernetic and agent-based conceptual repertoires mentioned above (section 2.1) is striking. Among the relevant cultural beliefs that habitually and, perhaps wrongly, are taken for granted are:

- that change and technological progress are the ideal and the norm,
- that agents somehow like us are basic (often with an implied mind/body dualism),
- that rationality is the ideal and the norm.

I suspect that we must follow the road that the hard sciences and mathematics have traditionally taken and make our assumptions precise and low level, and then observe what consequences flow from them. The implication is that the more complex behavior of social and world systems should emerge rather than be specified directly. The remainder of this chapter addresses some particular ways in which this approach might here be followed.

4.3.1   The Set of All Trajectories.

If we focus our attention on the set of *all possible trajectories* to complexity that an artificial society may follow, rather than those particular trajectories "of interest," we surely reduce the risk of our consciously or unconsciously selecting for particular attention trajectories which we, for unconsidered reasons, judge of special significance. The set of all trajectories to complexity is meaningful (on a computer) in the sense that given precise definitions of initial and terminal social formations in the multiple-agent system, and of the possible elemental system transitions, then the set of all possible system state sequences from initial to terminal formation must be well defined. Here "elemental system transitions" mean the possible changes that can take place, from one (simulated) time instant to the next, within the computational data structures that specify the state of the multiple-agent system (including the internal structures of agents) and its environment. In general these transitions are restricted only by the basic operations of whatever programming language is employed to implement the artificial society. Normally, of course, there is some attempt (which may or may not be made explicit) to implement an allowable set of elemental transitions which are judged to have some cognitive or social validity. Since different sets of elemental transitions must imply different sets of trajectories the choice of elemental transitions seems both critical and difficult, but it is often given little attention, at least as regards the internal cognition of agents.

Thus there are, unfortunately, major problems in addressing the set of all possible trajectories:

- As already indicated, there are a multitude of particular ways in which the task may be made precise (including alternative sets of elemental transitions of different granularity, and different initial conditions) and it is potentially prohibitively laborious to enumerate the set of possible trajectories, even to sample it adequately. We have to work on the assumption that there are relatively simple regularities waiting to be found.
- Even if enumerated, finding a useful description of the set of trajectories is a highly nontrivial task. It implies discovering and deploying an appropriate repertoire of descriptive concepts. To believe that a preexisting conceptual repertoire is sufficient, is to fall into the exact trap we are trying to avoid.

4.3.2 The "Memes" Perspective on a Society.

One possible shift in descriptive conceptual repertoire is to focus attention upon the dynamics of a population of "memes" in the sense of Dawkins (1989) and Hales (1997). Memes are entities such as tunes, ideas, catch-phrases, clothes fashions, ways of making pots or of building arches that propagate themselves by "leaping" from brain to brain (Dawkins 1989:192). If we focus on that subclass of memes which contains concepts and beliefs, then the analogous event to the actual emergence of a hierarchical society is presumably the emergence of *the concept* of a hierarchical society, with concrete instantiation of the concept (that is, the first coming into existence of an actual hierarchy) as merely a secondary matter.

It seems that this "dual" emergence problem may be posed without even using the notion of an agent, certainly without giving it primacy. By doing so, attention is turned firmly to the language of expression of beliefs/concepts and its limitations, and to the set of possible deformations/mutations of the belief system and the circumstances under which they occur. To date these matters have received relatively little attention. How significant would this shift of focus be? Is it a means for escaping from our concept of "self" and the undue impact it has for us?

Before turning to the question of agents and their relationship to our concept of self, we may ask a further question: are there different and effective perspectives on societies and their dynamics other than those that are agent-based or meme-based? Is there, for example, an essentially emotions-oriented view of society? Is it the ebb and flow of emotional "waves" (recall the quotation from Collins in section 3.4.1) that has primary importance in determining social dynamics, with the implication that our descriptions of society should be structured accordingly? As yet there is no answer to this question.

4.3.3   Agents and the Self.   The notion of an agent is, by definition, at the heart of agent-based simulation and of artificial societies. Most current definitions minimally require that an agent should act in the light of its situation. Yet these definitions then vary greatly along at least two dimensions: the external functionality that is to be expected of an agent (autonomous? social? pro-active? adaptive?), and the internal "cognitive" processes that an agent should contain (goal posting? using internal representations? planning?). We may reasonably suspect that part of the reason for this diversity of definition is that the notion of an agent, as used in this context, partly derives from our own diverse concepts of an individual and the self—in fact, that the notion of an agent is itself a questionable cultural construct.

This insight can be taken a little further. Cultures are often classified into those that take an *egocentric* view of the self, and those that take a *sociocentric* view (Mageo, 1995).[2] The former focuses attention on the internal experiences, feelings and goals of the individual, the latter on the role or roles that the individual is playing in society. The distinction is not clear cut, but it is useful and meaningful. Now it may be argued that the traditional artificial intelligence view of an agent is an egocentric one (as in, for example, the well-known BDI or "Beliefs, Desires, and Intentions" agent architecture) but that some of the more recent definitions of agents have moved much closer to the sociocentric perspective with emphasis on the agent's social roles.

The distinction may be drawn more operationally, if speculatively, as follows. An agent designed according to an egocentric perspective will act by having knowledge of its possible actions and their potential impact on the world, establishing its present circumstances, posting relevant preferences and goals, generating and committing to plans that promise the most benefit to itself, and attempting to execute its plans. On the other hand, a sociocentric agent will act by maintaining knowledge of a range of social situations, including the expected behavior of each participant in each situation, and then, as necessary, matching its current circumstances to a known situation and hence identifying its own appropriate action.

Which perspective is adopted seems likely to make a major difference in an agent-based model or artificial society. Most work to date has followed (albeit in a relatively simple way) the egocentric perspective. The implications of the sociocentric perspective remain largely unexplored.

The foregoing remarks concern alternative designs for agents in an artificial society. But there is a further complexity. Agents may have a view of themselves. That is, an agent may maintain within its own belief system a concept of itself. This is not technically particularly difficult at least in simple cases. It means that in an artificial society we may have agents designed according to an egocentric perspective, but with a sociocentric view of themselves, and vice versa. The impact at the macrolevel of such contrasts of design and self-view is quite unknown.

---

[2]I am grateful to Tim Kohler for drawing my attention to this distinction.

4.3.4 Foundations.   Most current definitions of agents explicitly or implicitly allow the possibility that agents may be composed of subagents. But this can easily become counterintuitive if the subagents may be deliberative in their own right, especially if they have no awareness of the part they are playing in the whole. And typically there is no restriction on the degree of nesting which is potentially infinite. Equally counterintuitive, but also allowed within standard definitions, is the possibility that (a) agents may partially spatially overlap or (b) that individual agents may be distributed in space in a disconnected form. These counterintuitive possibilities suggest systems of agents that are much more complex in their collective structure than our everyday intuitions would expect and call into question either the definitions or our intuitions. Could our intuitions about agents be downright misleading?

Unfortunately, to tackle these difficulties with the concept of an agent takes us into deep waters. Agenthood is bound up with (among other things) perception and action, both of which on close examination rely on uncertain notions of causality and time (Doran in preparation). Remarkably, this suspicion that the methodological foundations of artificial societies rest upon shifting sand jibes with arguments recently put forward by O'Meara (1997) who suggests:

- a reconsideration of our basic ontology and of how causality is viewed within it, and hence,
- a view of society in which the nature and existence of macrostructures is/are emergent from physical (that is, microlevel) processes rather than existing in a separate domain of thought and discourse, and in which cognitive phenomena are indeed significant but as physical phenomena.

5   CONCLUSIONS

What has been learned from these experiments and this discussion? There are two main insights. First, cognition and its wider aspects, for example, (mis)belief and the impact of emotional states, can be incorporated in agent-based (computer-based) models and artificial societies, even though the "technology" is as yet primitive (but fast moving). That does not of itself mean that collective beliefs and emotions, say, must be incorporated in our models and artificial societies if they are to be of value, but that often these complexities will be needed. Just how often and when remains to be discovered.

Second, if we move away from actual modeling and its concern with validation against specific instances, then we are also able to use artificial societies to investigate general social processes and how they interact. This prospect is very exciting. But then methodological problems begin to loom large, notably how to avoid building into our computer-based societies our own ill-considered expectations and cultural preconceptions. In fact, we may be forced to look again at fundamental questions that will not easily be answered.

REFERENCES

Binford, Lewis R.
1980 Willow Smoke and Dog's Tails: Hunter-Gatherer Settlement Systems and Archaeological Site Formation. American Antiquity 45(1):4–20.

Binmore, Ken, Cristiano Castelfranchi, James Doran, and Michael Wooldridge
In press Rationality in Multiagent Systems. The Knowledge Engineering Review 13(3).

Boehm, Christopher
1993 Egalitarian Behavior and Reverse Dominance Hierarchy. Current Anthropology 24(3):227–254 (with CA comment).

Brumfiel, Elizabeth M., and Timothy K. Earle
1987 Specialization, Exchange and Complex Societies: An Introduction. *In* Specialization, Exchange and Complex Societies. Elizabeth M. Brumfiel and Timothy K. Earle, eds. Cambridge UK: Cambridge University Press (New Directions in Archaeology Series).

Collins, Randall
1990 Stratification, Emotional Energy and the Transient Emotions. *In* Research Agendas in the Sociology of Emotions. T. D. Kemper, ed. Pp. 27–57. Albany: SUNY Press.

Dawkins, Richard
1989 The Selfish Gene. New edition. Oxford: Oxford University Press.

Doran, Jim
1990 Computer Based Simulation and Formal Modeling in Archaeology: A Review. *In* Mathematics and Information Science in Archaeology: A Flexible Framework. Albertus Voorrips, ed. Pp. 93–114. Studies in Modern Archaeology, Vol. 3. Bonn: Holos.
1997 From Computer Simulation to Artificial Societies. Transactions SCS 14(2):69–77.
1998 Simulating Collective Misbelief. Journal of Artificial Societies and Social Simulation 1(1). (http://www.soc.surrey.ac.uk/JASSS/1/1/3.html)
n.d. Time, Causality, Agenthood and Societies.

Doran, Jim, and F. Roy Hodson
1975 Mathematics and Computers in Archaeology. Edinburgh: Edinburgh University Press and Cambridge, MA: Harvard University Press.

Doran, Jim, Mike Palmer, Nigel Gilbert, and Paul Mellars
1994 The EOS Project: Modeling Upper Palaeolithic Social Change. *In* Simulating Societies. Nigel Gilbert and Jim Doran, eds. Pp. 195–221. London: UCL Press.

Doran, Jim, and Mike Palmer
1995 The EOS Project: Integrating Two Models of Palaeolithic Social Change. *In* Artificial Societies. Nigel Gilbert and Rosaria Conte, eds. Pp. 103–125. London: UCL Press.

Epstein, Joshua M., and Robert Axtell
    1996 Growing Artificial Societies: Social Science from the Bottom Up.
    Washington, DC: The Brookings Institution Press and Cambridge, MA:
    MIT Press.

Flannery, Kent V.
    1972 The Cultural Evolution of Civilisations. Annual Review of Ecology
    and Systematics 3:399–426.

Hales, David
    1997 Modeling Meta-Memes. *In* Simulating Social Phenomena. Rosaria
    Conte, Rainer Hegselman, and Pietro Terna, eds. Pp. 365–384. Lecture
    Notes in Economic and Mathematical Systems, 456. Berlin: Springer.

Halpin, Brendan
    To appear Computer Simulation in Sociology: A Review. American Be-
    havioral Scientist, late 1998.

Hoe, Kah E.
    1997 Emotional Dynamics in a Society of Agents. MSc. Computer Sci-
    ence Dissertation, Department of Computer Science, University of Essex,
    Colchester, UK.

Johnson, Allen W., and Timothy K. Earle
    1987 The Evolution of Human Societies. Stanford, CA: Stanford Univer-
    sity Press.

Mageo, Jeannette Marie
    1995 The Reconfiguring Self. American Anthropologist 97(2):282–296.

Manaloglou, Eva
    To appear Agent-Based Modeling of Prehistoric Hunting Strategies. MSc.
    Research dissertation, Department of Computer Science, University of
    Essex, Colchester, UK.

Mellars, Paul A.
    1985 The Ecological Basis of Social Complexity in the Upper Palaeolithic
    of Southwestern France. *In* Prehistoric Hunter-Gatherers: The Emer-
    gence of Cultural Complexity. T. J. Price and J. A. Brown, eds. Pp. 271–
    297. New York: Academic Press.

Mithen, Stephen J.
    1990 Thoughtful Foragers: A Study of Prehistoric Decision Making. Cam-
    bridge, UK: Cambridge University Press.
    1996 Anthropomorphism and the Evolution of Cognition. Journal Royal
    Anthropological Inst. 2(4):717–721. (With comment by P. Boyer.)

O'Meara, Tim
    1997 Causation and the Struggle for a Science of Culture (with comment
    by M. Harris). Current Anthropology 38(3):399–418.

Rappaport, Roy A.
    1971 The Sacred in Human Evolution. Annual Review of Ecology and
    Systematics 2:23–44.

1984 Pigs for the Ancestors. 2nd edition. New Haven and London: Yale University Press.

Read, Dwight
1987 Foraging Society Organization: A Simple Model of a Complex Transition. European Journal of Operations Research 30:230–236.

Renfrew, A. Colin
1987 Problems in the Modelling of Socio-Cultural Systems. European Journal of Operational Research 30:179–192.
1994 The Archaeology of Religion. *In* The Ancient Mind: Elements of Cognitive Archaeology. Colin Renfrew and Ezra B. W. Zubrow, eds. Pp. 47–54. New Directions in Archaeology Series. Cambridge, UK: Cambridge University Press.

Russell, Stuart J., and Peter Norvig
1995 Artificial Intelligence: A Modern Approach. Englewood Cliffs, NJ: Prentice-Hall.

Sanders, William T., and David Webster
1978 Unilinealism, Multilinealism, and the Evolution of Complex Societies. *In* Social Archaeology: Beyond Subsistence and Dating. C. L. Redman, M. J. Berman, E. V. Curtin, W. T. J. Longhorn, N. W. Versaggi, and J. C. Wanser, eds. Pp. 249–302. New York: Academic Press.

Sperber, Daniel
1994 The Modularity of Thought and the Epidemiology of Representations. *In* Mapping the Mind: Domain Specificity in Cognition and Culture. L. A. Hirschfeld and S. A. Gelman, eds. Cambridge, UK: Cambridge University Press.

Wright, Henry, and Melinda Zeder
1977 The Simulation of a Linear Exchange System Under Equilibrium Conditions. *In* Exchange Systems in Prehistory. Timothy K. Earle and J. E. Ericson, eds. Pp. 233–253. New York: Academic Press.

MAGICAL Computer Simulation of Mesolithic Foraging

Mark Winter Lake

INTRODUCTION

The MAGICAL (Multi-Agent Geographically Informed Computer AnaLy-sis) software described in this chapter was designed to integrate two of the most important computational methods used by archaeologists during the last decade: Geographical Information Systems (GIS) (e.g., Allen et al. 1990) and multiagent simulation (e.g., Lake 1995; Mithen 1990). At the outset of model development in 1995, it was recognized that GIS provide archaeologists with a sophisticated means of manipulating spatial data, but offer limited support for modeling change through time. Conversely, multiagent simulation models have allowed archaeologists to study change through time, but have either lacked or had simplistic spatial components. Consequently, the research described here aimed to combine the strengths of GIS and multiagent simulation in one software package so as to better facilitate the quantitative study of spatiotemporal variability in the archaeological record.

The MAGICAL software was developed within the broader context of the Southern Hebrides Mesolithic Project (SHMP). This project was established in 1988 by Dr. Steven Mithen (University of Reading) to acquire new data from the Scottish Islands of Islay and Colonsay and, by integrating this with existing data, to develop a regional perspective on the early postglacial set-

Dynamics in Human and Primate Societies, edited by T. Kohler and
G. Gumerman, Oxford University Press, 1999.

tlement of Western Scotland (Mithen and Lake 1996). The construction of a computer simulation model was considered a fundamental part of the postex-cavation studies of the SHMP (Lake in press). It was hoped that conceptual models which would otherwise remain largely intuitive could be more rigor-ously explored by formalizing them into mathematical algorithms, translating those algorithms into computer code, and then running simulation experi-ments.

This chapter describes how the MAGICAL software integrates GIS and multiagent simulation. It does so directly in section one and then by example in sections two, three, and four. Section two discusses the conceptual basis of the SHMP simulation model, and section three describes how this was implemented using the MAGICAL software. Section four presents the results of the SHMP simulations. Note that the SHMP simulation model is discussed primarily as a means of demonstrating the capabilities of the MAGICAL software. Those interested in the wider background to this particular modeling endeavor are urged to consult Mithen (ed., in prep).

1   THE MAGICAL SIMULATION PACKAGE

Although developed in the context of the SHMP, it was always intended that the MAGICAL software should have wider application. To that end it offers a compromise between flexibility and the need for specialist computing skills. The archaeologist who is not a computer programmer can quickly build a simulation model customized to his or her needs provided that it falls within the basic paradigm described below. Those who wish to move beyond this paradigm will need to write new program code, which should prove relatively straightforward since the software design and implementation has been docu-mented in considerable detail (Lake and Mithen 1998).

1.1   THE MODELING PARADIGM

In 1968 Clarke noted the potential for stochastic simulation in archaeology, and two years later Doran (1970) wrote a brief introduction to the subject. Since that time computer simulation has been used to address a variety of ar-chaeological problems ranging from the boundary conditions for Palaeolithic social systems (Wobst 1974) through Mycenaean settlement (Chadwick 1978) to the movement of artefacts as a result of modern ploughing (Boismier 1996). A particularly consistent and successful area of research has been the use of simulation to model hunter-gatherer societies (Mithen 1994), and, as already noted, this is the arena in which the MAGICAL project was originally con-ceived. Consequently, the range of behaviors currently implemented by the MAGICAL software (i.e., without the need for further programming) reflect a research tradition that has generally placed an emphasis on mobility, subsis-tence, and, more recently, "rational" decision making (Bettinger 1991; Mithen

1990). For example, the software allows each individual to rationally calculate the benefit of moving to a particular location in the landscape and to have an energetic state that may be decremented due to the cost of moving, or incremented as a result of resource capture. Although many of the implemented behaviors reflect those modeled in previous studies, the MAGICAL software nevertheless affords new possibilities within the broad evolutionary-ecological hunter-gatherer paradigm. It does so by providing a framework within which it is possible to explore what individuals might have been thinking in order for them to have produced an observed behavior.

Early (e.g., Thomas 1972) simulation models of hunter-gatherer societies that modeled decision making and/or learning typically assigned agency to the group. In a changed intellectual climate, which emphasizes the role of the individual in creating, sustaining, and dissolving larger scale regularities (e.g., Giddens 1984), such studies are now frequently criticized for having placed too much emphasis on the social or ecological system at the expense of the individual human agent (Shanks and Tilley 1987). For this reason researchers in ecology (DeAngelis and Gross 1992), economics (Holland and Miller 1991), and sociology (Gilbert and Doran 1994) have all turned to multiagent simulation, since it provides a means of explicitly modeling the interaction of individuals and the resulting emergence of group-level phenomena. Archaeologists have also adopted multiagent simulation for studies of hunter-gatherer behavior in which the ability to model decision making by individuals has allowed the application of insights from contemporary evolutionary theory (Mithen 1990; Lake 1995). These archaeological studies have not, however, harnessed the full potential of multiagent modeling. For example, although the individuals in Mithen's (1990) simulation of Mesolithic hunting each have their own internal states, they nevertheless share the principles governing their behavior. In contrast, the MAGICAL software allows each individual to behave according to a potentially unique set of principles, which means that it is possible to simulate individuals thinking and behaving differently according to factors such as age, gender, and social standing.

Figure 1 depicts the main elements of human cognition that can currently be modeled using the MAGICAL software: individual learning, cultural learning, and decision making. All three have been modeled previously; what is novel here is that the software allows them to be applied to spatially referenced data, which in turn requires the ability to model spatially referenced knowledge. The MAGICAL software achieves the latter through its close integration with GIS by allowing each individual to maintain its own cognitive maps in the form of GIS raster maps. The concept of a cognitive or mental map has been loosely invoked by archaeologists (e.g., Renfrew 1987) and given rather more careful consideration by cognitive scientists (e.g., Kuipers 1983; Tolman 1948) and geographers (Lloyd 1989). It appears that the Cartesian model of geographic space implied by a universal transverse mercator or $x - y$ referenced GIS raster map is probably very different from that used by humans to store spatial information (Mark and Frank 1990). Indeed it has been

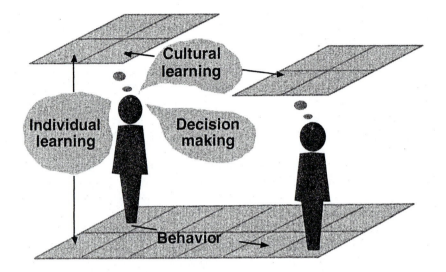

FIGURE 1   The elements of a multiagent GIS.

argued that for many people the development of a Cartesian cognitive model of space requires access to graphic, metrically correct maps (Mark and Frank 1990). Nevertheless, since even chimpanzees are apparently able to calculate transport costs as a function of both weight and distance (Boesch and Boesch 1984), it can be argued that humans are able to comprehend—and do use—at least some aspects of the metric implied by raster-based mapping. In other words, raster-based cognitive maps store relevant information even if they do not accurately model the underlying psychology.

1.2   THE SOFTWARE DESIGN

In architectural terms, MAGICAL software can be decomposed into three main elements which together reflect the modeling paradigm just described: the collection of agents, the event scheduler, and the spatial database. Each is discussed in turn.

1.2.1   The Collection of Agents.

The central tenet of agent-based modeling is that each agent, whether it is a theoretical construct, molecule, ant or human, has its own set of internal state variables affected by its own history. This principle is often extended so that each agent's behavior is governed by its own set of principles, and it may also be the case that each occupies a discrete spatial location in the environment (although this may not be modeled as a point in Cartesian space but, for example, a node on a network). As already noted, the MAGICAL software implements all aspects of the extended agent concept. Agents are entities that have a range of properties and possible behaviors (or actions) which are appropriate for modeling human behavior under the paradigm outlined above. They also possess a unique identifier and spatial location. Since the MAGICAL software was written in the C^{++} programming language, agents are realized as objects of a class, and their properties and actions are implemented as class member variables and functions. Implemented properties and actions include the agent's energy level, its current rate of return on foraging, various kinds of search, and the exchange of information. These and other examples are illustrated in the SHMP foraging simulation described later in this paper; a full list can be found in Lake and Mithen (1998) and Lake (in press). Researchers who wish to use the MAGICAL software outside the modeling paradigm in which it was originally conceived may need to add new member variables and functions to the agent class to meet their specific requirements.

The MAGICAL software offers nonprogrammers considerable flexibility for research within the evolutionary-ecological paradigm because agents' behavioral principles are not coded into the software, but instead provided at run time in the form of a user-specified genotype. Each agent may have a unique genotype which comprises a set of action and decision tokens that specify how its state variables are updated along with their subsequent role in decision making. Figure 2 depicts the genotype assigned to foragers in the SHMP foraging simulation and is best conceived as a table in which each row corresponds to one of the possible actions, identified by the appropriate token. It should be read as follows. In order to determine what an agent will do next, find the row corresponding to the action that the agent has just completed. This lists all the candidate actions and the conditions which must be true for each to be chosen. Each candidate is separated from its associated condition by a colon, with the whole unit enclosed inside square brackets. Each condition comprises a string of one or more decision tokens, each possibly followed by a map number (explained later) and one of the logical operators AND, OR, or NOT. Since each decision token represents a specific question, which can be answered TRUE or FALSE according to the agent's state or knowledge, it follows that the entire string constitutes a logical expression which will evaluate TRUE or FALSE (following the principles of Reverse Polish Notation). If the string evaluates TRUE then the condition is met and the agent will undertake the associated action.

1.2.2 **The Event Scheduler.** The way in which the MAGICAL software handles time is strongly influenced by the underlying agent-based philosophy. The event scheduler drives the dynamic process of simulation by receiving agents' requests to act and granting those requests at the appropriate time. Since agents are objects which contain logic about how they behave, it follows that the algorithms which implement agent behavior need not be repeated in the core simulation program code. Instead all that is required is a means of controlling when agents act. Broadly speaking there are two methods by which this might be achieved. One is to provide a scheduling mechanism that in-

2
Agent
BEGIN [rs: al][rd: al][rm: al][jg: al][shbp: al][atr: al][rav 0:
al][rvh: al];
DPH ;
DVH ;
MTD [atr: al][rav: al][datwo 2: al][dathree 3: s][dafour 4: s not][hv
1: al];
CRD [dvn 0: al][waitb: al];
MDN ;
ATR ;
RAV ;
MIDN ;
SHBP ;
MDHB [rgxid: s not dd not and][rd: dd][rvh: s not dd and][rgxis:
s][daone 1: al][datwo 2: al][dathree 3: al][dafour 4: al];
RS ;
IS [rvh: sd not][mdhb: sd s not and][id: sd s and];
JG ;
RGXID [id: al];
GIXI ;
SIXIG [aga: al];
AGA ;
RGA ;
WAITA [see 0: ndvz0 not][scrd: ndvz0];
GXI ;
GAMXI ;
GA ;
RVH [cvh 1: al][dvh 0: al][mcn 1: s not][crd: s];
DDM ;
MCN [cvn 1: al][dvn 0: al][waitc: al];
CVN ;
DVN ;
CUD [dvn 0: al][waitd: al];
CVH ;
GIMHB ;
GMHBV ;
GAMCMHB ;
MHBV [scvh 1: al][waitk: al];
RGMHB [im: al];
RD ;
ID [crod: dd s not and][im: dd s and][rvh: dd not][rs: al];
RM ;
IM [mdhb: s md and][rvh: s md not and][rd: s md not and][fs: s not md
and][waitg: s not md not and];
FS [rvh: al][rm: al][ddm: al][rd: al];

FIGURE 2   The foraging genotype.

```
HV [is: al];
EE [mtd: al];
RCB ;
GMEHB ;
SHV [sis: al];
SEE [smtd: al];
SCRD [dvn 0: al][waita: al];
SCUD [scvn 1: al][waith: al];
SIS [scvh 1: sd not][waiti: al];
SMCN [scvn 1: al][waitj: al];
SMTD [shv 1: al];
SCVN ;
SCVH ;
ES ;
CROD [rgmhb: al];
CROS ;
CSROS [aga: srgrd][rga: srgrd not][rs: al];
RR ;
RHB ;
GAMVMHB ;
GMHBC ;
MHBC ;
CDMHB ;
DAONE ;
DATWO ;
DATHREE ;
DAFOUR ;
RGXIM ;
RGXIS [fs: al];
GSNHB ;
WAITB [ee 0: ndvz0 not][crd: ndvz0];
WAITC [ee 0: ncgpc1 ndvz0 not and][cud 0: ncgpc1 not ndvz0 or];
WAITD [ee 0: ig ndvz0 not and][crd: ig not ndvz0 or];
WAITE [see 0: ncgpc1 ndvz0 not and][scrd: ncgpc1 not ndvz0 or];
```

FIGURE 2   Continued.

structs agents to act according to the cycle in the simulation. The problem with this approach is that it becomes cumbersome if different types of behavior are of differing duration: the scheduler must interrogate each agent in turn to establish whether it has finished the previous action, and further, it must be provided with information about any necessary sequence in which actions are to be performed. The alternative method is to provide a "clock" and a queue in which agents may place time-stamped requests to act; the scheduler continually traverses the queue and activates all requests whose time stamp matches the current time on the "clock." The rationale for this method is that since agents contain data about their current state and also the logic which governs their behavior, they are best placed to decide how to act next, and when. This is the approach adopted by the MAGICAL software, both because of its conceptual elegance and because it is particularly suited to an object-oriented implementation.

The key element in the MAGICAL software scheduling system is the event. Events are essentially agents' requests to act, which are held in a queue by the scheduler. Each event in the queue includes information about the time at which it is to be executed and by whom. Events do not contain information about how they are to be executed since agents "know" how to act and consequently this information need not be duplicated. The processing of events is continuous throughout the simulation and takes place as follows. An agent, having decided how it intends to act next and when, sends the appropriate event to the scheduler. The scheduler places the event in the queue in order of increasing time stamps. Meanwhile, on each increment of the simulation "clock" the scheduler starts at the head of the queue and removes all those events whose time stamps are less than or equal to the current time. On removing each event the scheduler instructs the appropriate agent that it may now perform the requested action. When this is complete the agent will, if necessary, send a new event to the scheduler. This process continues until the total simulated time has elapsed.

1.2.3   The Spatial Database.   Perhaps the single most important feature of the MAGICAL software is that agent activities and knowledge are spatially referenced through linkage with a GIS package. In this way any simulation model built using the MAGICAL software is closely integrated with a spatial database which potentially stores three types of data. The first two are compulsory and comprise information about the "real" landscape through which the agents move and the agents' own knowledge about that landscape (their cognitive maps). The third type of data is optional and comprises any output maps of agent activity that the user may have requested. All three types of data are stored as GIS raster maps. There may be more than one layer of each according to the number of variables that are relevant to the agents' behavior. If this is the case, each layer is assigned a unique map number by which it may be referenced in the agents' genotypes. Linking simulation and GIS in this way allows both input and output (spatial) data to be manipulated using any of the available GIS tools. Consequently, simulations can be run using spatial data which is well understood as a result of intensive analysis, or which is itself the outcome of a modeling process. The potential of the latter is demonstrated by the model of hazelnut abundance used as input for the SHMP foraging simulation. Similarly, the simulation results can be compared with spatial data held in the GIS, or even used as input into a further simulation.

The MAGICAL software is linked to the Geographical Resources Analysis Support System (GRASS) GIS package. GRASS (now distributed under the terms of the GNU Public License by Baylor University, Texas) was chosen because its open architecture permits the efficient temporal updating of raster maps from within a single end-user environment. A GRASS GIS basically comprises a collection of raster and/or vector maps of spatial phenomena (with lists of point attributes where appropriate) and a set of programs and scripts for operating on those maps. The UNIX shell mechanism and hierarchical file system are used to ensure that all programs and scripts can be accessed from the same command-line interface and that the maps are organized to form a simple database. Consequently, the GIS appears to the end-user as a tightly integrated whole even though it is actually made up of a number of essentially self-contained parts. This makes it relatively easy to add new functions that nevertheless appear to the user as though they are standard components of the GIS, and indeed the MAGICAL software is provided as three new GRASS functions: ma.set_genotypes, ma.set_agents, and ma.sim. The open architecture of GRASS also allows new functions to be implemented as native code programs rather than as scripts linking existing programs. A comparison of the two methods has demonstrated that the possibility of writing in native code is essential for computationally intensive methods such as simulation (Lake, Woodman, and Mithen 1998). GRASS aids the development of native-code programs by providing a well-documented library of routines for manipulating the spatial database. Indeed, at a software level this is the main link between the MAGICAL software and GRASS: each raster map in the simulation database is created or opened, read and/or written to, and finally closed or deleted using GRASS library routines.

2 A CONCEPTUAL MODEL OF MESOLITHIC FORAGING FOR HAZELNUTS

As noted in the introduction, the MAGICAL software has been used by the Southern Hebrides Mesolithic Project to examine whether the distribution of Mesolithic flint artefacts on the Southern Hebridean island of Islay could be explained in terms of small groups landing at the coast and then foraging for hazelnuts. The conceptual underpinnings of this endeavor are discussed here, starting briefly with the GIS model of relative hazelnut abundance, followed by the actual simulation model of foraging.

2.1 A MODEL OF HAZELNUT AVAILABILITY

In order to examine the extent to which the availability of hazelnuts influenced the movement of Mesolithic foragers around the landscape it was obviously necessary to build a model of the relative abundance of hazel in the prehistoric vegetation. It should be noted at the outset that the abundance of hazelnuts in a given area depends not just on the abundance of the tree, but also its productivity (Petra Dark personal communication). The factors used in this study to model the abundance of hazel included the most important of those that also influence productivity. Datable pollen evidence has been used to produce both isochrone and isopollen maps for the spread of various tree and vegetation species across northern Europe and the British Isles in particular (Birks 1989). Unfortunately such maps lack the resolution required to reconstruct the post-glacial vegetation of a relatively small region such as Islay. Since, for example, only one of the 135 cores used by Birks to construct his isochrone maps for the British Isles plus Ireland was from Islay, it was clear that pollen mapping could not be used as the sole source of data for the production of an island-specific vegetation map. Instead it was decided to use the pollen data to assess the plausibility of a map generated from environmental data and ecological principles.

Environmental factors such as climate and soil type play a significant role in determining the distribution and abundance of tree species. For example, decreasing temperature with increasing latitude delayed the northward spread of lime and ash in Scotland, while birch is better suited to acidic soils than hazel (Rackham 1980). Consequently, climatic reconstruction and evidence of prehistoric soils can be used to help estimate the capability of land for supporting the growth of specific species. Given this, two simple mathematical functions were used to model intolerant (Eq. (1)) and tolerant species (Eq. (2)) on the assumption that, in the absence of competition, the density of cover achieved by a species declines with decreasing land capability. In both functions the parameter a set the density of cover in the "best" environment while the parameter b determined how poor the environment must be for no trees to grow. The parameter k tuned the exact shape of the curve.

$$y = b - \frac{b - (x-1)^k}{(a-1)^k}, \tag{1}$$

$$y = \frac{b(a-x)^k}{(a-1)^k}. \tag{2}$$

In reality, a species may not achieve the density of cover predicted by land capability alone, either as a result of historical factors such as distance from refugia, or due to the effect of interspecies competition. At a relatively coarse resolution, the effect of competition can be seen in the general succession of tree species during the Early Holocene. Birch and hazel are both present in the British Isles by 10,300–9600 B.P. Hazel continues to increase in abundance between 9600–9000 B.P., but birch is increasingly restricted to the north as oak and elm appear (Rackham 1980). At a finer resolution the effect of competition depends on the species in question. For example, ash and hazel are not "gregarious" in that they can occur as isolated individuals scattered throughout many types of woodland (Rackham 1980). Consequently, while birch will not grow under hazel the converse is possible, although the two are mutually exclusive where they occur in competition with a third species such as oak (Peterken 1993). Competition was built into the model by assuming a strict succession of species, such that each more competitive species would always displace the preceding species to the extent required for it to achieve its maximum density of cover for the given land capability. Consequently, the adjusted abundance for a given species was calculated as: $DA_n = DS_n - DS_{\max(i<n)}$ where DS_n is the signal species abundance for species n and $DS_{\max(i<n)}$ is the greatest signal species density of any more competitive species.

Once the density of cover had been adjusted for each species, it was a simple matter to calculate any one species' density of cover expressed as a percentage of the total woodland cover as follows: $R = 100/(\sum_{i=o}^{i=n} DA_i)DA_j$ where DA_i is the abundance of species i, and DA_j is the abundance of the species in question.

2.2 A SIMPLE MODEL OF FORAGING

It was decided that the SHMP model should capture four aspects of foraging for hazelnuts: explicit decision making, the exchange of information, a seasonal round, and changes of base camp.

The rules governing animal decision making in the context of foraging have been extensively studied by behavioral ecologists (Stephens and Krebs 1986) and form the core of Optimal Foraging Theory (OFT). The choice principle most often used in OFT is the maximization of long-term energy gain (Stephens and Krebs 1986). In other words, it is usually assumed that animals attempt to maximize the ratio of benefit to cost, and there is indeed evidence that some animals, such as great tits (Krebs, Kacelnik, and Taylor 1978), are relatively successful in this. Although it is doubtful whether humans attain the optimal rate of energy gain (Martin 1983), they do, nevertheless, succeed in improving their foraging efficiencies, or "meliorizing" (Dawkins 1982). It is most likely that this is achieved through the use of rules of thumb rather than by complex calculation (Mithen 1990). Consequently, all foragers were given the simple rule that they should seek a neighboring map cell containing a greater relative abundance of hazelnuts. The fact that this rule prevented agents from attempting rate-maximization was particularly appropriate because colonizing Mesolithic foragers would not have possessed sufficient information to have identified the energetically optimal route to the location with the greatest hazelnut abundance.

The search for greater relative hazelnut abundance included an element of risk taking. Optimal foraging theory recognizes at least two types of risk. The most obvious is the risk associated with immediate survival. For example, a forager close to starvation should probably choose a patch offering a little energy with certainty over one offering more energy with a low probability, providing that the lesser amount of energy is minimally adequate. Such risk-reducing decisions have been observed in a range of animals (Caraco et al. 1980; Stephens and Krebs 1986), and indeed Mithen has suggested that Mesolithic hunters in Germany apparently adopted a risk-reducing strategy because the lack of alternative resources increased the cost of foraging failure. This type of risk aversion was not modeled because its inclusion could potentially have reduced search activity on the basis of an energetic shortfall that would, in fact, have been overcome with an alternative resource. The second type of risk is that of increasing short-term gain at the expense of a long-term increase in efficiency (Stephens and Krebs 1986). Aversion to this type of risk was included in the foraging model in order to increase the agents' willingness to explore unknown areas. To this end, the decision algorithm ensured that if none of the neighboring cells known to the agent contained more hazelnuts than its current location then it would instead move to a randomly chosen neighboring cell that was unknown. If none of the neighboring cells were unknown then the last resort would be to move to a randomly chosen known cell.

The decision algorithm was applied to knowledge stored in agents' cognitive maps of relative hazelnut abundance. It was assumed that Mesolithic foragers were exploring uncharted territory so that over time their initial ignorance about the availability of hazelnuts would have been replaced by a growing knowledge. It followed that the agents' cognitive maps should initially be empty but then gradually come to mirror the underlying GIS model of relative hazel abundance. For the sake of simplicity, such learning was modeled as a process whereby agents observed and then memorized the abundance of hazel in each map cell that they physically occupied. Furthermore, it was assumed that they could do this accurately and that the abundance of hazel was unchanging from season to season.

One of the most striking features of hunter-gatherer knowledge acquisition is the generally high intensity of information exchange between group members (Mithen 1990). This is not surprising, since from an evolutionary perspective one of the most important advantages of group living is that it allows more rapid updating of information than is possible by individual learning (Clark and Mangel 1984). Similarly it also permits the acquisition of information about larger areas. An extreme example of this is provided by the Cree when they undertake trapping expeditions to assess the suitability of an area for settlement (Tanner 1979). Given the ubiquity of information exchange among modern hunter-gatherers, it seemed likely to have been a feature of Mesolithic peoples' exploration of the Inner Hebridean islands and was therefore incorporated in the foraging model. This was achieved by merging all individual agent's cognitive maps to form a composite group map that could then be redistributed among the group members. Since the ethnographic record suggests that the evening is a particularly important time for information exchange (Mithen 1990), this process was scheduled to take place at the end of each simulated day during the hazelnut season.

Unlike most other animals, humans gather a large amount of information that is not immediately relevant to the task in hand, but which may be useful in the future (Estes 1984). Indeed, the opportunity for such information gathering may itself influence task choice. For example, Beckerman (1983) found that the Bari, a group of tropical-forest horticulturists who depend on hunting and fishing to obtain much of their protein, spend more time hunting than would be anticipated given its relatively low return, because it enables them to monitor the availability of fish stocks over a wider area. It was, there-fore, a minimal assumption that Mesolithic hunter-gatherers would have used information acquired out of season to inform their subsequent foraging for hazelnuts. This important aspect of hazelnut exploitation was modeled by the simple expedient of dividing the year into two seasons: one in which agents foraged for hazelnuts as already described and one in which they performed some other activity. The out-of-season activity was not explicitly modeled, since all that was required for the purposes of the simulation was the "inci-dental" acquisition of information about the distribution of hazelnuts. This latter was modeled by having foragers learn about the relative abundance of hazel while pursuing a random walk; a scenario which captured the assump-tion that the out-of-season activity was largely undirected with respect to hazelnut availability.

The SHMP model assumed that the Mesolithic seasonal round involved a spring and summer dispersal and that, consequently, group-wide informa-tion exchange would not have occurred outside the hazelnut season. It also assumed, however, that at the start of the hazelnut season all foragers would have gathered at the last common base camp to exchange information ac-quired during the dispersal. Regular information exchange would then have occurred for the rest of the season, and to this end foragers would have re-turned to a base camp at the end of each day. Since the initial base camp would not necessarily have been well placed for the harvest of hazelnuts it was thought likely that the group would have moved base camp from time to time, both in response to increasing knowledge about the distribution of hazel and so as to reduce the need for site maintenance activities, for which there is little archaeological evidence. Consequently, at the end of each month dur-ing the hazelnut-gathering season, the SHMP simulation modeled the group deciding whether and where to move camp.

In accordance with the multiagent paradigm, group decision making was modeled as arising through the interaction of group members. Group decision making is typically a complex process in which individual views are initially expressed tentatively and then more firmly argued before being suppressed in favor of the emerging consensus (Fisher 1980). The SHMP model captured some of this complexity by allowing foragers to vote on whether or not to move base camp. As the first stage of this process, it was proposed that the group should move to the map cell with the highest abundance known to it. This was done on the assumption that hazelnut abundance shows a degree of spatial autocorrelation, so that map cells with high values would be found clustered together. Note that foragers would not disagree about the location of the proposed camp because they all shared the same knowledge as a result of information exchange. They could, however, disagree about whether moving to the proposed camp would increase their foraging returns compared with staying put, or returning to any previously occupied camp. To model this possibility, each forager was required to conduct a mental simulation of one day's foraging, comparing the return with its own return from the present camp and all previous camps, and voting accordingly. If the foragers shared extensive knowledge about the area around the proposed camp, and if hazel was significantly more abundant than around the present camp, then the result would almost certainly be a vote in favor of moving. The likelihood of a positive vote decreased with increasing uncertainty, the latter arising as a result of insufficient information, similar hazel abundance figures, or highly variable individual returns from foraging around the present camp.

3 BUILDING THE SIMULATION

Having devised a conceptual model of foraging for hazelnuts, the next stage was to implement this using GRASS and the MAGICAL software.

3.1 THE GIS MODEL OF HAZEL AVAILABILITY

Full details of how the abstract mathematical model of species' relative abundance was implemented within the GRASS GIS can be found in Lake (in press). The key considerations were the choice of species to be modeled and the choice of factors determining land capability.

A combination of existing woodland reconstructions, pollen evidence, and ecological factors suggested that oak, hazel, birch, and alder should be included in the model. Pollen evidence indicates that birch and hazel were the dominant species on Islay between 9500–9000 B.P. with oak and elm becoming more important over the next 1,000 years. The presence of ash appears to have been limited while the appearance of alder is time transgressive, first appearing in the pollen record at dates ranging from 7500 B.P. to 4400 B.P. (Mithen, ed., in prep., chapter 3.5). Given that all the main species that would ever appear on Islay during the early and mid-Holocene were present by the Mesolithic, and that the Scottish woodland in general was stable until 5000 B.P. (Edwards and Whittington 1997), it was considered reasonable to use woodland reconstructions pertaining to the Neolithic as the starting point for a 7000 B.P. reconstruction. McVean and Ratcliffe (1962) suggested that the Rhinns of Islay was covered with birch forest, while the remainder of the island was predominantly oak with some birch. Bennett's more recent (1988) reconstruction retained the east-west differentiation in cover, showing birch as the dominant species on the Rhinns and the Mull of Oa, with oak dominant elsewhere. Tipping (1994) reconstructed the cover as a mixture of birch, hazel, and oak at 3000 B.C., and Edwards and Whittington (1997) accepted this with some modifications as the cover at 5000 B.P. Neither Tipping nor Edwards and Whittington suggested that the tree cover on the Rhinns varied significantly from that on the remainder of the island. Recent pollen evidence showing a high relative frequency of hazel on Islay (Mithen, ed., in prep.) favored the Tipping/Edwards and Whittington reconstruction of oak/hazel/birch woodland, although it may be that birch was more abundant in the west and hazel more abundant in the east. Given their predominance in the pollen record it was decided to limit the model to these three species plus alder, which also occurs with a relatively high frequency (although often not until after 6000 B.P.).

The classification of land capability for forestry on the basis of climate can be regarded as a "first sieve" (Bibby and Futty 1988), which indicates the best class for the area if no other limitations are present. The modern climate of Islay is characterized by a minimum mean annual wind speed of 4.4 m/s and a maximum accumulated temperature above 5.6 degrees centigrade of 1650. Land offering these "best" conditions is capable of supporting both broad-leaved and coniferous species, albeit with some restrictions. More typically, however, the range of species is limited to conifers, or conifers and the hardiest broad-leaves such as birch and alder. The highest and most exposed land is unsuitable for forestry. Windthrow, the availability of nutrients, local topography, draughtiness, wetness, and soil depth may all reduce land capability for forestry from that suggested by climate alone (Bibby and Futty 1988). For practical reasons (Lake in press) the SHMP model was based on climate modified in the light of local exposure. Together these provided the broad capability classes and went some way to modifying them on the basis of windthrow and, to the extent that exposure dictates local rainfall, draughtiness, and wetness. Aspect was used as a proxy for local exposure. Climate was modeled on the basis of modern annual windspeed and accumulated temperature. Although the accumulated temperature at 7000 B.P. was probably greater than at present (Edwards and Whittington 1997) there was no reason to suppose that the rank ordering of capability classes across the island would have been significantly different.

Figure 3 shows the completed GIS model of land capability for forestry on Islay. It codes each 50 m square unit of land with a value between 1 and 15, representing decreasing capability, or increasingly adverse conditions. This map was created in two stages. The first manipulated the digital elevation model (DEM) of Islay to imitate Bibby and Futty's (1988) climate map. This involved reclassifying the DEM to show just three categories: land below 80 m above sea level (OD) which was coded 1; land greater than or equal to 80 m OD but below 300 m OD (coded 6); and land greater than 300 m OD (coded 11). Buffers were then placed around one point on the Mull of Oa and one off the north coast in order to enclose relatively low land marked on Bibby and Futty's map as particularly exposed. These buffers were added to the reclassified DEM and assigned the same category value as land above 300 m OD. The result was a base map showing homogeneous areas coded 1, 6, or 11 according to their decreasing capability for forestry. The second stage modified the base map to include the effect of local exposure. This was achieved by using the GIS to produce an aspect map from the DEM and then reclassifying this to model five levels of local exposure, ranging from a maximum of 4 on slopes facing between 270 and 315 degrees from north and a minimum of 0 on slopes facing between 90 and 135 degrees from north. The aspect-based exposure

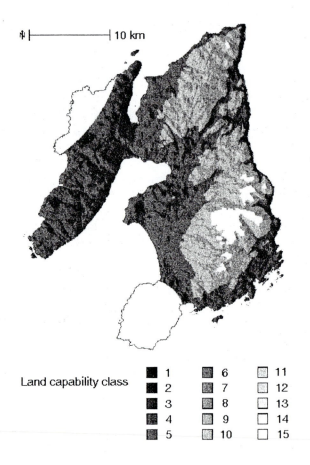

FIGURE 3   GIS raster map of land capability for forestry. © License No. MC/354. Reprinted by permission.

map was then added to the base map on a cell-by-cell basis to produce the final capability map coded from 1 to 15 according to the decreasing capability for forestry.

The relationship between single-species abundance and land capability for forestry (in the absence of competition) was specified by choosing the appropriate function and parameters for each species. The functions assigned to each species were chosen to reflect the relative intolerance of oak compared to the relative tolerance of birch and alder, with hazel occupying the middle ground. Consequently the concave function (Eq. (1)) was used with $k = 8$ to model a rapid decrease in the abundance of oak as land capability decreases. The convex function (Eq. (2)) was used with $k = 2$ to model a slow decrease in alder and with $k = 1.4$ to model an even slower decrease in birch. The convex function was also used for hazel, but with $k = 1.02$ resulting in an almost constant decrease in abundance. The maximum single-species abundances were controlled via the parameters b. These were set so that oak would cover 70% of land in the absence of competition, hazel would cover 85% and birch 100%. The b parameter for alder was also set so that the species would cover 100% of land in the absence of competition, but in this case the distribution was subsequently limited to areas near fresh water. The a parameters were set so that the abundance of oak decreased to near zero at land capability category nine, while hazel, birch, and alder all decreased to zero at category 14. According to the land capability model these parameter choices confined oak to land below 80 m OD, while permitting some growth of the other species in all but the most exposed locations on west-facing coasts and the highest land. This latter seemed reasonable given the warmer conditions, Pennington's suggestion that trees extended above 760 m OD in the English Lake District (Tipping 1994) and, most importantly, evidence that the more exposed Outer Hebrides and Shetland Isles were wooded (Edwards and Whittington 1997). Once all parameters had been chosen, the GRASS map algebra program, r.mapcalc, was used to calculate the single-species abundance maps for each species.

The effect of competition on species abundance was modeled according to the principle of succession described in Eq. (3), with some adjustment for alder. The pollen record indicates that the general succession in Worthwest Scotland was from birch through an increasing abundance of hazel to the appearance of oak and later, in wet areas, alder. Consequently, it was assumed that in areas of good land capability oak would outcompete hazel, and hazel would outcompete birch. This assumption was also supported by observations of modern woodlands that birch usually occurs as a primary colonizer and that hazel rarely overtops oak (Rackham 1980). The model also assumed that alder would outcompete all other species in wet areas, reflecting its preference for streamsides, depressions, and swampy ground (Rackham 1980). Before the single-species abundances were adjusted to reflect the effect of competition, alder was restricted to wet areas by using the GRASS GIS programs r.buffer and r.mapcalc to positively mask the alder abundance map with a 50-m-wide buffer placed around streams and inland lochs. This reduced the alder abundance values to zero in cells further than 50 m from fresh water. The adjusted abundance maps for each species were then calculated using the algebra program r.mapcalc to subtract the other abundance maps as dictated by Eq. (3), with alder, oak, hazel, and birch ordered $n = 1$ to 4, respectively.

FIGURE 4   GIS raster map of relative hazel abundance. © License No. MC/354.
Reprinted by permission.

The final stage in producing a map of relative hazelnut abundance on
Islay was to convert the adjusted hazel abundance map to show relative hazel
abundance. Recall that the adjusted abundance maps measure the contribution of a given species to the total land cover, whereas the relative adjusted
abundance maps measure the contribution of that species to the wooded land
cover. The map algebra program r.mapcalc was used to produce the relative
hazel map according to Eq. (4), with oak, hazel, and birch ordered $n = 1$ to
3. Alder was omitted for the sake of simplicity. The plausibility of the finished
map, shown in Figure 4, was assessed by comparing the cumulative relative
frequencies of tree pollen observed in cores from Islay with those predicted
from the land capability in the vicinity of the cores. Table 1 shows the frequencies of oak, hazel, and birch relative to total land pollen for the three datable
cores from Islay. It also shows these frequencies as percentages of their sum.
Figure 5 compares these latter with the cumulative relative frequencies predicted on the basis of the average land capability within a 5-km radius of the

TABLE 1 The relative frequencies of oak, hazel and birch in pollen cores from Islay.

Site	Oak	Hazel	Birch
Loch á Bhogaidh			
raw data	15	38	15
percentages	22.1	53.8	22.1
cumulative %	22.1	76.9	100
Loch Gorm (core A)			
raw data	1	40	15
percentages	1.8	71.4	26.8
cumulative %	1.8	73.2	100
Sorn Valley			
raw data	7	60	10
percentages	9.1	77.9	13
cululative %	9.1	87	100

relevant core. It can be seen that the overlain observed percentages fit the model remarkably well. Although the percentage of hazel is underestimated at the Sorn Valley site, it is correct for both Loch á Bhogaidh and Loch Gorm (core A). The percentage of oak is correctly predicted for all three pollen core sites. Admittedly, comparison with just three data points does not provide a robust test, but the level of fit does nevertheless suggest that the model captures the most important determinants of the relative abundance of hazel.

3.2 THE SIMULATION MODEL OF FORAGING

The first and most important step when building a simulation model using the MAGICAL software is to construct the agents' genotypes. These specify the agents' behaviors, which other agent parameters are relevant, and also the number and types of data maps that must be opened at the start of a simulation. Figure 2 shows the content of the text file that was used to specify the forager and group genotypes shared by all agents in the SHMP simulation. The MAGICAL program ma.set_genotpyes was invoked from within GRASS to parse the rules contained in this file and convert them to the internal format "understood" by agents. There is insufficient space here to provide a complete description of the foraging genotype, but as an example the flowchart in Figure 6 shows how it specifies the basic decision algorithm described earlier. In order to follow the logic of this it is necessary to know that a genotype may include actions from one or more of three classes, instrumental, minor, and major. Instrumental actions serve only to provide the user with information about the progress of the simulation. Since they have no analogue in the real world they should never influence subsequent behavior and consequently

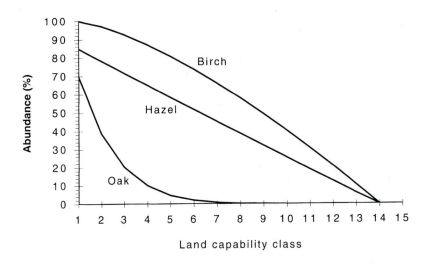

FIGURE 5   The fit between pollen data and predicted tree species' frequencies.

agents always "forget" that they had performed them when deciding what to do next. Minor actions are performed after instrumental actions, but prior to major actions. They are subtly different from instrumental actions in that while the fact of their having been performed is not pertinent to the decision process, the result may be. These actions are mostly those which move information around inside an agent's "brain" or which reset control counters such as the day of the month. Major actions are the last to be performed after a decision event, and since the fact of their having been performed is pertinent to the decision processes they form the basic building blocks of an algorithm. Some correspond to observable agent behavior, others represent complex cognitive processes that operate on the results of minor actions, and a third type control the flow of time in the simulation.

The foraging genotype specifies the basic decision algorithm as follows:

A At the start of the simulation an agent will always record the data value at its current location on its cognitive map (RVH). It will also always highlight its current location on the displayed base map (ATR) and mark that location as visited on output raster map number zero (RAV 0). Two points of general significance are worth noting. The first is that the decision token "a1" ensures that a condition is always met by the simple expedient of returning the logical value TRUE. The second is that the logical integrity of the genotype depends on the fact that only one of the three actions whose condition evaluates to TRUE is a major action. If this were not

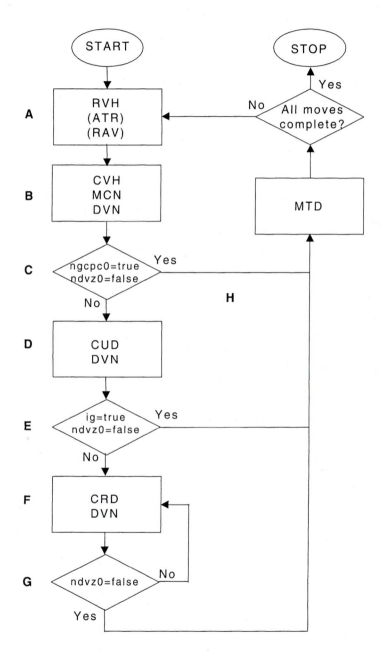

FIGURE 6   The foraging decision algorithm.

so, the flow of activity would fork causing each agent to make multiple parallel decisions.

B Having recorded the data value at its current location, the agent will then load that value into working memory (CVH) before searching its cognitive map (cognitive map 0) for the neighboring cell with the greatest value and proposing that cell as its destination (MCN). The agent loads the value at the chosen cell into working memory (CVN), while the user checks the corresponding data map (data map 0) for the actual value (DVN).

C The agent then waits (WAITA) for long enough to ensure that all the necessary information is available in working memory[1] before deciding whether to move to the proposed destination (MTD), or choose an alternative destination about which it has no knowledge (CUD). Since both MTD and CUD are major actions their conditions are necessarily mutually exclusive. They are also more complex than those encountered so far. The decision token "ncgpc0" returns the logical value TRUE only if the value of the cell at the proposed destination is greater than the value at the current location, where the values used are those previously loaded into working memory from cognitive map 0. The token "ndvz0" returns TRUE if the data value at the proposed destination is zero. The full condition ensures that the agent will only move to the proposed destination if ncgpc0 returns TRUE and ndvz0 returns FALSE, in other words, if the destination is both higher than the current location and on land. Conversely, if ncgpc0 returns FALSE and/or ndvz0 returns TRUE then the alternative condition will be met and the agent will choose an alternative destination.

D If required by the outcome of the previous step the agent randomly picks a neighboring cell about which it has no knowledge and then proposes this as its new destination (CUD). Should this action fail because all neighboring cells were known, the agent notes this fact and the proposed destination remains unchanged. In either case, the user then checks the appropriate data map (data map 0) for the actual value at the proposed destination (DVN).

E As previously, the agent waits (WAITB) for long enough to ensure that all the necessary information is available in working memory before deciding whether to move to the proposed destination (MTD) or randomly choose an alternative destination (CRD). And again, since both MTD and CRD are major actions their conditions are mutually exclusive. The decision token "ig" returns TRUE if the agent was able to identify a neighboring cell about which it has no knowledge, while ndvz0 functions as previously described. The full condition ensures that the agent will only move to the proposed destination if ig returns TRUE and ndvz0 returns FALSE,

---

[1]This delay is required because all conditions in any given row of a genotype are evaluated simultaneously before any resulting actions are invoked, from which it follows that it is impossible for a condition to test the results of any action invoked from the same row, even if it is a minor action such as CVN or DVN.

in other words, if it is unknown and on land. If ig returns FALSE and/or ndvz0 returns TRUE then the agent will choose an alternative destination.

F If the agent has still not moved then it randomly picks a neighboring cell without any qualification and proposes this as its destination (CRD). The user then checks the appropriate data map for the actual value at that location.

G The agent waits (WAITC) for long enough to ensure that all the necessary information is available to the user before the latter decides whether the move is permissible. At this stage the only criterion is that the proposed destination must be on land. Consequently, the condition for "move to proposed destination" (MTD) evaluates TRUE if the data value at the proposed location is not zero. If it is zero then the alternative condition evaluates TRUE, and the agent returns to step F to try another destination.

H Eventually, after step C, E, or G, the agent moves to its proposed destination (MTD). If the agent moves directly after step C then it will knowingly move to a cell with a greater abundance of hazelnuts. If it moves directly after step E then it may or may not move to a cell with a greater abundance of hazelnuts; if it does then this represents the satisfactory outcome of an episode of risk taking in the face of incomplete knowledge. Finally, if the agent moves after step G then it will not move to a cell with a greater abundance of hazelnuts, but instead moves to one with fewer hazelnuts so as to escape what it thinks might be a local optimum. After moving the agent records the data value at its new location on its cognitive map (RVH), highlights its new location on the displayed base map (ATR), and marks that location as visited on output raster map number zero (RAV 0). These three actions complete the basic foraging cycle, which the agent then starts over again by returning to step B.

Having constructed the foraging and group genotypes, the next stage in setting up the SHMP simulation model was to determine the region that the agents would inhabit. The appropriate GRASS command was used to give this the bounding Ordnance Survey National Grid coordinates 680025 (N), 638500 (S), 152500 (E), and 110500 (W), and a resolution of one map cell per 0.0025 square kilometres. The MAGICAL program ma.set_agents was then invoked to place agents in the region and specify their properties. Each simulation involved four agents belonging to one group, where the agents were conceived as representing a small family unit rather than individual foragers. The agents were placed at the appropriate initial base camp using the mouse. Each was then assigned the foraging genotype and suitable initial values for the other properties implicated in that genotype.

The step size was used to specify the number of neighboring cells that each agent should consider when deciding where to move and was therefore a vital parameter of the foraging algorithm because it determined the agents' willingness to take risks on arrival at a local optimum. This latter was varied within and between individual simulations, with the most conservative agents considering 24 neighboring cells and the most adventurous considering 80. Note that the increased risk implied by a greater number of cells was interpreted as a greater willingness to sacrifice short-term gain in the hope of achieving a greater long-term increase in efficiency. The number of steps, number of days, and number of months were all set so that each year was split into two equal seasons of six 30-day months during which agents would forage over distances of up to 12 km per day. During the hazel season information exchange would occur at the end of each day, while the group would consider whether to move base camp at the end of each month. Each agent was also assigned one of the standard GRASS colors in which to mark its location on the video monitor during the simulation. More importantly, all agents were given a 10% probability of discarding one knapped stone artefact in each of four categories after they had performed certain actions. For the purposes of the SHMP simulation model, the four categories were interpreted as: (1) primary debitage, (2) secondary debitage, (3) microliths, and (4) scrapers. The foraging genotype specified that all four categories of artefact could be discarded during each visit to a base camp, but only secondary debitage, microliths, and scrapers could be discarded away from a base camp. The exact combination depended on the season: secondary debitage and scrapers could be discarded while foraging for hazelnuts, whereas secondary debitage and microliths could be discarded during the dispersal. In both cases the possibility of discard arose on leaving each map cell.

The final stage in setting up the SHMP simulation model was to specify the maps $(0\ldots n)$ referred to in the foraging genotype. This was achieved using the MAGICAL program ma.sim, which assigns map 0 to the contents of the currently active GRASS display frame before prompting for the name of any other maps required by the agents' genotypes. Map 0 was assigned to the digital elevation model (DEM) of Islay so as to delineate the extent of the island. Map 1 was assigned to the raster map of hazelnut abundance.

4 EXPLORING ISLAY

It will be recalled that the SHMP simulation model was constructed to examine whether the distribution of Mesolithic flint artefacts on Islay could be explained in terms of small groups landing at the coast and then foraging for hazelnuts. To this end the MAGICAL program ma.sim was used to run a number of simulations with different combinations of starting point and risk taking. Several runs were made for each combination, but as the basic patterns of exploration proved insensitive to differences in the value used to seed the random number generator only one set of results is shown in each case. All runs lasted for a total of 216,000 increments of simulated time (over 8.5 million scheduling steps) representing approximately ten years foraging. Each simulation produced five raster maps of the region: one recorded the number of visits received by each map cell while each of the other four recorded the number of artefacts of a given category that were deposited in each cell.

4.1   ARRIVING BY SEA

The first simulations were run to discover how foragers landing on the coast of Islay might have explored the island if the harvest of hazelnuts was a major objective. Agents were started from three locations. Port Ellen would have provided a sheltered landing place at 7000 B.P., just as it does for vessels approaching from the mainland today. Landing at Port Askaig might have been more difficult at 7000 B.P. than is now the case, but it would nevertheless have allowed the shortest crossing from the island of Jura. Finally, Port Wemys provides one of very few sheltered landing places for an approach from the west. In the initial simulations from all three locations, three agents considered 24 neighboring cells when deciding where to move, while the fourth considered 48 and was therefore prepared to take more risks to increase long-term foraging gains. Note that as a result of information sharing the three conservative agents should eventually have benefited from the fourth agent's risk taking. (The long-term stability of this unequal distribution of risk constitutes an interesting research question which is, unfortunately, beyond the scope of the present study.) In some cases subsequent simulations increased the amount of risk taking so that all four agents considered 80 neighboring cells when deciding where to move.

Figure 7 shows the combined distribution of all artefacts discarded by foragers who landed at Port Ellen. It shows that relatively risk-averse agents who landed at Port Ellen did not explore much of the island. The distribution of primary debitage indicated that agents never moved their base camp more than 1 km from Port Ellen, and indeed, examination of the simulation report revealed that 12 out of 22 moves were to a previously occupied location. The distribution of secondary debitage and microliths was less localized, but still largely confined to within 10 km of Port Ellen. This restricted dispersal was probably at least partly a function of the random walk preventing easy passage through the narrow land bridge to and from the Mull of Oa.

Relatively risk-averse foragers agents who landed at Port Askaig explored rather more of Islay than those who landed at Port Ellen, reaching the northernmost and southernmost extremities of the island as well as part of the Rhinns. The distribution of primary debitage showed that the foragers set up base camps in a tightly constrained area around Port Askaig and another around Port Ellen. The distribution of scrapers (Figure 8) reveals that foraging for hazelnuts was largely confined within a 2-km radius of the base camps. The distribution of microliths (Figure 9) confirms that most of the exploration occurred out of the hazelnut season and, crucially, that it was information gathered during the dispersal which led the agents to move south into the Port Ellen area. No base camps were established on the Rhinns even though the northern and central part of the peninsula was explored.

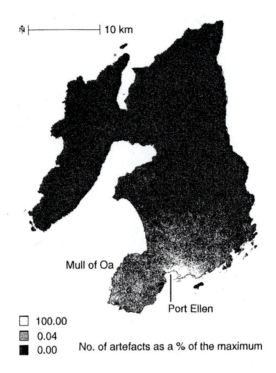

FIGURE 7 Artefacts discarded by risk-averse foragers who landed at Port Ellen. © License No. MC/354. Reprinted by permission.

Figure 10 shows the combined distribution of all artefacts discarded by risk-averse agents who landed at Port Wemys. It is clear that the long narrow shape of the Rhinns peninsula restricted movement during the summer dispersal much as the land bridge to the Mull of Oa restricted the movement of agents starting from Port Ellen. Nevertheless, it was clear from the distribution of scrapers that the agents found no reason to create a base camp in the central area of the Rhinns despite very extensive exploration of this area.

4.2   AVOIDING THE CENTRAL RHINNS

The failure of foragers who started from either Port Askaig or Port Wemys to establish even one base camp on the central Rhinns was considered highly significant given the concentration of archaeological evidence in this area (see below). The apparent conservatism of those who started from Port Wemys is especially remarkable and gave rise to a suspicion that their behavior might have been an artefact of some unidentified constraint imposed by the simu-

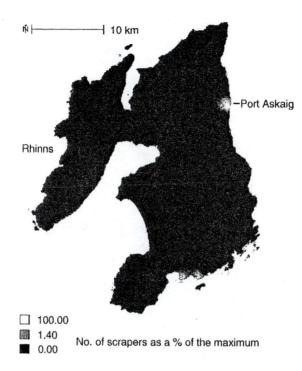

FIGURE 8   Scrapers discarded by risk-averse foragers who landed at Port Askaig.
© License No. MC/354. Reprinted by permission.

lation algorithm. Consequently it was decided to run a set of simulations in which foragers started from the Mesolithic site at Bolsay Farm.

Figure 11 shows the combined distribution of all artefacts discarded by risk-averse agents who started from Bolsay farm. Although it records a high concentration of artefacts around the Mesolithic site, it is clear that most discard occurred around Port Wemys. The distribution of scrapers confirmed that Port Wemys was the favored area for the harvest of hazelnuts. Indeed, the simulation report recorded that 32 out 45 decisions about whether to move base camp resulted in a move to, or to stay in the vicinity of Port Wemys.

Perhaps even more revealing was the distribution of artefacts discarded by agents who were prepared to take greater risks to increase their harvest of hazelnuts. Figure 12 shows that such agents rejected the Rhinns as a whole in favor of the area around Port Ellen. The simulation report recorded that the only base camp used on the Rhinns was the one initially established at Bolsay Farm, whereas six new camps were established around Port Ellen. The distribution of scrapers, which provides a proxy for the spatial extent of hazel-

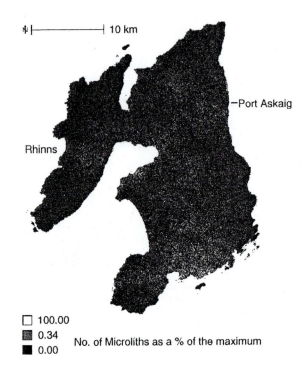

☐ 100.00
▦ 0.34   No. of Microliths as a % of the maximum
■ 0.00

FIGURE 9   Microliths discarded by risk-averse foragers who landed at Port Askaig.
© License No. MC/354. Reprinted by permission.

nut foraging, clearly indicated that foragers had to travel greater distances to increase their harvest at Bolsay Farm than was the case at Port Ellen.

4.3   WERE MESOLITHIC FORAGERS SEARCHING FOR HAZELNUTS?

Mesolithic artefacts have been found in three areas of Islay (see Figure 13): the central and northern Rhinns, a central region around the river Sorn, and a limited area at Kiells, near Port Askaig. This immediately presents a stark contrast with the results of the simulations, which showed a preference for the southern Rhinns, southern Islay and the area around port Askaig. The most important of these is southern Islay, since this was the only area "settled" by agents even when they had landed elsewhere. This strong preference has not been demonstrated for the southern Rhinns or Port Askaig because there is no evidence that agents would have used these areas had they not been selected as landing places. The fact that there is some evidence of Mesolithic activity around Port Askaig, which is only a short crossing from Jura, but none around Port Wemys, which is a far greater distance from the mainland,

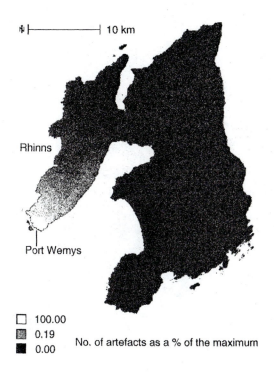

〵 ├──────────┤ 10 km

Rhinns

Port Wemys

☐ 100.00
▨ 0.19
■ 0.00

No. of artefacts as a % of the maximum

FIGURE 10   Artefacts discarded by risk-averse foragers who landed at Port Wemys.
© License No. MC/354. Reprinted by permission.

would thus be more interesting were it not for the generally poor fit between
the hazelnut foraging model and the artefact distribution. In this respect the
lack of evidence from southern Islay is quite striking given that this is the one
area where activity would be expected irrespective of the landing place. This
discrepancy is all the more noteworthy because southern Islay is not an area
that presents major methodological problems in the way that survey of the
central and northern uplands does (see Mithen, ed., in prep.).

The simulation output included the frequencies of four classes of artefact,
but the resulting assemblage composition does not fit the archaeological data
any better than the basic artefact distribution. The broad trend in the archaeological data is for a reduction in the relative frequency of cores and primary
debitage as one moves east from the flint-rich beaches of the west coast, with a
corresponding increase in retouched artefacts, blades, and microliths (Mithen,
ed., in prep, chapter 4.1). In contrast, if the principle determinant of land use
were hazelnut gathering, then following the assumptions built into the foraging model one would expect to see primary knapping debitage and scrapers

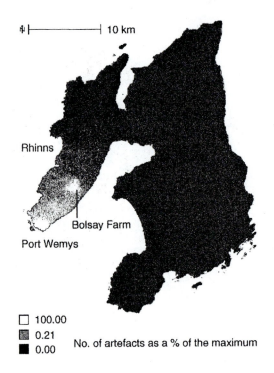

FIGURE 11   Artefacts discarded by risk-averse foragers who started at Bolsay Farm. © License No. MC/354. Reprinted by permission.

concentrated in sheltered east-facing coastal areas. The low frequency or absence of primary debitage in these areas could be accommodated by arguing that much initial flint reduction took place at specialized camps on the west coast, and there are indeed reasons to favor this scenario (Marshall 1997). This would also explain why occupation of the central and northern Rhinns did not produce the higher relative frequency of blades predicted by the hazelnut foraging model. Significantly, however, such a scenario does little to explain the discrepancy between actual and predicted assemblage composition at Kiells, located approximately 1 mile inland from Port Askaig. According to the simulation output, this assemblage ought to be dominated by heavy retouched artefacts such as scrapers, but it is actually characterized by the highest frequency of blades of any fieldwalked assemblage on the island.

How should one interpret the poor fit between the archaeological evidence and the simulation output given that there is, as discussed earlier, direct evidence for the exploitation of hazelnuts? Overall it seems that, given the assumptions built into the model, the distribution of Mesolithic flint artefacts

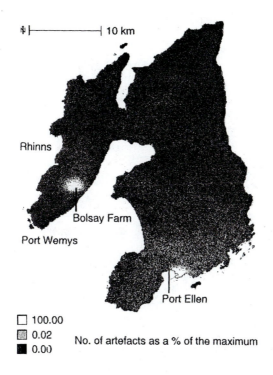

FIGURE 12   Artefacts discarded by risk taking foragers who started at Bolsay Farm. © License No. MC/354. Reprinted by permission.

on Islay cannot be explained in terms of small groups landing at the coast and then foraging for hazelnuts. Consequently, either the assumptions are wrong, or foraging for hazelnuts was not a major determinant of Mesolithic land use on Islay. The former is possible in respect of both assemblage composition and absolute visibility. It has already been suggested that primary debitage and cores might not be found at "normal" or hazelnut-related base camps if there were specialist reduction sites on the west coast. The near complete absence of artefacts in southern Islay, however, requires that hazelnut gathering was not just associated with different artefacts than those proposed, but involved virtually no artefact discard. This latter requirement tends to support the second interpretation, that foraging for hazelnuts was not a major determinant of Mesolithic land use on Islay. If it had been, then even if hazelnut gathering itself is of low archaeological visibility, other necessary activities should have resulted in the deposition of a significant number of artefacts in southern Islay. To argue that the Mesolithic land-use pattern was not predominantly determined by foraging for hazelnuts does not, of course, imply that hazelnuts

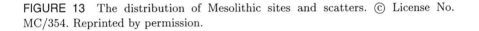

Mesolithic sites and scatters

FIGURE 13   The distribution of Mesolithic sites and scatters. © License No.
MC/354. Reprinted by permission.

were not an important resource, merely that if they were then their harvest
must have been embedded in a land-use system which was subject to other
stronger spatial determinants.

5   CONCLUSION

The MAGICAL software successfully integrates GIS and mutliagent simulation to provide a means of exploring the behavior responsible for spatiotemporal variability in the archaeological record. Three achievements, all at least
minimally demonstrated by the simulation model described here, are worthy
of emphasis:

1. Its close integration with a GIS package permits far greater spatial realism
   than has hitherto been typical of archaeological simulation modeling, and
   also opens up the possibility of direct comparison with digitally stored
   archaeological data. Moreover, it allows the full range of GIS analysis,

management, and presentation tools to be applied to simulation input and output.

2. The MAGICAL software is the first archaeological simulation package designed to allow research into a class of problems rather than one specific problem. Most significantly, the genotype mechanism allows users to build their own simulation models without recourse to computer programming. Any competent user of the GRASS GIS package should be able to master the steps required to do this. In addition, comprehensive documentation has been provided for those who wish to further extend the capabilities of the software by programming, and to that end care has been taken to ensure that the source code compiles with freely available software engineering tools.

3. The MAGICAL software's extensive support for agent-based modeling opens up new possibilities for the computer simulation of hunter-gatherers. The provision for explicitly modeling agent's spatial knowledge is perhaps the most obvious of these. Other advances include the possibility of group behavior emerging from the decisions of individual members and also the ability of agents to conduct their own mental simulations.

ACKNOWLEDGMENTS

Development of the MAGICAL software was supported by award GR3/9540 from the U.K. Natural Environment Research Council to Dr. Steven Mithen, University of Reading. Steven Mithen proposed to the N.E.R.C. that there was a pressing need to integrate multiagent simulation and GIS for archaeological purposes; I am grateful to him for the opportunity to help make that a reality and, of course, for his encouragement and advice.

I am also grateful to Petra Dark and Martin Bell for guidance concerning the reconstruction of past vegetation, although they can in no way be held responsible for the simplistic nature of the hazelnut availability model. Paddy Woodman kindly provided access to landscape data generated in the course of her doctoral research.

Finally, I must thank Tim Kohler and George Gumerman for inviting me to participate in the workshop that gave rise to this volume, along with the staff of the Santa Fe Institute for their part in making it such an enjoyable occasion.

REFERENCES

Allen, K. M. S., S. W. Green, and E. B. W. Zubrow
  1990 Interpreting Space: GIS and Archaeology. London: Taylor and Francis.

Beckerman, S.
1983 Carpe Diem: An Optimal Foraging Approach to Bari Fishing and Hunting. *In* Adaptive Response of Native Amazonians. R. Hames and W. Vickers, eds. Pp. 269–299. New York: Academic Press.

Bennett, K. D.
1988 A Provisional Map of Forest Types for the British Isles 5000 Years Ago. Journal of Quaternary Science 4:141–144.

Bettinger, R. L.
1991 Hunter-Gatherers: Archaeological and Evolutionary Theory. New York: Plenum.

Bibby, J. S., and D. W. Futty
1988 Land Capability Classification for Forestry in Britain. Aberdeen: The Macaulay Land Use Research Institute.

Birks, H. J. B.
1989 Holocene Isochrone Maps and Patterns of Tree-Spreading in the British Isles. Journal of Biogeography 16:503–540.

Boesch, C., and H. Boesch
1984 Mental Map in Chimpanzees: An Analysis of Hammer Transports for Nut Cracking. Primates 25:160–170.

Boismier, W. A.
1996 Modelling the Effects of Tillage Processes on Artefact Distributions in the Ploughzone: A Simulation Study of Tillage-Induced Pattern Formation. Unpublished Ph.D. thesis, Cambridge University.

Caraco, T., S. Martindale, and T. S. Whitham
1980 An Empirical Demonstration of Risk-Sensitive Foraging Preferences. Animal Behaviour 28:820–830.

Chadwick, A. J.
1978 A Computer Simulation of Mycenaean Settlement. *In* Simulation Studies in Archaeology. I. Hodder, ed., Pp. 47–57. Cambridge, UK: Cambridge University Press.

Clark, C. W, and M. Mangel
1984 Foraging and Flocking Strategies in an Uncertain Environment. American Naturalist 123:626–641.

Clarke, D. L.
1968 Analytical Archaeology. London: Methuen.

Dawkins, Richard
1982 The Extended Phenotype. Oxford: Freeman.

DeAngelis, D. L., and L. J. Gross
1992 Individual-Based Models and Approaches in Ecology: Populations, Communities and Ecosystems. New York: Chapman & Hall.

Doran, Jim
1970 Systems Theory: Computer Simulations and Archaeology. World Archaeology 1:289–298.

Edwards, K. J., and G. Whittington
1997 Vegetation Change. In Scotland: Environment and Archaeology, 8000 B.C.–A.D. 1000. K. J. Edwards and I. B. M. Ralston, eds. Pp. 63–82. Chichester: Wiley.

Estes, W. K.
1984 Human Learning and Memory. In The Biology of Learning. P. Marler and H. S. Terrace, eds. Pp. 617–628. Berlin: Springer-Verlag.

Fisher, B. A.
1980 Small Group Decision Making. New York: McGraw Hill.

Giddens, A.
1984 The Constitution of Society. Cambridge, UK: Polity Press.

Gilbert, N., and J. Doran, eds.
1994 Simulating Societies: The Computer Simulation of Social Phenomena. London: UCL Press.

Holland, J. H., and J. H. Miller
1991 Artificial Adaptive Agents in Economic Theory. American Economic Review, Papers and Proceedings 81:365–370.

Krebs, J. R., A. Kacelnik, and P. Taylor
1978 Test of Optimal Sampling by Foraging Great Tits. Nature 275:27–31.

Kuipers, B.
1983 The Cognitive Map: Could It Have Been Any Other Way? In Spatial Orientation: Theory, Research and Application. H. L. Pick, Jr., and L. P. Acredolo, eds. Pp. 345–359. New York: Plenum.

Lake, Mark W.
1995 Computer Simulation Modelling of Early Hominid Subsistence Activities. Unpublished Ph.D. thesis, Cambridge University.
In press Magical Computer Simulation of Mesolithic Foraging on Islay. In Hunter-Gatherer Landscape Archaeology: The Southern Hebrides Mesolithic Project, 1988–1998. S. J. Mithen, ed. Cambridge: The McDonald Institute for Archaeological Research.

Lake, Mark W., and S. J. Mithen
1998 The MAGICAL Project: Integrating Simulation Modelling and GIS Analysis in Archaeology with an Application to Mesolithic Scotland. Unpublished manuscript in possession of the authors, University of Reading.

Lake, Mark W., P. E. Woodman, and S. J. Mithen
1998 Tailoring GIS for Archaeological Applications: An Example Concerning Viewshed Analysis. Journal of Archaeological Science 25:27–38.

Lloyd, R.
　1989 Cognitive Maps: Encoding and Decoding Information. Annals of the Association of American Geographers 79:101–124.

Mark, D. M., and A. U. Frank
　1990 Experiential and Formal Models of Geographic Space. *In* Language, Cognitive Science, and Geographic Information Systems. D. M. Mark and A. U. Frank, eds. Pp. 1–24. Santa Barbara, CA: National Center for Geographic Information and Analysis.

Marshall, G. D.
　1997 Mesolithic South West Scotland, Lithic Raw Materials and Regional Settlement Structure. Unpublished Ph.D. thesis, University of Southampton.

Martin, J. F.
　1983 Optimal Foraging Theory: A Review of Some Models and Their Applications. American Anthropologist 85:612–629.

McVean, D. N., and D. A. Ratcliffe
　1962 Plant Communities of the Scottish Highlands. London: HMSO.

Mithen, S. J.
　1990 Thoughtful Foragers: A Study of Prehistoric Decision Making. Cambridge, UK: Cambridge University Press.
　1994 Simulating Prehistoric Hunter-Gatherer Societies. *In* Simulating Societies: the Computer Simulation of Social Phenomena. N. Gilbert and J. Doran, eds. Pp. 165–193. London: UCL Press.

Mithen, S. J., ed.
　In prep Hunter-Gatherer Landscape Archaeology: The Southern Hebrides Mesolithic Project, 1988–1998. Cambridge: The McDonald Institute for Archaeological Research.

Mithen, S. J., and M. W. Lake
　1996 The Southern Hebrides Mesolithic Project: Reconstructing Mesolithic Settlement in Western Scotland. *In* The Early Prehistory of Scotland. T. Pollard and A. Morrison, eds. Pp. 123–151. Edinburgh: Edinburgh University Press.

Peterken, G.
　1993 Woodland Conservation and Management. 2nd ed. London: Chapman & Hall.

Rackham, O.
　1980 Ancient Woodland, Its History, Vegetation and Uses in England. London: Edward Arnold.

Renfrew, A. C.
　1987 Problems in the Modelling of Socio-Cultural Systems. European Journal of Operational Research 30:179–192.

Shanks, M., and C. Tilley
1987 Reconstructing Archaeology: Theory and Practice. Cambridge, UK: Cambridge University Press.

Stephens, D. W., and J. R. Krebs
1986 Foraging Theory. Princeton, NJ: Princeton University Press.

Tanner, A.
1979 Bringing Home Animals: Religious Ideology and Mode of Production of the Mistassini Cree Hunters. London: C. Hirst.

Thomas, D. H.
1972 A Computer Simulation Model of Great Basin Shoshonean Settlement Patterns. *In* Models in Archaeology. D. Clarke, ed. Pp. 671–704. London: Methuen.

Tipping, R.
1994 The Form and Fate of Scotland's Woodlands. Proceedings of the Society of Antiquaries of Scotland 124:1–54.

Tolman, E. C.
1948 Cognitive Maps in Rats and Men. Psychological Review 55:189–208.

Wobst, H.
1974 Boundary Conditions for Palaeolithic Social Systems: A Simulation Approach. American Antiquity 36:127–138.

Be There Then: A Modeling Approach to Settlement Determinants and Spatial Efficiency Among Late Ancestral Pueblo Populations of the Mesa Verde Region, U.S. Southwest

Timothy A. Kohler
James Kresl
Carla Van West
Eric Carr
Richard H. Wilshusen

The archaeology of southwestern Colorado from A.D. 900 to 1300 presents a number of interesting problems, including population aggregation and abandonment. We report on an on-going project, implemented using the modeling libraries of Swarm, to model the settlement dynamics of this region, treating households as agents. Landscape detail includes an annual model of paleoproductivity, soils, vegetation, elevation, and water resource type and location. Individuals within households reproduce and die; households farm, relocate, and die; children within households marry and form new households. Household location is responsive to changing productivity (depleted in some scenarios) and, in some scenarios, water resources. Comparison of simulated settlement with the archaeological record highlights changes in the settlement and farming strategies between Pueblo II and Pueblo III times, including the increasing importance of water- and sediment-control, and other alternatives to extensive dry farming. Our results suggest that degradation of the dry-farming niche may have contributed to these changes.

Dynamics in Human and Primate Societies, edited by T. Kohler and
G. Gumerman, Oxford University Press, 1999. **145**

1 MOTIVATION

This project began with a desire to understand why, during certain times in prehistory, most Pueblo peoples lived in relatively compact villages, while at other times, they lived in dispersed hamlets (Cordell et al. 1994). Our approach to this problem is based on a thread of accumulating research begun in the early 1980s when a dissertation from the University of Arizona by Barney Burns (1983) showed that it was possible to retrodict potential prehistoric maize yields in a portion of Southwest Colorado by combining prehistoric tree-ring records with historic crop-production records of local farmers. A few years later, Kohler et al. (1986; see also Orcutt et al. 1990) simulated agricultural catchment size and shape in a northern portion of the present study area, to arrive at the suggestion that avoiding violent confrontation over access to superior agricultural land was a major force in forming the villages that appeared in this area in the late A.D. 700s and again in the mid-800s. Shortly after that, Carla Van West, in a 1990 dissertation (published 1994), used a different and larger set of tree-ring data to produce spatialized Palmer Drought Severity Indexes (or PDSIs, a measure of meteorological drought) in 1,070 GIS data planes, one for each year from A.D. 900–1970, for the portion of southwestern Colorado shown in Figure 1, at a spatial resolution of 4 ha. Construction of these landscapes is described briefly below. Van West was the first to use a series of local weather stations and specific soil types to reconstruct PDSI in a way that made these measures respond to very local conditions.

Finally, Kohler and Van West (1996) examined these production landscapes against the known record of aggregation in this area and came to the tentative conclusion that microeconomic processes, at the level of the household, could successfully explain whether settlement was dispersed or aggregated at any time. Specifically, we suggested that villages tended to form during periods when it was in the best interests of households to share food with other households. On the other hand, villages tended to dissolve during periods when it was in the best interests of households (as predicted by a utility function) to hoard their production. Our arguments were based on comparing the relative payoffs to households of sharing vs. hoarding under various production regimes, using sigmoid-shaped utility curves. The underlying model for aggregation, then, is that it is an epiphenomenon of dense local networks of interhousehold maize exchange. To test this model more rigorously, however, we needed to simulate household placement, maize production, consumption, and exchange with other households in considerable detail, rather than at an aggregate level for the landscape as a whole.

This chapter (see also Kohler and Carr [1997]) lays the groundwork for that study. Here we study how varying a series of parameters relating to paleoproductivity, water resources, and anthropogenic degradation changes the settlement pattern produced by a population of agents. These agents represent households inhabiting a space that resembles, in some characteristics, the en-

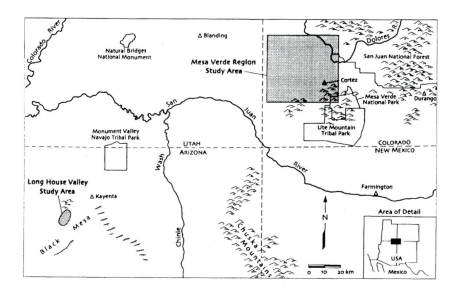

FIGURE 1   Study area in Southwest Colorado, with Long House Valley (see Dean et al. [this volume]) also located for comparison.

vironment of Southwest Colorado between A.D. 901 and 1287. Our study area (Figure 1) comprises most of what Varien et al. (1996:86) recently defined as the McElmo/Yellowjacket District, as well as small adjacent portions of their Ute Mountain, Montezuma Creek, and Dolores Valley districts.

1.1   ENVIRONMENTAL DETERMINANTS OF SITE LOCATION IN THE UPLAND SOUTHWEST

Given the huge literature on southwestern archaeology, relatively little has been written about the large-scale determinants of settlement location on this landscape. Janet Orcutt (1986) noted that habitation sites in the Dolores area between A.D. 600 and 920 were located so as to have catchments with significantly more good-quality agricultural land than did a series of random points. She was unable to demonstrate that the catchments surrounding the many fewer sites in this same area after A.D. 920 still contained disproportionate amounts of good agricultural land, though poor-quality agricultural lands were still demonstrably avoided. Nearly all the known Pueblo I (PI: A.D. 700–900) villages within and near our study area, which are the primary residences of entire communities and typically contain more than 120 surface rooms and 16 pitstructures, are at an elevation of about 2,100 m with a standard deviation of only 50 m, and are typically close to locales with deep loess soils (Wilshusen 1997).

Sarah Schlanger (1988) examined three elevationally distinct portions of the present study area. She perceived a generally good fit between the population movement within this region from A.D. 600 to 1200 and the changing opportunities for agricultural production as reconstructed from proxies for low- and high-frequency climate change. In a more detailed study of local population movement in the Dolores area, Schlanger and Wilshusen (1993) documented that abandonments of a particular locale for several decades were closely tied to high-frequency variation in precipitation and maize harvests.

Pueblo II (PII: A.D. 900–1140) communities are typically more dispersed than the PI villages. Varien et al. (1996:106) note that these dispersed communities "were characterized by small habitation sites located on what are today the most productive arable soils." The wide range of Pueblo II habitation and field house locations (on mesa tops, at high elevations, and in canyon bottoms) suggests that already a more diverse set of agricultural strategies was in place than in the earlier Pueblo I period (Wilshusen 1997). Schlanger (1988) has suggested that there was a pervasive shift in the area after about A.D. 1100 from rainfall-dependent farming on mesa tops to farming in canyons and watercourses, accompanied by water-harvesting techniques. This innovation was necessitated, she suggests, by the combination of a low-frequency trend toward decreased precipitation (especially winter precipitation), which would have made higher elevations attractive for dry farmers, and a (somewhat controversial) high-frequency trend toward shorter growing seasons, which would have made those same areas quite risky (Petersen 1988). More recent studies (Wilshusen 1997) emphasize that sediment and water-controlling features become increasingly common in our area even earlier, after the A.D. 940s, making a climatic explanation for them more problematic.

Just outside of our study area, in southeastern Utah, Matson et al. (1988) show that both Basketmaker III and Pueblo II/III habitations and field stations on Cedar Mesa are concentrated at relatively high elevations, in dense pinyon-juniper, within a putative dry-farming zone, in contrast with the settlement shift seen further east.

Finally, for the Pueblo III (PIII: A.D. 1140–1285) period Varien et al. (1996:106) note that "after A.D. 1200, settlement moved away from the mesa tops, and the direct association of habitation sites with the best agricultural soils no longer existed."

More studies could be cited, but there is clear and completely unsurprising agreement that opportunities for farming were important in the locational decisions of these farmers, although the extent to which habitations themselves are directly adjacent to fields may vary. It is also quite probable that mesa-top dry farming becomes less important throughout much of our area during the A.D. 900–1300 period.

Less systematically studied is the role of water sources in determining site location. Wilshusen (1997) reports that Pueblo I villages are typically within 1 km of permanent water sources such as the Dolores River. Mark Varien et al. (1996:106) suggest that after A.D. 1200 "securing a domestic water source appears to have been a central concern, as many of the large sites surround a spring at the head of the canyon [with] small sites located toward the canyon rims, at the base of cliffs, on talus slopes, in alcoves, or on terraces." Varien (1997) provides a comprehensive overview of all the known late, large PIII canyon-oriented sites and their associated communities. Sites such as Woods Canyon (Kelley 1996) or Sand Canyon Pueblo (Bradley 1992) illustrate how central these canyon drainages are in the design and layout of these PIII villages.

It is widely agreed that climate affects resource distributions for these farmers. Over the last 15 years research has also demonstrated that anthropogenic impact on potential resources may have an equally profound influence on farming decisions. Kohler, for example, has argued that widespread deforestation within the northern portions of our study area contributed to the departure of the Dolores Anasazi just before A.D. 900 (Kohler and Matthews 1988). Eric Force and Wayne Howell (1997) report very high sedimentation rates building fans into the north side of McElmo Creek (toward the maximum density of human occupation), but not also into the south side of the drainage (as would be expected if the erosion were climatic in origin). These depositional episodes are concentrated in Basketmaker III times, and in the PII/III periods. Force and Howell suggest that these high rates are caused in part by agricultural practices which disturb the natural cover of the mesa-top headwaters for the north-side drainages. They further suggest that the aggrading low-elevation floodlands on the margins of places like McElmo Canyon provided good farming opportunities for PIII farmers. By their analysis, then, PIII settlements may be located along canyon rims to be near both mesa-top and flooplain farms.

1.2 PLAN OF ARGUMENT

Our task in this chapter is to exercise several different models for site location within this area between A.D. 900 and 1300. We examine, in a systematic and additive way, how much we improve random guesses as to site location by using a model in which paleoproductivity alone affects agents' locational decisions. We then ask whether we further improve the fit between our simulated locations and the known sites of the PII and PIII periods by requiring agents to locate within different radii of known water sources of different types. Finally, we combine all of these models with two degradation scenarios in which agents either degrade all lands which they farm, or only those lands supporting a pinyon-juniper vegetation and those which are characterized by thin soils on slopes.

Some of what we do here could be studied by traditional statistical techniques. For example, it would be possible to build associations between water sources of various kinds and the presence/absence of site locations. Other aspects of this study would be more difficult or impossible to duplicate using such techniques. Our paleoproductivity data change every year, and so would have to be averaged for a specific spot over many years to be used statistically. This procedure, however, could hide spikes of productivity that might be sufficient to induce relocation. Finally, it is hard to imagine how the dynamic impact of agents on these changing environments could be studied in the absence of simulation.

Our long-term agenda is to move beyond an investigation of the environmental determinants of site location. In many areas the process of aggregation in Neolithic societies comes early in a sequence of changes that often eventually includes increasing task specialization, reorganization of storage in a way that alienates a portion of it from the household, the addition of new layers of ceremonial organization focused on the community rather than on its constituent kin groups, and the appearance of ranked kin groups. Not all of these changes apparently took place in our study area, perhaps in part because of a series of deleterious climatic events in the late 1200s, but there is no reason that, eventually, we cannot use the machinery we are building here as the basis for exploring various assumptions about the operation of such processes in similar societies.

2 METHODS

2.1 CONSTRUCTING THE PALEOPRODUCTION LANDSCAPES

The yearly maps of potential agricultural potential used in this simulation were produced by Van West (1994) as follows:

1. A study area was defined. The area selected had to have sufficiently diverse landforms, variable elevational settings, and well-documented archaeological sites dating from the appropriate time periods. Further, it had to exist as 7.5-minute DEMs (Digital Elevation Models). Eventually, Van West selected an area equivalent to 12 7.5-minute topographic maps to represent the maximum study area.
2. A base map for the study was produced by mosaicking the 12 DEMs into a single image.
3. The spatial resolution of the analysis was established. The image was partitioned into rows and columns, where each cell was 4 ha (200×200 m) in area. After trimming, the final image was organized as 200 rows and 227 columns.
4. Van West recorded selected attributes for each of the 45,400 cells in the image. Soil data in the form of soil series information, soil depth, available water capacity, and natural plant productivity, as well as agricultural yield

information, were recorded for each cell. The soil series information was used to create a second data layer or map which depicted the distribution of 98 distinct soil types. A total of 36,759 cells representing 81% of the study area (1,470 km^2) had complete soils information when this study was originally undertaken; these cells were used in all subsequent steps.

5. Derivative maps, which reduced the elevational and soils data into more interpretable forms, were produced. A third map was derived that depicted the 98 soil types classified into one of 11 soil-moisture classes, which could be used to calculate Palmer Drought Severity Index (PDSI) rankings. A fourth map that classified the 1,512 different elevational values into one of five elevational bands also was created. Each elevational band was associated with the instrumented records of an appropriate and proximate weather station (Bluff, Utah; Cortez, Ignacio, Mesa Verde, and Fort Lewis, Colorado).

6. The climatic and the soils data were used to calculate PDSI values. These took the form of monthly precipitation and temperature data from the five, elevationally diverse weather stations, as well as data on the available water capacities and soil depth for the 11 contrasting soil-moisture classes. PDSIs are temporally sensitive indicators of soil moisture; they are commonly used to model the success of dry-farming agriculture. Negative values indicate dry conditions, and positive values indicate moist conditions. As with tree-ring width data, PDSIs integrate the effects of precipitation and temperature on available stores of soil moisture and incorporate the balance from previous months into the estimate for the current month. In this study, PDSIs calculated for the month of June during the historic instrumented period were correlated with tree-ring width data for the same set of years. This produced a calibration, or transfer function, that was applied to the full length of the tree-ring series, A.D. 901 to 1970. In this way, 55 long-term reconstructions of PDSI were produced, one for each combination of the five elevational strata with the 11 soil-moisture groups.

7. Van West created a fifth map illustrating the precise spatial distribution of each of the 55 long-term reconstructions. It combined data from the 11 soil-moisture classes and the five elevation bands.

8. The 55 long-term reconstructions were used to assign annually specific PDSI values to each cell in the image. Consequently, 1,070 data planes were created and represented a continuous record of potential soil-moisture conditions for the A.D. 901 through A.D. 1970 period. Each summarizes spatially variable soil-moisture conditions as they existed across the study area on July 1, just before the advent of typical summer rains.

9. All the PDSI values compiled for a single year were reexpressed as potential crop yields (first as beans and later as maize) and summed. This was accomplished through regression analysis and estimation. The relationship between natural plant productivity data and historical crop yield data for 44 of the 98 soil types in the study area were used to estimate

potential yield on soils without crop yield data. The end products of these GIS-coordinated steps were the creation of 400 annual maps (A.D. 901 to 1300) depicting the distribution of climatically conditioned yield values for potential maize production and a tabular summary of yearly yield estimates for the four century-period.

10. Finally, for this study, Van West updated the paleoproductivity and soils data bases using newly available and still unpublished soils maps, filling in many gaps in her original study.

Although these reconstructions are based on the best data available, and although we believe them to be the best ever produced, it is important to be frank about their limitations. Because of selection and filtering processes on the tree-ring samples on which they are based, they may not accurately reflect low-frequency climatic trends (on time scales of several decades of more). They will also be relatively insensitive to growing-season length. It is possible, therefore, that they may overestimate production at the highest elevation areas in the study area, or in times and places where cold-air drainage would be a problem. They may also over- or underestimate potential production in periods that are at the peaks or troughs of low-frequency climatic trends. Finally, they provide a model for dry-farming potential. Potential for plots that profit from surface-water flows or alluvial ground-water levels may be underestimated, or in fact considered here to be zero since soils data are missing from some canyon-bottom locations.

2.2   BUILDING THE DATABASE OF ACTUAL SITE LOCATIONS

Included in the model are all the prehistoric sites known for the study area that exhibit surface evidence of architecture and thus represent some minimal amount of investment. They were drawn in 1997 from the database maintained at the Colorado State Historic Preservation Office. These data contained fields with the UTM (Universal Transverse Mercator) coordinates, as well as fields identifying the "site type" and "culture" attributed to the site. In the present version of the model, these are the only site features utilized. All the sites identified as architectural under the "site type" field were sorted from the list. We assume that most of these were habitations, although some could be seasonal sites such as field houses. Then from those, any assigned through the "culture" field to a Pecos Classification type of PI, PII, or PIII were pulled out and placed into a text file. Several of the sites were labeled in the listing as belonging to more than one culture type, and therefore appear in more than one file.

The three text files, one for each period, contained only UTM coordinates. These files were then transferred to a GIS application and converted into grid layers, each with 45,400 cells (200 rows and 227 columns). These data planes contain 435 cells with PI sites, 783 cells with PII sites, and 485 cells with PIII sites. These grid layers were then incorporated into the Swarm model.

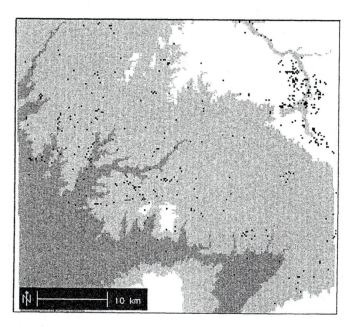

FIGURE 2   Pueblo I period (A.D. 700–900) site distribution overlaid on a simplified digital elevation model. Lighter areas are higher; the middle-elevation zone runs from about 6100′ (1860 m) to 6900′ (2100 m).

These data are of great intrinsic interest and to our knowledge have not been mapped previously. Figure 2 shows the PI period sites concentrated at relatively high elevations in the northeastern portion of our area (many within the former study area of the Dolores Archaeological Program). Figure 3 shows the PII sites, the most numerous, as relatively ubiquitous, but especially common within the northwest-to-southeast mid-elevation band running diagonally across the study area. Figure 4 shows further contraction within this band and large areas that seem unused in the northern and eastern portions of our study area during the PIII period.

Known problems with the site data include questions of dating, location, function, and coverage. First, each site was assigned to a single 200×200 m cell, even though some may in fact spread over more than one cell.[1] Second, we do not at present have satisfactory measures of site size or estimated population.

---

[1]In the future we may move to a representation of the actual sites as objects (in the object-oriented programming sense of the word) within the model. They could then, if necessary, be entities that cover several cells. Then the agent populations could be compared to site populations, as object attributes to object attributes, rather than having to compare the number of agents to the number of cells holding an appropriate site-type value. Since the prehistoric site objects created would hold data about geographic cell location, they could still be used for spatial analysis, but would not be restricted to this.

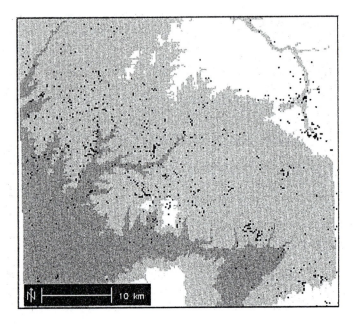

FIGURE 3   Pueblo II period (A.D. 900–1140) site distribution overlaid on a simplified digital elevation model.

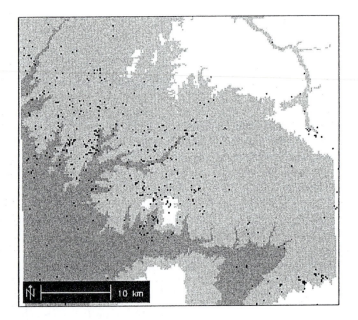

FIGURE 4   Pueblo III period (A.D. 1140–1285) site distribution overlaid on a simplified digital elevation model.

Third, we do not have satisfactory measures of estimated population for many of the sites, so the issue of individual site population is not addressed in the present model. Finally, it will eventually be necessary to identify areas that lack sites because of little or no systematic survey rather than because of unsuitable conditions. At present we simply assume that lacunae in our site database are either absent (extremely unlikely) or random with respect to the resources our agents seek (and, hence, their chosen site locations).

2.3 BUILDING THE DATABASE OF WATER TYPES AND LOCATION

Various sources contributed to the present state of the plane containing water data. Initially, all hydrographic information shown on the twelve USGS 7.5' maps that cover the area was manually digitized using the ARC-INFO GIS package. Subsequent data were added from the Colorado Division of Water Resources database, and the Bureau of Land Management Hydrographic Inventory records.

The USGS maps used were the same hard-copy versions used by Van West to previously build the soils and maize potential data planes. This was done in order to make sure declinations and datums used were consistent. The water data were digitized onto three layers with differing values, so they could easily be considered separately later. First the springs and rivers appearing on the map were entered and coded with a value of three. Then streams shown as solid and therefore considered perennial were added to their own layer and coded with a value of two. Finally, all the streams represented by a sashed or broken lines fell into the category of intermittent, and were added with a code of one.

Additional data on springs were retrieved from the Colorado Division of Water Resources. These data were taken from all the recorded filings for water rights on private lands within the study area. They were recorded by legal location, and needed to be manually plotted onto the USGS maps. Then, their UTM location could be ascertained. This same process was conducted for all the recorded data concerning water sources on public lands and held on file at the Bureau of Land Management. The inclusion of these data increased the number of springs the model considers by a factor of five. Moreover, these data sets include attributes of the water sources beyond just type, most notably flow rates and consistencies. We plan to use some of this information in the next version of the model.

The resultant 36 maps, 12 for each layer, were then edgematched and joined into a single coverage for the entire study area. Drainages and streams that crossed the map boundaries were joined, and it was verified that the union did not alter position of either stream by more than one percent.

The coverages were then converted from their appropriate map projection to UTM, the coordinate system used in the next stage, and converted from the vector-based data layers into a raster (or cell-based) grid. The grid, as before, consisted of 200 rows and 227 columns, where each cell was 200 m square and the grid origin was at UTM 676000mE 4126000mN Zone 12. A background or NODATA value of zero was used. After successfully creating a grid where the highest coded values were used in the case of a cell that encompassed more than one possible value, the grid was then converted to a text file. This file is read by the Swarm simulation and used by the agents to determine water resource availability.

It is likely that gaps remain in the coverage for springs. Areas not considered for modern development or not the target of past projects would be absent from the Colorado Division of Water Resources records (though some of these may be included in the USGS data). Further sources of information concerning water use historically and prehistorically are being pursued in order to add to our knowledge of water availability in the region.

2.4 BRIEF DESCRIPTION OF AGENTS' ACTIONS IN THE CURRENT MODEL

The simulation is implemented in Swarm 1.3, which itself is built in Objective-C, an object-oriented version of the C language.[2] The most important "objects" in this simulation are listed in Table 1, and the principal actions (called methods in Swarm) of the households are listed in Table 2. The basic structure of the model world is a rectangular lattice representing the study area. Each cell in this model consists of a 4-ha square cell, which retrieves the information describing it from the databases describing the world as well as a record of the current number of its households and farm plots. Upon this landscape exist numerous households.

We use the populations from the archaeological record for this area within 40-year periods as estimated by Wilshusen and Varien (1996), and begin the simulations with the population they estimate for the early A.D. 900s. In our study area, this is a population minimum; the large PI populations have departed, apparently for northwestern New Mexico (Wilshusen 1997). At the beginning of the simulation, in year A.D. 901, 154 households are created and placed randomly on the landscape. At initialization parents are the same age, drawn from a random uniform distribution from 16–30, with from 1 to 3 children, depending on their age. Because at least a few agents will land on uninhabitable locations, all are told to move at the end of the creation phase. The criteria the households use in this process are variable according to the parameters we set at the beginning of each run (see Table 3), but if they move, they will always try to find a place (within their potential search radius) with a higher maize productivity than has been realized, on average, at their present location over the last two years. They may also require water of a certain type (permanent springs and rivers [$H_2O\_TYPE=3$], perennial streams [$H_2O\_TYPE=2$], or intermittent streams [$H_2O\_TYPE=1$]) within a specifiable radius ($H_2O\_RAD= 2$ or 5) of their new location. If they cannot find a better location by these

---

[2]Swarm is in the public domain. See http://www.santafe.edu/projects/swarm/ for more information.

TABLE 1   Principal objects in the model and their most important attributes.

AgentModelSwarm:	maintains lists of agents (households) and cells, adds and removes agents;
AgentObserverSwarm:	sets up display of world, probes (windows into agents), and graphs;
DataBase:	reads in various external databases (for example, annual maize yields) or generates random or peaked yields;
Cell:	maintains x, y locations, information on maize potential (read in each year), elevation, water, soils, actual archaeological sites, the list of households in any cell ("settlerSet"), and the number of simulated farming plots (limited to 10/cell); draws itself onto the raster display;
Exchange:	maintains sets of traders, tags, and balances (not implemented in version discussed here);
Agent:	households which contain up to 2 parents, up to 8 children, which carry out the activities ("methods") listed in Table 2.

criteria, they stay where they are. If the production they realize is sufficient to see them through the year, they can try to move again the following spring. Our agents are not strict maximizers. When they move they attempt to go to the most productive location within their search radius that satisfies possible constraints on domestic water, but once they are there, they stay as long as their situation remains tenable.

Households begin their year with spring activities, which include assessing whether or not they need to add or shed plots based on their yields over the last two years and their anticipated caloric needs for the coming year. Planting is done within .4-ha plots; there are potentially 10 such plots in each cell. Households attempt to plant enough to get them through two years, taking into account the storage presently on hand; however, their estimates about their needs are based on the recent climatic conditions and cannot take into account the possibility of changes in the number of people in the household through birth, marriage or death. Moreover, they are limited in the number of plots they are allowed to plant to no more than the number of workers in the household + 1, where workers are generously defined as members older than 7. There are caloric penalties for cultivating plots outside the household's home cell, and for the clearing involved in bringing new plots into cultivation. We drew heavily on Forde (1931) as a source in making estimates as to how long various agricultural activities would require.

TABLE 2   Principal Methods for Agents (households).

Agent creation:	−setTag (unique for each household)
	−setFormationDate
	−setMySwarm (for kinship recognition among households; not implemented in current version)
	−setWorld (world typed as an instance of class Grid2d)
	−setX:Y (sets location of agent and sets up a local 3×3 neighborhood)
	−setParentAges
	−setRandNumKids
Setting agents' internal states:	−setCells
	−setFamilyTag
	−setMaizeStorage
	−setFarmPl
	(most of the above have equivalent—get methods to allow this information to be seen)
Agent actions:	−step (one year per step; resets calorie counter; invokes seasons)
	−spring (calculates changes in number of plots needed; moves if necessary; sheds or adds plots; plants; eats)
	−summer (weeds; eats)
	−fall (weeds; harvests; eats)
	−winter (eats)
	−updateFamily (age members; calculate probability of dying, marriage, and giving birth; evaluate and update state; add or remove people and households)
	−moveHouse (variable radius)
	−searchNeighborhood (used by agents to look for a desirable location when they need to add plots, change residential location, or form a new household through marriage)
	−evalCell (called by searchNeighborhood to evaluate possible cells based on variable criteria)

Each household makes planting decisions (to add or shed plots, or to stay with those planted last year) based upon past harvests in its home cell and on the current potential productivity of its nine neighbors. Depending on its recent local success and whether it can add more local plots, the household might opt to search a wider area and possibly relocate if the internal storage of maize is dangerously low and better areas are available. The household is subject to probabilistic fertility and mortality rules specifying the likelihood of adding or subtracting members (Table 4). New household formation or "marriage" provides a dynamic element to planting and location considerations

TABLE 3 Parameters that may be varied during simulation (those "slanted" were experimentally varied in the results reported below).

Parameter	Value(s) in simulation	Comment
H₂O_TYPE	1, 2	0 in data indicates no data or no known water source; 1 indicates intermittent stream (from USGS 7.5′ Quads); 2 indicates perennial stream; 3 indicates permanent rivers (i.e., Dolores River) and springs
H₂O_RAD	2, 5	search radius (in pixels) for water of type specified in H_2O_TYPE; irrelevant if $NEEDS\_H_2O = 0$
NEEDS_H₂O	0, 1	if 0, agents will disregard water in their locational decisions for residences; if 1, they will look for water of type specified in H_2O_TYPE (or better) within the radius specified in H_2O_RAD
FALLOW_FACTOR	1.3, 1.5	intensity of planting relative to Van West's historic calibration data for maize yields. This acts as a divisor so that 1.5 results in a 33% reduction in yields and 1.3 results in a 23% reduction in yields
DEGRADE_FACTOR	0, 1, 10	0 for no degradation; 1 for degradation only in pinyon-juniper belt; 10 for degradation everywhere
MOV_RAD	20	radius (in pixels) within which households will search for a new location if a residential move is dictated by their state
BUD_OFF	MOV_RAD/2	radius searched around parent household when a new household is formed via marriage
STATE_GOOD	0.10	increases fertility and decreases mortality relative to our standard life table (see Table 4) by this proportion when agents are experiencing good yields and meeting storage goals. Applied to households in states 2 or 3.
STATE_BAD	−0.10	decreases fertility and increases mortality relative to our standard life table (see Table 4) by this proportion when agents are experiencing poor yields and not meeting storage goals. Applied to households in state 0.
HOUSE_LIMIT	400	max n households per cell
PLOTS	10	max plots of .4 ha (about 1 ac) per cell
STORAGE_DECR	0.1	maize decrement from year to year in storage due to spoilage, use for seed, etc.

TABLE 3   (continued)

Parameter	Value(s) in simulation	Comment
BASE_CAL_MAN	70820	1872 Cal * 91.25 days; base estimate for a 3-month season, drawing on Wing and Brown (1979:17–72) for completely sedentary people
BASE_CAL_WOM	142350	1560 Cal * 91.25 days; as above, for women
BASE_CAL_KID	91250	as above, for children
WORK_CAL_MAN	240	caloric increments per hour work for men
WORK_CAL_WOM	200	caloric increments per hour work for women
WORK_CAL_KID	92	caloric increments per hour work for children
MAIZE_KG_CAL	3560	kcal per kg maize
MAIZE_PER	0.6	prop. of calories in diet assumed to come from maize

since neighbors will influence how much available land there is for planting in any local environment. Children greater than 14 years old get married with a probability of 0.8 (each year until married), and move away upon marriage with a probability of 0.5. If they stay they find the best nearby location, where "best" and "nearby" are subject to experimental variation. Children are not differentiated by sex in the model.[3]

Summer household activities now include weeding, and fall activities are weeding and harvesting. In the winter households at present have only to eat maize, as they also do in all other seasons. All work contributes to household caloric needs. At the end of the year household storage and demographic parameters are updated, new households are formed, and the condition or "state" of the household is also evaluated. The result of this evaluation influences birth and death probabilities within the household, and household decisions to add or shed plots, or relocate, in the coming spring (Table 5).

2.5   MODELING DEGRADATION

We use the "DEGRADE_FACTOR" to simulate reduction in maize production under continuous farming in a specific location. If DEGRADE_FACTOR is set to 10, or if DEGRADE_FACTOR is set to 1 and the cell in question is in the pinyon-juniper belt, a cell slowly loses up to half of its potential productivity if it is under more than 20% cultivation. It loses productivity at the rate of 10% per year if it is completely farmed (all 10 of the available .4 ha plots are under cultivation), at the rate of 1.25% per year if only 30% is farmed, and at intermediate rates that are a linear function of the percentage under

---

[3]For this reason, we double Weiss' age-specific birth rates in our Table 4, since his rates report the probability that a mother in a specific age category will bear a daughter.

TABLE 4   Mortality and Fertility Schedules adopted from Weiss' (1979:156) 27.5–55.0 Model Table.

Age	Age-Specific Probability of Dying	Age-Specific Birth Rates (Females)[a]
<1	.2330	0
3	.1400	0
8	.1000	0
13	.0735	0
18	.1305	.098
23	.1336	.264
28	.1367	.264
33	.1400	.214
38	.1432	.148
43	.1466	.062
48	.1500	.012
53	.1536	0
58	.1879	0
63	.2513	0
>64	1.0	0

[a]No woman, however, may have more than 8 children.

TABLE 5   Factors affecting calculation of state and adding or shedding plots for households.

	Condition of Household (HH) Storage in Winter after Harvest		
Average of household production for last 2 years	≤ next year's anticipated needs	> next year's anticipated needs but < maximum storage	> next year's anticipated needs and ≥ maximum storage
≤ next year's anticipated needs	HH desperate; search widely (radius MOVE_RAD) for different plot and residence location (state 0)	HH unhappy; search locally (radius 1) for additional .4-ha parcel (state 1)	HH overproducing; shed one plot (state 3)
> next year's anticipated needs	HH unhappy; search locally for additional .4-ha parcel (state 1)	HH satisfied; no search needed for additional parcels (state 2)	HH overproducing; shed one plot (state 3)

cultivation. If 10% or less is farmed, cells regain their potential productivity at the rate of 1% per year. If exactly 20% of the cell is under cultivation, production remains unchanged. These potential reductions due to degradation act as multipliers for the cell-specific paleoproductivity data read in for each year; they do not displace the climatic signal but rather modify it.

These rates are simply experimental parameters and have little empirical basis. In an analysis of Dolores-area soils, Decker and Petersen (1986) have suggested on the basis of very sparse data that the sorts of cropping systems employed by the Anasazi would probably not have depleted local soils of major nutrients, although field rotations might have been useful in mitigating weed infestations and crop disease. On the other hand, Sandor and Gersper (1988) seem to have shown that prehistoric agriculture in highland south-central New Mexico resulted in nutrient depletion that remains unabated today, 600 years after the cessation of cultivation. Moreover, the study by Force and Howell cited above seems to demonstrate that many sediments, probably including once-fertile topsoils, were being repositioned downslope during the occupation of our study area.

The decision to limit degradation in one set of runs to the pinyon-juniper belt attempts to implement suggestions by Matson et al. (1988), Kohler

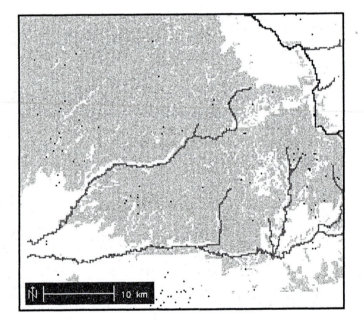

FIGURE 5   Water sources and area subject to degradation when Degrade_Factor=1 (light gray). Permanent water (type 3; Dolores River and the known springs) shown in black; perennial water (type 2; mainly McElmo Creek and Yellow Jacket Canyon) shown in medium gray.

(1992), and others that mesa-top dry farming was typically extensive in nature and involved short-term use of plots cleared by burning which were quickly depleted of nutrients, water, and topsoil reserves. We identified a set of soils that we thought would be most heavily impacted by such practices. These soils, as a group, tend to support a pinyon-juniper vegetation, are on mesa tops or are thin and rocky and on areas with relatively steep slopes. Their distribution is shown in Figure 5 along with the water sources coded as types 2 and 3.

2.6 DISPLAY AND ANALYSIS TOOLS AND TECHNIQUES

At this stage in our cycle of model development and testing, we are interested in seeing how well various combinations of parameters perform in reproducing the partially known site distribution and the estimated paleodemographic trajectory for the study area. We have two types of tools available to assess the performance of the model with different sets of parameters. The first is a rich set of tools available through Swarm's graphical user interface. We presently build a two-dimensional map display showing the locations of the simulated households relative to the known sites of various periods and various environmental parameters, and three graphs, which show:

- the simulated number of households relative to the estimated actual numbers;
- the average maize production being realized by the simulated households relative to that across the entire landscape; and
- the average number of (.4-ha) plots that each household has, and the average number of people in each household.

We also build additional two-dimensional maps that cumulate the occupational history for each cell across whatever period we choose. Swarm also provides the capability of "probing" each cell and each agent during the simulation to see whatever internal states we might find useful to monitor. Taken together these tools are very helpful in debugging a model and in building an intuition for its behavior.

For more extended and less anecdotal analyses we also write to external files:

- the cumulated history of occupation from A.D. 910 to 1140 to compare with the PII site distribution[4];
- the cumulated history of occupation from A.D. 1140 to 1285 to compare with the PIII site distribution; and
- annual simulated population size and the other data automatically graphed during the simulation, noted above.

---

[4]Settlement data from A.D. 901–909 are discarded, since they contain many transient locations as households seek acceptable locations by the current criteria.

In the current model, we stop the simulation at 1287. For this chapter, 30 different combinations of parameters have been explored (Table 6). Only one run, with the same random seed each time, has been attempted for each of these combinations. The variability in results using different seeds has not been explored thoroughly, but seems to be small in general, becoming smaller as household search radii become larger and as any single run progresses though time.

The output maps of cumulated occupation histories are matrices with 227 columns and 200 rows, with the number of household-years that cell was occupied in the period of interest stored in each element. Using a GIS (GRASS) we first processed these maps to change all numbers greater than 0 to 1; since we presently do not have population size or duration of occupation estimates for our actual sites such data become irrelevant too in our simulated data set.

We then multiply these maps with a version of the actual site maps that had been processed to store the distance to the closest actual site in each period. The new map then stores, in each cell, the distance to the closest (say, PII) site, or a zero in the case where no site is simulated for that cell. For each period these distances are summed across the map and divided by the number of cells containing simulated sites. The resultant measure is the mean distance of all simulated sites to the closest actual PII or PIII site. The smaller these distances, the more accurately the decision rules in question reproduce the pattern of actual occupation (as measured simply by structural site presence or absence). Without further examination, even a perfect fit would not be sufficient evidence to claim that we have reproduced the actual decision rules, since, even in our limited explorations, we have discovered different decision rules that produce exactly the same pattern of occupation.

2.7 SUMMARY

We have conducted 30 experimental runs, testing 15 different sets of site location rules on landscapes tuned to two different productivity levels using the FALLOW_FACTOR parameter. For comparison we also generated two sets of random locations, one, with 1,219 cells, for comparison against the simulated PII locations, and the other, with 1,067 cells, for comparison against the simulated PIII locations. These have been chosen to match the average number of cells occupied during the simulations of the PII and PIII periods, respectively.

In modeling site location relative to dry-farming opportunities and water, we have tried to account for the most common and calorically expensive activities of these farmers. The degradation scenarios begin to consider the locations of more ephemeral resources such as topsoil, soil nutrients, and, more indirectly, wood for fuel and construction. We simply ignore a wealth of other possible subsistence-related, economic, and social criteria that undoubtedly impinged on real decisions. The simulated locations provide a first approximation to the locations that would have been chosen if access to dry-farming

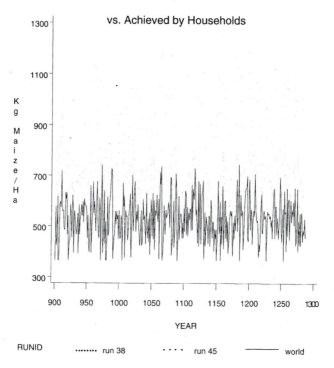

FIGURE 6 Average maize production in kg achieved per ha farmed by households in runs 38 and 45 (dotted lines) relative to potential production rates on the landscape as a whole (solid line).

possibilities and (variably) domestic water were primary considerations in site location. To the extent that the actual sites were near our simulated locations, we consider them to have been efficiently located relative to those resources.

3 RESULTS

The first unexpected thing we discovered is that runs 39–41 yield results identical to runs 30–32, as was also the case for runs 45–47 and 54–56. This is because, as we learned, there are no locations more than 5 cells from a type 1 (or better) water source on this landscape with production sufficiently high to cause agents to locate there. If having an ephemeral water source within 1 km is sufficient, water can be ignored as a locational criterion.

TABLE 6 Parameter combinations explored in these experiments (see Table 3 for definitions of parameters).

FALLOW. FACTOR	NEEDS. H_2O	RADIUS. H_2O	H_2O_TYPE ($\geq$)	DEGRADE. FACTOR	Run #[a]	Type Designator[b]
1.5	0	-	-	0	30	P
1.5	0	-	-	1	31	P & D1
1.5	0	-	-	10	32	P & D10
1.5	1	2	1	0	33	P & W1_R2
1.5	1	2	1	1	34	P & W1_R2 & D1
1.5	1	2	1	10	35	P & W1_R2 & D10
1.5	1	2	2	0	36	P & W2_R2
1.5	1	2	2	1	37	P & W2_R2 & D1
1.5	1	2	2	10	38	P & W2_R2 & D10
1.5	1	5	1	0	39	P & W1_R5
1.5	1	5	1	1	40	P & W1_R5 & D1
1.5	1	5	1	10	41	P & W1_R5 & D10
1.5	1	5	2	0	42	P & W2_R5
1.5	1	5	2	1	43	P & W2_R5 & D1
1.5	1	5	2	10	44	P & W2_R5 & D10
1.3	0	-	-	0	45	P
1.3	0	-	-	1	46	P & D1
1.3	0	-	-	10	47	P & D10
1.3	1	2	1	0	48	P & W1_R2
1.3	1	2	1	1	49	P & W1_R2 & D1
1.3	1	2	1	10	50	P & W1_R2 & D10
1.3	1	2	2	0	51	P & W2_R2
1.3	1	2	2	1	52	P & W2_R2 & D1
1.3	1	2	2	10	53	P & W2_R2 & D10
1.3	1	5	1	0	54	P & W1_R5
1.3	1	5	1	1	55	P & W1_R5 & D1
1.3	1	5	1	10	56	P & W1_R5 & D10
1.3	1	5	2	0	57	P & W2_R5
1.3	1	5	2	1	58	P & W2_R5 & D1
1.3	1	5	2	10	59	P & W2_R5 & D10

[a]runs 1-28 were reported in the original oral version of this paper, but due to a modified search algorithm are not strictly comparable.
[b]used in figures 8 and 9.

TABLE 7   Measures of Model Performance in these experiments (see Table 3 for definitions of parameters). Boxed cells designate minima for distance measures.

RUN #	Maximum Population in Households (cf. 2828)	Year Maximum reached (cf. 1240–1285)	Mean Distance (km) from simulated to real sites, A.D. 910–1139	Mean Distance (km) from simulated to real sites, A.D. 1140–1285
30	3534	1274	1.11	1.54
31	1412	1119	1.06	1.43
32	775	1131	1.17	1.79
33	3435	1199	1.06	1.48
34	1407	1132	1.00	1.57
35	760	1131	1.12	1.75
36	2205	1277	1.22	1.71
37	681	1127	1.11	1.72
38	412	1132	1.20	1.89
39	3534	1274	1.11	1.54
40	1412	1119	1.06	1.43
41	775	1131	1.17	1.79
42	2121	1274	1.14	1.71
43	849	1131	1.09	1.92
44	618	1127	1.06	1.68
45	4338	1199	1.11	1.59
46	2059	1132	1.05	1.45
47	1714	1132	1.08	1.75
48	4102	1286	1.10	1.49
49	2322	1132	1.01	1.45
50	1910	1132	1.10	1.73
51	3391	1287	1.26	1.76
52	1608	1274	1.20	1.82
53	733	1132	1.20	1.80
54	4338	1199	1.12	1.59
55	2059	1132	1.05	1.46
56	1714	1132	1.08	1.75
57	3467	1284	1.20	1.77
58	1723	1127	1.22	1.83
59	1717	1275	1.17	1.89
Random	–	–	1.62	2.23

3.1   MAIZE PRODUCTION HISTORIES

Because some of highest-producing lands are not very close to water of type 2 or 3, the average maize production that households can achieve on this landscape, in these models, depends on whether they are constrained to live near water of type 2 or 3, and also on whether they deplete part or all of the landscape as they use it. If households are severely enough constrained, they will reproduce less, since they spend more time in state 0 (Table 5), where their mortality is slightly inflated, and their natality suppressed, relative to the rates in Table 4. The magnitude of this effect is shown in Figure 6, which compares the average maize production (in kg/ha) achieved by households in run 45, which offered the least constraints, and run 38, which imposed the most. Even in run 38, however, households produce more per hectare farmed than they would were they locating themselves randomly relative to production opportunities (solid line, Figure 6).

3.2   POPULATION TRAJECTORIES

The possible combinations of the parameter values identified in Table 6 therefore result in markedly different population histories, varying from a low maximum population of 412 in run 38 to more than 4,300 households in runs 45 and 54 (see Table 7 and Figure 7). Runs 30 and 45, in which households required maize production only, result in the highest populations for given levels of Fallow_factor. Adding additional settlement constraints generally result in lower populations, with models requiring settlement within 2 cells of a water source of type 2 or greater, and models in which households engender degradation wherever they farm, resulting in the lowest populations.

All models result in population increases in the early-to-mid-A.D. 900s, after which population growth ceases or slows dramatically in the most severely constrained models on the less productive landscape. In models with degradation, population usually peaks in the early-to-mid-1100s. Populations in models without degradation peak in either the late 1100s or the mid-to-late-1200s. None of the runs resulted in a dramatic decrease of population in the late A.D. 1200s, as seen in the record, although in several runs populations decline slightly in the 1280s.

3.3   SETTLEMENT PATTERNS

In general, Table 7 shows that the less productive landscapes (where "Fallow_factor" was set to 1.5) result in a better fit to the settlement pattern, suggesting that scaling up production allows simulated households to live in some places where they could not in fact have successfully farmed. The mean distances from the simulated to the actual sites for both landscape settings are compared in Figures 8 and 9 for each of the 15 sets of locational rules.

For both the PII and PIII periods, our agents use a set of locations that are markedly closer to the actual sites than are the same number of random

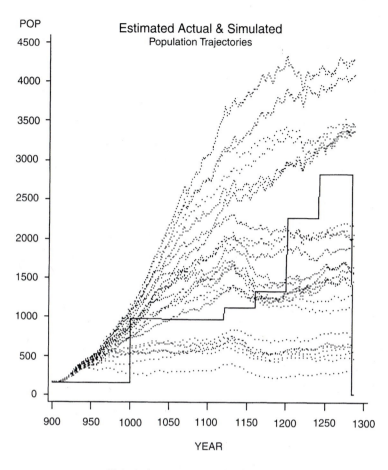

POP

Estimated Actual & Simulated
Population Trajectories

YEAR

Trajectories on more productive landscapes
Shown with more closely spaced dots

FIGURE 7 Estimated actual (solid line) and simulated population trajectories (in number of households). Runs with FALLOW_FACTOR set to 1.5 are shown with widely spaced dots.

points. Comparison of the two figures shows that the worst models for the PII period performed better than the best models for the PIII period.

For both periods, the simple model in which agents are constrained only to live near the best dry-farming land provides relatively good results. In both cases, to our surprise, models in which location is constrained only by ephemeral (or better) water sources often provide a better fit than models in which agents required a perennial (or permanent) source. We have not attempted to differentiate among the models to see if the fits were statistically different.

Dist (m)

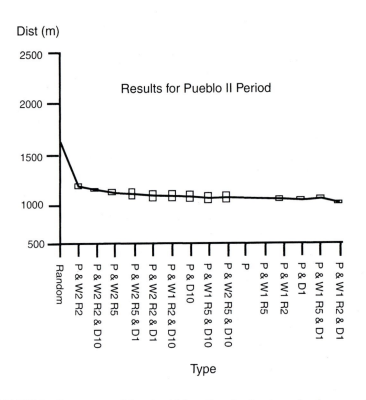

FIGURE 8 Fit generated by the 15 locational rulesets on landscapes at two levels of productivity, and a set of random points, to the known PII sites. Y axis shows average distance in m from each cell occupied in the simulation between A.D. 910 and 1139 to the nearest cell with an actual PII site.

For the PII period, the best fit is provided by runs 34 and 49, in which agents are constrained to be within 2 cells (.4 km) of a type 1 or better water source, and are subject to degradation if they are within the area shaded in Figure 5. The errors made by the run providing the best fit (34) are mapped in Figure 10 in white and light gray. In general this model performs well in the large (dark) central and eastern portion of the study area, but somewhat overestimates sites in the north-central and south-central areas.

The next-best models for the PII period are the best models for the PIII period. These constrain agents to live within 1 km of a type 1 or better water source, which is to say anywhere that also has a reasonable productivity, but also with the condition that when they farm within the shaded area of Figure 5 their fields will be subject to degradation. Figure 11 has been produced to be numerically and graphically comparable to Figure 10. By contrast, however, Figure 10 shows that run 31 greatly overestimates the number of PIII sites through a large swath of the northern and eastern study area and, throughout

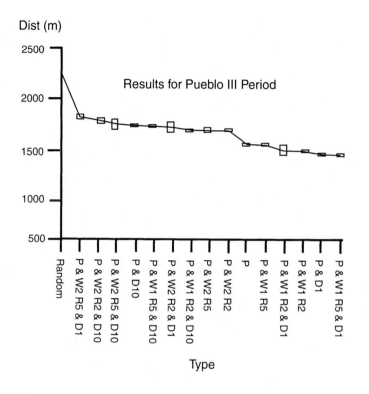

FIGURE 9 Fit generated by the 15 locational rulesets on landscapes at two levels of productivity, and a set of random points, to the known PIII sites. Y axis shows average distance in m from each cell occupied in the simulation between A.D. 1140 and 1285 to the nearest cell with an actual PIII site.

nearly all our range, provides a poorer fit to the actual site distribution. The white corridor in the southeastern portion of the figure is a fair mapping of Montezuma Valley and U.S. Highway 666; the white areas to the north are the forested uplands of the Dolores Rim. The model fits better in the incised canyon and mesa country of the central and western portions of the study area.

Models in which agents are closely or loosely tethered to type 2 or better water sources perform poorly in both periods, as did models in which the agents degrade all locations equally.

3.4 SUMMARY OF RESULTS

Any variation of this model we attempted does better—probably significantly better—than the random model in predicting site location; all models for the PII period perform better than any model for the PIII period. Paleoproduc-

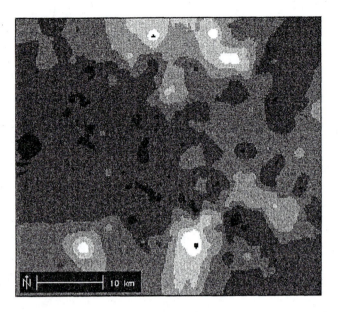

FIGURE 10 Surface generated from measures of distance between cells occupied between A.D. 910 and 1139 in run 34 and the known PII sites. Lighter areas indicate poorer fits (longer distances).

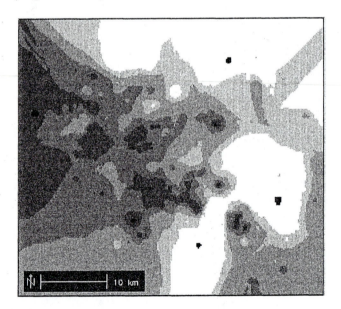

FIGURE 11 Surface generated from measures of distance between cells occupied between A.D. 1140 and 1285 in run 31 and the known PIII sites. Lighter areas indicate poorer fits (longer distances).

tivity is the single most significant explanatory variable; alone it reduces the mean distance between simulated sites and real sites an average of 31% for the PII period and 30% for the PIII period.

Surprisingly, requiring agents to locate near a type 2 or better water source never improves results over the paleoproductivity models. The best models for the PII period constrain households to live within 2 pixels of a type 1 or better water source. The best models for the PIII period ignore water entirely (or constrain households only to live within 5 pixels of a type 1 or better source, which amounts to the same thing).

Models in which households degrade all locations equally always result in a poorer fit to the known settlements than result from requiring households to track productivity alone. In both the PII and PIII cases, however, the best-fitting models are those in which households did degrade locations in the belt defined in Figure 5.

4 DISCUSSION

Undoubtedly some of our results are due to weaknesses in our empirical database. Perhaps we would have better results for models requiring perennial or permanent water if we had a better mapping of springs, including knowledge about when in prehistory springs were active. (We must also add lists of known constructed reservoirs, many of which appear to have been first constructed in the PII period [Wilshusen et al. 1997], to our database.) Some of our apparent errors of fit may result from growing sites in areas where sites in fact exist but have not been recorded. There may also be some systematic overestimation of production (and hence population) in the upper portions of the study area, if these were differentially affected by high-frequency short-growing seasons, or deleterious low-frequency change poorly reflected in the tree-ring data. Moreover, in the early A.D. 900s our agents confront a landscape with no history of use; in fact, as Figure 2 shows, the northern portions of the study area had been abandoned recently by large populations. We do not take into account any degradation due to this occupation.

The improvement in fit caused by forcing degradation in the pinyon-juniper zone is interesting but needs to be examined more carefully in future work. In our model degradation has two somewhat contradictory effects. First, it increases local mobility, resulting in more cells occupied in the degrading area. Households that would otherwise complacently persist are forced to move. This effect allows the model to better match the relatively dense settlement in fact found in this zone. At the same time local degradation slightly suppresses local population growth by keeping more households in state 0, where fertility is slightly depressed and mortality increased (Tables 4 and 5), and by keeping fewer in states 2 and 3, which have the opposite effect. This has the opposite (but probably weaker) effect on the number of occupied cells in this zone. A much more powerful test of our models, for this and other parameters, would be to compare the simulated household-years with a measure of household-years estimated for the actual sites. This unfortunately is impossible at present. We need better measurements of the known archaeological record to improve our metric for determining the best models.

5 CONCLUSIONS

Despite these problems we can draw a number of legitimate if tentative conclusions from this work. First and most apparent is that *either* the importance of dry farming was decreasing through the PII/PIII periods, or that, for some other reason, the PIII farmers were accepting inefficient locations relative to their fields. The latter could be the case, for example, if water sources were becoming much more limited on the landscape, or if social or economic considerations dictated that community members live in face-to-face circumstances. The relatively minor role played by the better (known) water sources in our models somewhat weakens the argument that late sites were first and foremost protecting water sources. Still, we can not eliminate this argument until we can differentiate between habitations and fieldhouses in evaluating our model performance (since it is probable that only habitations require dependable domestic water) and until we have more confidence in our mapping of water resources.

Second, and somewhat more speculatively, we suggest that the mid-1100s cessation in population growth in many of the models with degradation may accurately represent both the comfortable maximum for dry farmers on this landscape, and the approximate time at which that might have been reached. The fact that we do not reproduce the observed subsequent population growth in these models may reflect the fact that our agents cannot intensify; they can, in effect, only dry farm. The difference between the actual population curve and the family of curves peaking in the early-to-mid-1100s estimates the importance of the population size effect resulting from the increasingly active water and sediment management techniques, including floodplain farming, of the last 150 years of occupation. Opportunities for this type of farming are greatest in the incised canyon and mesa portions of our area, in which our PIII models perform adequately. The possibility that these changes may have been precipitated as much by degradation of the dry-farming niche as by climate change is perhaps slightly strengthened by our results. If the suitable portions of the uplands had lost their attractiveness after centuries of dry farming, farming innovations such as check dams, terraces, and increased use of the conveniently aggrading floodplains were perhaps the only alternatives to long-distance migration.

6 FUTURE DIRECTIONS

Aside from the obvious high-priority work to be done with the database of archaeological sites to sharpen our understanding of their temporal placement, function, and size, and other empirical work on the database of water sources, our primary area of research in the immediate future will be to examine the effect exchange relationships have upon the formation of larger social groups. Now that a reasonable model of agent planting and movement has been constructed, we can begin to endow agents with balanced reciprocity behaviors and adaptive encodings of exchange, placing the households into social and economic networks of other (related and unrelated) households. These networks will be flexible enough to evolve according to agent interactions and changes in the world environment.

We share with many other members of the modeling community, and contributors to this volume, a desire to move beyond the deterministic agents used here to agents who can learn, who can emulate successful neighbors, and who can draw on and modify a domain of norms and concepts that they share with other agents. Although agent-based modeling has many advantages, it is also important to realize that real societies are not composed of uncoordinated atoms. Starting from there, however, assuredly will help us to understand how coordination arises.

ACKNOWLEDGMENTS

The original paleoproductivity data planes that provide so much of the dynamism for this model were generated by Carla Van West with support from the Wenner-Gren Foundation for Anthropological Research (grant 4799). The original coding for the "village" simulation was undertaken as a prototype Swarm application by Eric Carr when he was in residence at the Santa Fe Institute, and immediately afterwards, with support from the National Center for Preservation Technology and Training (grant R-47 to Kohler). Since then additional coding has been completed by Eric Nelson (University of Illinois), Kresl, and Kohler. Kresl is responsible for adding the databases on actual site distributions, kindly provided for our use by Victoria Atkins of the Anasazi Heritage Center, Dolores, Colorado, and for developing the water distribution data, which involved a great deal of hand work and archival research. Bureau of Land Management hydrologist Dennis Murphy, Montrose, Colorado, was a great help in acquiring and interpreting these data sets. We had advice on demographic matters from Alan Swedlund, University of Massachusetts-Amherst, and very helpful comments on a first draft from Lorene Yap. When we had problems installing Swarm on our H-P, we got generous assistance from Rick Riolo of the Program for the Study of Complex Systems at the University of Michigan. At critical times we have received help and support from other members of the Swarm Hive, especially Chris Langton (Swarm-Corp) and Marcus Daniels (Santa Fe Institute). Figure 1 was drafted by Sarah Moore of Pullman. Thanks everyone.

REFERENCES

Bradley, Bruce A.
1992 Excavations at Sand Canyon Pueblo. *In* The Sand Canyon Archaeological Project: A Progress Report. William D. Lipe, ed. Pp. 79–97. Occasional Papers 2. Cortez, CO: Crow Canyon Archaeological Center,

Burns, B. T.
1983 Simulated Anasazi Storage Behavior Using Crop Yields Reconstructed from Tree-Ring Records, A.D. 652–1968. 2 vols. Ph.D. Dissertation, University of Arizona. Ann Arbor, MI: University Microfilms.

Cordell, Linda S., David E. Doyel, and Keith W. Kintigh
1994 Processes of Aggregation in the Prehistoric Southwest. *In* Themes in Southwest Prehistory. George J. Gumerman, ed. Pp. 109–133. Santa Fe, NM: School of American Research Press.

Decker, Kenneth W., and Kenneth Lee Petersen
1986 Sediment and Chemical Analyses of Soil Conservation Service Designated Soils. *In* Dolores Archaeological Program: Final Synthetic Report. D. A. Breternitz, C. K. Robinson, and G. T. Gross, comp. Pp. 133–146. Denver, CO: Bureau of Reclamation Engineering and Research Center.

Force, Eric, and Wayne Howell
1997 Holocene Depositional History and Anasazi Occupation in McElmo Canyon, Southwestern Colorado. Arizona State Museum Archaeological Series 188. Tucson, AZ: The University of Arizona.

Forde, C. D.
1931 Hopi Agriculture and Land Ownership. Journal of the Royal Anthropological Institute of Great Britain and Ireland 61:357–405.

Kelley, Jeffery P.
1996 Woods Canyon Pueblo: A Late Pueblo III Period Canyon-Oriented Site in Southwest Colorado. Unpublished M.A. Thesis, Department of Anthropology, Washington State University, Pullman.

Kohler, Timothy A.
1992 Prehistoric Human Impact on the Environment in the Upland North American Southwest. Population and Environment: A Journal of Interdisciplinary Studies 13:255–268.

Kohler, Timothy A., and Eric Carr
1997 Swarm-Based Modeling of Prehistoric Settlement Systems in Southwestern North America. *In* Proceedings of Colloquium II, UISPP, XIIIth Congress, Forli, Italy, Sept 1996. I. Johnson and M. North, eds. Sydney University Archaeological Methods Series 5. Sydney, Australia: Sydney University.

Kohler, Timothy A., and Meredith H. Matthews
1988 Long-Term Anasazi Land Use and Forest Reduction: A Case Study from Southwest Colorado. American Antiquity 53:537–564.

Kohler, Timothy A., Janet D. Orcutt, Kenneth L. Petersen, and Eric Blinman
1986 Anasazi Spreadsheets: The Cost of Doing Agricultural Business in Prehistoric Dolores. *In* Dolores Archaeological Program: Final Synthetic Report. D. A. Breternitz, C. K. Robinson, and G. T. Gross, comp. Pp. 525–538. Denver, CO: Bureau of Reclamation Engineering and Research Center.

Kohler, Timothy A., and Carla R. Van West
1996 The Calculus of Self-Interest in the Development of Cooperation: Sociopolitical Development and Risk Among the Northern Anasazi. *In* Evolving Complexity and Environment: Risk in the Prehistoric Southwest. Joseph A. and Bonnie B. Tainter, eds. Pp. 169–196. Santa Fe Institute Studies in the Sciences of Complexity, Proceedings Vol. XXIV. Reading, MA: Addison-Wesley.

Matson, R. G., W. D. Lipe, and W. R. Haase IV
1988 Adaptational Continuities and Occupational Discontinuities: The Cedar Mesa Anasazi. Journal of Field Archaeology 15:245–264.

Orcutt, Janet D.
1986 Settlement Behavior Modeling Synthesis. *In* Dolores Archaeological Program: Final Synthetic Report. D. A. Breternitz, C. K. Robinson, and G. T. Gross, comp. Pp. 539–576. Denver, CO: Bureau of Reclamation Engineering and Research Center.

Orcutt, J. D., E. Blinman, and T. A. Kohler
1990 Explanations of Population Aggregation in the Mesa Verde Region prior to A.D. 900. *In* Perspectives on Southwestern Prehistory. Charles Redman and Paul Minnis, eds. Pp. 196–212. Boulder, CO: Westview Press.

Petersen, Kenneth Lee
1988 Climate and the Dolores River Anasazi. Anthropological Papers 113. Salt Lake City, UT: University of Utah.

Sandor, J. and P. L. Gersper
1988 Evaluation of Soil Fertility in Some Prehistoric Agricultural Terraces in New Mexico. Agronomy Journal 80:846–850.

Schlanger, Sarah H.
1988 Patterns of Population Movement and Long-Term Population Growth in Southwestern Colorado. American Antiquity 53:773–793.

Schlanger, Sarah H., and R. H. Wilshusen
1993 Local Abandonments and Regional Conditions in the North American Southwest. *In* The Abandonment of Settlements and Regions: Ethnoarchaeological and Archaeological Approaches. C. M. Cameron and S. A. Tomka, eds. Pp. 85–98. Cambridge, UK: Cambridge University Press.

Van West, Carla
    1994 Modeling Prehistoric Agricultural Productivity in Southwestern Colorado: A GIS Approach. Department of Anthropology Reports of Investigations 67. Pullman, WA: Washington State University.

Varien, Mark D.
    1997 New Perspectives on Settlement Patterns: Sedentism and Mobility in a Social Landscape. Unpublished Ph.D Dissertation, Department of Anthropology, Arizona State University, Tempe, AZ.

Varien, Mark D., William D. Lipe, Michael A. Adler, Ian M. Thompson, and Bruce A. Bradley
    1996 Southwestern Colorado and Southwestern Utah Settlement Patterns: A.D. 1100 to 1300. *In* The Prehistoric Pueblo World A.D. 1150–1350. Michael A. Adler, ed. Pp. 86–113. Tucson, AZ: The University of Arizona Press.

Weiss, Kenneth M.
    1973 Demographic Models for Anthropology. Memoirs of the Society for American Archaeology 27.

Wilshusen, Richard H.
    1997 Big Shifts in Small Sites: Changes in Fields, Field Houses, Check Dams, and Other Agricultural Features Between A.D. 760 and 1280 in the Mesa Verde Region. Paper presented at the 62nd Annual Meeting of the Society for American Archaeology, Nashville, TN.

Wilshusen, Richard H., Melissa J. Churchill, and James M. Potter
    1997 Prehistoric Reservoirs and Water Basins in the Mesa Verde Region: Intensification of Water Collection Strategies During the Great Pueblo Period. American Antiquity 62:664–681.

Wilshusen, Richard H. (with the assistance of Mark D. Varien)
    1996 Estimating Prehistoric Population for the Mesa Verde Region: Using New Methods to Interpret Old Data. Report submitted to the Colorado Historical Society, 1300 Broadway, Denver, CO.

Wing, Elizabeth S., and Antoinette B. Brown
    1979 Paleonutrition: Method and Theory in Prehistoric Foodways. New York: Academic Press.

Understanding Anasazi Culture Change Through Agent-Based Modeling

Jeffrey S. Dean
George J. Gumerman
Joshua M. Epstein
Robert L. Axtell
Alan C. Swedlund
Miles T. Parker
Stephen McCarroll

1 INTRODUCTION

Traditional narrative explanations of prehistory have become increasingly difficult to operationalize as models and to test against archaeological data. As such models become more sophisticated and complex, they also become less amenable to objective evaluation with anthropological data. Nor is it possible to experiment with living or prehistoric human beings or societies. Agent-based modeling offers intriguing possibilities for overcoming the experimental limitations of archaeology by representing the behavior of culturally relevant agents on landscapes. Manipulating the behavior of artificial agents on such landscapes allows us to, as it were, "rewind the tape" of sociocultural history and to experimentally examine the relative contributions of internal and external factors to sociocultural evolution (Gumerman and Kohler in press).

Agent-based modeling allows the creation of variable resource (or other) landscapes that can be wholly imaginary or that can capture important aspects of real-world situations. These landscapes are populated with heterogeneous agents. Each agent is endowed with various attributes (e.g., life span, vision, movement capabilities, nutritional requirements, consumption and storage capacities) in order to replicate important features of individuals or relevant social units such as households, lineages, clans, and villages. A set of

Dynamics in Human and Primate Societies, edited by T. Kohler and
G. Gumerman, Oxford University Press, 1999. **179**

anthropologically plausible rules defines the ways in which agents interact with the environment and with one another. Altering the agents' attributes, their interaction rules, and features of the landscape allow experimental examination of behavioral responses to different initial conditions, relationships, and spatial and temporal parameters. The agents' repeated interactions with their social and physical landscapes reveal ways in which they respond to changing environmental and social conditions. As we will see, even relatively simple models may illuminate complex sociocultural realities.

While potentially powerful, agent-based models in archaeology remain unverified until they are evaluated against actual cases. The degree of fit between a model and real-world situations allows the model's validity to be assessed. A close fit between all or part of a model and the test data indicates that the model, albeit highly simplified, has explanatory power. Lack of fit implies that the model is in some way inadequate. Such "failures" are likely to be as informative as successes because they illuminate deficiencies of explanation and indicate potentially fruitful new research approaches. Departures of real human behavior from the expectations of a model identify potential causal variables not included in the model or specify new evidence to be sought in the archaeological record of human activities.

2 THE ARTIFICIAL ANASAZI PROJECT

The Artificial Anasazi Project is an agent-based modeling study based on the Sugarscape model created by Joshua M. Epstein and Robert Axtell (1996), both of The Brookings Institution and the Santa Fe Institute. The project was created to provide an empirical, "real-world" evaluation of the principles and procedures embodied in the Sugarscape model and to explore the ways in which bottom-up, agent-based computer simulations can illuminate human behavior in a real-world setting. In this case, the actual "test bed" is prehistoric Long House Valley in northeastern Arizona, which, between roughly 1800 normalfontB.C. and A.D. 1300, was occupied by the Kayenta Anasazi, a regionally distinct prehistoric precursor of the modern Pueblo cultures of the Colorado Plateau (Figure 1). Archaeological information on the Kayenta Anasazi provides an empirical data set against which simulations of human behavior in Long House Valley can be evaluated. The actual spatiotemporal history is the "target" we attempt to recreate and, hence, explain with an agent-based model. Ultimately, this target is constructed from the research of the Long House Valley Project, a multiyear research effort of the Museum of Northern Arizona and the Laboratory of Tree-Ring Research at The University of Arizona, which primarily involved a 100-percent survey of the valley (Dean et al. 1978). Directly, however, the data were extracted from the Long House Valley database in the computer files of the Southwestern Anthropological Research Group (SARG), an effort at large-scale data accumulation and management and cooperative research (Gumerman 1971; Euler and Gumerman 1978). These data were downloaded from the SARG master file, modified through the elimination of many categories of data deemed extraneous for our purposes, and then imported into the Artificial Anasazi software. These locational and site data serve as the referents against which the simulations are evaluated.

The simulations take place on a landscape (analogous to Epstein and Axtell's Sugarscape) of annual variations in potential maize production values based on empirical reconstructions of low- and high-frequency paleoenvironmental variability in the area. The production values represent as closely as possible the actual production potential of various segments of the Long House Valley environment over the last 1,600 years. On this empirical landscape, the agents of the Artificial Anasazi model play out their lives, adapting to changes in their physical and social environments.

3 CHARACTERISTICS OF THE STUDY AREA

Long House Valley (Figure 1), a topographically discrete, 96 km^2 land form on the Navajo Indian Reservation in northeastern Arizona, provides an intensively surveyed archaeological case study for the agent-based modeling of settlement and economic behavior among subsistence-level agricultural societies in marginal habitats. This area is well suited for such a test for four reasons. First, it is a topographically bounded, self-contained landscape that can be conveniently reproduced in a computer. Second, a rich paleoenvironmental record, based on alluvial geomorphology, palynology, and dendroclimatology (Gumerman 1988), permits the accurate quantitative reconstruction of annual fluctuations in potential agricultural production (in kilograms of maize per hectare). Combined, these factors permit the creation in the computer of a dynamic resource landscape that replicates conditions in the valley. On this landscape, our artificial agents move about, bring new sites under cultivation, form new households, and so on. Third, detailed regional ethnographies provide an empirical basis for generating plausible behavioral rules for the agents. Fourth, intensive archaeological research, involving a 100-percent survey of the area supplemented by limited excavations, creates a database on human behavior during the last 2,000 years that constitutes the real-world target for the modeling outcomes (Dean et al. 1978; Gumerman and Dean 1989). Between roughly 7000 and 1800 normalfontB.C., the valley was sparsely occupied by, first, Paleoindian big game hunters and, second, Archaic hunters and gatherers. The introduction of maize around 1800 normalfontB.C. initiated a long transition to a food-producing economy and the beginning of the Anasazi cultural tradition, which persisted until the abandonment of the area about A.D. 1300. Long House Valley provides archaeological data on economic, settlement, social, and religious conditions among a localized western Anasazi population. The archaeological record of Anasazi farming groups from A.D. 200–1300 provides information on a millennium of sociocultural stasis, variability,

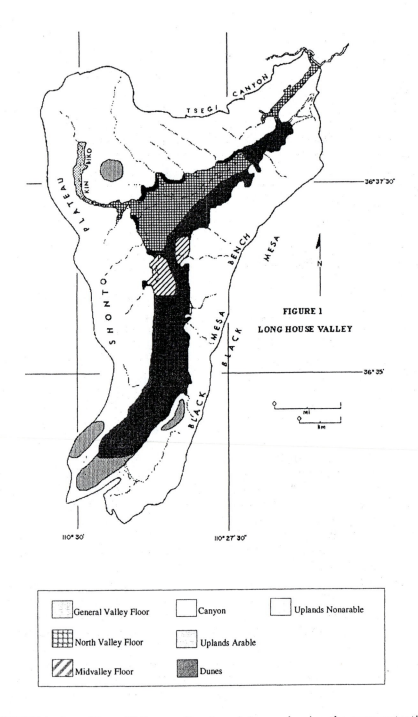

FIGURE 1
LONG HOUSE VALLEY

General Valley Floor
North Valley Floor
Midvalley Floor
Canyon
Uplands Arable
Dunes
Uplands Nonarable

FIGURE 1   Long House Valley, northeastern Arizona, showing the seven potential production zones.

change, and adaptation to which the model can be compared. The valley's geologic history has produced seven different environmental zones (Figure 1) with vastly different productive potentials for domesticated crops and various degrees of suitability for residential occupation. One of these habitats, the Uplands Nonarable zone consists of exposed bedrock and steep, forested colluvial slopes with no farming potential. Different soil and water characteristics impart different agricultural potentials to the remaining habitats, in order of increasing potential productivity the Uplands Arable, General Valley Floor, Midvalley Floor, North Valley Floor and Canyon, and Sand Dunes zones.

Because the local environment is not temporally stable, modern conditions, which include three soil types, heterogeneous bedrock and surficial geology, sand dunes, arroyos, seeps, springs, and varied topography, are only imperfect indicators of the past environmental circumstances that influenced how and where the Anasazi lived and farmed. Accurate representations of these circumstances, however, can be achieved through paleoenvironmental reconstruction. Low- and high-frequency variations in alluvial hydrologic and depositional conditions, effective moisture, and climate have been reconstructed in unprecedented detail using surficial geomorphology, palynology, dendroclimatology, and archaeology. High-frequency climatic variability is represented by annual Palmer Drought Severity Indices (PDSI), which reflect the effects of meteorological drought (moisture and temperature) on crop production (Palmer 1965). Low-frequency environmental variability is characterized primarily by the rise and fall of alluvial groundwater and the deposition and erosion of floodplain sediments. Based on relationships among these variables provided by Van West (1994), these measures of environmental variability are used to create a dynamic landscape of annual potential maize production, in kilograms, for each hectare in the study area for the period A.D. 382 to 1400.

4 CONSTRUCTING THE PRODUCTION LANDSCAPE

Because there are no crop yield data for any nearby or comparable areas, maize production in Long House Valley (LHV) cannot be reconstructed directly from tree growth or from dendroclimatically reconstructed PDSI values, as was done by Burns (1983) and Van West (1994) for southwestern Colorado, which possesses the only reliable dry-farming crop yield data in the entire Southwest. Rather, the integration of information from several different sources was necessary to extrapolate the likely production record. The sources utilized include Burns' (1983) and Van West's (1994) dendroclimatic research and the Dolores Archaeological Project's soils work (Becker and Petersen 1987; Leonhardy and Clay 1985) in southwestern Colorado, E. and T. Karlstrom's (Karlstrom 1983, 1985; Karlstrom and Karlstrom 1986; Karlstrom 1988) soil and geomorphological studies and Lebo's (1991) dendroagricultural research on nearby Black Mesa, Bradfield's (1969, 1971) Hopi farming studies, and Soil Conservation Service (SCS) soils surveys in Apache (Miller and Larsen

1975) and Coconino (Taylor 1983) counties in Arizona. LHV crop yields were estimated by using relationships between PDSI values and maize production worked out for southwestern Colorado by Van West. In order to employ these relationships, the existing PDSI reconstruction for the LHV area (the Tsegi Canyon reconstruction produced by the Tree-Ring Laboratory's Southwest Paleoclimate Project) had to be related to one (or more) of Van West's 113 PDSI reconstructions. Because PDSI is calculated using specific water-holding attributes of the soils involved, LHV soils had to be matched as closely as possible to one (or more) possible southwestern Colorado equivalents.

The first step in matching LHV and Colorado soils involved characterizing the former so that attributes comparable to the latter might be identified. Because there are no soils data from LHV, one or more LHV soils had to be classified in order to acquire the necessary attributes. Soils research by the Black Mesa Archaeological Project identified possible analogs to one LHV soil, that of the area defined as the General Valley Floor environmental zone, hereafter referred to as LHVgensoil. This soil and several Black Mesa soils are clayey units derived principally from the Mancos shale. Furthermore, the Black Mesa soils were equated with T. Karlstrom's x and y chronostratigraphic units, which are coeval with the prehistoric LHV soils of interest here. Using these criteria, it was possible to identify six of E. Karlstrom's profiles that contained units potentially equivalent to LHVgensoil: Profiles 3, 4, and 9 (Karlstrom 1983), and 3, 4, and 5 (Karlstrom 1985) in Moenkopi Wash and Reed Valley, respectively.

Although E. Karlstrom provides considerable information on his soil units, he does not include the critical water-holding data necessary to derive PDSIs. Therefore, we had to identify analogs to his soils that had the requisite water capacity data. This was done by using SCS surveys of Apache and Coconino counties to find shale-derived soils that fell into the same typological classes as the Black Mesa soils: soil families fine, loamy, mixed mesic Typic Camborthids, Typic Haplargids, and Ustollic Haplargids. Potential analogs with adequate water capacity data included the Clovis Soil (Ustollic Haplargid) from Apache County and the Epikom Soil (Lithic Camborthid) from Coconino County. These preliminary identifications were checked against Bradfield's data for soils along Oraibi Wash that should share most characteristics with Black Mesa soils farther up the drainage. These procedures led to the recognition of E. Karlstrom's Ustollic Haplargid x/y alluvial soils from Profiles 3 and 4 (Karlstrom 1983) and 4 and 5 (Karlstrom 1985) as satisfactory analogs for LHVgensoil.

At this point, we intended to use the typological and water capacity characteristics inferred for LHVgensoil to identify one or more analogs among the 113 soils Van West used for PDSI calculations. Two problems arose in this regard. First, the Tsegi PDSI values had been calculated using NOAA's (the National Oceanic and Atmospheric Administration) generic soil moisture values of $1''$ in the first six inches of soil and $5''$ in the rest of the column (the $1''/5''$ standard). These values clearly did not mimic the $1''/10+''$ attributes inferred for LHVgensoil. Two options were open: (1) recalculate PDSI using more realistic water capacity values or (2) find a Colorado analog for the $1''/5''$ default PDSIs. Lacking resources to do the former, we opted for the latter.

Finding a Colorado analog for the default PDSIs involved identifying a soil (or soils) with attributes that mimicked those of the postulated LHVgensoil. Potential analogs had to have the following characteristics: (1) they had to duplicate the LHV soil families, (2) they had to represent the same elevational range as the floor of LHV, roughly 6,000 to 7,000 feet, (3) they had to have a comparable silt-loam-sand composition and shale derivation, and (4) they had to exhibit the default $1''/5''$ water capacity used in calculating the Tsegi PDSIs. The first criterion was rejected because, although Van West gives the series names for the 113 soils she used, she does not give their family assignments. Luckily, the Dolores Archaeological Project provided both series and family names and allowed us to assign family designations to Van West's series names. With this information, it was a simple matter to identify soils that exhibited the four characteristics listed above. Two soils came closest to meeting the criteria: Sharps-Pulpit Loam (R7C) and Pulpit Loam (ROHC), both fine, loamy, mixed mesic Ustollic Haplargids that occur between 6,000 and 7,000 feet in elevation. Fortunately, Van West had chosen each of these soils to represent one of eleven soil moisture classes. The ROHC class came closest to LHVgensoil and was chosen as the Colorado analog for that taxon.

The selection of ROHC as the working analog for LHVgensoil permitted the use of PDSI to estimate annual maize crop yields in LHV. Through a series of statistical operations, Van West calculated the yield of maize in pounds per acre or kilograms per hectare for each representative soil type, including ROHC, under five different growing season conditions: Favorable, Favorable-to-Normal, Normal, Normal-to-Unfavorable, and Unfavorable. She also assigned each yield category a range of PDSI values: Favorable (PDSI ≥ 3.000), Favorable-to-Normal (1.000 to 2.999), Normal (-0.999 to 0.999), Normal-to-Unfavorable (-2.999 to -1.000), and Unfavorable (≤ -3.000). These concordances allow crop yields to be estimated for each PDSI category. It then becomes a relatively "simple" matter to convert the Tsegi PDSI values to LHV maize crop yields.

Before conversion could begin, some way of integrating the LHV PDSI, Hydrologic Curve (HC), and Aggradation Curve (AC) representations of past environmental variability into a single measure useful for estimating crop yield had to be devised. This was necessary because, during periods of rising and stable high water tables, groundwater basically supports crop production and overrides climatic fluctuations. Therefore, there are long periods when PDSI does not adequately represent environmental potential for farming. We handled this issue by generating Adjusted PDSI values that incorporate HC and AC effects on crop production. This was done by assigning arbitrary PDSI values corresponding to Favorable or Favorable-to-Normal conditions during periods of deposition and rising or stable high water tables. At other times, climate is the primary control on crop yield, and straight PDSI values express environmental input. The new series of Adjusted PDSI values reflects this operation. But, this procedure applies only to the General Valley Floor zone of LHV and not to the five other farmable environments in the valley, the North Valley Floor, Midvalley Floor, Canyon, Uplands Arable, and Sand Dunes zones (Figure 1). Because the HC and AC are different for each of the environmental zones, a set of Adjusted PDSI values was created for each of five groups of zones: (1) General Valley Floor, (2) North Valley Floor East and West and Canyons, (3) Midvalley Floor East and West, (4) Shonto Plateau-Black Mesa Uplands Arable, and (5) the Sand Dunes along the northeastern margins of the valley. Each set of Adjusted PDSI values is used for its corresponding environmental zone. The four series of Adjusted PDSI values are then converted to maize crop yields for each hectare in each zone.

The conversion takes place by equating specific crop yields in kg/ha with specific PDSI ranges as indicated in Table 1. Thus, for example, on the General Valley Floor and Midvalley Floor East, a PDSI between 1.000 and 2.999 equals a yield of 824 kg/ha of shelled corn, a PDSI greater than or equal to 3.000 equals a yield of 961 kg/ha, and so forth. This transformation applies only to General Valley Floor and Midvalley Floor East, however, because the other environmental zones have different productivities. For example, the North Valley Floor, Midvalley Floor West, and Canyon zones produce higher yields under identical climatic, hydrologic, and aggradational conditions, while the Arable Uplands produce less. These differences are expressed by increasing the yield for the North Valley Floor-Midvalley Floor West-Canyons zones by 20 percent and decreasing the yield of the Uplands zones by 20 percent relative to the General Valley Floor yield as shown in Table 1. Thus, a PDSI between 1.000 and 2.999 equals crop yields of 988 (North Valley Floor) and 659 (Uplands) kg/ha, and a PDSI $\geq$ 3.000 produces yields of 1153 and 769 kg/ha, respectively. Yields for the particularly favorable dune areas in the North Valley and Midvalley Floor West zones are calculated by increasing the General Valley Floor yields by 25 percent as shown in Table 1. Here, a PDSI between 1.000 and 2.999 equals a crop yield of 1030 kg/ha, and a PDSI $\geq$ 3.000 equals a yield of 1201 kg/ha. Carrying these conversions of Adjusted PDSI values through for each of the environmental zones produces four series of annual crop yield estimates in kg/ha. Multiplying these by the hectarage of each zone produces estimates of total potential crop yield if every bit of land is farmed.

5   AGENT (HOUSEHOLD) ATTRIBUTES

The constructed physical and resource landscape of Long House Valley is the changing environment on which the agents described here act. Artificial agents representing individual households, the smallest social unit consistently definable in the archaeological record, populate the landscape. These household agents have independent characteristics such as age, location, and grain stocks, and shared characteristics such as death age and nutritional need.

TABLE 1 Factors for converting Long House Valley Adjusted PDSI Values to maize crop yields in kilograms/hectare.

ADJUSTED PDSI	MAIZE YIELD (kilograms/hectare)			
	General Valley Floor[a]	North Valley Floor/Can[b]	Upland Areas[c]	Sand Dune Areas[d]
3.00 to ∞	961	1153	769	1201
1.00 to 2.99	824	988	659	1030
−0.99 to 0.99	684	821	547	855
−2.99 to −1.00	599	719	479	749
−∞ to −3.00	514	617	411	642

[a]Used with General Valley Floor Adjusted PDSIs to estimate crop yields for the General Valley Floor and Midvalley Floor East environmental zones.

[b]Used with North Valley Floor and Canyons Adjusted PDSIs to estimate crop yields for the North Valley Floor East and West, Canyon, and Midvalley Floor West environmental zones.

[c]Used with Upland Adjusted PDSIs to estimate crop yields for the Shonto Plateau-Black Mesa Uplands Arable environmental zones.

[d]Used with North Valley Floor East and West and Canyons Adjusted PDSIs to estimate crop yields for the dune areas in the North Valley Floor and Midvalley Floor West environmental zones.

Distinctions between independent and shared characteristics are not always certain. For example, in the current model, nutritional need is the same for all agents but, in other models, nutritional need might be varied stochastically across agents. Agent demographics, nutritional requirements, and marriage characteristics were derived from ethnographic and biological anthropological studies of historic Pueblo groups and other subsistence agriculturalists throughout the world (Hassan 1981; Nelson et al. 1994; Swedlund 1994; Weiss 1973; Wood 1994).

In the archaeological view of Long House Valley, five surface rooms or one pithouse is considered to represent a single household, which, based on numerous archaeological and ethnographic analyses, is assumed to comprise five individuals. In our Artificial Anasazi model, household size is fixed at this number for all households at all times. Each simulated household is conceived to be both matrilineal and matrilocal, and so assumptions governing household formation and movement center on females. Males are included in maize consumption calculations.

Every year, household agents harvest the grain that is available at the location they have chosen to farm, as determined by environmental data and modified by stochastic factors. These factors are intended to grossly approximate location-to-location soil quality variation, as well as year-to-year fluctuations caused by weather, blight, and other factors not available in the data.

The agents then consume their nutritional requirements, 800 kg of maize per year, based on an approximation of individual consumption of 160 kg (560 kcal) per year. Households can store any remaining grain for later consumption, but grain that is not consumed within two years of harvest is lost. At this point households may cease to exist, either because they do not have enough grain to satisfy their nutritional needs or because they have aged beyond a certain maximum, 30 years in the current model. Note that a household "death" is not imagined to represent the literal death of all household members. Instead, it represents that a given household no longer exists as a single unit in the valley. Members might die, but they also might be absorbed by other households or simply migrate out of the valley altogether.

Next, household agents estimate the amount of grain that will be available the following year, based on current year harvest and grain stores. If this amount will not satisfy minimum requirements for a given household, the household moves. Determining how, and thus where, a household moves is a critical factor in designing a model that has a meaningful relationship to the historical record. First, the agent finds a new location to farm. In the current model, agents simply search for the most productive land that is available and within 1,600 m of a water source. Household farmlands each occupy one cell in the model, with each cell comprising one hectare. Household residential locations, or settlements, also occupy one cell. To be considered available, land must be unfarmed and unsettled.

Second, the agent looks for a settlement location. The agent finds and settles on the location nearest the farmland that contains a water source. In the current model, if the closest water source is located in a flood plain, the agent instead occupies the closest location to the water source that is on the border of or outside of the floodplain area.

Note that the requirement that a farmland site be within 1,600 m of a water source is not dictated by an overriding need to farm near a water source; water sources in the context of the model provide potable water suitable for household consumption, and they are not important to agriculture. Rather, the farmland must be near water because proximity to water sources is a critical factor in choosing residence locations and because farmplots must be located within reasonable distances of residences. In fact, farm and residence siting searches are really inseparable parts of single decisions on residence and farm locations. This is one reason households are not initially assigned historical settlement locations. As historical farmland locations are not known, they cannot be supplied as initial conditions for running the model and have to be selected by the agents according to the rules of the model. To attempt to constrain farming location choice by using contextually meaningless and predetermined residence locations would be arbitrary and inconsistent.

Finally, household agents may fission. If a household is older than a specified fission age (16 years), it has a defined probability (0.125) of triggering the formation of a new household through the "marriage" of a female child. This summary value is derived from the combined demographic inputs. The use of a minimum fission age combined with fission probability is designed to approximate the probability a household would have daughters, the time it would take such daughters to reach maturity, and the chances of their finding a mate, conceiving a child, and forming a new household. As discussed for household deaths above, the fission process is not meant to be a strict measure of new births within a household. For instance, fission might partially represent immigration, as new arrivals to the valley combine with existing households.

The above completes the specification of agent attributes. Artificial Anasazi household agents are endowed with behavioral rules governing consumption, reproduction ("fissioning"), movement, the selection of farm and residential sites, and ultimately decisions to abandon LHV, which the actual Anasazi did around 1300. Can we explain all or part of local Anasazi history—including the departure—with agents that recognize no social institutions or property rights (rules of land inheritance), or must such factors be built into the model? At present, our agents do not invoke such considerations; they respond purely to environmental stimuli. These are the simplest plausible rules that we could devise. Both the strengths and weaknesses of these rules will prove revealing.

6 RUNNING THE MODEL

Although the LHV production landscape has been reconstructed for the period A.D. 382 to 1450, our study period runs from A.D. 800 to 1350. The initial agent configuration for each run uses the historically known number of agents but, to be consistent with the agent design, does not use historical settlement locations. Each household executes its full behavioral repertoire (e.g., moving, consuming, reproducing, storing food, and, if need be, leaving) each year. The program tracks household fissions, deaths, grain stocks, and internal demographics. If felicitous decisions are made, the household produces enough food to get through another year; if not, the household runs out of food and is removed from the simulation as a case of either death or emigration.

While a single simulation run may produce plausible and interesting outcomes, many iterations involving altered initial conditions, parameters, and random number generators must be performed in order to assess the model's robustness. Some model outputs (e.g., total population) can be characterized statistically across runs and can be compared to LHV data. Other outputs (e.g., spatial distributions of agents) are not easily characterized statistically, but can be visually compared to real-world patterns.

7 COMPARING THE SIMULATION WITH THE ARCHAEOLOGICAL DATA

Graphical output of the model includes a map for each year of simulated household residence and field locations, which runs simultaneously with a map of the corresponding archaeological and environmental data. These paired maps facilitate comparison of historical and simulated population dynamics and residence locations. Simultaneously, "real time" histograms and time series plots illustrate annual simulated and historical population numbers, zonal aggregation of population, location and size of residences by environmental zone, the simulated amounts of maize stored and harvested, the zonal distribution of simulated field locations, and the number of simulated households that fission, die out, or leave the valley. Figures 2 through 5 illustrate representative results for many simulations, all using the parameter values listed in Table 2. Unless otherwise indicated, the graphs represent mean values for 35 runs, a procedure that characterizes general trends across a number of iterations rather than the idiosyncrasies of individual runs.

Population size curves representing iterations of the model and archaeological estimates are shown in Figure 2(a) and 2(b), respectively, at different scales to facilitate comparison. The stepped appearance of the archaeological population graph is an artifact of the estimation procedure in which ceramic dates for sites begin and end on full, half, or quarter centuries (e.g., 1000, 1150, or 1275). Simulated population typically tracks the archaeological population trajectory; that is, both exhibit similar relative variation. If it were smoothed, the archaeological curve would even more closely resemble the simulated graph. Each shows an increase up to about 900, a leveling off in the tenth century, a major growth surge between 1000 and 1050, another leveling from 1050 to 1150, a drop in the middle 1100s, resurgence in the late 1100s to a peak in the thirteenth century, and a major crash in the late 1200s. The simulated and archaeological curves also exhibit important qualitative differences including a greater and more prolonged simulated population decline in the twelfth century, a more immediate, more gradual, and relatively higher post-1150 recovery in the archaeological population, a slightly earlier thirteenth century decline in the simulated curve, and the failure of the simulated curve to drop to zero at 1300. While there is general qualitative agreement between these two curves, there are significant quantitative disparities in the household numbers and settlement sizes. Both total population (Figure 2) and individual settlement sizes (Figure 3) are much larger in the typical simulation than what we infer to have been the actual case. Population aggregation occurs earlier and with greater frequency in the typical simulation than in the historical record (Figure 3).

Although simulated Long House Valley population aggregation (Figure 3) departs quantitatively from the archaeological situation, it is nonetheless quite revealing about settlement dynamics. The simulation's tendency to generate aggregation of greater magnitude than that of the study area is evident in the large number of households distributed across settlements larger than 40 households beginning in the early 1100s. This pattern varies considerably from the real situation in which a few large sites appeared only after 1200. The peak at 1180 means that nearly 800 simulated households were living in fewer than 20 sites of 40 or more households, when during that period

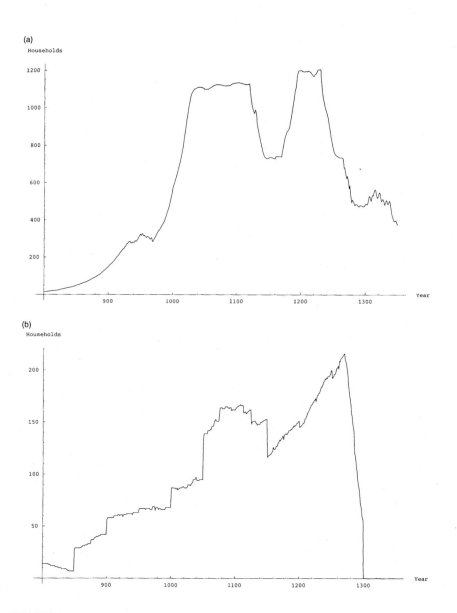

FIGURE 2 Simulated population (a) compared to archaeologically estimated population (b) in numbers of households through time, A.D. 800 to 1360. Numbers of households are graphed at different scales to allow easier comparison of the time series.

TABLE 2   Long House Valley Model Parameter Summary.

PARAMETER	VALUE
Random Seed	Varies
Simulation Begin Year	A.D. 800
Simulation Termination Year	A.D. 1350
Minimum Nutritional Need	800 kg
Maximum Nutritional Need	800 kg
Maximum Length of Grain Storage	2 yr
Harvest Adjustment	1.00
Harvest Variance, Year-to-Year	0.10
Harvest Variance, Location-to-Location	0.10
Minimum Household Fission Age	16 yr
Maximum Household Age (Death Age)	30 yr
Fertility (Chance of Fission)	0.125
Grain Store Given to Child Household	0.33
Maximum Farm-to-Residence Distance	1,600 m
Minimum Initial Corn Stocks	2,000 kg
Maximum Initial Corn Stocks	2,400 kg
Minimum Initial Agent Age	0 yr
Maximum Initial Agent Age	29 yr

in the real valley there were no sites of the requisite size (200 rooms). The peak around 1260, with 600 households in fewer than 15 sites of more than 40 households, conforms more closely to archaeological reality. Although only one or two individual sites had as many as 200 rooms during the 1250–1300 period (Long House had more than 300), there were at least four clusters of sites each of whose total room count equaled or exceeded that number. Clearly, the simulation packs more households into single residential loci than did the real Anasazi who tended to distribute members of a residential unit across a number of discrete but spatially clustered habitation sites (Dean et al. 1978).

On a larger scale, the qualitative aspects of the aggregation graphs (Figure 3) replicate important aspects of the settlement history of Long House Valley and the surrounding region with uncanny accuracy. Fluctuations in the numbers of simulated households in the two smaller site categories (1 to 9 and 10 to 39 households) parallel one another and, together, exhibit a strong reciprocal relationship with the largest sites (40 and more households). When the simulated population is concentrated in large aggregated sites, there are few small-to-medium-sized sites and, when most of the population is distributed among small-to-medium sites, there are few large sites. Thus, from 900 to 1000, the population was concentrated in large and medium sites and from 1150 to 1200 and 1260 to 1300 it was concentrated in large sites. Conversely, from 1000 to 1150 and 1200 to 1260 it was distributed among small and medium sites.

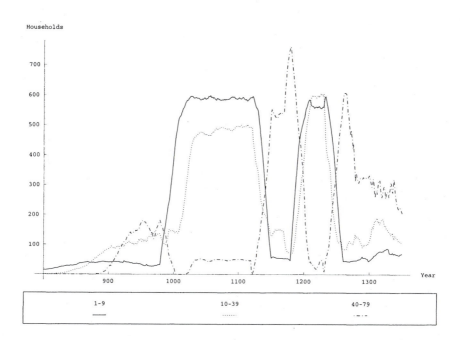

FIGURE 3   Simulated household aggregation represented by the number of households grouped into settlements of 1 to 9 rooms, 10 to 39 rooms, and more than 40 rooms.

These patterns of aggregation and dispersal virtually duplicate the settlement history of the eastern Kayenta Anasazi area, which includes Long House Valley (Dean 1996). During Pueblo I times (850–1000), the real population was aggregated into medium-to-large pithouse villages. Large villages disappeared abruptly after 1000, and, in the Pueblo II period (1000–1150), the population dispersed widely across the landscape, living in small-to-medium-sized unit pueblos that rarely comprised more than 30 rooms. During the Transition period (1150–1250), settlements once again exhibited a tendency toward aggregation, although not nearly as strong as that produced by the simulation between 1150 and 1200. After 1150, people began moving out of upland and outlying areas and concentrating in lowland localities like Long House Valley. Although they did not yet aggregate into extremely large sites or unified clusters of sites, site size tended to be larger than that of the Pueblo II period. The magnitude of the simulated return to a dispersed small-to-medium site distribution from 1200 to 1260 also far exceeds the archaeological situation during the second half of the Transition period in which there were minor settlement adjustments toward a more dispersed pattern in the valley (Effland 1979). The simulated shift to residence in large sites between 1260 and 1300 duplicates the Tsegi phase (1250–1300) pattern of aggregation into fewer but larger sites and into organized site clusters throughout Kayenta Anasazi territory.

Eastern Kayenta Anasazi settlement shifts between 800 and 1300 are related to low- and high-frequency environmental fluctuations (Dean et al. 1985:Figure 1). During periods of depressed alluvial water tables and channel incision (750–925, 1130–1180, 1250–1450) populations tended to aggregate in the few localities where intensive flood plain agriculture was possible under these conditions, a process of compaction that produced large sites or site clusters. During intervals of high groundwater levels and flood plain deposition (925–1130, 1180–1250), farming was possible nearly everywhere, and people were not constrained to live in a few favored localities. In the 1000–1130 period, a combination of salubrious flood plain circumstances and unusually favorable high-frequency climatic conditions allowed the population to disperse widely across the landscape. Given the simulation outcomes illustrated in Figure 3, it seems clear that the Artificial Anasazi Project has successfully captured the dynamic relationship between settlement aggregation-dispersal and low- and high-frequency environmental variability in the study area.

After 1250, the area was afflicted with simultaneous low and high frequency environmental degradations. Falling alluvial water tables, rapid arroyo cutting, the Great Drought of 1276–1299, and a breakdown in the spatial coherence of seasonal precipitation (Dean and Funkhouser 1995) combined to create the most severe subsistence crisis of the nearly 2000 years of paleoenvironmental record, an event that was accompanied by the abandonment of the entire Kayenta region. As was the case with population, simulated aggregation does not duplicate the Anasazi abandonment of the valley after 1300. Nonetheless, the behavior of artificial aggregation after 1250 is extremely instructive about the possibilities of human occupancy of the area during intervals of environmental deterioration and high population densities. The number of large settlements (more than 40 households) drops precipitously, but they do not disappear entirely. Conversely, the numbers of small and medium settlements continue unchanged through the period of greatest stress and increase noticeably after 1300. These results, coupled with paleoenvironmental evidence that the valley environment could have supported a reduced population, clearly indicate that many Anasazi could have remained in the area had they disaggregated into smaller communities dispersed into favorable habitats, especially the North Valley Floor. Thus, the model supports extant ideas that environmental factors account for only part of the exodus from the study area and that the total abandonment must be attributed to a combination of environmental and nonenvironmental causes (Dean 1966, 1969). The delicate balance between environmental "push" factors and nonenvironmental (cultural) "pull" factors suggested by the artificial Long House Valley results is compatible with long-standing, archaeologically untestable hypotheses (Dean 1966; Lipe 1995) about the real Anasazi world. The failure of this aspect of the simulation to quantitatively replicate the case study results provides valuable insights into what humans might have done in the real Long House Valley but did not.

The similarities between the simulated and real Long House Valley settlement patterns far outweigh the differences. Figure 4(a)–(c) gives side-by-side comparisons of simulated and archaeological site distributions for three years (1000, 1144, and 1261) selected to illustrate relationships between the simulated and known distributions of sites against the backdrop of increasing hydrologic potential represented by progressively darker shades of gray. Figure 4(a) shows the paired situations at 1000 when there was considerable hydrologic variability coupled with high corn production potential across the landscape. While the number of simulated sites far exceeds the actual numbers, the simulation accurately reflects the distribution of real sites along the periphery of the flood plain throughout the entire valley. Although crowded, the simulated distribution is what would be expected given the relatively uniform productive potentials across all farmable zones. The large simulated sites along the northeastern margin of the valley represent population aggregates held over from the Pueblo I interval (850–1000) of low alluvial water tables and flood plain erosion. Apart from these similarities, however, the model performs only moderately well for this period.

Figure 4(b) represents a year (1144) in which both hydrologic conditions and potential crop production varied across the landscape. The simulation mimics the spread of sites throughout the valley, particularly along the margins of the flood plain, and captures the initial shift in settlement density toward the north end of the valley that occurred during the environmental degradation of the middle twelfth century. The simulation replicates the twelfth century clustering of settlements into five groups, one at the southwestern extremity of the valley, one in each of the Midvalley Floor localities, one at the mouth of Kin Biko on the northwestern margin of the valley floor, and one at the northeastern corner of the valley. In the northeastern corner of the valley, a real group of eight sites is matched in the simulation by two aggregated sites. In addition, the simulation reproduces the scatter of sites in the nonagricultural uplands on the western and northern sides of the valley. In the northeastern corner of the valley, a real group of eight sites is matched in the simulation by two aggregated sites. In addition, the simulation reproduces the scatter of sites in the nonagricultural uplands on the western and northern sides of the valley. Finally, the simulation accurately locates settlements in the appropriate environmental zones, with the heaviest concentrations in the Midvalley Floor and the North Valley Floor. Major differences between the simulated and real situations are the greater size and number of simulated settlements in the north-central uplands and upper Kin Biko.

Figure 4(c) depicts a year (1261) near the beginning of the period of severe environmental stress that began about 1250. This year was characterized by extremely high spatial differentials in hydrologic conditions and crop production potential. The model spectacularly duplicates the abandonment of the southern half of the valley as a place of residence and the concentration of the

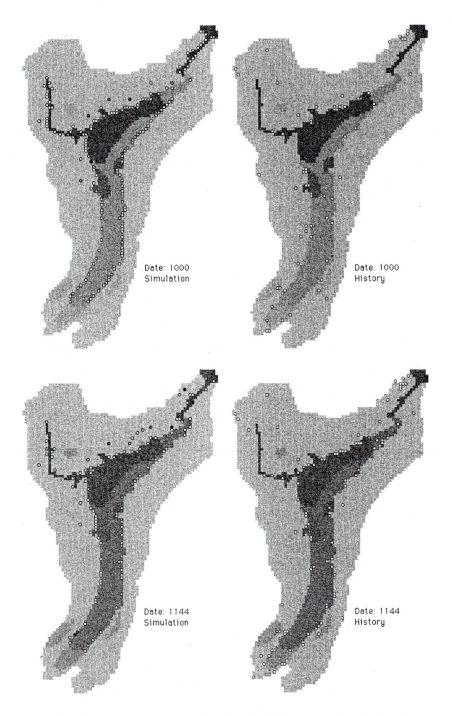

FIGURE 4 Long House Valley showing simulated site size and spatial distributions at three selected years: (a) [top] A.D. 1000, (b) [bottom] A.D. 1144, (c) [next page] A.D. 1261. Sites are represented by circles; the darker the circle, the greater the number of households in the settlement. (continued)

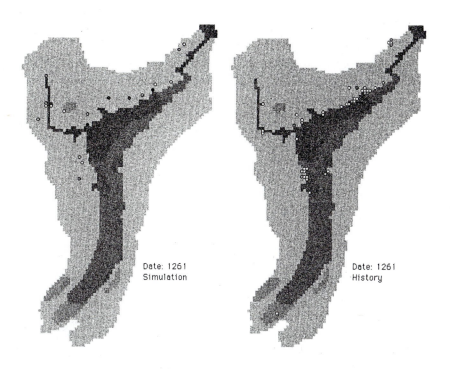

FIGURE 4   (continued) Long House Valley showing simulated site size and spatial distributions at three selected years: (c) [above] A.D. 1261. Sites are represented by circles; the darker the circle, the greater the number of households in the settlement.

population along the northwestern edge of the flood plain near the remaining patches of productive farmland. The simulation also reproduces four of the five settlement clusters that characterized Tsegi phase settlement. An upland cluster of four sites at the northeastern end of the valley is represented in the simulation by two aggregated sites. A larger cluster of large and small sites along the northern margin of the flood plain is matched by a single, very large site and a row of small to large sites. The Long House cluster at the mouth of Kin Biko is represented in the simulation by a couple of large sites. The simulated Midvalley Floor West settlement group, consisting of two aggregated and two small sites, is displaced into the uplands compared to the actual cluster of nine sites, which adjoins the farmland. In three of the clusters, the simulation reproduces the site size distribution of the actual situation in which the cluster comprises one or two large pueblos and a few smaller sites. In addition, the model located a large site in exactly the same positions as the Anasazi situated Long House in the cluster at the mouth of Kin Biko and Tower House in the cluster along the northern margin of the valley. Significant discrepancies between the artificial and real site distributions are the absence of a Midvalley Floor East group from the simulation and the model's placement of too many settlements in Kin Biko.

Another aspect of the simulation reveals much about general patterns of subsistence farming in the valley, even though real-world information on the utilization of farmland for detailed testing of the simulation is unattainable. The order in which different environmental zones are exploited by the Artificial Anasazi (Figure 5) is in exact accordance with expectations of the real world (Dean et al. 1978). The simulation begins during a period of low-frequency environmental stress, and most fields are located in the zones that are productive during episodes of depressed alluvial water tables and arroyo cutting: the North Valley Floor, Kin Biko, and, to a lesser degree, the Midvalley Floor. Fields saturate the North Valley Floor and Kin Biko by 1000, and farming of these areas fluctuates only slightly thereafter. The Midvalley Floor reaches capacity by 1030. During the 800–1000 period, use of the Uplands Arable and General Valley Floor zones remains low because neither area has groundwater available to support crop production, which would have depended solely on the unreliable and generally deficient rainfall. This dependency is indicated by the high variability in farmland use on the General Valley Floor before 1000. By 1000, changes in flood plain processes that begin early in the tenth century enhance productivity in the General Valley Floor and impact the agricultural decisions made by the agents. Rising alluvial water tables and flood plain deposition provide a stable water supply for crops in the General Valley Floor and replace precipitation as the primary control on production. The result is a major "land rush" to establish fields in the newly productive General Valley Floor that begins around 980 and approaches the zone's carrying capacity within 50 years. Again as would be expected, large-scale use of the Upland Arable Zone, where production is controlled primarily by rainfall, does not begin until after 1020 when all the other zones have achieved virtual saturation. The salubrious agricultural conditions that began around 1000 supported the huge population growth and settlement expansions of the 1000–1120 period in both the artificial and the real Long House Valleys.

After about 1030, Figure 5 reflects varying use of different farming environments by a population of agents that approaches the carrying capacity of the simulated area. The North Valley Floor, General Valley Floor, Midvalley Floor, and Kin Biko were fully occupied by fields, and because crop production was controlled by stable flood plain conditions, use of these areas exhibits minimal variability. In contrast, field use in the Upland zone varies considerably because production there depends on precipitation rather than hydrologic conditions. Fields in both the General Valley Floor and Upland zones are severely reduced by the secondary fluvial degradation and drought of the middle twelfth century. The greater sensitivity of the Upland farms to environmental perturbations is indicated by the facts that farming in these areas begins to decline before that on the General Valley Floor and that Upland farmland is abandoned during the depth of the crisis. Upward blips in Midvalley Floor and North Valley Floor field numbers reflect the establishment of fields in these more productive areas by a small number of agents forced out of the General Valley Floor and Uplands. Displaced agents that cannot be accommodated in the favorable areas are removed from the simulation (through death or emigration), which accounts for the decline in simulated population during this interval (Figure 2(a)). When favorable groundwater conditions return, more fields are once again established in the General Valley Floor and Uplands. Once again, the inferior quality of Upland farmland is indicated by the fact that it was not reoccupied until all other zones had been filled to capacity. The Uplands' continued sensitivity to environmental variation is shown by the fluctuations in use between 1190 and 1230 and its abandonment before the primary effects of the next environmental degradation are felt in the other zones. The major low- and high-frequency environmental crisis of the last half of the thirteenth century have major repercussions for Artificial Anasazi field selection. Groundwater depletion and arroyo cutting virtually destroy the farming potential of the General Valley Floor and make production there totally dependent on precipitation, which itself is depressed by the Great Drought of 1279–1299. Upland fields are abandoned by 1240, the number of fields on the Midvalley Floor decreases after 1270, and the Gen-

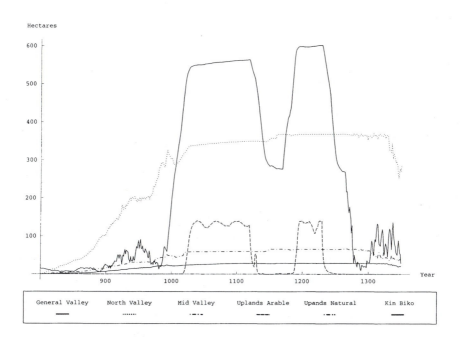

FIGURE 5   Distribution of simulated Artificial Anasazi farms among five arable environmental zones expressed as the number of hectares under cultivation in each zone from A.D. 800 to 1360.

eral Valley Floor is virtually abandoned as a farming area by 1280. Only the North Valley Floor and Kin Biko, where local topographic and depositional factors mitigate the effects of fluvial degradation, retain their farming potential. These areas, already completely filled, remain fully utilized but lack the capacity to absorb agents displaced from the General Valley Floor, Midvalley Floor, and Uplands zones. The disappearance of these agents from the simulation accounts for the major population decline of this period (Figure 2(a)). Unlike the real Anasazi, simulated agents continue to locate fields in Long House Valley after 1300 but under vastly altered environmental conditions. Far fewer fields are located on the General Valley Floor and, as shown by the rapid fluctuations after 1280, this area is far less productive and far more vulnerable to high-frequency productivity fluctuations caused by the greater control exercised by precipitation. The North Valley Floor continues to be highly productive but even there, after about 1280, high-frequency climatic variability becomes a more important factor in productivity. The decline in field locations on the North Valley Floor after 1320 is due to the depopulation of the virtual valley; for the first time in about 200 years, the population of agents falls below what can be supported on the landscape.

As was the case with simulated population (Figure 2(a)) and aggregation (Figure 3), the simulated distribution of farmland clearly shows that the Anasazi need not have totally abandoned Long House Valley as a result of environmental deterioration comparable to that presently built into the model. Instead, a substantial fraction of the population could have stayed behind in small settlements dispersed across suitable farming habitats located in areas (primarily in the North Valley Floor zone) still suitable for agriculture given the detrimental environmental conditions of the post-1250 period. The fact that in the real Long House Valley, that fraction of the population chose not to stay behind but to participate in the exodus from the area, supports the assertion that sociocultural "pull" factors were drawing them away from their homeland.

All runs described above use the parameter estimates of Table 2. These were deemed the most plausible values. But they are not the only possibilities. In research to be presented elsewhere, these values are systematically varied over a range in which the Table 2 values are intermediate. It is striking that over that entire range of plausible environments—including some severely degraded ones—we have not observed the complete abandonment of the real Long House Valley that occurred after A.D. 1300. This outcome strongly reinforces the idea that the valley could have supported a reduced, but still viable, population. Thus, the comparison of the results of the simulation with the real world helps differentiate external (environmental) from internal (cultural) causation in cultural variation and change and even provides a clue, in the form of the proportion of the population that could have stayed but elected to go, as to the relative magnitude of these factors. This finding highlights the utility of agent-based modeling in archaeology by demonstrating a predicted response (Dean 1966) that never could be tested with archaeological data. Because the purely environmental rules explored thus far do not fully account for the Anasazi's disappearance from LHV, it could be argued that predominantly nonenvironmental sociological and ideological factors were responsible for the complete abandonment of an area still capable of supporting a substantial population.

8 CONCLUSIONS

How has agent-based modeling improved understanding of culture change in Anasazi country? First, it allows us to test hypotheses about the past for which we have only indirect evidence. For example, the simulations support predictions about the use of different kinds of farmland under different low- and high-frequency environmental conditions. Second, it illuminates the relative importance of and interactions among various demographic and environmental factors in the processes of sociocultural stability, variation, and change. Third, the generation of similar macroscale results from different microscale specifications elucidates the role of equifinality in sociocultural processes and archaeological analysis. Fourth, progressively augmenting agent specifications allows the experimental manipulation of behavioral modes and assessment of their incremental effects on agent responses to environmental variability.

Finally, agent-based modeling encourages the consideration of previously unspecified, ignored, or discounted factors as consequential mechanisms of cultural adaptation and change. In this regard, Stephen Jay Gould (1989) among others has emphasized that a problem with historical sciences—such as astronomy, geology, paleontology, and archaeology—is that we cannot rewind and rerun the tape of history. While this may be literally true, with agent-based modeling we can execute numerous simulations to investigate alternative outcomes of sociocultural processes under different initial conditions and operational procedures. We can systematically alter the quantitative parameters of a model or make qualitative changes that introduce completely new, and even unlikely, elements into the artificial world of the simulation. Thus, in terms of the Artificial Anasazi model, we could change agent attributes, such as fecundity or food consumption, or introduce new elements, such as mobile raiders, environmental catastrophes, or epidemics.

Ultimately, "to explain" the settlement and farming dynamics of Anasazi society in Long House Valley is to identify rules of agent behavior that account for those dynamics; that is, generate the target spatiotemporal history. Agent-based models are laboratories where competing explanations—hypotheses about Anasazi behavior—can be tested and judged in a disciplined empirical way. The simple agents posited here explain important aspects of Anasazi history while leaving other important aspects unaccounted for. Our future research will attempt to extend and improve the modeling, and we invite colleagues to posit alternative rules, suggest different system parameters, or recommend operational improvements. Agent-based models may never fully explain the real history—these, after all, are simple instruments—but they enable us to make scientific progress in a replicable, cumulative way that does not seem possible with other modeling techniques or through narrative methods alone, crucial as these are in formulating the principles, hypotheses, and experiments that can carry us forward.

ACKNOWLEDGMENTS

We thank David Z. C. Hines of the Brookings Institution and Carrie Dean of the Laboratory of Tree-Ring Research for valuable assistance. The following organizations provided funding and institutional assistance: The Brookings Institution, The National Science Foundation, The John D. and Catherine T. MacArthur Foundation, The Alex C. Walker Educational and Charitable Foundation, the Santa Fe Institute, the Arizona State Museum, and the Laboratory of Tree-Ring Research.

REFERENCES

Bradfield, Maitland
    1969 Soils of the Oraibi Valley, Arizona, in Relation to Plant Cover. Plateau 41:133–140.
    1971 The Changing Pattern of Hopi Agriculture. Royal Anthropological Institute Occasional Paper No. 30. London: Royal Anthropological Institute of Great Britain and Ireland.

Burns, Barney Tillman
    1983 Simulated Anasazi Storage Behavior Using Crop Yields Reconstructed from Tree Rings: A.D. 652–1968. Ph.D. dissertation, Department of Anthropology, The University of Arizona, Tucson, AZ. Ann Arbor, MI: University Microfilms International.

Dean, Jeffrey S.
    1966 The Pueblo Abandonment of Tsegi Canyon, Northeastern Arizona. Paper presented at the 31st Annual Meeting of the Society for American Archaeology, Reno, NV.
    1969 Chronological Analysis of Tsegi Phase Sites in Northeastern Arizona. Papers of the Laboratory of Tree-Ring Research, No. 3. Tucson, AZ: The University of Arizona Press.
    1996 Kayenta Anasazi Settlement Transformations in Northeastern Arizona, A.D. 1150 to 1350. In The Prehistoric Pueblo World, A.D. 1150–1350. Michael A. Adler, ed. Pp. 29–47. Tucson, AZ: The University of Arizona Press.

Dean, Jeffrey S., Robert C. Euler, George J. Gumerman, Fred Plog, Richard H. Hevly, and Thor N. V. Karlstrom
  1985 Human Behavior, Demography, and Paleoenvironment on the Colorado Plateaus. American Antiquity 50:537–554.

Dean, Jeffrey S., and Gary S. Funkhouser
  1995 Dendroclimatic Reconstructions for the Southern Colorado Plateau. *In* Climate Change in the Four Corners and Adjacent Regions: Implications for Environmental Restoration and Land-Use Planning. W. J. Waugh, ed. Pp. 85–104. Grand Junction, CO: U.S. Department of Energy, Grand Junction Projects Office.

Dean, Jeffrey S., Alexander J. Lindsay, Jr., and William J. Robinson
  1978 Prehistoric Settlement in Long House Valley, Northeastern Arizona. *In* Investigations of the Southwestern Anthropological Research Group: An Experiment in Archaeological Cooperation: The Proceedings of the 1976 Conference. Robert C. Euler and George J. Gumerman, eds. Pp. 25–44. Flagstaff, AZ: Museum of Northern Arizona.

Decker, Kenneth W., and Kenneth Lee Peterson
  1983 Simulated Anasazi Storage Behavior using Crop Yields Reconstructed from Tree-Ring Records, A.D. 652–1968. 2 vols. Ph.D. Dissertation, University of Arizona, Ann Arbor, MI: University Microfilms.

Effland, Richard Wayne, Jr.
  1979 A Study of Prehistoric Spatial Behavior: Long House Valley, Northeastern Arizona. Ph.D. dissertation, Department of Anthropology, Arizona State University, Tempe. Ann Arbor, MI: University Microfilms International.

Epstein, Joshua M., and Robert Axtell
  1996 Growing Artificial Societies: Social Science from the Bottom Up. Washington, DC: The Brookings Institution Press and Cambridge, MA: MIT Press.

Euler, Robert C., and George J. Gumerman, eds.
  1978 Investigations of the Southwestern Anthropological Research Group: An Experiment in Archaeological Cooperation: The Proceedings of the 1976 Conference. Flagstaff, AZ: Museum of Northern Arizona.

Gould, Stephen J.
  1989 Wonderful Life: The Burgess Shale and the Nature of History. New York: W. W. Norton.

Gumerman, George J., ed.
  1971 The Distribution of Prehistoric Population Aggregates: Proceedings of the Southwestern Anthropological Research Group. Prescott College Studies in Anthropology, No. 1. Prescott, AZ: Prescott College Press.
  1988 The Anasazi in a Changing Environment. Cambridge, UK: Cambridge University Press.

Gumerman, George J., and Jeffrey S. Dean
   1989 Prehistoric Cooperation and Competition in the Western Anasazi
   Area. *In* Dynamics of Southwest Prehistory. Linda S. Cordell and George
   J. Gumerman, eds. Pp. 99–148. Washington, DC: Smithsonian Institution Press.

Gumerman, George J., and Timothy A. Kohler
   In press Creating Alternative Culture Histories in the Prehistoric South-
   west: Agent-Based Modeling in Archaeology. Durango, CO: Fort Lewis
   College Press.

Hassan, Fekri A.
   1981 Demographic Archaeology. New York: Academic Press.

Karlstrom, Eric
   1983 Soils and Geomorphology of Northern Black Mesa. *In* Excavations
   on Black Mesa, 1981: A Descriptive Report. F. E. Smiley, Deborah L.
   Nichols, and Peter P. Andrews, eds. Pp. 317–342. Research Paper No. 36.
   Center for Archaeological Investigations, Southern Illinois University,
   Carbondale.
   1985 Soils and Geomorphology of Excavated Sites. *In* Excavations on
   Black Mesa, 1983: A Descriptive Report. Andrew L. Christenson and
   William J. Perry, eds. Pp. 387–409. Research Paper No. 46. Center for
   Archaeological Investigations, Southern Illinois University, Carbondale.

Karlstrom, Eric, and Thor N. V. Karlstrom
   1986 Late Quaternary Alluvial Stratigraphy and Soils of the Black Mesa–
   Little Colorado River Areas, Northern Arizona. *In* Geology of Central
   and Northern Arizona. J. D. Nations, C. M. Conway, and G. A. Swann,
   eds. Pp. 71–92. Rocky Mountain Section Guidebook. Flagstaff, AZ: Geological Society of America.

Karlstrom, Thor N. V.
   1988 Alluvial Chronology and Hydrologic Change of Black Mesa and Nearby Regions. *In* The Anasazi in a Changing Environment. George J.
   Gumerman, ed. Pp. 45–91. Cambridge, UK: Cambridge University Press.

Lebo, Cathy J.
   1991 Anasazi Harvests: Agroclimate, Harvest Variability, and Agricultural
   Strategies on Prehistoric Black Mesa, Northeastern Arizona. Ph.D dissertation, Department of Anthropology, Indiana University, Blooming-
   ton.

Leonhardy, Frank C., and Vickie L. Clay
   1985 Soils. *In* Dolores Archaeological Program: Studies in Environmental Archaeology. Kenneth Lee Petersen, Vickie L. Clay, Meredith H.
   Matthews, and Sarah W. Neusius, comp. Pp. 139–153. Denver: USDI
   Bureau of Reclamation.

Lipe, William D.
  1995 The Depopulation of the Northern San Juan: Conditions in the Turbulent 1200s. Journal of Anthropological Archaeology 14:143–169.

Miller, Mack L., and Kermit Larsen
  1975 Soil Survey of Apache County, Arizona, Central Part. Washington, DC: USDA Soil Conservation Service.

Nelson, Ben A., Timothy A. Kohler, and Keith W. Kintigh
  1994 Demographic Alternatives: Consequences for Current Models of Southwestern Prehistory. *In* Understanding Complexity in the Prehistoric Southwest. George J. Gumerman and Murray Gell-Mann, eds. Pp. 113–146. Santa Fe Institute Studies in the Sciences of Complexity, Proceedings Volume XVI. Reading, MA: Addison-Wesley.

Palmer, William C.
  1965 Meteorological Drought. Research Paper No. 45. USDC Office of Climatology, U.S. Weather Bureau, Washington, DC.

Swedlund, Alan C.
  1994 Issues in Demography and Health. *In* Understanding Complexity in the Prehistoric Southwest. George J. Gumerman and Murray Gell-Mann, eds. Pp. 39–58. Santa Fe Institute Studies in the Sciences of Complexity, Proceedings Volume XVI. Reading, MA: Addison-Wesley.

Taylor, Don R.
  1983 Soil Survey of Coconino County Area, Arizona, Central Part. Washington, DC: USDA Soil Conservation Service.

Van West, Carla R.
  1994 Modeling Prehistoric Agricultural Productivity in Southwestern Colorado: A GIS Approach. Department of Anthropology Reports of Investigations 67. Pullman, WA: Washington State University.

Weiss, Kenneth M.
  1973 Demographic Models for Anthropology. Memoirs of the Society for American Archaeology, No. 27.

Wood, James W.
  1994 Dynamics of Human Reproduction: Biometry, Biology, Demography. New York: Hawthorne.

Anti-Chaos, Common Property, and the Emergence of Cooperation

J. Stephen Lansing

'Ητοι μὲν πρώτιστα χάος γένετ' αὐτάρ ἔπειτα / Γαῖ'
(First Chaos came into being, but next Gaia)

Hesiod, *Theogony*, 116–117

Complex adaptive systems, as conceived by John Holland, are groups of agents engaged in a process of coadaptation, in which adaptive moves by individuals have consequences for the group. Holland and others have shown that under certain circumstances simple models of this process show surprising abilities to self-organize (Holland 1993; Kauffman 1993). Complex adaptive systems have interesting mathematical properties, and the process of "anti-chaos"—the spontaneous crystallization of ordered patterns in initially disordered networks—has become a new area of interdisciplinary research. But the question of whether these models can illuminate real world processes is still largely open. Not long ago John Maynard Smith described the study of complex adaptive systems as "fact-free science" (1995).

This chapter has two purposes. First, in response to Maynard Smith, I will show how the concept of ecological feedback in complex adaptive systems provides a simple and powerful explanation for the

Dynamics in Human and Primate Societies, edited by T. Kohler and
G. Gumerman, Oxford University Press, 1999. **207**

structure and persistence of cooperative networks among Balinese rice farmers. Second, I will generalize this explanation to shed light on the emergence of cooperation in a class of social systems where interactions with the natural world create both rewards and punishments. But before turning to these examples, in line with the purposes of this volume I will comment on the ideas and assumptions that underlie the use of models in this analysis.

1 INTRODUCTION: COMPLEXITY AND SOCIAL THEORY

"Society is a human product. Society is an objective reality. Man [sic] is a social product." With this epigram Peter Berger and Thomas Luckmann neatly encapsulated a fundamental problem in social theory (1967:61). In American anthropology today this paradox is often posed as a conflict between "structure" and "agency," where the former refers to ideational, economic, institutional, or psychological systems that are represented as generating social reality; and the latter to the ability of individual social actors to modify their own social worlds. The same paradox recurs in classical social theory, such as Jürgen Habermas' insistence on the need to somehow reconcile actor-focused and system-level social theories (Habermas 1985, 1987).

Complexity theory offers several new avenues from which to approach this problem. The most straightforward method involves the construction of simulation models, typically consisting of artificial worlds inhabited by populations of heterogeneous actors who interact with one another and with their environments. The behavior of the actors changes their world, and over time global macroscopic patterns of behavior—"emergent properties"—may appear. In this way, "agency" (the behavioral patterns of the agents) generates "structure," which in turn constrains or liberates "agency" in a changing world. An example of this type of model is "Sugarscape," a tool for simulating artificial societies recently developed by Joshua Epstein and Robert Axtell. "Sugarscape" is a simulated landscape consisting of a lattice with resource-bearing sites. Populations of "adaptive agents" are created and endowed with internal states, behavioral rules, and the capability to move around on the landscape. Some internal states are fixed for the agent's life span, while others change in response to interaction with other agents or with the external environment. Sugarscape has been used to test hypotheses about economic, psychological, and social behavior, and the spread of disease (Epstein and Axtell 1996).

On a more abstract level, complexity theory offers new tools with which to explore such questions as preconditions for the emergence of cooperation. For example, Lindgren and Nordahl (1994) have studied the evolution of cooperation in games during which individual "adaptive agents" are placed on a lattice and interact with their immediate neighbors. In a simple version of this experiment, individuals play two-person games like the iterated Prisoner's Dilemma, deciding whether to cooperate with each of their neighbors.

The interesting result is that the details of the games which are played are rather unimportant; whole classes of games lead to the emergence of spatial patterns of cooperation and defection that improve the payoffs for all players. In this way, complex adaptive systems may emerge from the interactions of heterogeneous collections of agents.

Perhaps the most intriguing aspect of these models is the opportunity they provide to search for the drivers of historical change. If we could rewind an imaginary videotape of the evolution of life, as Stephen Jay Gould observes in a recent book, each sequence would show us not design but contingency: "The divine tape player holds a million scenarios, each perfectly sensible. Little quirks at the outset, occurring for no particular reason, unleash cascades of consequences that make a particular future seem inevitable in retrospect" (1990:320). Paleontologists continue to debate whether Gould is right about the Cambrian explosion. But in the models to be described below, we have the opportunity to "rewind the tape" of the formation of cooperative associations among Balinese farmers, to see whether or not a certain model of "agency" will yield the predicted structural patterns.

Perhaps the most important issue with respect to the use of simulation models is the question of how to test them. The strategy I employ in this chapter derives not from complexity theory (where models are most often viewed as mathematical abstractions) but from systems ecology. Systems ecologists create models in order to test their understanding of complex interactive processes. Imagine that you wish to understand the growth of a species of moss in an Alaskan forest. The growth rate should depend on temperature, light, nutrients, and perhaps some other, unknown factors. The behavior of most of these parameters is already fairly well known. One builds a model to predict the growth rate on the basis of values observed in the field and then compares these predictions with field observations. One can also vary each parameter sequentially, both in the model and on the ground, and compare the results. In this way, it is possible to test each of the components of the model, so that in the end one can predict what a change in a single parameter (say, light levels) will do to the growth of the moss.

An alternative strategy is the "kitchen sink" approach (as in "throw in everything including the kitchen sink," and keep tinkering with the model until it acquires the desired level of approximation to the phenomenon under study). The problem with this approach is that it is always possible, with enough tinkering, to make a model do what you want, but then you still do not understand why it behaves the way it does. A model that accurately predicts the growth of the moss to nine decimal places but includes false assumptions about the physics of how moss responds to light is useless. To understand why the model behaves as it does, it is vital to be able to test each of its assumptions. It follows that the best model is not necessarily one that comes closest to predicting the behavior under study but rather one that captures and illustrates the underlying dynamics driving the behavior.

Models like "Sugarscape" are quite different from systems-ecological models, for the reasons we have just considered. "Sugarscape" is an abstract model in the sense that neither the actors nor the landscapes of "Sugarscape" are meant to resemble reality. Such models are intended to illustrate fundamental processes and cannot be tested. In contrast, this chapter describes the creation and testing of a series of different models, in a process of reasoning designed to illuminate the driving forces behind a particular historical process.

2 COOPERATION AND COMMON PROPERTY

One of the best-known examples of common property management in a traditional society is the subak system of Bali. Subaks are egalitarian, cooperative farmers' associations that manage the flow of irrigation water into rice terraces and carry out agricultural rituals associated with the Balinese "rice cult." The membership of each subak generally consists of all of the farmers who obtain irrigation water from a common tertiary irrigation source, most often a canal. Subak members meet regularly to actively manage their irrigation system, to decide on cropping schedules, and to organize annual cycles of agricultural rituals in their fields. The common interest of subak members in irrigation management and spiritual welfare is obvious to the farmers, and subaks play an active role in managing the rice terraces (Lansing 1993).

But the average size of a subak is less than 50 hectares and 100 members. A much more complicated pattern of multisubak cooperation is apparent from aerial photographs of Balinese rice terraces. These photographs show large blocks of terraces in which all of the rice is at the same stage in its growing cycle. Such synchronous planting is surprising for several reasons:

- The amount of water needed to flood the terraces at the start of a planting cycle is three to five times greater than later on, when the ground is saturated. Synchronous planting is therefore likely to lead to water shortages at the start of a planting cycle, followed by an overabundance of water a few weeks later.
- Labor requirements are also greatest at the start and end of the planting cycle. Synchronous planting can thus create a labor bottleneck.

Yet despite these disadvantages, synchronous planting is the norm for most Balinese communities, and appears to be an ancient pattern. In earlier publications, my colleagues and I have proposed an explanation for synchronous planting based on the farmer's desire to control rice pests (including rats, insects, and insect-borne diseases) (Lansing and Kremer [1993]). The idea is quite simple: if all of the fields in a sufficiently large area are harvested at the same time, and subsequently flooded, rice pests are deprived of their habitat. If no alternative hosts are available, the pest population will drop (Aryawan et al. 1993). The need to minimize losses from pests provides a strong motivation for farmers to cooperate with their neighbors in synchronous planting schedules, even though this forces everyone to plant exactly the same crops and may lead to the water and labor bottlenecks mentioned above.

In computer simulations, we have compared the effectiveness of different scales of synchronized cropping on harvest yields. The problem is quite complicated. Choosing the best cropping pattern involves finding the scale of spatial synchronization that optimizes the trade-off between water shortages (caused by too many synchronized subaks experiencing peak irrigation demand at the same time) versus pest damage (caused by too little synchronization of cropping patterns). When a subak selects its cropping pattern, it actively modifies ecological conditions for its neighbors (pest populations and irrigation water flows). With hundreds of subaks distributed in many branches along a typical river, there are an enormous number of possible cropping schedules. Yet our computer simulations of the actual pattern of syncronization and offsets along two rivers show that they achieve a near-optimal solution, minimizing pest damage and maximizing water usage along the entire watershed. How do the farmers get it right, given that the units actively managing irrigation are the subaks?

Before trying to answer this question, let me pause to restate it: Imagine a jigsaw puzzle of a watershed with 100 subaks, where each color signifies a cropping plan for the year: yellow might mean "plant a particular rice variety the week of February 15, and a different rice variety the week of July 20." Groups of subaks up and down the river choose this plan, while others choose different plans, symbolized by different colors. The result, for the whole watershed, is a patchwork of colors. An almost infinite number of different-sized and different-colored patches is possible, but nearly all of them would lead to acute water shortages and pest outbreaks. For example, if everyone followed the yellow plan, pests would be minimized by a fallow period extending over the whole watershed. But water shortages would be disastrous, because all fields would experience peak irrigation demand at the same times.

My point is that the subaks do not consciously attempt to create an optimal pattern of staggered cropping schedules for a whole watershed. Nonetheless, such patterns occur and are probably typical. Management at the local level, by many small groups of neighboring subaks, leads to region-wide solutions. But how?

3 WHY DO THE FARMERS COOPERATE?

In the absence of a central authority with the ability to calculate, and impose, an optimal cropping pattern for an entire watershed, it must be the case that the subaks somehow find their way to this global solution, even though each individual subak is only trying to find the optimal cropping pattern for its own immediate neighborhood. To simulate this we need a simple model that will predict whether any given pair of subaks will decide to synchronize their

$$
\begin{array}{ccc}
 & \mathbf{D_A} & \mathbf{D_B} \\
\mathbf{U_A} & 1,1-w & 1-p,1-p \\
\mathbf{U_B} & 1-p,1-p & 1,1-w
\end{array}
$$

FIGURE 1

cropping pattern. There should be two players in each game: an upstream subak, which by virtue of its location controls water flow, and a downstream subak, which needs some of this water. To simplify the problem, let's assume that these players can adopt one of two possible cropping patterns, A and B (for example, A could mean planting on January 1 and May 1, while B means planting on February 1 and June 1). Further assume that the water supply is adequate for both subaks if they stagger their cropping pattern. But if both plant at the same time, the downstream subak will experience water stress and its harvests will be somewhat reduced. Finally, assume that pest damage will be higher if plantings are staggered (because the pests can migrate from one field to the next), and lower if plantings are synchronized. Let $p(0 < p < 1)$ represent the damage caused by pests, and $w(0 < w < 1)$ represent the damage caused by water shortage. Given these assumptions, the payoff matrix is in Figure 1, where $\mathbf{U}$ and $\mathbf{D}$ designate the actions of the upstream and downstream subaks, respectively:

Here the first number is the payoff (harvest) for the upstream subak, and the second is the harvest for the downstream subak. Thus, if both subaks plant on the same schedule (either A or B), the harvest for the upstream subak is 1, but it is $1 - w$ for the downstream subak because of insufficient irrigation water. If the two subaks choose different schedules (U choosing A and D choosing B, or vice versa), then each subak achieves a harvest of $1 - p$.

We can immediately draw several conclusions about the payoffs for alternative strategies. The upstream subaks do not care about water stress (they are never affected by w), but their downstream neighbors do. (This is the well-known "tail-ender" problem, common to most irrigation systems: the farmers at the tail end of an irrigation system are at the mercy of their neighbors upstream, who control the irrigation flow). But the upstream subaks *do* care about pest damage, since pests, unlike water, are quite capable of moving upstream. So a strategy of synchronized cropping patterns to control pests will always produce higher yields for the upstream subaks. When $p > w$, the downstream subak will also achieve higher yields by synchronizing. Note that if they do so the aggregate harvest is higher (i.e., mean harvests for both subaks goes up). If $w > p$, adding more pests to the fields actually increases the aggregate harvest for the two subaks, since it encourages cooperation. But if the farmers are not worried about pests, the upstream subak has little

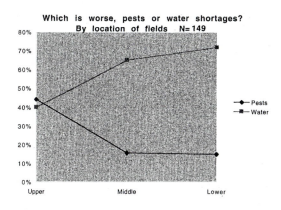

FIGURE 2 Responses of Balinese farmers to the question "which is worse, pests or water shortages?" by location of their fields. Downstream farmers worry more about water shortages; upstream farmers worry more about pest damage.

incentive to give up some of its water in a synchronized cropping plan with its downstream neighbor.

How well does this simple model capture the actual basis for decision making by the farmers? In the summer of 1998, with the help of Balinese colleagues, I undertook an extensive survey of farmers in ten subaks located in the Tegallalang district of south-central Bali. In each of the ten subaks, we chose a random sample of fifteen farmers. Of these fifteen, five were selected whose fields are located at the upstream region of their subak; five more from the middle of the subak, and the last five from the downstream area of the subak. In order to test the predictions of the simple two-player game outlined above, we asked "Which problem is worse, damage from pests or irrigation water shortages?" The results, shown in Figure 2, clearly confirm the model.

But in the end it is whole subaks, rather than individual farmers, which must decide whether to cooperate. In our sample, six of the ten subaks are located in upstream/downstream pairs, where the downstream subak obtains most of its water from its upstream neighbor. Thus it was also possible to compare the aggregate response of all the farmers in each subak, to the response of their neighbors. Figure 3 shows this result.

These results are also supported by our videotaped records of monthly meetings in which elected representatives of all ten subaks (plus four others not included in the survey) discuss matters of mutual interest. The willingness of upstream subaks to synchronize cropping patterns seems to be strongly related to the perceived threat of pest invasions. It is important to note that which subaks synchronize cropping plans with their neighbors varies from year to year. An increased threat of pest damage, such as has occurred re-

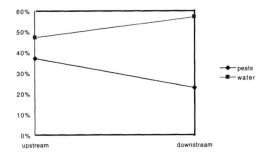

FIGURE 3   "Which is worse, pests or water shortages?" Aggregate responses of farmers in 3 upstream subaks and 3 downstream subaks $N = 90$. As with individual farmers, the aggregate response of all the farmers in each subaks series systematically depending on its relative location (upstream or downstream).

cently in several cycles of pest infestations (brown planthoppers, rice tungro virus), quickly leads to larger sychronized groups; while a year of light rains encourages greater fragmentation.

   Thus we appear to have a decent working understanding of the trade-offs that are involved when subaks decide whether or not to synchronize cropping patterns with their neighbors. But how do the decisions made by interacting pairs of subaks lead to region-wide cropping patterns that apparently optimize conditions for everyone?

4   COADAPTIVE DYNAMICS ON A LATTICE

To answer this question we need to shift our attention from the interaction of pairs of autonomous agents (the upstream and downstream subaks in the two-player game) to the entire dynamic system; in this case all of the subaks in a watershed. Intuitively, this is reasonable since the actual flow of water in the rivers and irrigation systems will depend on the cropping schedules set by all the subaks, not just pairs of subaks. We can speculate that the patterns of cooperation (synchronization of cropping patterns) among the subaks could be the outcome of an historical process in which the subaks sought to find the best balance between water sharing and pest control. Using real data on the location, size, and field conditions of 172 subaks in the watershed of the Oos and Petanu rivers in southern Bali, we modeled changes in the flow of irrigation water and the growth of rice and pests as subaks chose whether to cooperate with their neighbors. Here each subak behaves as an "adaptive agent" that seeks to improve its harvest by imitating the cropping pattern of more successful neighbors:

As a new year begins, each of the 172 subaks in the model begins to plant rice or vegetables. At the end of the year, harvest yields are calculated for each subak. Subsequently, each subak checks to see whether any of its closest neighbors got higher yields. If so, the target subak copies the cropping pattern of its (best) neighbor. The model then simulates another year of growth, tabulates yields, and continues to run until each subak has reached its local optimum [Lansing and Kremer 1993:212].

The simulation begins with a random distribution of cropping patterns (Figure 4). After a year the subaks in the model begin to aggregate into patches following identical cropping patterns, which helps to reduce pest losses. As time goes on these patches grow until they overshoot and cause water stress. Yields fluctuate but gradually rise. The program ends when the model generates a distribution of cropping patterns that optimizes both pest control and water sharing (Figure 5(a)). The close relationship between this pattern as calculated in the model (Figure 5(a)), and the actual pattern of synchronized planting units (Figure 5(b)) is apparent. In the model, as patterns of coordination resembling the water temple networks emerge, both the mean harvest yield and the highest yield increase, and variance in yield across subaks declines (Figure 6). Subsequent runs showed that if the environment was perturbed dramatically by decreasing rainfall or increasing the virulence of pests, a few subaks change their cropping patterns, and within a few years a new equilibrium is achieved (Lansing and Kremer 1993:215–216).

Clearly, the model accurately predicts the broad patterns of spatial cooperation. Interestingly, the model also predicts that variance in harvest yields will decline, while average yields increase. This also appears to be empirically accurate: in the areas of Bali where synchronous planting is the norm, there is very little variation in harvest yields. In the region where we conducted the survey described above, variance in yields from test plots seldom exceeds 5%. This suggests an explanation for the stability of these patterns of cooperation. In game theory, a Nash equilibrium is a state in which each player can do no better by imitating the strategy of a neighbor. Such an equilibrium is more stable than a nonequilibrium state, in which strategies and players continue to compete. Evolutionary game theorists observe that if a game includes evolutionary dynamics, then a Nash equilibrium is also an evolutionarily stable strategy, or ESS (Maynard Smith 1982). Once the players have found an ESS, the system becomes stable. In Bali, it appears that patterns of cooperation among subaks are ancient and very stable; this is easier to understand if we imagine that all of the farmers over large areas obtain harvest yields that are indistinguishable from their neighbor's. But this observation raises another question: if the pattern of interaction between subaks were different, could the system still self-organize?

FIGURE 4 Initial conditions for a simulation model of irrigation flows and rice and pest growth for 172 subaks. Differences in cropping patterns are indicated by different symbols (subaks with the same symbols have identical cropping patterns).

5 CONSTRAINTS ON SELF-ORGANIZATION

In the Balinese example we have just considered, the subaks turned out to inhabit a world in which self-organization was relatively easy to achieve. In the model, the opposing constraints of pests and irrigation flows created variation in harvests that enabled a process of coadaptation to occur. This model result suggests it is relatively easy, in the real world, for subaks to find their way to a complex cropping pattern that benefits everyone. In the model, this process occurs as each subak checks its four closest neighbors to determine whether any of them have a better (more productive) cropping plan. If so, the subak copies its (best) neighbor's plan. But what if each subak only compared itself with one neighbor, or with 12 neighbors, or 57? Does the structure of the connections between the subaks (considered as adaptive agents) influence the ability of the entire collection of subaks to self-organize? This question—the structure of relationships between social actors—is seperate from the ecological problem they are trying to solve: the subaks could be growing roses and

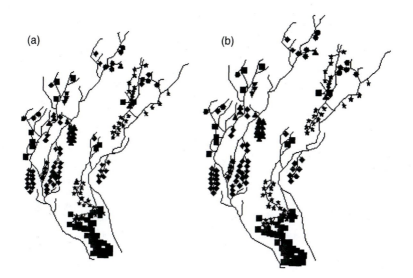

FIGURE 5   (a) Model cropping patterns after 11 years. (b) Cropping patterns in the real water temple system.

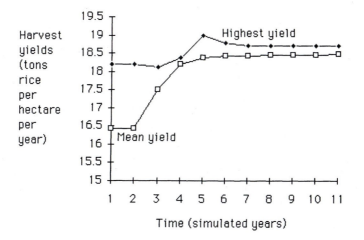

FIGURE 6   Increase in harvest yields in the Bali model. Variance in yields also declines, as they converge on the mean yield.

Time 1   2   3   4   5

FIGURE 7   Five successive states of a lattice model. Here each site is wired to 2
other sites. Whether a site changes color depends on the state of its neighbors (on
or off) in the previous time step.

trying to minimize aphids. Here again, recent work in complexity theory offers
some useful insights.

Once again, we begin by simplifying the problem and creating a model.
Imagine a lattice, like the Bali model described above, in which the behavior
of each agent in the lattice is affected by the behavior of some of its neighbors.
Stuart Kauffman's NK model is appealingly simple (Kauffman 1993). Imagine
a collection of N Christmas tree lights. Each bulb has one of two possible
states: on or off, and is wired up to k other bulbs. A simple rule tells each
bulb what to do. For example, set $k = 3$, meaning that each bulb is wired to
3 other bulbs. At each time step, each bulb decides whether to turn itself on
or off in accordance with the state of the majority of its neighbors. A typical
rule is "majority wins," meaning that if 2 or 3 of its neighbors are on, the bulb
will itself turn on; otherwise it will turn off. How will such a system behave?

There are three possible patterns of behavior:

1. Frozen stability: if k is very large, the bulbs are subject to many conflicting
   constraints. Frustrated, some flip on and off few times, and very soon the
   whole array of lights stops twinkling.
2. Chaos: if k is small ($k = 1$), the bulbs keep twinkling chaotically as they
   switch each other on and off.
3. Complex: if k is around 2, complex patterns are likely to appear, in which
   twinkling islands appear, spread, and vanish, as in Figure 7.

In this type of model, there are two parameters to consider with respect
to the interconnection of agents: how many agents are interconnected, and
where the agents are located in space. Figure 8 shows a pattern in which each
agent is connected to its four or eight immediate neighbors. This is the Nash
neighborhood (as in Nash equilibrium), consisting of the closest neighbors of
an agent in a two-dimensional grid.[1]

In the Bali model described above, each agent checks its four neighbors
to the north, south, east, and west, so $k = 4$ and all connections are local.
But what if each subak were connected to fewer (or more) neighbors? Is there

---

[1]The Nash neighborhood consists of the four nearest neighbors, and the von Neumann
neighborhood of the eight nearest neighbors.

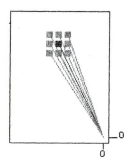

FIGURE 8   The Nash neighborhood (an agent and its surrounding immediate neighbors), as indicated by the four colored lines.

an optimum number of connections to facilitate solving problems like the pest-water dynamics? It is immediately obvious that if each subak based its cropping pattern on the state of ALL of its neighbors ($k = N - 1$) then the subaks would be frozen into place. At the opposite extreme, if each subak acts independently ($k = 0$) then no learning is possible and coadaptation cannot occur. Is there an optimal k?

Figure 9 shows the results of varying k from 3 to 13. As long as the subaks connect only with their closest neighbors, expanding the search space increases the speed of the coadaptive process. But if k includes distant neighbors the process of coadaptation ceases. When $k = 4$ subaks from anywhere in the watershed, the system remains chaotic. The reason, obviously, is that distant neighbors are not responding to the same environmental signals as one's immediate neighbors.

This may seem like much ado about a seemingly trivial result, but consider the implications. For example, most agricultural extension plans are based on the results from experimental plots located at research stations. Farmers are encouraged to imitate these distant models. But if the farmers react to these signals, rather than those emanating from their immediate neighborhoods, the process of coadaptation will cease.

How typical is this result? A recent comparison of steppe pastures in Central Asia found an enormous disparity between the regions where local pastoralists have been left to themselves, as compared to regions subject to government planning and active intervention (Table 1). In the regions where the state was actively engaged in agricultural extension efforts, the steppe grasslands have been severely degraded (defined as "a more or less permanent decline in the rate at which land yields livestock products") (Sneath 1998). In contrast, pastures remained intact in regions where local pastoralists were allowed freedom of movement. It is worth noting that in the traditional herding system of the Mongols, the density of herders and animals on the landscape

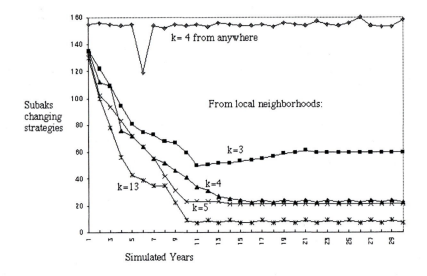

FIGURE 9 Effects of various k on the coadaptation of subaks in the Bali model. Increasing k from 3 to 4, 5, and 13 progressively enlarges the search space and increases the speed at which most of the subaks arrive at a Nash equilibrium, with high mean yields. But if subaks compare their harvests to those of distant neighbors ($k = 4$ from anywhere in the landscape), the system becomes chaotic and mean yields do not improve.

varies dramatically by season: the pattern is not static. Perhaps here, as in Bali, the key to a stable and productive adaptation is the ability to respond to local environmental cues. Encouraging farmers or pastoralists to imitate an "optimal" model derived from research stations may carry the hidden cost of the loss of information gained from interactions with their neighbors and the local environment.

6 CONCLUSION

In the Balinese example, each subak decides whether or not to cooperate with each of its neighbors using a myopic strategy ("might as well try what the neighbors are doing") that ignores the real and formidable complexity of their problem. Luckily for the subaks, the mathematics of complex adaptive systems are such that this ill-informed collection of strategies is all that is needed for them to rapidly climb the foothills of their local adaptive landscapes. Within a few short years, a collection of autonomous agents (the subaks) has become a network, with islands of cooperation where all the farmers enjoy nearly identical, relatively bountiful harvests. The structure of these networks bears a remarkable resemblance to the lattice configurations of spatial games, for

TABLE 1   Relationship between active state control and degradation of pastures.

	Degradation of grasslands
Regions with active state intervention:	
Inner Mongolia	"more than a third"
Buryatia	79%
Chitia	77%
Regions without active state planning:	
Independent Mongolia	9%
Tuva	"negligible"

the excellent reason that both solutions are driven by the same coevolutionary dynamics. The entire network has a structure, in which the value of both cooperation and noncooperation varies according to spatial location. This structure is itself adaptive: perturbations that change local payoffs trigger small cascades of change that allow the entire network to respond effectively to events such as the addition of a new irrigation system or a new rice pest.

Elsewhere I have described the ritual system of agricultural rites and "water temples" that create symbolic ties between subaks (1993). I have also argued that the practical role of the patterns of cooperation created by water temples went unnoticed by generations of agricultural researchers in Bali, for whom the synchronization of agricultural rites had no connection with harvests. The water temple networks articulate patterns of cooperation and facilitate communication among subaks. But the ritual system alone does not appear to have the capacity to generate the overall structure of the patterns of cooperation in a watershed. In this chapter, I have proposed an explanation for how these patterns could have developed.

I suspect that the water temple networks of Bali are probably far from unique: if the arguments described above are valid, then we need to revise our models of the world of peasant agriculturalists. From Marx, who famously dismissed the "idiocy of rural life," to the latest Five Year Plans, social scientists have generally assumed that one bit of countryside is much like the next. It may be, however, that wherever groups of farmers are engaged in iterative games with nature, the mathematics of anti-chaos have created complex patterns that await our discovery. Perhaps, indeed, we are fortunate that these new mathematical tools have appeared while there is still some countryside left! For history shows that systems like the water temple networks of Bali, and the steppe grasslands of Central Asia, are highly vulnerable to centralized development policies that replace adaptive patchiness with monocrop uniformity.

REFERENCES

Aryawan, I. G. N., I. N. Widiarta, Y. Suzuki, and F. Nakasuji
  1993 Life Table Analysis of the Green Rice Leafhopper, *Nephotettix virescans* (Distant), an Efficient Vector of Rice Tungro Disease in Asynchronous Rice Fields in Indonesia. Res. Popul. Ecol. 35:31–43.

Berger, Peter, and Thomas Luckmann
  1967 The Social Construction of Reality. Garden City, NY: Doubleday.

Epstein, Joshua M., and Robert Axtell
  1996 Growing Artificial Societies: Social Science from the Bottom Up. Washington, DC: The Brookings Institution and Cambridge, MA: MIT Press.

Gould, Stephen Jay
  1990 Wonderful Life: The Burgess Shale and the Nature of History. New York: W. W. Norton.

Habermas, Jürgen
  1985 The Theory of Communicative Action, vol. 1. Boston: Beacon Press.
  1987 The Theory of Communicative Action, vol. 2. Boston: Beacon Press.

Holland, John H.
  1993 Adaptation in Natural and Artificial Systems. Cambridge, MA: MIT Press.

Kauffman, Stuart
  1993 The Origins of Order: Self-Organization and Selection in Evolution. Oxford: Oxford University Press.

Lansing, J. Stephen
  1993 Priests and Programmers: Technologies of Power in the Engineered Landscape of Bali. Princeton, NJ: Princeton University Press.

Lansing, J. Stephen, and James N. Kremer
  1993 Emergent Properties of Balinese Water Temple Networks: Coadaptation on a Rugged Fitness Landscape. *In* Artificial Life III. C. G. Langton, ed. Pp. 201–224. Santa Fe Institute Studies in the Sciences of Complexity, Proceedings Volume XVII. Reading, MA: Addison-Wesley.

Lansing, J. Stephen, James N. Kremer, and Barbara B. Smuts
  1998 System-Dependent Selection, Ecological Feedback and the Emergence of Functional Structure in Ecosystems. J. Theor. Biol. 192:377–391.

Lindgren, Kristian, and M. G. Nordahl
  1994 Evolutionary Dynamics of Spatial Games. Physica D 75:292–309.

Maynard Smith, John
  1982 Evolution and the Theory of Games. Cambridge, UK: Cambridge University Press.

1995 Life at the Edge of Chaos. The New York Review of Books, March, 2:28–30.

Sneath, David
1998 State Policy and Pasture Degradation in Inner Asia. Science, 21 August, 281:1147–1148.

Wilson, David S., and Elliot Sober
1994 Reintroducing Group Selection to the Human Behavioral Sciences. Behav. & Brain Sci. 17:585–654.

The Political Impact of Marriage in a Virtual Polynesian Society

Cathy A. Small

Computer modeling, because it abstracts cultural processes and quantifies social variables, is often seen as contradictory to the rich qualitative rendering of culture that ethnography offers. In this chapter, I attempt to show that computer modeling and ethnography can go hand-in-glove. Using an agent-based model of Polynesian social dynamics, I demonstrate how simulation can aid an ethnographer in better understanding the ethnographic record, in this case, the relationship between marriage customs and stratification in Tonga. In a more abstract sense, I suggest that agent-based models, simulated over time, can elucidate the relationship between individual or group (human) decisions and the social structures which both result from and constrain those decisions. In so doing, simulation can provide new insights into the ethnographic record, edifying structural relationships, helping to generate explanations for phenomena, or pointing to the most fruitful places to go in the ethnographic record for new insights.

1 MARRIAGE IN POLYNESIA

Marriage in Polynesia both reflects and creates political fortunes by affecting the kinship and exchange relationships among lines, the pattern of chiefly

Dynamics in Human and Primate Societies, edited by T. Kohler and
G. Gumerman, Oxford University Press, 1999.   **225**

alliances, and the transmission of rank over generations (Sahlins 1958; Biersack 1982; Huntsman 1975; Goldman 1970; Linnekin 1990; Shore 1976; Kaeppler 1971; Gailey 1987; Valeri 1972). The significance of marriage preferences or restrictions in the political process is often understood by historical example, that is by the advantages that accrued to particular lines or chiefs who enacted particular types of marriages. Thus, for instance, to understand Tongan "kitetama" marriage (where a man marries his mother's brother's daughter), Bott (1982:77) generalizes from particular examples of kitetama marriages, suggesting that this marriage custom strengthens a man's tie with his mother's people and, over time, serves to reinforce kinship and alliance ties over generations between a brother's and sister's lines.

What we cannot tell from such an analysis is if this marriage form has any implications for the development and evolution of chiefdoms as a whole. In the example above, for instance, one might ask: what does the continual reinforcement of brother-sister alliance ties *mean* to the political structure or functioning of the chiefdom? Looking at marriage and chiefdoms more generally, we can ask: how do the marriage decisions of particular chiefs and chiefly lines (or the conventions, like kitetama, they exemplify) relate to emergent features in Polynesian history and structure, like stratification? In its most abstract form we are asking, what is the relationship between human agency, social institutions, and social structure?

This experiment in modeling is designed to explore such questions. I use modeling to compare the implications of different sets of marriage conventions or constraints on the way simulations (or virtual history) unfold and the pattern and degree of stratification that develop. I am interested here in three aspects of marriage, discussed later in fuller detail: (1) the degree of incest prohibitions, (2) the marriage prohibitions placed on the eldest sister of a high chief, and (3) the ability of a chiefly woman to bring minor co-wives into a high marriage. Simulations are used to trace the effects of variations in these marriage customs on the larger dynamics and history of the chiefdom. Other computer simulation attempts to better understand the implications of kinship-based structures and institutions within a society have been completed by Read (1990, 1995) and Nardi (1977).

In this chapter, I play out the results of different types of marriage rules within a computer-based cultural testbed. By cultural testbed, I mean a modeled society in which the seminal processes of the society and its reproduction are represented. The modeled society I use, which I will call "TongaSim," has been constructed on the basis of ethnographic, oral history, and archaeological evidence from The Kingdom of Tonga, a Western Polynesian society. [1]

---

[1] TongaSim is not complete in its level of detail. However, the model is being built to approximate a plausible physical and demographic environment, based on estimated measures of arable land, population size, production, and growth (Kirch 1984; Green 1973; Cowgill 1975; Crane 1979; Burley 1994; Cook 1972; Thaman 1975). The modeler used archaeological, ethnohistorical, and oral history accounts of Tongan social structure to construct the rules of the model including information about social change in prehistory (Spennemann

Earlier iterations of this system were developed and presented in 1995, at the SimSoc Conference in Boca Raton, Florida (Small et al. 1995). TongaSim was developed to look at a number of processes, including but beyond marriage, involved in the development of chiefdoms.

TongaSim is conceived as a dynamic and interacting system of linked processes (production and redistribution, marriage and kinship, growth and stratification) within which chiefly agents (familial lines, headed by chiefs) compete for status and ascendancy. It is capable of simulating up to 50 chiefly lines that reproduce themselves, produce and redistribute agricultural wealth, expand territory, grow in population, and split into branch lines over a specified number of generations.

2 THE MODELING APPROACH

I am a cultural anthropologist who has worked closely with a computer programmer to model the social dynamics of a Polynesian society. My modeling approach departs somewhat from conventional modeling wisdom, which strives toward ends of "elegance" and "simplicity." The TongaSim model, although a clear simplification of social dynamics, attempts to preserve much of the social complexity of decision-making contingencies. I have tried to represent the processes that anthropologists would say were culturally significant in reproducing the social order. [2]

1986; Dye 1988; McKern 1929; Poulsen 1987; Davidson 1979), historical Tongan social structure (Biersack 1990; Mahina 1990; Kirch 1980, 1982:41–69, 1988), the Tongan construction of authority and leadership (Coult 1959; Gunsen 1979; Korn 1978; Bott 1981; Gunsen 1979), marriage and exchange patterns (Earle 1977; Kaeppler 1978; Collocott 1923; Biersack 1982), and kinship, fahu, and gender (Spennemann 1990; Valeri 1989; Korn 1974, 1978; Rogers 1977; James 1981, 1983). The most directly valuable sources were anthropological studies and descriptions of Tonga that relate specifically to the period between 1000 A.D. and 1600 A.D. (Gailey 1987; Bott 1982; Kirch 1982:220–242; Wood 1943:3–14; Mahina 1986, 1990; James 1992; Spennemann 1986, 1990; Korn 1978). Where the historical record is incomplete, evidence from other important ethnographic and oral history sources in Tonga (Mariner 1827; Gifford 1924, 1929; Beaglehole 1941; Collocott 1929; Aoyagi 1966; Cummins 1972; Rogers 1975; Ve'ehala 1977; Marcus 1975; Herda 1987; Wood Ellem 1987) and relevant archaeological and ethnohistorical evidence from other stratified Polynesian chiefdoms will be considered to aid in the social reconstruction process (Langevin 1990; Marshall 1983; Thomas 1989; Valeri 1985; Sahlins 1958, 1981; Goldman 1955, 1970; Kirch 1984:17–67, 243-262; Marcus 1989; Gunsen 1987; Ralston and Thomas 1987; Burrows 1938; Hocart 1915; Kirch 1989; Schoeffel 1987; and Shore 1989).

[2] Although there are clear benefits to "simplicity" in simulation, I have found that the credibility of modeling work for cultural anthropologists rests with its details—its ability to take into account a number of factors that enter into human decision making. In this sense, then, I have constructed what modelers would call an "inelegant" model that is difficult to evaluate without being highly familiar with Polynesian ethnography/archaeology. As a result of my approach, I am having to develop a detailed rule book to accompany my simulations, which includes not only programming information but (1) how the algorithms were constructed; (2) the ethnographic principles, in English, that the algorithms are designed to enact or preserve; and (3) the supporting evidence for the principle in the literature. I do not include all of this in this chapter.

The model, thus, aims toward "holism" in the anthropological sense. As a result, although the focus of the model is "marriage," the modeled society performs many operations beyond marriage: it expands territory and splits lines, creates kinship ties and economic obligations, selects heirs, produces agricultural wealth, and redistributes wealth to commoners. It does this because, from an ethnographic perspective, a number of other subsystems impinge on marriage contingencies and choices, even if indirectly, just as marriage decisions have implications for a wide range of system components.

In the next two sections, I explain some of what the model does and how it was programmed.

3 BUILDING THE MODEL: FROM ETHNOGRAPHY TO ALGORITHM

I begin with the admission that at this early stage of modeling (and perhaps at later stages as well), computers will not be able to match the richness of the ethnographic record nor the complexity of human behavior. However, even though computer models necessarily simplify human decisions and behaviors, the final product need not be simplistic.

For example, selecting a titled heir within a chiefly line is one process I model that is central to the reproduction of the Tongan chiefdom. The ethnographic record offers detailed insight into heir selection conventions both through numerous examples in history and myth and through principles indicated directly by Tongan nobility (Collocott 1923, 1928; Gifford 1924; Mahina 1990; Bott 1982:56-155; Gailey 1987). Bott (1982:123), for instance, through discussions with Queen Salote of Tonga, reports three characteristics of children that influenced their selection as heirs: their personal rank (this includes their birth order), their personal ability, and the support of their mother's people. Although personal rank was primary, all influenced the final choice and various circumstances, exemplified in the historical record, could alter the priorities.

How is this ethnographic information translated into TongaSim? In the case of heir selection, the modeler developed a set of situation-specific rules for rank-ordering priorities and then choosing an heir from a larger pool. In most cases, the priority order is (1) personal rank (this takes into account primogeniture), (2) support, and (3) ability. Each potential heir (i.e., child of titled chief) is ranked according to all three factors against the other potential heirs, receiving a specified number of points for the ranking in each category. For instance, these are the points earned in the current model:

Priority Ordering	Position 1	Position 2	Position 3
1 Rank	5	3	1
2 Support	3	1	0
3 Ability	1	0	0

In this system, a potential heir who was first in rank would earn 5 points, and would be the likely heir. However, if another potential heir was second in rank (earning 3 points) and then also first in support of their mother's line (earning another 3 points), he would be selected over the highest ranking choice.

Specific circumstances can alter the priority ordering (column 1), and these are also defined by rules. A line that is high in rank relative to other lines, but proportionally lower in wealth, may wish to choose a son whose mother's line is large and wealthy. A line which has been losing kin (because of poor redistribution rates) would prioritize an heir with high personal ability (as priority 1) and support (as priority 2), but might not continue to do so in a different generation.

While not a perfect representation of "reality," this translation system is faithful to the basic principles involved: the existence of a limited number of distinct priorities for decision making, the line's evaluation of the individual merit of each heir, and flexible priorities based on the specific situation of a line. In this way, many factors enter into the decision, and the outcome is something more than a rote calculation. Moreover, the algorithms can be changed as our ethnographic knowledge increases or changes.

Some variables that are extremely important as cultural concepts are not particularly amenable to mathematical definition. The "status of a line," for instance, is an elusive concept in chiefdoms that can be translated as "social prestige" or "prominence" and that is effectively used to socially rank chiefly lines. The concept is "real" in the sense that people have an idea of which line is higher, lower, falling or rising but it is "unreal" in the sense that it is not a quantity and it is always relative to other lines. How then do you quantify it?

With many such social variables, I program based on the supposition that "if it looks like a duck, walks like a duck, and quacks like a duck, then it is a duck." So, regarding "line status," I have attempted to program its properties: it was durable over time and depended on past reputation; yet, a line could rise and fall in its line status, depending on which other chiefly lines were attracted to it, and the personal status of its title-holder. The literature suggests that a series of bad marriages and heir choices could change the "status" of a line but it would probably take 4–5 generations for a line to lower its rank position relative to other lines. This description is what I attempted to match in devising the algorithm for line status: line status $= [(.5(\text{statusGen}^{-2}) + \text{statusGen}^{-1})/1.5] + [\text{current chief} - \text{past chief}) + \text{earned status points}]$. Stated in plain English, the algorithm calculates current status as a function of the past reputation of the line, the personal rank of the current title holder (and his difference $+$ or $-$ from the past title holder), and the status accrued through marriages to important lines during the past generation.

Chance or natural variation can be and is also built into the algorithms. In the example of heir selection, "personal ability" is an individual attribute that may be important to the operation of the line. "Ability" is considered to be distributed normally, along a bell curve and the program assigns a random ability value to each child born, based on this distribution. When a line chooses an heir based on "ability," these values become primary in the heir selection process, and may be affected by the particular pool of potential heirs in that generation; in turn, an heir's "ability" may affect other model outcomes, such as the production level of his people.

The operating model for this chapter is based on a number of such rules. To date, much of the work involved in producing the TongaSim model has comprised designing these rules and basing them on an analysis of ethnographic examples and relevant archaeological evidence. Although considerable work has already been done on the social system and the rules, the model is not yet complete. It does not, for instance, allow for the possibility and ramifications of warfare, and the marriage choices associated with creating military alliances and avoiding war. This is the next step in its development.[3]

Below is a brief summary of the current model, and how it reproduces itself. The full exposition here of all the rules and processes would occupy more than a paper-length manuscript so, in the following section, I offer simply an overview of the model and its operation. It is within this cultural "testbed" that we will compare the effects of different application of marriage rules.

4   AN OVERVIEW OF MODEL DYNAMICS

TongaSim recreates cyclical processes involved in the operation and reproduction of the Tongan chiefdom over time. The model begins with ten chiefly lines (an arbitrary number) that are related to one another and hierarchically ranked. The population of the chiefdom grows (at two percent per year currently, or at any rate I specify) and, in so doing, lines may split into separate branches and move into new territories when their population density becomes substantial. The model handles up to 50 hierarchically chiefly lines that each pay tribute to the higher node of the structure in which they are embedded. The rank (or relative status) of each line is capable of rising and falling over generations as lines and chiefs "behave." In the Tongan system, neither wealth nor power can directly buy rank. To increase in rank, one must use wealth to attract hypergamous marriages that, because personal rank is inherited, will devolve on the next generation. Marriage, then, is a central political process.

On the basis of knowledge about Tongan incest restrictions and marriage aims, the program begins a marriage process by having each line rank potential spouses in priority order. The prototypic Polynesian marriage is hypergamous; women marry up in status. Men marry first for status, then for wealth. Although the model allows us to alter marriage priorities, this is the default. The marriage process results in several hundred chiefly "marriages" in

---

[3]I am now looking at the effect of line expansion, migration, and warfare on the system, and gender-related features of the system, in a project funded by a POWRE grant (SBR 9753111) from the National Science Foundation.

the simulation, producing a complex web of economic and kin ties. Following Tongan custom, the simulation institutionalizes what Tongans call *fahu* privileges, i.e., the regular flow of wealth from wife-receiving lines to wife-giving lines.

Marriages also result in children. The existing model uses an average of four living children per marriage, but this will ultimately be refined using available data about fertility rates and what we know of Tongan genealogies. Each child inherits a personal rank, a combination of its mother's and father's personal rank. Personal rank (*eiki*) varies with birth order such that older children are higher in personal rank than younger children and girls' rank exceeds boys. Consistent with the Tongan system, all children receive a personal rank but only boy children have authority or *pule*, and *pule* is a function of actual title holding. Every generation, an heir to the title is chosen from the pool of possibilities, based on priorities discussed in the preceding section.

Each line in each generation produces agricultural wealth. The major constraining factor in production is labor (really, kin size) (Bott 1982) but land can limit production if it is insufficient for the number of kin. Production is thus affected by kin numbers, land, and a third factor, chiefly leadership ability (which is capable of affecting the production level per person).

The wealth produced by a line is used to satisfy a line's various obligations. These include *fahu* obligations, mentioned previously, wherein a line gives support to the lines of its daughter's (sister's) children. A yearly first-fruits tribute is made to the highest ranked line (called *inasi* in Tongan) and lines make regular tribute to their immediately superior lines in the system. Tribute patterns may be altered with the addition of new titles or by the absorption of titles. The third obligation in a line is of a chief to his commoner retinue. In the simulation (and depending on level of stratification), most of wealth produced is redistributed to the commoners who produced it. A line that has incurred greater obligations may, however, redistribute less than others. This lesser redistribution, however, will result in a loss of loyalty and some commoners will leave for other lines.

The modeler is able to chart the system's growth, marriages, status, wealth, and land holding, kinship and tribute relationships, and numbers of chiefs and commoners over several hundred years.

5 SIMULATING WITH DIFFERENT MARRIAGE RULES

The question I attempt to answer through simulation is how marriage rule constraints or preferences affect the dynamic operation and virtual history of a chiefdom. TongaSim has been programmed with an interactive screen that allows me to specify a series of marriage rules that will apply to the simulation. I can easily change particular rules or a combination of rules without changing any other component of the system. I am able to hold steady the stochastic factors of the simulation by providing seeds that will reproduce the same simulation run.[4] Comparing simulations within the model, thus, can allow me to trace the effects of marriage prescriptions and constraints on the system.

In this chapter, I focus on three specific marriage variations, all of which have relevance in Tongan history.

5.1   INCEST RULES

The first area of marriage that I manipulate is *incest rules*. Over a number of centuries, Polynesian chiefdoms tended to develop marriage rules that allowed high chiefly people to marry close relatives. Although incest taboos remained a defining feature of commoner marriages, high chiefs were able to marry progressively closer relatives. This happened in a number of different Polynesian systems, including Tonga. Although Tongan commoners are enjoined to marry nonrelatives, and it is considered scandalous to marry blood kin (*kainga*), Tongan high chiefs have a marriage preference for cross cousins. In Hawaii, the highest and most sacred marriages occurred between sister and brother.

In individual cases, the advantages of close kin marriages to high chiefs are politically transparent. "Personal status," the primary factor in determining one's place in a chiefdom, is inherited. By marrying a close relative, a high chief is attempting to preserve his or her "blood line" by marrying a person who will contribute equally high blood to their child (who will inherit blood from both lines) and who, conversely, will not dilute the high blood of one parent. The further a high chief gets away from his/her own line for marriage, the more likely that he/she will be marrying someone of lower blood.

But did this marriage transformation do more than secure a particular status for a particular line? How important was this marriage shift to the development of stratification more generally in Polynesia? Sahlins (1958:9) suggests that these endogamous developments in marriage were one among the defining features of stratification. Was it also a necessary condition, or enabling feature?

I can toggle among three levels of incest prohibitions, as defined below, to begin any simulation.

1. *No relatives (Exogamous)*: this rule will stop marriage if the potential spouses are related by having a great grandparent in common. This rule disallows all "first and second cousins."

---

[4]Stochastic factors are chance elements, such as the natal ability of a child. This is built into the simulation as an element that is distributed normally in the simulation. However, because runs may differ slightly because of these random effects, it is advisable to hold the random elements constant when comparing simulation runs, by providing a seed that will produce the same chance effect for the runs under consideration.

2. *Cross-Cousin Marriage*: This rule disallows sibling marriages, or the marriage of parallel cousins. Cross-cousin marriages are permitted. This rule is designed to approximate the Tongan chiefly system of marriage.

3. *Sibling Marriage*: No marriages are disallowed within this system. As in the ethnographic record, however, this rule may be differentially applied so that only high chiefs may marry this way. For purposes of the simulation, I define as "high chiefs" all chiefs whose personal status is within 20 percent of the highest chief.

For this chapter, I will run a simulation based on each of the incest rule variations and then compare the outcomes of the simulations to see if marriage customs themselves influence the social structure of the simulated society and, if so, in what ways.

5.2 VIRGIN SISTER

The second marriage custom I look at is called the "sacred sister" or "virgin sister," a convention that exists throughout Western Polynesia. While the particulars of the custom differ slightly cross-culturally, the gist of the "sacred sister" rule is that the eldest sister of the highest line remains a virgin, neither marrying nor having children through childbirth or adoption. Tonga apparently had a sacred sister custom historically (Bott 1982:67), but it was later replaced by a new version that allowed the highest sister to marry (as long as she married outside the culture) but required that *her* daughter remain a virgin.

In this chapter, I test a hypothesis advanced by Hecht (1977) about why this occurs. She argues that the custom is political. Sisters in Western Polynesia carry high status, and their marriage into another line carries with it the possibility that a high-ranked sister will pass on her high rank to the heir of another line, i.e., her husband's line, providing the genealogical fuel to potentially eclipse her natal line in status. TongaSim has an "on" or "off" switch enabling or disabling a virgin sister rule requiring the eldest sister of the highest line to remain unmarried. I test Hecht's proposition by comparing the fortunes of the highest line with and without the virgin sister custom. I ask whether the introduction of the virgin sister rule, in fact, stabilizes an otherwise unstable future for a chiefdom's highest lines. (Eventually, I will simulate a number of variations on this theme that happened historically.)

5.3 FOKONOFO

The third custom I consider is called "*fokonofo*" in Tonga. Tonga was a polygynous society, where chiefly men took several wives, often as many as fifteen. The *fokonofo* was a convention wherein a high chiefly wife, entering into marriage with a politically significant chief, would bring other wives with her into marriage, often as her husband's only other wives. These secondary *fokonofo* wives were often her younger sisters or inferior cousins, but always women who were subordinate to her in rank and who owed her kinship allegiance. For a woman, it was presumably a way of ensuring that her son would be chosen heir over potentially competing wives. For the system as a whole, the custom limited the competition of multiple children of a man for heirship or title. This custom is not frequently discussed in the literature, except that numerous case examples are mentioned, so I wanted to see whether modeling could reveal anything about its operation, function, or implications in the system at large.

The outcomes of these simulations are traceable through a series of outputs that give various assessments of each line and the system as a whole over time. For any time period or any series of generations, one can look at kin size, kin relations among lines, status, land holding, and wealth production figures.

For purposes of this chapter, I am interested in tracking stratification. I look at several related outputs to measure stratification in the system:

1. the range and variation $[\sum(x - x)^2/x]$ of line statuses in the system (how big are the differences in status among chiefly lines within the system?);
2. the range of personal status that chiefs have inherited by birth in the system;
3. the concentration of "high chiefly people" in the system (how are "high" chiefly people—those within the top 20 percent in their rank—distributed across lines? Do lines develop with no high chiefly people while others have several?); and
4. the mobility of lines (how much do line ranks, i.e., relative line statuses, shift upward or downward from their initial position?).

6   SIMULATION RESULTS AND ANALYSIS

The first set of results concerned incest rules, specifically, the differences in stratification within the model that proceeded from adjusting the closeness of kinship relationships allowed in marriage. To evaluate stratification, I looked at four sets of outputs that assessed differences in social prestige or "status" among chiefly lines and chiefly individuals.

"Status" in Polynesia indicates the "high-ness" with which a line or person is held by others, and has many other social, economic, and political correlates. Individuals accrue "status" by birth alone, whiles lines have status based on their past status, the personal status of the chief of their line, and the success of the line in forging high alliances with other high-status lines. The status of the line will determine who will wish to marry into it and, thus, what economic and kinship relationships a line is able to create.

One measure of system stratification was Line Status Variability—the sum of the distances of each line's status from the mean of the sample. I used

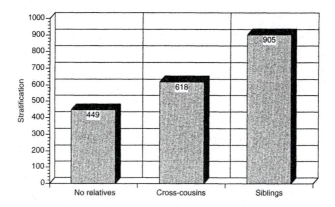

FIGURE 1   Incest rule variation and stratification in initial ten lines at generation 20.

this measure to answer the question: how much internal variation in status is there among the lines of the system and how is this variation affected by the incest level allowable in marriage rules? Figure 1 compares the "stratification" among the initial 10 lines of the system after 20 generations under three different conditions of incest rules: (1) no relatives may marry, (2) cross cousins (MoBroDa or FaSiSo) or more distant relatives may marry, and (3) siblings may marry (if top 20 percent of chiefs).

The actual numbers in Figure 1 are less meaningful than their relative values. When we compare column 1 (where no relatives can marry), to either column 2 (the Tongan case where cousins may marry) *or* to column C (the Hawaiian case where siblings of high lines may marry) it is clear that relaxing incest rules increases our measure of stratification. The more the incest restrictions are loosened to allow close marriages, the greater the internal variation (or the larger the overall number). The initial ten lines of the system are twice as stratified (905 vs. 449) when siblings may marry than when no relatives may marry, while cross-cousin marriage shows two-thirds the stratification of sibling marriage and 38 percent more stratification than "no relative" marriage. Conversely, high restrictions on marriage—prohibiting marriage with any relative (column 1)—results in the most "converged" line status variation, an indicator of least stratification.

The stratification pattern evident at the line level is also true at the level of the chiefly individual. Personal status in Polynesia, as in the computer model, is a basic social distinction that is inherited through one's parents. It is through marriage that the fate of one's children is sealed. Marrying up, to someone of higher status, increases your children's status relative to your own, while marrying down causes the reverse to be true.

In Figures 2(a)–(c), we can see the values and ranges of personal status that developed over time, as chiefly people married and had children over 20

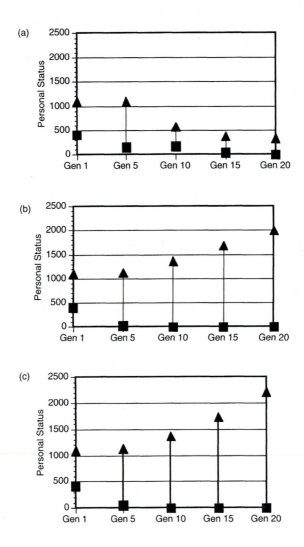

FIGURE 2   Incest rules and personal status.

generations. Each of the three companion charts that follow (Figures 2(a), 2(b), and 2(c)) show the high and low values of chiefly personal status that existed in the chiefdom at five-generation intervals from generation 1 to 20 of the simulation.

Comparing the three figures shows that status distinctions among chiefs vary markedly with changes in marriage rules. When chiefs cannot marry their relatives, chiefly statuses converge. In other words, high and low chiefs in the system lose their status distance from each other and from commoners (0 status). Allowing endogamous marriages results in an increasing trajectory of status ranges; at the "cousin" level of marriage (Figure 2(b)), high chiefs become higher and more differentiated from lower chiefs and commoners. This pattern is even more pronounced at the sibling level of incest (Figure 2(c)).

These findings demonstrate the logical processes associated with exogamy over time. When high chiefs are forced to marry "out" (that is, marry non-relatives) over generations, they necessarily must marry lower chiefs at some point, causing the personal status of their progeny to spiral downward. Conversely, lower chiefs have increasing opportunities to marry "up" since high chiefs run out of appropriate marriage partners. Their hypergamous marriage increases the status of their children.

There are many noted historical examples of hypogamous and hypergamous marriages and what they meant for the particular lines in question. What the model and its output makes clearer is the systemic effect of marriage choices. When chiefs must marry nonrelatives, as in Figure 2(a), the status distinctions among chiefs in the system narrow markedly. When high chiefs are allowed to marry closer relatives (Figure 2(b) and 2(c)), they do—with the effect that the distance in status among individuals widens in the system over time. High chiefs marry high chiefs, bolstering status among a small class of individuals, while lower chiefs must marry other lower chiefs or even commoners, resulting in a downward status trend and a widening gap between high and low chiefs. These findings suggest that the development of endogamous marriage rules may have been a necessary or enabling condition for the development of stratification.

Endogamous marriage patterns are also associated with an uneven concentration of high chiefs within TongaSim. In our virtual system, lines may split to form new lines up to a limit of 50 chiefly lines. By the twentieth generation of the simulation, this limit has been reached, and we can trace how chiefly people are distributed among the 50 lines at the end of the simulation run. While all lines in the system contain some "chiefly people," not all lines have "high chiefs"—those whose personal status falls within the top 20 percent. The "donut" figures that follow indicate what number and percentage of lines of the total 50 lines contains high chiefly people under three simulation conditions. Comparing Figures 3(a)–(c) shows that stricter marriage rules (e.g., no marriage of relatives) are associated with a much wider distribution of high chiefs. Conversely, when cross-cousin and sibling marriage are permitted, there is a corresponding reduction in the number of lines that hold high chiefs. High chiefly blood becomes more concentrated in a few high lines, another sign of increasing stratification.

A fourth measure of stratification is designed to represent the stability/mobility of lines within the system. Each line has a rank, depending on the status that it holds relative to every other line at the same point in time. Ranks in the system go from 1–50, and in the real as in the virtual world, the behavior of lines (marriages, heir choices, etc.) may cause them to rise or fall relative to other lines.

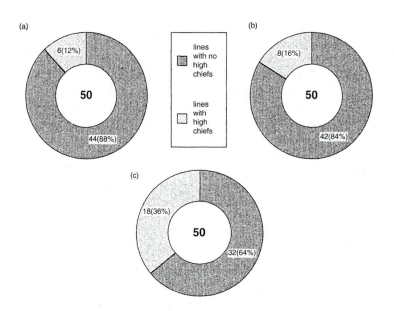

FIGURE 3   The concentration of High Chiefs under three marriage conditions: (a) siblings, (b) cross-cousins, and (c) no relatives.

The rising and falling of lines—which I call Rank Variation—is an important property of the system, a component of what I am calling "stratification." From the point of view of a *high* line, this property is an indication of how unstable or volatile the system is and, thus, the extent to which a high line's position might be at risk. From the point of view of a *low* line, rank variation can be used to assess how much mobility is in the system and what are a lower line's chances for increasing in rank.

Table 1 shows the total ranks gained and the total ranks lost by a line over 20 generations under different marriage rule conditions. For instance, $-10/+5$ for Line B (column 1) means that in the course of 20 generations where sibling marriage was permitted, Line B had dropped ten ranks, while it increased five ranks. Drops or increases in rank are measured from the previous generation. A line that drops from rank 2 to rank 4 in a generation is thus assigned a number of -2. All the drops and increases are added together to give a 20-generation total for each line, the numbers in each cell. Then the drops and increases of all ten initial lines over all generations are represented in the final row. The totals in the last row give a measure, then, of the "rank variation" in the system over time. Again, it is not absolute numbers that matter. The lines represented here are only the first ten, for simplicity's sake, and which lines increased or which decreased are not of particular consequence. What is interesting is the relative degree of stability or mobility in the system.

TABLE 1   Rank variation and incest level change over 20 generations.

Line	Incest Level 1 (siblings–applies to only top 10% of chiefs)	Incest Level 2 (cousins)	Incest Level 3 (no relatives)
A	−3/ + 1	−14/ + 11	−16/ + 12
B	−10/ + 5	−14/ + 6	−15/ + 16
C	−1/ + 3	−5/ + 6	−22/ + 15
D	−6/ + 6	−2/ + 5	−21/ + 16
E	−6/ + 5	−9/ + 5	−18/ + 9
F	−7/ + 8	−9/ + 7	−5/ + 9
G	−4/ + 9	−7/ + 8	−14/ + 8
H	−5/ + 5	− 7/ + 10	−13/ + 14
I	−8/ + 3	−9/ + 3	−21/ + 27
J	−7/ + 2	−5/ + 3	−12/ + 16
Total Rank Changes	−57/ + 47 = 104	−81/ + 64 = 145	−157/ + 142 = 299

As one can see in Table 1, the stability of the system (as measured by rank variation) varies markedly with the incest level permitted in marriage. Incest level 3 (marrying nonrelatives) results in three times as many rank variations as incest level 1 (siblings) and twice as many as incest level 2.

In descriptive terms, marrying one's siblings results in a more stable or rigid system, where lines keep their position and are less mobile compared to both of the other marriage conditions. Marrying nonrelatives, by contrast, produces a highly mobile or unstable system (depending on one's point of view). To evolve a rigid stratified system, then, kinship-restrictive marriage rules would need to be replaced by rules that permitted close family marriages.

6.1   TWO OTHER MARRIAGE RULES

Simulations were also used to explore the nature of two specific marriage rules that were present in Tongan ethnohistory: (1) a "virgin sister" rule where the eldest sister of the chief of the highest line would be prevented from marrying and (2) a "*fokonofo*" rule that enabled a first wife to choose successive wives for her husband from among her relatives.

6.1.1   The "Virgin Sister."
Hecht (1977) and others have argued that the virgin sister rule is a way of "holding on" to the high rank of an eldest sister, and preventing the highness of her blood from being passed to another line that might otherwise eclipse her natal line. This is a perfect problem for modeling because it posits a "what-if?" scenario that did not actually occur at the time the virgin sister rule was in operation. In other words, it proposes that had the virgin sister rule *not* existed, then the highest chiefly line might have been eclipsed by another line. The virgin sister rule exists in this theory to prevent

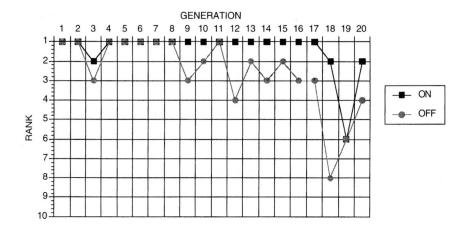

FIGURE 4 Virgin Sister.

a status eclipse from occurring. Modeling allowed me to introduce the "what if" proposition by turning the virgin sister "on" and "off" and comparing the outcomes of the simulation runs with regard to the highest line. (When the virgin sister rule was on, the eldest sister of the highest chief had to marry, according to the rules that were operating within the system.)

To see the political effect of the virgin sister rule in Tonga, I compared the ranks of Line A, the highest line in the system, over 20 generations with the rule "on" and "off" (under the single condition of "cousin marriage," the level of incest allowed chiefs in Tonga). Figure 4 gives an overall visual sense of the stability of Line A under the two conditions.

As Figure 4 shows, although the eclipse of the highest line is never completely prevented, Line A is much more stable when the virgin sister rule is ON than when it is OFF. Tables 2(a) and 2(b) attempt to quantify this difference by indicating line ranks in each generation and the SUM of all rank decreases and increases. Line A is more than twice as stable with the virgin sister rule in operation than when the rule is off. Turning OFF the virgin sister rule causes much greater instability for line A (25 as opposed to 11 changes in rank, or 14 rank declines as opposed to 6), and the eclipse of line A occurs 12 times, three times more frequently than with the custom ON. The eclipse is also more severe with the absence of the virgin sister rule; only in one generation does line A fall more than one rank away from the #1 rank position with the virgin sister custom ON while, with the custom OFF, Line A occupies a subordinate rank in nine of twenty generations.

TABLE 2　Line ranks, change in line ranks, and total line rank variation (SUM) over 20 generations.

(a) With Virgin Sister Custom OFF

ON	Generation																				SUM
	1	2	3	4	5	6	7	8	9	10	11	12	13	14	15	16	17	18	19	20	
Rank	1	1	3	1	1	1	1	1	3	2	1	4	2	3	2	-3	3	-8	6	4	
Change in Rank	0	-2	2	0	0	0	0	-2	1	1	-3	2	-1	1	-1	0	-5	2	2		25 changes -14/+11

(b) With Virgin Sister Custom ON

ON	Generation																				SUM
	1	2	3	4	5	6	7	8	9	10	11	12	13	14	15	16	17	18	19	20	
Rank	1	1	2	1	1	1	1	1	1	1	1	1	1	1	1	1	1	2	6	2	
Change In Rank	0	-1	1	0	0	0	0	0	0	0	0	0	0	0	0	0	1	-4	4		11 changes -5/+6

6.1.2　The *Fokonofo* Custom.　What about the *fokonofo* rule, which allows a first wife of a high chief to bring "friendly wives" (usually her close relatives) into marriage as co-wives? Ethnographically, the custom occurs when a female chief marries a high male with an important title. It is presumably a political strategy to increase the chances that the female chief's son will inherit her husband's title, by limiting other competition. Since there is no specific hypothesis to be tested here, I just sought to explore the nature of the custom by looking at its effect on stratification within the system, as seen during a simulation run of 40 generations.

I found that the *fokonofo* rule was somewhat variable in its effect on stratification, depending on the point in the simulation it was examined and the degree of marriage exogamy that applied. The custom, then, had no obvious systemic or implications in itself for stratification. Unlike certain customs (such as incest prohibitions) whose effects are consistent throughout the time span of the simulation and under varying parameters, the *fokonofo* custom was very context dependent. For this reason, I looked at the *fokonofo* custom in the virtual context that best approximated its historical appearance, i.e., a late point in the simulation and in a virtual society that permitted cross-cousin marriages for chiefs.

Under these conditions, the effect of the *fokonofo* custom was to increase stratification on all measures. At generation 30 (which was typical of other late generation results), the system was 26 percent more stratified with the custom ON than with it OFF and the initial 10 lines were 93 percent more stratified. The custom also resulted in a much greater concentration of chiefly blood. With the custom ON, only 7 of the existing 50 lines contain chiefly people that are within 50 percent of the personal status of the highest chief. With the *fokonofo* custom OFF, there are 32 lines holding people with this degree of high chiefly blood.

TABLE 3   The number and proportion of High, Mid, and Low Chiefs, with the *Fokonofo* Custom on and off.

Chiefly Status[a]	Fokonofo ON	Fokonofo OFF
High Chiefs	32 (.03)	32 (.03)
Mid Chiefs	43 (.05)	327 (.31)
Low Chiefs	893 (.92)	685 (.66)

[a]High chiefs are defined as being within 10 percent of the status of the highest chief, mid-chiefs within 50 percent, and lower chiefs as less than 50 percent of the status of the highest chief in the system.

The virtual history of the simulation suggests why this is so. With the *fokonofo* custom in place (and with the condition that marriages could occur between relatively close relatives), a *fokonofo* marriage doubly limits the pool of high-born women available for marriage and rank transmission because marriage obligates not only a high chiefess but also her younger or minor female relatives. Monopolizing more women of high lines in fewer marriages statistically decreases the marriageable pool of high women, resulting in fewer chances for lower chiefs to contract a marriage with a higher woman. By reducing the number and probability of high chiefly marriages to lower lines, the *fokonofo* custom has the ultimate effect of lowering mobility in the system and gutting the ranks of middle-level chiefs, as Table 3 indicates.

Table 3 indicates the numbers and proportion of chiefs who fall into HIGH, MID, and LOW chiefly ranks with the custom ON and OFF after 30 generations. With the *fokonofo* custom OFF (column two), 31 percent of all chiefs are in a middle tier of chiefly status. Turning the custom ON, however, in column one, results in a more class-like two-tiered rank system, with very few middle-level chiefs (5 percent) and most chiefly people (92 percent) having a more distant rank from the high chiefs.

In real history, the *fokonofo* custom is a minor one that persisted for a limited number of generations, and it probably did not have far-reaching structural effects. The simulation results then do not reenact history. What the simulation *does* do, though, is show the researcher what variables seem to be important to insight and the logical implications of patterned choices. In this way, it can help researchers to frame their investigations and point them in more fruitful directions within the ethnographic and archaeological records.

These findings suggest that, in interpreting the *fokonofo* or other sororate-type custom in chiefdoms, it is crucial to know particular features of context, namely, the status of the *women* entering into these marriages, the type of incest prohibitions that apply in the society, and the degree of existing stratification. If the *fokonofo* is seen to consistently occur in the ethnographic record with high-status women, and under stratified conditions that permit cross-cousin marriage, then the *fokonofo* convention may possibly be understood as part of a complex of customs that contributes to state development in highly stratified chiefdoms. This is a possibility that could be fruitfully pursued through a focused investigation of *fokonofo*-type customs within the ethnographic and ethnohistorical record.

7 SUMMARY AND IMPLICATIONS

These simulations give clearer insight into marriage rules and their relationship to stratification in Polynesia. The main insight to emerge from three different simulation tests was that changes in the parameters of Polynesian marriage rules had significant implications for the internal stratification that developed in the system.

The ability to marry close relatives significantly increased all indicators of stratification, including the status variability that existed among chiefly lines and the status differences that developed among chiefly individuals. The results of the simulation suggested further that marriage rules might have been necessary to the system in order for stratification to occur because, without the presence of endogamous customs, the trajectories of chiefly statuses converged. The history and dynamics surrounding changes in marriage rule customs takes on new ethnographic significance in this light.

Specific marriage customs also came into sharper focus. Simulations gave support for existing theories which argue that the virgin sister rule is a custom developed and used to stabilize the highest lines in a system. This clearly was the case in our virtual world where the withdrawal of the virgin sister rule caused the instability of the system's highest line to double. The *fokonofo* marriage custom was seen to increase stratification in the virtual system. While the custom may have served to bolster the heirship chances of a woman's son, it also may be one of a number of developments that strengthened stratification in the late history of chiefdoms, raising interesting questions about the articulation of individual choices and structural change.

Simulation results such as these, while they do not represent actual history, can spur some fruitful new avenues for further ethnographic investigation. The development of endogamous marriage conventions, for example, takes on new ethnographic meaning in light of the virtual results connecting marriage and stratification. How did cross-cousin or sibling marriages come to be? Given their political significance, it would make sense that lower lineages or lower ranks would balk at close marriages, realizing that such rules would ultimately limit their own mobility. This simulation does not explain how endogamous marriage conventions came to be, but it does point to the fact that the absence of this explanation is problematic. One implication, then, of TongaSim's virtual history is to lead us to question the details of the ethnographic context that would give rise to new marriage rules. Is there evidence that endogamous marriages were contested in the historical record? Was a developing warrior class associated with the adoption of endogamous marriage rules (suggesting that social force and the consolidation of ranks were parallel developments)? What other social developments allowed chiefly groups to institute their course toward marriage endogamy, especially when it was disadvantageous to the population on whom chiefs depended? It becomes highly significant here that brother-sister marriages in Hawaii were socially understood as "sacred" suggesting, perhaps, how sacredness has played a role in furthering rank stratification.

Virtual history can usefully serve as probe of our ethnographic and archaeological models of reality. Although simulations may not mirror the historical record, they often reflect back to us the logical implications of our assumptions in a way that promotes new and creative avenues for ethnographic inquiry.

REFERENCES

Aoyagi, M.
  1966 Kinship Organization and Behavior in a Contemporary Village. Journal of the Polynesian Society 75:141–176.

Beaglehole, Ernest, and Pearl Beaglehole
  1941 Pangai, Village in Tonga. Wellington: The Polynesian Society.

Biersack, Aletta
  1982 Tongan Exchange Structures: Beyond Descent and Alliance. Journal of the Polynesian Society 91(2):181–212.
  1990 Blood and Garland: Duality in Tongan History. *In* Tongan Culture and History. P. S. Herda, J. Terrell, and N. Gunson, eds. Pp. 46–58. Canberra: Australian National University.

Bott, E.
  1981 Power and Rank in the Kingdom of Tonga. Journal of the Polynesian Society 90:7–81.

Bott, Elizabeth, with the assistance of Tavi
  1982 Tongan Society at the Time of Captain Cook's Visits: Discussions with Her Majesty Queen Salote Tupou. Wellington: The Polynesian Society.

Burley, David
  1994 Settlement Pattern and Tongan Prehistory: Reconsiderations from Ha'apai. Journal of the Polynesian Society 103(4):379–409.

Burrows, Edwin G.
  1938 Western Polynesia: A Study in Cultural Differentiation. Ethnologiska Studier 7:1–192.

Collocott, E. E. V.
  1923 Marriage in Tonga. Journal of the Polynesian Society 32:221–228.
  1928 Tales and Poems of Tonga. Bulletin No. 46. Honolulu: Bernice P. Bishop Museum.

Cook, S.
1972 Prehistoric Demography. Reading, MA: Addison-Wesley.

Coult, Allan D.
1959 Tongan Authority Structure. Kroeber Anthropological Society Papers 20:56–70.

Cowgill, George
1975 On the Causes and Consequences of Ancient and Modern Population Changes. American Anthropologist 77(3):505–525.

Crane, E. A.
1979 The Geography of Tonga. Nuku'alofa: Government of Tonga.

Cummins, H. G., ed.
1972 Sources of Tongan History: A Collection of Documents, Extracts, and Contemporary Opinions in Tongan Political History 1616–1900. Nuku'alofa.

Davidson, J.
1979 Samoa and Tonga. In Prehistory of Polynesia. J. Jennings, ed. Pp. 82–109. Cambridge, MA: Harvard University Press.

Doran, Jim, Mike Palmer, Nigel Gilbert, and Paul Mellars
1994 The EOS Project: Modelling Upper Paleolithic Social Change. In Simulating Societies: The Computer Simulation of Social Phenomena. N. Gilbert and J. Doran, eds. Pp. 195–222. London: UCL Press.

Dye, T. S.
1988 Social and Cultural Change in the Prehistory of the Ancestral Polynesian Homeland. Ph.D. dissertation, Yale University, New Haven, CT.

Earle, T. K.
1977 Exchange Systems in Prehistory. New York: Academic Press.

Gailey, Christine Ward
1987 Kinship to Kingship: Gender Hierarchy and State Formation in the Tongan Islands. Austin, TX: University of Texas Press.

Gifford, Edward W.
1924 Tongan Myths and Tales. Honolulu: Bernice P. Bishop Museum.
1929 Tongan Society. Bulletin 61. Honolulu: Bernice P. Bishop Museum.

Goldman, Irving
1955 Status Rivalry and Cultural Evolution in Polynesia. American Anthropologist 57:680–697.
1970 Ancient Polynesian Society. Chicago, IL: University of Chicago Press.

Green, R. C.
1973 Tonga's Prehistoric Population. Pacific Viewpoint 14:61–74.

Gunsen, Neil
1979 The "Hau" Concept of Leadership in Western Polynesia. The Journal of Pacific History 14:28–49.

1987 Sacred Women, Chiefs, and Female "Headmen" in Polynesian History. The Journal of Pacific History 22(3):139–172.

Hecht, Julia
1977 The Culture of Gender in Pukapuka: Male, Female and Mayakitanga "Sacred Maid." Journal of the Polynesian Society 86:183–206.

Herda, Phyllis, Jennifer Terrell, and Niel Gunson, eds.
1987 Tongan Culture and History, Papers from the 1st Tongan History Conference 14–17 January 1987. Canberra: Department of Pacific and Southeast Asian History, Research School of Pacific Studies, Australian National University.

Hocart, A. M.
1915 Chieftainship and Sister's Son in the Pacific. American Anthropologist 17(4):631–646.

Huntsman, Judith, and Anthony Hooper
1975 Male and Female in Tokelau Culture. Journal of the Polynesian Society 84(4):415–430.

James, Kerry
1983 Gender Relations in Tonga. Journal of the Polynesian Society 92(2):233–243.
1991 The Female Presence in Heavenly Places: Myth and Sovereignty in Tonga. Oceania 61(4):287–308.
1992 Tongan Rank Revisited: Religious Hierarchy, Social Stratification and Gender in the Ancient Tongan Polity. Social Analysis 31(July):79–102.

Kaeppler, Adrienne
1971 Rank in Tonga. Ethnology 10:174–193.
1978 Exchange Patterns in Goods and Spouses: Fiji, Tonga, and Samoa. Mankind 11(3):246–252.

Kirch, Patrick Vinton
1980 Burial Structures and Societal Ranking in Vava'u, Tonga. Journal of the Polynesian Society 89:291–308.
1984 The Evolution of Polynesian Chiefdoms. Cambridge, MA: Cambridge University Press.
1988 Niuatoputapu: The Prehistory of a Polynesian Chiefdom. Seattle: Burke Museum.
1989 Prehistory. In Developments in Polynesian Ethnology. A. Howard and R. Borofsky, eds. Pp. 13–46. Honolulu: University of Hawaii Press.

Korn, Shulamit Decktor-
1974 Tongan Kin Groups: The Noble and the Common View. Journal of the Polynesian Society 85:5–13.
1978 Hunting the Ramage: Kinship and the Organization of Political Authority in Aboriginal Tonga. The Journal of Pacific History 13(2):107–113.

Langevin, Christin
1990 Tahitiennes de la Tradition à l'Integration Culturelle. Paris: Editions l'Harmattan.

Linnekin, Jocelyn
1990 Sacred Queens and Women of Consequence: Rank, Gender and Colonialism in the Hawaiian Islands. Ann Arbor, MI: University of Michigan Press.

Mahina, Okusitino
1986 Religion, Politics and the Tu'i Tonga Empire. M.A. Thesis, University of Auckland.
1990 Myths and History: Some Aspects of History in the Tu'i Tonga Myths. In Tongan Culture and History. P. Herda, J. Terrell, and N. Gunson, eds. Pp. 30–45. Canberra: Research School of Pacific Studies, Australian National University.

Marcus, George E.
1975 Alternative Social Structures and the Limits of Hierarchy in the Modern Kingdom of Tonga. Bijdragen Tot De Taal-Land-En Vol Ken Kunde 131(1):34–66.
1989 Chieftainship. In Developments in Polynesian Ethnology. A. Howard and R. Borofsky, eds. Pp. 175–209. Honolulu: University of Hawaii Press.

Mariner, William
1827 An Account of the Natives of the Tongan Islands. John Martin, ed. Edinburgh: John Constable.

Marshall, Mac, ed.
1983 Siblingship in Oceania: Studies in the Meaning of Kin Relations. Volume ASAO Monograph #8. Lanham: University Press of America.

McKern, W. C.
1929 The Archaeology of Tonga. Honolulu: Bernice P. Bishop Museum.

Nardi, Bonnie A.
1977 Demographic Aspects of Lineage Exogamy in Small Populations: A Microsimulation Model. Ph.D. Dissertation, University of California, Irvine.

Poulsen, J.
1987 The Prehistory of the Tongan Islands. Canberra: Terra Australis.

Ralston, Caroline, and Nicholas Thomas
1987 Sanctity and Power: Gender in Polynesian History. Special Issue. The Journal of Pacific History 22(3–4):114–122.

Read, Dwight W.
1995 Kinship-Based Demographic Simulation of Societal Processes. Modelling Gender and Social Change in a Polynesian Society. Simulating Societies '95, Approaches to Simulating Social Phenomena and Social Processes, Pre-Proceedings for the 1995 SIMSOC Conference in Boca Raton, FL, Department of Sociology. University of Surrey.

Read, Dwight W., and Clifford A. Behrens
  1990 An Expert System for the Algebraic Analysis of Kinship Terminologies. Journal of Quantitative Anthropology. 2(4):353.

Rogers, Garth
  1975 Kai and Kava in Niuatoputapu: Social Relations, Ideologies, and Contexts in a Rural Tongan Community. Ph.D. Thesis, University of Auckland.
  1977 The Father's Sister Is Black: A Consideration of Female Rank and Powers in Tonga. Journal of the Polynesian Society 86:157–182.

Sahlins, Marshall
  1958 Social Stratification in Polynesia. Seattle: University of Washington Press.
  1981 Historical Metaphors and Mythical Realities. Ann Arbor: University of Michigan Press.

Schoeffel, Penelope
  1987 Rank, Gender, and Politics in Ancient Samoa. Sanctity and Power: Gender in Polynesian History, Special Issue. The Journal of Pacific History 22(3-4):174–194.

Shore, Bradd
  1976 Incest Prohibitions and the Logic of Power in Samoa. Journal of the Polynesian Society 85:275–296.
  1989 Mana and Tapu. In Developments in Polynesian Ethnology. A. Howard and R. Borofsky, eds. Pp. 137–173. Honolulu: University of Hawaii Press.

Small, C. A., J. Tumlinson, and V. Blankenship
  1995 Modelling Gender and Social Change in a Polynesian Society. Simulating Societies '95, Approaches to Simulating Social Phenomena and Social Processes, Pre-Proceedings for the 1995 SIMSOC Conference in Boca Raton, FL, Department of Sociology. University of Surrey.

Spenneman, Dirk H. R.
  1986 'Ata 'a Tonga Mo 'Ata 'o Tonga: Earlier and Later Prehistory of the Tongan Islands. Ph.D. Thesis, Australian National University.
  1990 Changing Gender Roles in Tongan Society: Some Comments Based on Archaeological Observations. In Tongan Culture and History. P. Herda, J. Terrell, and N. Gunson, eds. Pp. 101–109. Canberra: Department of Pacific and Southeast Asian History, Research School of Pacific Studies, Australian National University.

Thaman, R. R.
  1975 The Tongan Agricultural System. Ph.D. dissertation, University of California, Los Angeles.

Thomas, Nicholas
  1989 Domestic Structures and Polyandry in the Marquesas Islands. *In* Family and Gender in the Pacific. M. Jolly and M. Macintyre, eds. Pp. 65–83. Cambridge, UK: Cambridge University Press.

Valeri, Valerio
  1972 Le Fonctionnement du Systeme des Rangs a Hawaii. L'Homme 12(1): 29–66.
  1985 Kingship and Sacrifice: Ritual and Society in Ancient Hawaii. Chicago: Chicago University Press.
  1989 Death in Heaven: Myth and Rites of Kinship in Tongan Kinship. History and Anthropology 4:209–247.
  1994 On Female Presences and Absences in Heavenly Places. Oceania (65):75–93.

Ve'ehala, Hon, and Tupou Posesi Fanua
  1977 Oral Tradition and Prehistory. *In* Friendly Islands: A History of Tonga. N. Rutherford, ed. Melbourne: Oxford University Press.

Wood, A. H.
  1943 A History and Geography of Tonga. Canberra: Kalia Press.

Wood Ellem, E.
  1987 Queen Salote Tupou of Tonga as Tu'i Fefine. The Journal of Pacific History 22(4):209–227.

The Impact of Raiding on Settlement Patterns in the Northern Valley of Oaxaca: An Approach Using Decision Trees

Robert G. Reynolds

1 INTRODUCTION

A growing body of data indicates that armed conflict played a role in the creation of complex societies such as chiefdoms and states (Wright 1984; Spencer 1998). For example, according to Wright (1977:382), "most ethnographically reported chiefdoms seem to be involved in constant warfare," and large chiefdoms grew by absorbing their weaker neighbors. Marcus and Flannery suggest that warfare was often used to create a state out of rival chiefdoms:

> We do not believe that a chiefdom simply turns into a state. We believe that states arise *when one member of a group of chiefdoms begins to take over its neighbors*, eventually turning them into subject provinces of a much larger polity. (Marcus and Flannery 1996:157)

As an example of this process, the authors cite Kamehameha's creation of a Hawaiian state out of five to seven rival chiefdoms between 1782 and 1810. They suggest that something similar happened in the Valley of Oaxaca, Mexico, when a chiefdom in the Etla region seized the defensible mountain top of Monte Albán and began systematically subduing rival chiefdoms in

Dynamics in Human and Primate Societies, edited by T. Kohler and
G. Gumerman, Oxford University Press, 1999. **251**

the southern and eastern parts of the valley. If this is the case, there should be a point in the sequence when considerations of defense began to influence settlement choice.

In this chapter, our goal is to provide a preliminary description of our efforts in testing the suitability of this model to the Oaxacan case, and its potential use as the basis for a more general model of state formation. In order to test this hypothesis we need some way to operationalize it in terms of the archaeological record in the Valley of Oaxaca. The key phases of the model can be expressed as follows:

1. An early period in which raiding was minimal, and variables relevant to successful agriculture predominate in settlement choices.
2. A gradual rise in friction between social groups prior to state formation. This friction can be represented by archaeological evidence for raiding, the principle form of warfare in tribes and chiefdoms. Excavations indicate that wattle-and-daub buildings (especially temples and elite residences) were burned in raids, making the presence of burned daub (and other signs of heavy burning) one indicator of raiding (Marcus and Flannery 1996:124–130).
3. A period of increased raiding in a given region, which makes it advantageous for one or more groups to consider a more proactive approach to warfare in order to protect the society's elite decision makers.
4. This proactive response can be seen in terms of decisions to locate some new, particularly administrative, sites in defensible areas in order to consolidate the resources necessary for prolonged conflict.
5. If one major vehicle for chiefly expansion, and in some cases state formation, is warfare, then one should be able to see a pattern of warfare beginning in one region and spreading to neighboring regions. Each of these regions in turn should experience increased attacks and eventually move the elite to more defensible positions as a defensive tactic.
6. The conquest of a region should bring about a reduction in evidence for conflict, and a shift in site location priorities back to those that reflect agricultural production considerations.

One should be able to test the validity of this model by examining the correspondence between (1) changes in site settlement decisions over time and (2) changes in the pattern of raiding over the same periods. The basic data set to be employed comes from the Oaxaca Settlement Pattern survey conducted by Kowalewski et al. (1989) for over a decade. The goal of the full-coverage survey was to locate all archaeological sites in the valley based on the presence of surface remains. In all more than 2,700 sites, dating from the archaic hunting-gathering period to the Spanish Conquest of 1521, were identified. The specific archaeological periods covered by the survey of concern for this paper are given below:

Period	Approximate Date
Tierras Largas Phase	1400–1150 B.C.
San José Phase	1150–850 B.C.
Guadalupe Phase	850–700 B.C.
Rosario Phase	700–500 B.C.
Monte Albán Ia	500–300 B.C.
Monte Albán Ic	300 to c. 150/100 B.C.
Monte Albán II	150/100 B.C. to A.D. 200
Monte Albán IIIa	roughly A.D. 200–500

The settlement pattern survey recorded more than 100 variables in connection with each site (Kowalewski et al. 1989). Sites were numbered in terms of the region of the valley in which they occurred, with the basic spatial regions used being: Monte Albán itself (located in the Central Valley), Etla (the northwest arm), the Central Valley (the area surrounding Monte Albán), the Valle Grande (the southern arm), Tlacolula (the eastern arm), and Ocotlán (the southeastern portion of the valley). These basic geographic regions can be seen in Figure 1. The shaded areas correspond to piedmont, and the darkest regions represent higher mountains.

Although our overall goal is to test our hypothesis against trends over the entire valley for all relevant time periods, in this study we focus on the northwest, or Etla region, from the Tierras Largas phase (early egalitarian villages) through Monte Albán IIIa (the mature Zapotec state). Etla was chosen for this chapter since it was the arm of the valley in which population grew most rapidly and trends appeared first; it was also the home of the chiefdom ancestral to Monte Albán. As a result, it should be one of the first regions to be affected by the state formation processes centered at Monte Albán. Once we are able to identify basic patterns in the Etla arm, we will in future work examine how the other regions behaved, both synchronically and diachronically, in relation to Etla.

As mentioned earlier, each site, for each region and time period, was described in terms of over 100 variables relating to the environment, agriculture, economy (e.g., craft production and trade), and architecture variables. Additional information based upon excavated sites was also added to the survey data. The resultant data set was stored as a Microsoft ACCESS database. This database was used as the basis for testing our hypotheses here.

Using this database as our knowledge source, our goal was to extract trends in settlement decision making using techniques from Machine Learning, a subfield of Artificial Intelligence. These trends will be expressed in terms of *decision trees*. A decision tree is a hierarchically structured collection of decisions, each based on the value for a particular variable, that can be used to classify objects of interest into various categories or classes. Here we want to produce a decision tree that is able to predict correctly whether or not a site is likely to have evidence for raiding in a given time period for a given region of the valley. While the resultant decision trees need not correspond to

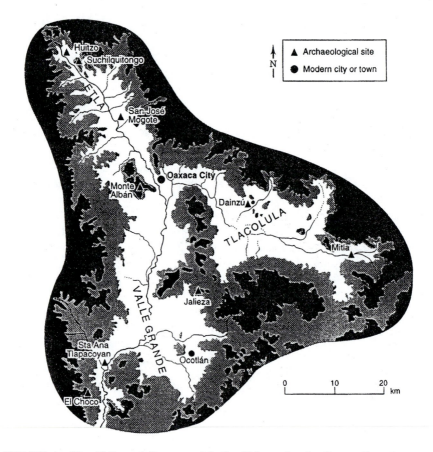

FIGURE 1   The Valley of Oaxaca with the Etla region in the northwest corner. Light shading highlights the piedmont; and, dark shading highlights the mountains.

a specific real-world procedure for making site location decisions, the relative importance of variables in predicting the distinction between the classes of interest can be seen in their relative positions in the tree. The most important (or "key") variables will be found higher up on the tree, while secondary or tertiary variables tend to be found lower down. Our expectation, therefore, is that need for defense from raiding will gradually "climb the tree" over time.

An example of a decision tree is given in Figure 2. Each rectangle represents a variable about which a decision is to be made in the settlement process. Proceeding from the topmost, or key variable, this tree first separates sites into those that are located on the boundary of the loam and the swampy floodplain and those that are not. If a site is on the boundary of the

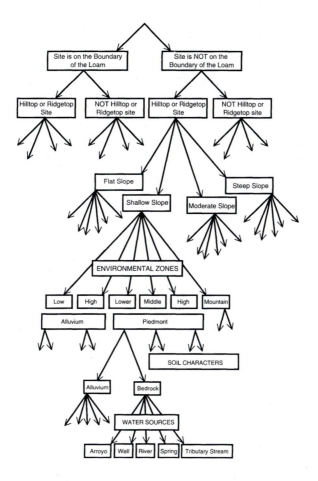

FIGURE 2   A hypothetical decision tree that may be produced for classifying sites that are likely to be targets for warfare. Rectangles represent variables used to make decisions. A given site is classified using this tree by following a path from the apex to a leaf (class) based on the values for its relevant variables.

loam and the swampy floodplain, the process will proceed down the leftmost branch. If it is not, the process proceeds to the right. At the next level, the site is checked to see whether it is situated on a hilltop or not. Again, there are two choices. The third level sorts sites based upon the degree of slope at a site. There are four basic categories used here: flat, shallow, moderate, and steep. One of the four branches is selected for the site based upon the recorded value of slope. At the next level, the environmental zone in which the site is located is used. Here there are five outcomes: low alluvium, high alluvium, low piedmont, high piedmont, and mountain zones. Next, soil character (two outcomes) is used, followed by the principal water source. The process proceeds until an outcome is reached. Outcomes are labeled + or −, depending on whether burnt daub or other evidence for burning is present (+) or absent (−) at the site. A detailed discussion of specific trees is deferred to section 4.

This example describes only one of many possible trees that can be used to classify sites. This tree is homogeneous in its terms since no matter which branch is taken at a previous level, the same choice variable is used at the next. Trees can also have different variables at different levels; variables can be of different types (categorical, ordinal, interval); a variable can be used more than once; and a few or perhaps even all of the variables may be used. Thus the search for a tree that can efficiently and accurately classify each site for a given spatiotemporal grouping is not an easy task.

In the next section we identify the basic variables used to monitor raiding at a site. Sites will then be classified into those that do have evidence for raiding in terms of these variables, and sites that do not, for each phase in the Etla region. This data will be given to a machine learning algorithm ID5R, developed by Utgoff (1989), which constructs a decision tree to separate the sites efficiently and accurately into the two categories based upon their environmental attributes. The decision-tree algorithm used here is detailed in section 3. Section 4 describes the decision trees produced for the time periods of interest and the extent to which they support our hypotheses. Section 5 presents our conclusions and plans for future work.

2   ARCHAEOLOGICAL MANIFESTATIONS OF RAIDING

While warfare has been viewed by some authors as an important force in state formation, archaeologists have usually concentrated their efforts on activities that are more easily detectable. Redmond, in a study of aboriginal warfare in Latin America, suggests possible manifestations of chiefly warfare that can be detected archaeologically (Redmond 1994). Several phases of the warfare process were identified there, based upon ethnographic and ethnohistoric information—preparations and planning for warfare, prewar rituals, offensive tactics, defensive tactics, and postwar rituals. We will focus on offensive and defensive tactics here.

In terms of offensive tactics, Redmond suggests that raiding parties are the principle vehicles for warfare in chiefly societies, and that they often leave archaeological evidence of their activity that is visible on the surface of a site.

> The destruction and violence wrought by raiding parties should leave discernible archaeological evidence at target settlements. The offensive tactic of setting target settlements on fire will produce widespread evidence of burning in the form of an ashy stratum throughout the settlement and unusually dense carbonized remains, usually accompanied by signs of settlement abandonment. (Redmond 1994:64–65)

Two of the variables recorded during the site settlement survey pertain directly to this activity. One variable is the presence of burnt daub at the site. Daub was used as a material for the construction of buildings, and becomes as hard as brick when burned. Unusual quantities of burnt daub on the surface of a site suggest that buildings there were burned at some point. For example, Mackey and Green found that approximately 34% of all surveyed New Mexican Largo-Gallina phase (A.D. 1100–1300) sites were burned based upon the presence of carbonized remains on the surface. Upon excavation, some sites that had been recorded as unburned were found to exhibit evidence for burning in earlier occupations. Thus, they suggested that their surface estimate of burned sites was a conservative one (Mackey and Green 1979:145–146). In the Etla region of Oaxaca, Drennan found that some sites with no surface evidence for burning turned out to have burnt houses when excavated (Drennan 1976).

The other variable was labeled as "other evidence for burning" by the survey team. This evidence took the form of massive areas of burned earth such as occurs when mud brick (adobe) buildings are burned. The Pearson R correlation for "other evidence for burning" with burned daub is −.45 for the entire valley over all periods. This reflects the possibility that the two types of evidence reflect different architecture or different tactics with regard to burning. Since we know that some houses were burned without leaving surface evidence, the variables recorded by the settlement pattern survey probably underestimate the true levels of raiding and warfare for some periods.

Additional evidence for a proactive approach to raiding and warfare can be seen in fortifications or defensible locations at the site (Elam 1989). The presence of defensive walls at a site was recorded as part of the settlement survey. As with the offensive variables, this is certainly a conservative index of site targeting. There may be additional evidence for defensive pallisades below the surface at some sites (Flannery 1998), evidence that will show up only during excavation.

Here, the key to assessing the role of conflict in the evolution of more complex societies lies in determining how site settlement patterns were adjusted in response to observed raiding patterns. The goal then is to distinguish between (1) sites that are targets for attack and (2) those that are not, in terms of their basic site location variables. The locations of sites that are targets for raiding should shift over time in ways that are consistent with the predictions made by the model. The variables used to represent the environmental location of each site in this study are given on the following page. In each case, the variable name is followed by the set of possible values that it can take enclosed in set brackets.

Our goal will be to develop a decision tree that is able to distinguish, as well as possible, between the location of sites that are targets for raiding and those that are not for each time period in terms of a subset of these variables. Not all of these variables need be used to construct the tree. It is up to the algorithm to select the subset of variables that are most effective in generating the tree. What we expect to see happen is a shift over time of those environmental variables that are associated with targets for warfare. These shifts can be observed in terms of the environmental variables used to construct the tree and their relative positioning. The higher the variable in the tree, the more important it is in discriminating between the categories. The next section discusses the algorithm or procedure used to generate the classification trees in this chapter.

Environmental Zone:	{low alluvium, high alluvium, lower piedmont, high piedmont, mountains}
Slope:	{flat, shallow, moderate, steep}
Hilltop or Ridge top:	{Yes, No}
Soil Character:	{Alluvium, Bedrock}
On the boundary between the loam and the swampy region:	{Yes, No}
Water Source:	{main river, tributary stream, arroyo, spring, and well}
Depth to Water Table:	{Real-valued with a minimum of 0}
Type of irrigation:	{none, well, valley floor canal irrigation, piedmont canal irrigation, flood water farming, and terracing}
Land Use Type:	{Class I, Class II, Class III 100% arable, Class III 10% arable, and uncultivated}

3 DECISION-TREE GENERATION

The basic approach that we take to decision-tree construction here is based on the ID3 family of algorithms. ID stands for Induction of Decision Trees, which was developed by Quinlan (1987). The original ID algorithm constructs decision trees from a set of examples in a nonincremental fashion. It is given a training set of site examples, each of which is described in terms of a set of categorical variables, along with the class that the site belongs to. In the Etla case, the predictor variables are the environmental variables for each site. The relevant categories for a site are + (target of warfare) if it exhibits one or more of the three tactic variables described earlier, and a − (not a target) otherwise. Each site must belong to only one class or the other, there can be no inconsistent examples where an example is both positive and negative.

The goal of the decision-tree learning algorithm is to construct a tree that allows each member of the training set to be predicted correctly. That is, there is a path, or sequence of decisions, which leads to a leaf node that is labeled by one of the categories under consideration, + or −. If a current leaf node contains both + and − examples, the algorithm attempts to separate the two groups by adding another decision at that point. This results in the generation of the tree in a "top down" fashion from the key variable at the apex. For example, initially the key or apical point is a leaf node containing all of the examples in the training set. If they are homogeneous, all from the same category, then nothing else needs to be done. If the node contains examples from both classes, the system attempts to select a variable that will be most effective in separating the two groups of examples that are currently there. The measure used to determine which variable to apply is based on information theoretic principles. The best candidate variable is selected based on its E-score (or entropy), and the current node is replaced by a new subtree with the selected variable as the apex. The process continues until the leaf node is homogeneous or no new decisions or extensions can be made.

In this algorithm, knowledge is represented as a decision tree, and the search space for a particular problem consists of all trees that can be constructed from the attributes and categories in the test set. The quality function, i.e., the quality of a tree, depends on both the classification accuracy and the size of the tree. Trees that classify all objects in the test set correctly, and are simple as well, are preferred. ID3 constructs a tree as follows (Quinlan 1987):

1. If all the instances are from exactly one class, then the decision tree is the apical node that is labeled by the class of sites that it contains, + or −.
2. Otherwise,
   a. Define a(best) to be the attribute with the lowest E-score.
   b. For each of the i values of v(best), grow a branch from a(best) to a decision tree constructed recursively based on all of those training instances that have the value of v(best).

However, there are several basic drawbacks to using this approach in the Valley of Oaxaca case:

1. The number of instances can change as new site instances are added or the classifications of existing sites are changed. Since the approach is nonincremental, the entire tree will need to be produced again.
2. The presence of missing data and noise can make over-fitting of the tree to the data more likely. Due to the extensive temporal and spatial nature of the survey, there is bound to be both noise and missing data involved.
3. The variables to be used range from real-valued variables to binary variables. The basic approach requires categorical variables with a limited number of possible categories.

Incremental Tree Induction (ITI) is a machine learning system developed at the University of Massachusetts by Utgoff (1989) for building decision trees incrementally from examples. The main feature of the algorithm is that it can incorporate instances incrementally, instead of requiring all of the examples to be present at once. A particularly interesting and proven characteristic of ITI is that it builds trees independently of the order in which the instances are processed, and the resultant tree can be shown to be equivalent to that produced if all examples were available from the beginning.

The basic approach is to apply a set of transformations to the current tree rather than throwing away all of the learned information each time a new example is added. As stated by Utgoff:

> When given a new training instance that is to be incorporated into the tree, pass it down the proper branches as far as possible. This includes updating the test information kept at each node through which it passes (including marking each such node stale). It also includes the process of incorporating an instance at a leaf, which may cause additional growth of the tree below that leaf. After the instance has been incorporated, visit each stale node recursively, as described above, ensuring that the desired test is installed at that node. (Utgoff 1989)

The algorithm is given below.

1. If the tree is empty, then define it as the unexpanded form, setting the class name to the class of the instance, and the set of instance to the singleton set containing the instance.
2. Otherwise, if the tree is in unexpanded form and the instance is from the same class, then add the instance to the set of instances kept in the node.
3. Otherwise.
   a. If the tree is in unexpanded form, then expand it one level, choosing the test attribute for the root arbitrarily.
   b. For the test attribute and all nontest attributes at the current node, update the current node, update the count of positive or negative instances for the value of that attribute in the training instance.
   c. If the current node contains an attribute test that does not have the lowest E-score, then:
      - Restructure the tree so that an attribute with the lowest E-score is at the root.
      - Recursively reestablish a best test attribute in each subtree except the one that will update in step 3d.
   d. Recursively update the decision tree below the current node along the branch for the value of the test attribute that occurs in the instance description. Grow the branch if necessary.

A variable is considered best if it exhibits the best performance relative to an E-metric. This metric is called the *gain ratio*. This ratio is a variation on the information theoretic measure, entropy. In order to compute this ratio, one first calculates the amount of information needed to identify the class of a case in the training set T.

$$\text{info}(T) = -\sum_{j-1}^{k} \frac{\text{freq}(C_j, s)}{|S|} \times \log_2 \frac{\text{freq}(C_j, s)}{|S|} \text{bits} .$$

This is also known as the entropy of the set T. The information content of the partition of the training set produced by applying a test using attribute X is:

$$\text{info}x(T) = -\sum_{i=1}^{n} \frac{|T_i|}{|T|} \times \text{info}(T_i), .$$

The gain is the amount of information gained by partitioning T according to X and is given by:

$$\text{gain}(X) = \text{info}(T) - \text{info } x(T) .$$

The original ID3 algorithm then selects the next attribute based upon the gain. That approach is shown to be biased toward variables with many categories. The gain ratio has been suggested by Quinlan for use in C4.5 (Quinlan 1993) to rectify the impact of differences in multiple categories among the predictor variables.

The gain ratio is: gain ratio $(X) = \text{gain } (X)/\text{split\_info } (X)$, where the split_info for X is the potential information content produced by dividing T into subsets.

$$\text{split info}(x) = -\sum_{i=1}^{n} \frac{|T_i|}{|T|} \times \log_2 |T_i| .$$

The attribute with the highest gain ratio is then selected.

The basic goals behind the design of the ITI algorithm are to make the update cost as independent of the number and the order in which the training instances are presented. In addition, the use of tree reformulating techniques is designed to reduce the cost of updating the tree over that of developing the tree from scratch. The system also has been designed to handle numeric and symbolic attributes, missing data, multiple categories, and inconsistent data. Given that both numeric and symbolic variables are allowed here, it is necessary to insure that one test is not preferred over another in terms of the number of choices it offers. The use of the gain-ratio performance function has been suggested for this reason.

4 THE DECISION TREE RESULTS

The decision trees for the Etla region from the Tierras Largas phase through Monte Albán II are given in Figures 3 through 9. (One of the phases, Guadalu-

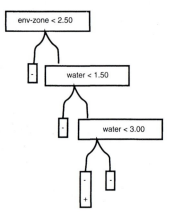

FIGURE 3   The decision tree for the location of sites with evidence for raiding in the Tierras Largas phase in the Etla region. There were 16 sites located in the Etla region during this period. The factors most influencing site location here are environmental zone and water source. The top level factor is the environmental zone for the site; 4 sites in the low or high alluvium (env-zone < 2.50) were not attacked (−). The second level decision separates out 3 sites whose water source is a main river or a tributary (water< 1.50) from the remaining sites. These 3 sites were not attacked (−). The third level decision separates out the remaining sites on piedmont arroyos (< 3.00). Of these 8 sites, 7 were not attacked (−) and one may have been (+).

pe, is not presented since the decision tree produced for that phase is essentially the same as that for the previous San José phase.) Each tree contains two types of nodes, decision nodes and leaf nodes. For example, in Figure 3 the top-level decision node is "environmental zone." All sites with a value for "environmental zone" of less than 2.5 take the leftmost branch in the classification process while the others take the rightmost branch. The numbers given at this point reflects a straightforward encoding of the values for each of the variables given earlier. For example, environmental zones are coded in the order listed earlier from 1 (low alluvium) through 5 (mountains) so "env-zone < 2.5" would indicate sites in the low alluvium or high alluvium. The leftmost branch consists of a single leaf node. A leaf node represents the category associated with the sites that it contains. Here, no sites in the low or high alluvial zones are classified as targets of warfare (−).

Notice that some nodes are labeled with both a + and a −. These nodes contain both categories of sites and are termed *nonhomogeneous*. A decision tree that perfectly classifies the training set will not contain any nonhomogeneous leaf nodes. The presence of nonhomogeneous nodes here means that the survey did not recover sufficient information to allow any additional differentiation between the categories in such cases. This early phase, Tierras

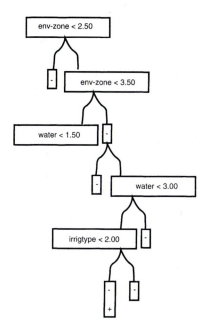

FIGURE 4   The decision tree for the location of sites with evidence for raiding in the San José phase in the Etla region. There were 20 sites recorded for the Etla region during this period. Again, environmental zone and water source were the most important factors in the location of sites in the upper four levels of the tree. However, a new variable, irrigation type, is used to identify sites with evidence for raiding at the fifth level of the tree. In this phase, the number of sites in the low and high alluvium (env-zone < 2.50) has increased from 4 to 6. There are now 2 sites on the middle piedmont or higher, both of which were not attacked. The 2 sites in the lower piedmont with a main river or tributary water source were not attacked. There were now 9 sites in the lower piedmont region with an arroyo water source. The site that exhibits signs of attack is one of the 8 sites that did not need irrigation.

Largas, was one of egalitarian villages, where almost all of these village sites were located in similar environmental settings for agricultural reasons. This means that location alone is not sufficient to predict site attacks here. Redmond (Redmond 1994:3) suggests that raiding at the egalitarian village level is often the result of individual feuds or vendettas, which means that it might be hard to tie it to specific environmental factors. It is expected, however, that as social structure and settlement choice become more sophisticated, the patterns of warfare and response may become more predictable in terms of such environmental factors.

A brief description of each individual decision tree is given in its caption. Here we will attempt to describe the overall trends in terms of the changes predicted by the model presented earlier. Each phase of the model and its corresponding expression in terms of the resultant trees will now be discussed.

Hypothesis 1: An early period in which raiding was minimal, and variables relevant to successful agriculture predominate in settlement choices.   If there were no raiding at all in the Tierras Largas phase, Figure 3 would consist of a single key node containing all sites and be labeled as a (−) node since it contained only sites that did not exhibit evidence for raiding. The more frequent and complex the pattern of raiding, the more complicated the tree becomes. Thus, even in the egalitarian Tierras Largas phase we have to suggest that occasional raiding took place. However, the tree is very small with only two variables, and needed only 3 decision nodes to distinguish the one site that may have been raided.

Hypothesis 2: A gradual rise in friction between social groups prior to state formation. This friction can be represented by archaeological evidence for raiding, the principle form of warfare in egalitarian village societies and chiefdoms. Excavations indicate that wattle-and-daub buildings (especially temples and elite residences) were burned in raids, making the presence of burned daub one indicator of raiding (Marcus and Flannery 1996:124–130).   The size of the decision tree for each phase can tell us something about the complexity or intensity of raiding. The tree for the egalitarian Tierras Largas phase uses two variables and 3 decision nodes. In the San José phase, the first period with evidence of social rank, this increases to three variables and 5 decision nodes (Figure 4). In the subsequent Guadalupe phase (not shown) there are still just four variables and 4 decision nodes used. But in the next phase, Rosario (700–500 B.C.), the number of variables used has increased to five, and the number of decision nodes to 9 (Figure 5). In other words, the number of decision nodes has almost doubled from that of the previous two phases. The Rosario phase was one in which rival chiefdoms arose in various parts of the valley, and burned daub was seven times as frequent on the surface as on the average valley site (Kowlewski et al. 1989:70). Soon defensive location would become a key variable (below).

Hypothesis 3: A period of increased raiding in a given region which makes it advantageous for one or more groups to consider a more proactive approach to warfare in order to protect the society's elite decision makers.   In all of the phases prior to Monte Albán Ia, the first variable to be selected for the key or apical node of the tree is "environmental zone." However, this changed in Monte Albán Ia (Figure 6), the first period whose decision tree shows "hill" as the key variable. The leaders of San José Magote set the example by moving themselves and all of their followers to the top of the defensible mountain known as Monte Albán. Some of their rivals also sought to defend themselves. In addition to "hill," the related variable "slope" rose from nowhere to become the second highest decision in the tree. This suggests that elevation and defensibility were becoming as important as agricultural variables in settlement location.

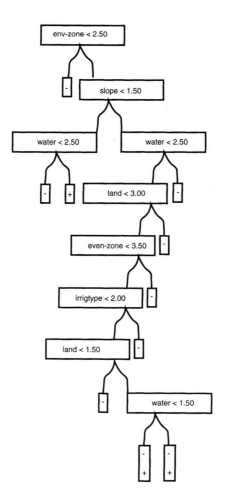

FIGURE 5   The decision tree for the locations of sites with evidence of raiding in the Rosario phase in the Etla region of the valley. Although environmental zone was still the dominant variable along with water source in determining the location of sites, other factors such as slope, irrigation type, and land use classification have now become important; so now a maximum of 8 decisions are needed to group the sites. The increase in the size of the tree reflects an increase in the complexity of site settlement along with increased signs of raiding. There are now 36 sites in the region, one fourth of which were located on the low or high alluvium. Fourteen other sites (up from 9 in the San José phase) were located in the lower piedmont. These sites used little or no irrigation, and were located on class II land. Seven of the sites had a main river or tributary water source, while 7 more had a piedmont arroyo water source. One site out of each group of 7 was attacked. Another site, above the lower piedmont on flat land with an arroyo water source, was attacked. As in the previous two phases, the sites that were attacked were in more peripheral locations.

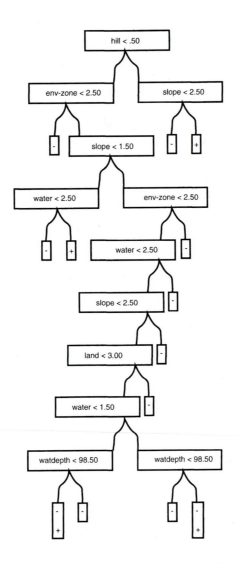

FIGURE 6   The decision tree for the locations of sites with evidence of raiding in the Monte Albán Ia phase in the Etla region of the valley. There were now 77 sites recorded in the region. While environmental zone and water source are both still important, hilltop location had now become the uppermost variable in determining site location, probably because of a need for defense. Hilltop location divides the tree into two subtrees. The left subtree corresponds to the traditional agricultural strategy observed in the region, the one used in previous phases. This subtree contains the majority of sites, 71. Two of these sites exhibit evidence for raiding. As before, the majority of sites were on good land with good (cont'd)

FIGURE 6 (continued) access to water for irrigation. The right subtree corresponds to a new settlement category that is focused on defensible locations. Of the 6 sites that were on hills, one third of them were attacked. Apparently, the hilltop locations were the principle targets for raiding in this period.

Hypothesis 4: This proactive response can be seen in terms of decisions to locate some new, particularly administrative sites, in defensible areas in order to consolidate the resources necessary for prolonged conflict. With the movement of population from San José Mogote and its subject villages to Monte Albán in Period Ia, hilltop location now becomes the dominant variable in distinguishing sites that are targets for raids and those that are not. In fact, it is now the dominant variable in distinguishing between sites that are targets for warfare and those that are not. Figure 6 shows six sites in the right-hand subtree (those on a hill) and one third of them show signs of raiding. The 71 sites in the left-hand subtree are further separated by variables such as environmental zone, land qualities, and water source. Of these, only two show signs of raiding.

The Monte Albán Ia decision tree indicates the emergence of a distinction between administrative sites with hilltop locations and sites mainly identified by variables related to agriculture. While raids could affect either site type, the fact that one third of the local hilltop centers show raiding suggests that Monte Albán was engaged in subjugating potential rivals.

By Monte Albán Ic (300–150/100 normalfontB.C.), Monte Albán had surrounded itself with 155 satellite communities, located within 15 km of the mountaintop city and providing it with farmers, warriors, and artisans. Since many of these sites were in the piedmont canal irrigation settings, this pattern has been called the "piedmont strategy" (Kowalewski et al. 1989).

The piedmont strategy shows up in the decision tree for Monte Albán Ic; it is the subtree marked "B" in Figure 7. While subtree A contains hilltop administrative centers, B contains sites on class III land in the piedmont that can produce good yields with canal irrigation. We presume that this intensive use of the piedmont near Monte Albán was designed to provision the latter city while it gradually subdued the rest of the valley during Period Ic. The piedmont strategy had been previously observed by Kowalewski for the Central Valley region around Monte Albán, and its extension into the Etla region shows how strong the political ties were between the mountaintop city and the region from which its founders had come.

Hypothesis 5: If one major vehicle for chiefly expansion, and in some cases state formation, is warfare, then (if the chronology is fine enough) one should be able to see a pattern of warfare beginning in one region and spreading to neighboring regions. Each of these regions, in turn, should experience increased attacks and eventually move elites to more defensible positions as a defensive tactic. While it is hard to assess this hypothesis in terms of the Etla region alone, some of its manifestations can be visualized here. With the founding of Monte Albán and its

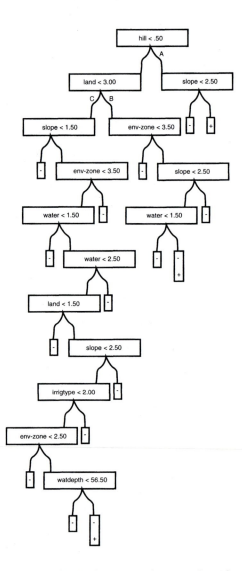

FIGURE 7   The decision tree for the locations of sites with evidence of raiding in the Monte Albán Ic phase in the Etla region of the valley. There were now 212 sites in the region. Hilltop location and slope were still in the top two levels of the tree. This suggests that defense was still a key issue in determining site location. But another variable had become important as well: land use type now divides sites into two subtrees. The subtree labeled C corresponds to sites that were on good agricultural land. This contains the majority of sites occupied in previous periods. These were sites with a tributary or main river water sources, and needed little or no irrigation. There were 169 sites in this group. One site in that group exhibited evidence of raiding. Subtree B corresponds to a new category of sites that were located on less productive land in the piedmont zone, requiring canal irrigation (the "pied- [cont'd]

FIGURE 7 [continued] mont strategy" of Kowalewski et al. [1989]). There were 32 sites in this category, and one of them shows signs of warfare. It is suggested that this new farming strategy had been motivated by the need to have high populations close to the city of Monte Albán in order to provide food, warriors, and craftsmen for the urban population. Subtree A contains 11 sites. This is the explicit hilltop class that had emerged in Monte Albán Ia. All 3 hilltop sites on moderate or greater slope had been attacked which suggests that this type of site was still a prime target.

subsequent expansion, there is a marked increase in the complexity of decision trees. In particular, the emergence of the three subtrees in Monte Albán Ic (Figure 7) reflects both a need for defense and for intensive irrigation to support expansion. "Hill" is a key apical node in Period Ic.

In Figure 7 the presence of subtrees A and B seems to have reduced the likelihood of attack for sites in more traditional agricultural settings, subtree C. Sites in subtree A now have the greatest likelihood of attack ($\sim$30%), followed by B($\sim$ 3%), and then finally C ($\sim$.6%). In the Rosario phase, sites in traditional agricultural settings exhibited an 11% likelihood of attack. By Monte Albán Ic, elite families in traditional small agricultural sites may have relocated to sites in subtrees A and B, making the smaller sites less attractive targets. Rival elite centers (subtree A) were now more likely to be raided than simple farming communities.

Hypothesis 6: The subjugation of a region should bring about a reduction in evidence for conflict, and a shift in site location priorities back to those that reflect variables of agricultural production. By the end of Period Ic, Monte Albán had subjugated the entire valley and the Zapotec state had formed. Decision trees become much more simplified in Monte Albán II (Figure 8) and IIIa (Figure 9) reflecting the reduction in conflict and shift in site location priorities associated with a mature state. In both Figures 8 and 9, subtrees A, B, and C are still present, although each is of reduced complexity. The greatest decrease in complexity can be seen in subtree C, which contains the bulk of the small agricultural sites. None of the 121 subtree C sites in Monte Albán II and the 65 subtree C sites in Monte Albán IIIa exhibit evidence of raiding. All of the sites that do show raiding in both phases belong to subtrees B and A. Again, sites associated with hilltop locations (subtree A) were more likely to be attacked, followed by subtree B.

Notice in Monte Albán IIIa (Figure 9) that only three variables and 4 decisions are needed to separate out those sites that are targets for raiding. Three of the decisions reflect land use or environmental zone variables that are closely tied to agriculture. "Environmental zone" has now begun to regain the importance that it had prior to state formation, e.g., from the Tierras Largas through Rosario phase.

Notice, however, that these variables are now associated with the new category of piedmont sites rather than sites in traditional locations. This may

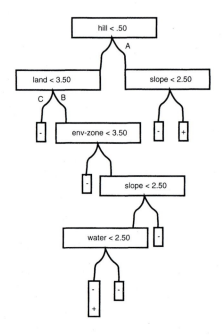

FIGURE 8   The decision tree for the locations of sites with evidence of raiding in the Monte Albán II phase in the Etla region of the valley. Hilltop location, slope, and land use type were still the main factors used to determine site location. Again we see 3 major subtrees. Subtree C, representing sites in the traditional locations for agriculture, contains 121 sites, none of which exhibit evidence for attack. Subtree B represents the "piedmont strategy" sites that emerged in the previous phase. These had dwindled to 14 sites, however, far fewer than before; it is believed that the piedmont strategy had become less important now that Monte Albán had gained control of the entire valley. Subtree C has 9 sites, down slightly from 11. Of those, the 2 on steeper slopes had both been attacked.

reflect a shift from traditional to piedmont sites as canal irrigation increased in importance.

Another interesting observation emerges when we compare the Monte Albán IIIa decision tree (Figure 9) with the Tierras Largas decision tree (Figure 3). We mentioned that although the Tierras Largas phase tree was simple, the environmental variables were not sufficient to distinguish between sites that were targets for raiding in all situations. We suggested that this might be due to the more personal ("vendetta") nature of warfare in egalitarian times. In contrast, in Monte Albán IIIa there are no nonhomogeneous leaf nodes. Although there are many more sites—and the settlement pattern is inherently more sophisticated—the business of warfare has now become more

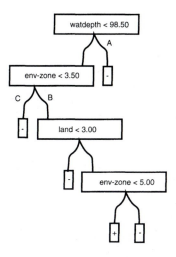

FIGURE 9   The decision tree for the locations of sites with evidence of raiding in the Monte Albán IIIa phase in the Etla region of the valley. There were now just 74 sites in the region. Vestiges of subtrees A, B, and C are apparent, but the variables that were most important in the early periods, such as land use and environmental zone, have now become important once again. "Hilltop location" has been replaced at the top of the tree by "water depth." Subtree C, representing the traditional agricultural location strategy, now has 65 sites. None of these sites exhibited evidence for attack. Subtree B, representing "piedmont strategy" sites, now contains only 8 sites, down substantially from the previous period. One site in this group was attacked. Subtree A had just one site with a hilltop location. That site, as expected, was attacked.

focused and predictable. This, it is suggested, reflects the nature of warfare as it is now conducted by the Zapotec state rather than by simpler societies.

5 CONCLUSIONS

In this chapter we have investigated the extent to which evidence from Etla region of the Oaxaca Valley Settlement survey can be used to monitor the role of conflict in chiefdom and state formation. Decision trees were used as a vehicle to express changes in the environmental variables used to predict the locations of targets for raiding and warfare in the Etla region over time, from egalitarian village societies to a mature state. The results suggest that a decision tree is an expressive vehicle for monitoring these temporal and spatial changes and appear to support our model. But since the results represent only a portion of the entire valley, further evaluation requires the production of decision trees for each of the remaining four regions.

One potential problem is that the number of sites (and the variety of possible variables) make it essential that each tree produced be as accurately and as efficiently as possible. Some of the regions of the valley have several hundred sites during a given period. If the algorithm is not able to produce an accurate and efficient scheme, the resultant tree may contain a large number of decisions and will be difficult, if not impossible, to analyze.

The ITI algorithm was selected for use since it is best suited to the needs of the current application. However, while it exhibits many improvements over existing systems, there is no guarantee that it will always be able to produce an optimal tree in all situations. If we can guarantee that there is no biasing in the selection of attributes for decision nodes based upon the number of choices as well as other factors, then an optimal tree should be produced each time.

In future work, we suggest an extension to ITI that uses an evolutionary computational approach, based upon the Cultural Algorithms program developed by Reynolds (1986), to "pull up" those variables that are the best discriminators, regardless of how they are measured. That is, in situations where biasing occurs, the best variables are often found near the bottom of the tree, while less useful variables are found near the key node. This will often occur if there is a bias toward variables with many choices, as opposed to conceptually more important variables with fewer choices. We would like to "pull up" the more conceptually important variables to make the tree more optimal in structure.

In particular, we want to "pull up" variables in order to:

1. Reduce the number of decision nodes.
2. Reduce the number of variables used in the tree.
3. Reduce the number of nonhomogeneous nodes.

In order to do this, we will try embedding the ITI algorithm within the framework of an evolutionary optimizer based upon Cultural Algorithms, CAEP (Reynolds 1994a, 1994b; Chung 1997). The principle behind this embedding is to allow the evolutionary system to experiment with the types of trees produced by ITI for different subsets of attributes in the data set. Those subsets that prove to be most useful in optimizing the performance function, which is a combination of classification accuracy and tree structure, are likely to be inherited as parts of the next generation of selector strategies by the evolutionary population. While this process uses ITI to generate a number of subtrees automatically, if the subtree is sufficiently smaller than that produced by using all of the variables, the additional cost can be reduced. This will be the subject for future work.

REFERENCES

Chagnon, N. A.
1983 The Fierce People. New York: Holt, Reinhart & Winston.

Chung, C.
1997 Knowledge-Based Approaches to Self-Adaptation in Cultural Algorithms. Ph.D. Thesis, Wayne State University, Detroit, Michigan.

Elam, J. M.
1989 Defensible and Fortified Sites. *In* Monte Albán's Hinterland, Part II, Vol. I. Memoirs of the Museum of Anthropology, Number 23. Pp. 385–408. Ann Arbor, MI: University of Michigan.

Flannery, K.
1998 Personal communication.

Kowalewski, S. A., G. M. Feinman, L. Finsten, R. E. Blanton, and L. M. Nicholas
1989 Monte Albán's Hinterland, Part II, Vol. I–II. Memoirs of the Museum of Anthropology, Number 23. Ann Arbor, MI: University of Michigan.

Mackey, J., and R. C. Green.
1979 Largo-Gallina Towers: An Explanation. American Antiquity 44(1): 144–154.

Marcus, J., and K. Flannery.
1996 Zapotec Civilization: How Urban Society Evolved in Mexico's Oaxaca Valley. London: Thames and Hudson.

Quinlan, J. Ross
1987 Decision Trees as Probabilistic Classifiers. *In* Proceedings of the Fourth International Workshop on Machine Learning. P. Langley, ed. Pp. 31–37. Irvine, CA: Morgan Kaufmann.

Quinlan, J. Ross, and R. L. Rivest
1989 Inferring Decision Trees Using the Minimum Description Length Principle. Information and Computation 80:227–248.

Quinlan, J. Ross
1993 C4.5: Programs for Machine Learning. San Mateo, CA: Morgan Kaufmann.

Redmond, E.
1994 Tribal and Chiefly Warfare in South America. Memoirs of the Museum of Anthropology 28. Ann Arbor, MI: University of Michigan.

Reynolds, R. G.
  1986 An Adaptive Computer Model for the Evolution of Plant Collecting and Early Agriculture in the Eastern Valley of Oaxaca Mexico. *In* Guilá Naquitz: Archaic Foraging in Oaxaca Mexico. K. V. Flannery, ed. Pp. 439–500. San Diego, CA: Academic Press.
  1994a Learning to Cooperate Using Cultural Algorithms. *In* Simulating Societies: The Computer Simulation of Social Phenomena. N. Gilbert and J. Doran, eds. Pp. 223–229. London: UCL Press.
  1994b An Introduction to Cultural Algorithms. *In* Proceedings of the 3rd Annual Conference on Evolutionary Programming. A. V. Sebald and L. J. Fogel, eds. Pp. 131–139. River Edge, NJ: World Scientific.

Spencer, C. S.
  1998 A Mathematical Model of Primary State Formation. Cultural Dynamics 10(1):6–20.

Utgoff, P. E.
  1989 Incremental Induction of Decision Trees. *In* Machine Learning. P. Langley, ed. Pp. 161–186. Boston, MA: Kluwer.

Wright, H. T.
  1977 Recent Research on the Origin of the State. Annual Review of Anthropology 6:379–397.
  1984 Prestate Political Formations. *In* On the Evolution of Complex Societies: Essays in Honor of Harry Hoijer. T. K. Earle, ed. Pp. 41–77. Malibu, CA: Udena Press.

Fractal House of Pharaoh: Ancient Egypt as a Complex Adaptive System, a Trial Formulation

Mark Lehner

1 ANCIENT EGYPT AS AN EARLY FORM OF SOCIAL COMPLEXITY

In addition to understanding small-scale societies in their own right "from a complex systems perspective" (Boekhorst and Hemelrijk this volume), workshop participants expressed a goal of using insights about the dynamics of small-scale societies to better understand the "evolution of state-like structures" (Small this volume), or "the 'emergence' trajectories by which a small-scale society, in its environment, may move autonomously from relatively simple (distributed, no ranking or centralized decision making) to complex (ranking/hierarchy, with centralized decision making and a degree of specialization)" (Doran this volume). Small-scale societies are seen as "preceding conditions" to the development of "rank vs. egalitarian ideologies" (Wright this volume) such as are found in archaic states.

Ancient Egypt is a salient example of such an archaic state. In the comparative study of civilizations, ancient Egypt has stood out as the quintessence of a centralized nation-state ruling a large territory. Egyptologists often operate through a vision of ancient Egyptian society, whether explicit or assumed, as highly absolutist. Pharaoh's control of society is complete, effected through an invasive and pervasive centralized bureaucracy. Anthropologists, taking their cue from Egyptologists, see Egypt as one of the earliest examples of a unified nation-state, with a redistributive economy centrally administered over the entirety of the Egyptian Nile Valley.[1]

I offer a prospectus for approaching Egyptian civilization as a complex adaptive system (CAS) based on loose analogies with concepts of emergent order and self-organization. This a narrative exploration of ways that ancient Egyptian society may be amenable to the kind of agent-based modeling applied to small-scale societies. Although I recognize that in discussions of "complexity theory" there is nothing close to unanimity or an agreed paradigm (Wilson 1998), some of the more general concepts may at least offer insightful new ways to view social complexity in Egypt. My prospectus is a work-in-progress. My sources for complex systems studies are "the literature of metaphor (e.g., Cowan et al. 1994), and the popularizations of metaphysics"; that is to say, what follows is most certainly in Morowitz's (1998) category of meta-metaphor (and I will try to refrain from "word magic"). If "complexity theory needs more information" (Wilson 1998:19), ancient Egypt may offer candidate data sets to study complex adaptive systems in human societies.

2   METAPHORS AND MODELS TO BETTER UNDERSTAND EGYPT

There is as much historical and archaeological evidence that ancient Egypt did not really operate as a centrally controlled organization and large-scale redistributive system as there are more obvious signs of royal power, like the giant pyramids of the early Old Kingdom, the crystallization of Egypt's first great period of efflorescence. The pyramids are products of "direct control mechanisms" (Gell-Mann 1994:20) imposed by authority on high, accurately oriented to the cardinal directions, and flanked by the stone tombs of officials laid out in gridded streets and avenues rank and file. But what was the broader social and economic context that made possible such hallmarks of central control as the giant pyramids of Giza? Was the more inclusive order of Egyptian polity and civilization likewise created by the imposition of centralized will, planning, and power?

In contrast to the orderly world of the Giza Necropolis, Egyptologists recognize "intermediate periods," the first (2134–2040 normalfontB.C.), following the breakdown of the Old Kingdom or Pyramid Age (2575–2134 normalfontB.C.), and the second (1640–1532 normalfontB.C.) following the Middle Kingdom (2040–1640 normalfontB.C.) and preceding Egypt's classic age of empire, the New Kingdom (1550–1070 normalfontB.C.). In the Third Intermediate Period (1070–712 normalfontB.C.), once called the period of the Libyan

---

[1]See Kemp (1989:232–234) for references to studies which apply the redistributive model to ancient Egypt and contrary arguments.

Anarchy, Egypt fragmented into a patchwork of rival principalities, each ruled by "great chiefs," four of whom called themselves King of Egypt. During a fifth, and possibly for as much as nearly a third (905 years), of ancient Egyptian history, the "state" was in its formative or intermediate phases.[2] Rather than seeing these times merely as exceptions to the normative Egyptian state, with the curtain of royalty lifted the intermediate periods may offer windows onto the real social-economic texture that made Egypt work in all periods. What was the nature of ancient Egyptian society that would allow the rise of a nation-state across a large territory, its endurance over long-lived dynasties and kingdoms, its periodic dissolution into competing smaller scale polities, and its reemergence in great cycles?

2.1 SEGMENTARY SYSTEMS

In Egypt, the territorial structure of the state was segmentary, consisting of homologous, though hierarchical units. (Hassan 1993:568)

Anthropological theory includes models of "segmentary systems" for polities that collapse into parts and then reassemble themselves. British social anthropologists Radcliff-Brown, Evans-Pritchard, and Fortes, known as structural-functionalists, developed the concept of the segmentary lineage from their studies of tribal societies in Africa. Marshall Sahlins (1961) further developed the model in an essay, "The Segmentary Lineage: An Organization of Predatory Expansion." Segmentary models have been applied to states (Stein 1977; Southhall 1988; Bakker 1988[1995]) as well as tribes. The model[3] may be applicable to the geographic and political fragmentation of the Third Intermediate Period, which may have corresponded to kinship units and lineage splits (Ritner 1990). However, the segmentary lineage is not easily applied to most periods of Egyptian society. For one thing, the long genealogies characteristic of the Third Intermediate Period, perhaps reflecting the tribal and pastoral ancestry of prominent Libyans of that period (Leahy 1985; Lloyd 1983), are not so evident in the earlier, greater part of Egyptian history.

Nonetheless, there does seem to have been a segmental character to Egyptian society, not just in the intermediate periods, but also during the great dynasties of the consolidated kingdom.

There also seems to have been a certain degree of similarity in patterns of small structures to larger ones at more than one scale in a vertical hierarchy.

---

[2] One could lower the total of fragmentation periods by arguing that in Dynasty 1 and 3, included in the formative Early Dynastic or Archaic periods, the country was unified (but probably less so in Dynasty 2). On the other hand, Egypt was scarcely unified at all times in the Late Period, which I have not included in the non-unified third of pharaonic history. The dodecarchy of the Delta, as Herodotus called it, persisted into Persian times.

[3] Follow-up studies of the some of the same societies from which Radcliff-Brown, Evans-Pritchard, and Fortes derived the segmentary lineage model argue that, while the model may be characteristic of the actors' own model of categories of people, it does not conform to the way they actually behave or distribute themselves across territory (Holy 1996:71ff).

For example, large tombs are often surrounded by, or sometimes contain, smaller tombs of dependents. In the Old Kingdom, the owners of large tombs were often priests and officials in the temples of the royal pyramids, but in like manner the large tomb owner had his own cult and priesthood that served in his tomb chapel; "the funerary service was simply a reduced continuation of the household after death." Membership made people "approximate to family members under the authority of the chief heir" (Eyre 1987:31).

> The officials had their own houses (*pr ḏt*), made up of land and peas-antry exploited to provide their income, manors in the form of villages and estates throughout the country, together with craft personnel, administrators, and personal servants. This is essentially the typical economic unit of the great estate, held in origin and principle from the king in return for performance of office. *Within such a house the personnel were in the same way dependent on the favour, patronage, and provision of the official as he was on the king.* (Eyre 1987:40, emphasis mine)

There also appears to have been a horizontal repetition, or redundancy, of patterns of dependency and authority along the ancient Egyptian Nile Valley. Bakker, who compares the segmentary state with other state models, includ-ing Weber's patrimonialism (see below), quoted Durkheim on the self-similar character of the segmentary state: "We say of these societies that they are seg-mental in order to indicate their formation by the repetition of like elements in them, analogous to the rings of an earthworm" (Durkheim 1964[1893]:175; Bakker 1995[1988]:296, n. 6). This seems true of ancient Egypt, even though the segmentary state, thought to be weak and decentralized, has been taken as the opposite of the centralized bureaucratic state.

2.2 PATRIMONIAL HOUSEHOLD MODEL

The German sociologist Max Weber recognized the family as the most fun-damental *social* unit, minimally a mother-child relationship that forms "a biologically-based household unit" (Weber 1978:357).[4] The management or regulation of domestic or household affairs—the original sense of the word "economy"—involves mechanisms that in ancient Egypt allowed the house-hold to evolve into what Weber called an *oikos* (house), whose essence is or-ganized want satisfaction (Weber 1978:381). The relationship between family (or kin) and household is close but problematic.[5] Gelb pointed out that

---

[4]While the idea of the "mother-child bond as naturally constituted and biologically determined" was accepted by many anthropologists, it has come under scrutiny and criticism in feminist anthropology. A distinction can be made between mater (a social, adapting, or nurturing mother) and genetrix (birth mother), like that between genitor and pater (Holy 1996:20–29).

[5]For one discussion see Holy (1996:51–70): "All the distinctions between family and household draw on residential propinquity as the defining criterion of the household."

The term "household": extends in meaning to cover social groupings ranging from a small family household living under one roof to a large socio-economic unit, which may consist of owners and/or managers, labor force, storage bins, animal pens, as well as fields, orchards, pastures, and forests.... In civilizations based mainly on agriculture, such as early Mesopotamia was, household stands for a primary unit of agricultural production. (Gelb 1979:3)

Gelb further commented about the polysemic nature of the term household in the textual record of Mesopotamia:

In my past work of many years, I have found no other word so full of weight for the proper understanding of the texts bearing on social and economic history. A study of ration texts, lists of personnel, or a division of a harvest is well-nigh meaningless unless it is framed within the socio-economic unit with which these texts are concerned; and this *Sitz im Leben* is provided by the concept "household." (Gelb 1979:3)

The same is true for ancient Egypt. Kemp concluded:

Belonging to a household, either as a relative or a receiver of patronage, seems to have been an important Egyptian wish...and some of the households, as officially recognized, could have been represented on the ground by several houses in a contiguous group, as can frequently be picked out in the Amarna suburbs. This points to a major question in the social history of the ancient world which we are unable to answer: when did cities begin to acquire a significant urban proletariat, a population of men, women, and children who were simply workers, and who looked for their employment to a source outside of their own household? The rise of this group would have been at the expense of the "households" which seem to have been of great importance to the Egyptians, but we cannot be sure if there was any change at all on this front during pharaonic times. (Kemp 1989:308)

It was the "household that provided the model and social vehicle where none yet existed." Evidence from ancient Egypt indicates that preferred property inheritance was through "a single male line": the eldest son, in the line "his son to son, his heir to heir, forever" (Eyre 1994b:112–113). However, "the key social unit was not the individual but a larger family grouping, whose head needed to marshal the resources of an essentially communal property to promote the socially necessary family solidarity, to make social alliances, especially through marriages, and to ensure provision for individual family members" (Eyre 1994b:113).

A variety of historical sources indicate that ancient Egyptian householders at all scales were maximizers. At all times in Egypt's first three thousand years, and probably for much of the last two millennia, there were mechanisms that allowed households to expand, sometimes into estates that could grow to gargantuan proportions along the lines for patrimonial regimes that Weber discussed (Bendix 1962:334). Much of the Egyptian infrastructure operated on the basis of large manors and estates through the ages. Egyptian estates and households, even a peasant's, could grow to *contain* smaller households in a nested or embedded pattern. Gelb (1979:7–8, 41) discussed ways in which large households contained or subsumed smaller households in Mesopotamia, basically through, "a socio-economic dependence of a lower-standing individual and his household on a higher standing individual and his household." Mesopotamian texts make such embedded hierarchical relationships explicit in what Gelb called "household-of-a-household" classification, of the sort, N dwells within N_2, of N_3 three or more levels deep.

Such relationships were key to much of Max Weber's study of society and economy and his contrasts between ancient and modern forms of domination. In Weber's patrimonial regime, the households it contained, at their respective scales, and "in their sphere of activity and power of command," were each "a mirror-image of that master a lower level" (Bendix 1962:295). Although his own treatments of ancient Egypt (Weber 1978, 1988[1909]:105–133) are outdated, a strong case can be made that, true to Weber's vision, the Egyptian state emerged from, was conceived as, and operated as an extended household-of-households, the word "pharaoh" deriving, in fact, from the Egyptian term, "Great House." Some Egyptologists (Janssen 1978:224–225; Eyre 1987:39–40) have recognized that the ancient Egyptian state, at least in its earliest phases, operated as a large patrimonial household. Yet notions of an invasive and pervasive rational centralized bureaucracy, and of a private-public dichotomy, remain deeply entrenched. In the Patrimonial Household Model (PHM):

> Patrimonialism is the antithesis of rational bureaucracy. In a patrimonial regime the entire social order is viewed as an extension of the ruler's household (and ultimately the god's household), and it consists of a hierarchy of sub-households linked by personal ties at each level between individual "masters" and "slaves" or "fathers" and "sons." There is no distinction between the "private" and "public" sectors of society, because government administration is effected through personal relationships on the household model rather than through an impersonal bureaucracy. (Schloen 1995:3)

The Patrimonial Household Model predicts the following:

- No political/economic distinction between *public* and *private*;
- No notion of rationalized bureaucracy, impersonal state;

- No structural or conceptual difference between governmental fiscal systems (taxation) and smaller personal exchanges;
- No structural or symbolic dichotomy between *urban* and *rural* (vertically merged by dyadic ties);
- No structural or symbolic dichotomy to ruling elite, legitimation is embedded in traditional social networks; authority is structurally similar at all ranks; and
- No fundamental structural difference among *tribes*, *chiefdoms*, and *states* (Schloen 1995).

2.3 COMPLEX ADAPTIVE SYSTEMS

To the extent that the ancient state arose and operated as the household-of-households, explanations for the origin of the state in Egypt must be sought in the basic mechanisms of the household at all its levels, "bottom-up" from the components of local hierarchies, and from the social rules from which households themselves emerge, for these are the seed beds from which Egypt's "Great Tradition" of divine kingship rose and resurrected itself in great cycles of unity and fragmentation. This makes a complex society like ancient Egypt approachable in terms of concepts and metaphors belonging to the "complexity paradigm" or "the complex systems perspective."

But describing ancient Egypt in these terms, and comparing a whole civilization to other CAS, is certain to be received with skepticism from several directions. First, practitioners of hard computational science, the "*sine qua non* of a science of complexity" (Morowitz 1998:20), may see the application of agent-based models and complexity concepts to human systems, to say nothing of three millennia of a complex society, as intractable. It is not at all obvious a priori that a civilization is susceptible to these methods of analysis, "because of the fact that it is so different from what we know from physical science. What is the scope of things that we can look at, and what is the scope of things that we're really presumptuous to be thinking about at this point?" (Discussion by Jen in Gell-Mann 1994:33).

Egyptologists have been trained by tradition to focus on particulars of language, history, art, and architecture, and they tend to shy away from general models and broad theoretical perspectives. Treating ancient Egypt as a complex adaptive system may therefore seem presumptuous and foolhardy by complex systems theorists and Egyptologists alike. However, even if, at this level of coarse graining, we are far from computational modeling, the local to global perspective on complex systems offers heuristic and integrative approaches to ancient Egypt; integrative of Egyptology and the other social sciences, but also in the vertical integration between numerous particularistic studies of Egyptian art, material culture, language, and history and better understandings of how Egyptian civilization as a whole worked, survived, and evolved. It is also my hope that this generalized meta-metaphorical (Morowitz

1998) prospectus of Egypt as a CAS will set the stage for more rigorous computational modeling studies that utilize the very finite and quantifiable major parameters of its traditional, pre-twentieth-century society and ecology.

In Weber's social theory, "collectivities like a state, or a nation or a family do not 'act' or 'maintain themselves' or 'function'" (Bendix 1962:262), rather they emerge "bottom up" from "meaningful action" when individuals pursue their interests. This aspect of his thought provides a segue from studies of nonhuman to human social complex systems. Weber's is one approach to a "focus on relationships" in human CAS; he already articulated the concept, now applied to corporate structure, of "a nested hierarchy of interactions within and between organizations. . . that each domain of relationship is dependent on the quality of relationship in the domain below it" (Lewin et al. 1998:38–39).

Rather than simply a strengthening of standard archaeological theory, which has tended toward a top-down "highly aggregate perspective" (Epstein and Axtell 1996:16), complexity theory may require new definitions of social complexity. Applied to ancient Egypt, long considered the quintessence of an early centralized nation-state, CAS studies may suggest that there are more useful ways to define social complexity than by focusing on noncentralized vs. centralized decision making, or on managers at the top who have global and strategic information, and workers at the bottom who are restricted to local information. Mitchell Resnick (1994) advises us that "people assume centralized control where it doesn't exist, and they impose centralized control where it isn't needed." To emphasize central control as *the* principal feature of archaic complex societies makes them appear significantly different than CAS in which control is highly dispersed, where coherent behavior emerges from competition and cooperation among the agents themselves, where there are "many levels of organization, with agents at one level serving as the basic building blocks for agents at a higher level" (Waldrop 1992:145–147), and which evolve in part by revision and recombination of building blocks.

3 PARTS

Ancient Egyptian civilization is as large, long-lived, and well-defined a macro-level, human, social CAS as one could hope to find among the ancient societies of this planet. It owed collective life to an exogenous energy source, the central artery of the Nile River and its annual inundation, and in its earliest periods it was enclosed membranelike on east and west by desert. Its southern border was gated by the Nubian cataracts and the thinning away of the Nile alluvium. On the north lay the Mediterranean Sea and, by about 6000 normalfontB.C., a coastal series of lagoons and marshes behind barrier beaches.

It was about this time (6500–5500 normalfontB.C.) that a deceleration in sea-level rise, a lowering of the Delta gradient, and, consequently, greater meander of the Nile tributaries lead to the deposit of a mantle of silt in the Delta supporting a rich cover of grasses and other plants (Stanley and Warne

1993a). This was also a period of heightened aridity which saw the drying of playas and the retreat of grasslands in the Western Desert. Archaeological evidence suggests a migration of cattle pastoralists and incipient farmers toward the Nile Valley occurred prior to 5000 normalfontB.C., when the first Neolithic sites appear in the Egyptian valley (Wendorf et. al. 1992; Holmes 1993). It was the sequence of continuous silt aggradations after 6000 normalfontB.C. that made agriculture possible in the Delta (Stanley and Warne 1993b). The organization of that alluvial carpet in the Egyptian Delta and valley, a very finite, well-defined 34,000 km², comprising only three percent of modern Egypt's territory, is what allowed Egyptian complex society to rise and resurrect itself in great cycles spanning three millennia.

In order to assess ancient Egypt in terms of CAS models, I attempt to outline basic components and processes. It is necessary to generalize over long periods that saw many significant changes. I try to abstract structures and processes that remained the same up to recent centuries. Many of the issues and patterns of centralized state vs. local control in Egypt may be general to other premodern states (Scott 1998). But it goes without saying that in recent centuries Egypt was a very different country than during the pharaonic period. Scholars have said that some of the basic structures and processes, such as basin irrigation, remained relatively constant over these millennia. I use studies of all premodern periods, for which historical documentation increases over time, to open up topics like village organization and land tenure for the pharaonic period, to draw analogies, and to pose questions. Analogies with more recent premodern Egypt may help us think about what is feasible in terms of central vs. local control, and how local control operated in the same environmental niche, with the same flood regimen. In most cases, there is evidence of parallel parts and processes in the textual and archaeological records of the pharaonic period. If approaching ancient Egypt as a CAS proves useful, we should investigate the structural depth and systemic impact of dramatic changes in religion (Christianity, Islam), crops (e.g., sugar cane, cotton), materials and industries (bronze and iron), and the advance of perennial irrigation over the five millennia of premodern Egypt. Tracing the parts and processes of Egypt civilization as a CAS from pharaonic periods to recent centuries would have to follow a rich body of primary documents through the Graeco-Roman period and Egypt in late antiquity, a period I have mostly leapt over.

3.1 HOUSEHOLDS

As a window onto the local rules of a mid-size household, Egyptologists are privy to the set of three undelivered letters and some accounts written by Hekanakht. Originally thought to date to 2002 normalfontB.C., just at the end of the First Intermediate Period and on the cusp of the reunification of the country under the Eleventh Dynasty pharaoh Mentuhotep Nebhepetre (James 1962; K. Baer 1963; Goedicke 1984), Allen (n.d.) now dates the letters to the

Twelfth Dynasty reign of Senwosret I (1971–1926 B.C.). Hekanakht wrote from Thebes, where he seems to have been carrying out duties as a funerary priest of the Vizier, to the center of his household located somewhere in the north, probably near Memphis or the Fayum (Allen n.d.). His was a relatively small farming household. Five men, some of whom were probably his sons, and a hired hand worked land that was owned and rented. As a young man, Hekanakht himself, a literate priest for a high official, may have also worked the land (Allen n.d.). In Letter II, vs. 7–23 Hekanakht lists the rations (ᶜqw, lit. "income") for 14 people. Included are "Merisu (and) his dependents" (ẖrw, literally, "those under him"; this is probably Hekanakht's eldest son and his household), and "Heti's son Nakht and his dependents, probably a hired man and his household" (K. Baer 1963:7). Hekanakht says, "The entire household is like [my] children and everything is mine."

Textual and archaeological evidence suggests a certain degree of modularity, the repetition of basic structures, in the organization of large household estates throughout ancient Egypt. Old Kingdom tombs give us glimpses in words and pictures. The Fifth Dynasty tomb of Nikanesut at Giza documents a household that included 2 overseers of the property in charge of his estates, 11 scribes, a director of the work force in charge of fields and peasants, 2 directors of the dining hall, 2 overseers of linen, a seal bearer, 3 butchers, 2 bakers, a cook, and 5 butlers (Malek and Foreman 1986:93). From the Middle Kingdom we have the better part of the footprint of a town attached to the pyramid temple of Senwosret II (1897–1878 B.C.) at Illahun, near the entrance to the Fayum (Figure 1). Ten large houses are found with 220 smaller houses (perhaps originally nearly double the number), all within a rectangular compound reflecting the ordered, "legible" way that a state sees complex social reality (Scott 1998). Each large house consisted of a core residence surrounded by small structures. In the more complete plans of the large houses in the northern row (Figure 1, right), each was entered through a common plain façade shared by all the large houses running the length of the street. Inside the doorway, a small antechamber gave access to a long narrow corridor running along the east length of the core house to the back of the compound. Here, a colonnade that faced north, away from the direction of the street entrance, gave shade to the "front" of the house. Before the colonnade lay an open court with a garden and grove. Behind the colonnade the large Illahun houses had a central room with four columns where the householder could formally greet his visitors. Off to one side or deeper into the house, there were bedrooms with sleeping niches set into one wall. It was Kemp's (1989:149–157) insight that the daily life and functions of the components traced in the ground plan of these large houses are represented in the wooden models of daily life that appear in the archeological record from the end of the Old Kingdom into the early Twelfth Dynasty. A particularly complete cache was discovered in the Middle Kingdom tomb of Meketre, Chancellor to pharaoh Mentuhotep II (Nebhepetre). Herbert Winlock (1955), who made the discovery, published the set with architectural plans of each boxed component,

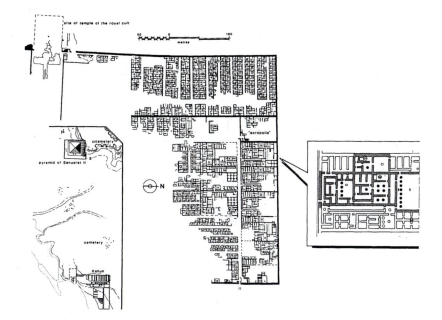

FIGURE 1   From Kemp (1989:150, Figure 53, and 152, Figure 54). The Middle Kingdom, Twelfth Dynasty town (near the modern site of Illahun) was attached to the pyramid complex of pharaoh Senwosret II. The inset is the ground plan of one of the large town houses occupying the northern part of the town. Kemp based his illustration on Petrie and Flinders (1891:pl. XIV) and Petrie et al. (1923:pls. XXXIII and XXXVIa).

including a porticoed house with a courtyard pool in a grove of trees, a bakery and brewery, carpentry and weaving shops, and a granary. Kemp matched the gridded ground plan of the granary with the footprint of structures in one corner of the large Illahun house compounds. Senwosret II's pyramid town was one of the rare sites from ancient Egypt where archaeology and texts directly complement one another. Fragments of papyrus with "specifications of members of a household," i.e., a census, list a house, probably one of the few larger ones, in which a priest of Senwosret II named Khakaura-Senefru, lived with his son, daughter and "serfs," some of whom were also priests. The list is incomplete, but a comparable list of the same period lists 95 serfs of an official, women outnumbering men by 2:1. In this document the men's titles include domestic servant, field labourer, brewer, cook, tutor, sandal maker (Kemp 1989:156).

At Amarna, the short-lived capital of the New Kingdom, Eighteenth Dynasty pharaoh, Akhenaten, we have a large part of the footprint of a New Kingdom city. The plan of the city and of the individual large house compounds, is less tightly organized than at Illahun, but again the larger houses, or "urban estates," consisted of a core residence surrounded by granaries, animal byres, wells, kitchens, weaving facilities, pottery kilns and other workshops (Kemp 1989:296–309).

3.2 VILLAGES

The roles and patterns of villages in the more recent, yet premodern, Egyptian landscape offer a starting point for assessing evidence for villages in the pharaonic periods. During the seventeenth to the early nineteenth centuries A.D. the village was a basic unit of Egyptian agrarian administration, although whole villages could be subsumed into so-called "private" estates. Within the span of decades, scores and hundreds of villages could fall into ruin and abandonment, or rise again and thrive, depending upon politics, patronage, protection, or plunder by the powerful. Whole villages or parts of villages were divided into zones of *iltizams*, "tax farms," over which the absentee patron, a *multazim*, acted as an exogenous government, collecting taxes, maintaining infrastructure, assigning land to cultivate (Cuno 1992).

Even as they contributed to the land use portfolios of absentee holders, the villages were traditionally autonomous units (Lyons 1908). Parts of villages were ruled by *shaykhs* who represented their clan-affiliated dependents. From several shaykhs in each village emerged a "shaykh-of-shaykhs," a leader who was called *umda*, "mayor" after 1820. These head shaykhs were the agents of the governmental authorities, even at the height of centralization. They also represented the village to the multazims and to urban merchant-creditors. They managed the operations of flood recession agriculture, until this century the primary infrastructure of Egyptian society (Cuno 1992). Their households could grow into extended joint households, "being divided into families living each, under a separate roof and the whole forming a city..." (Hekekyan, quoted by Cuno 1992:176), within the larger settlement.

Each village was a complex adaptive system unto itself. Each shaykh ruled a village part, or *hara*, sometimes related to north, south, east, and west quarters, even if the streets and paths did not correspond closely to the theoretical intersecting diagonals that would so divide the town physically. Certain families or clans could be identified with one of the quarters (Figure 2). The houses of older family lineages might occupy the center of the village, near an older religious shrine (Berque 1957; Cuno 1992:89–92). Jacques Berque (1957), who did an ethnographic study of a Delta village in the 1950s, noted that the cadastral quarters were an approximate match to the village quarters. The agricultural holdings in the sub-basins around the village were a radiation of the village proper, northern families farming plots in northern basins, etc. (Figure 2). This patterning was in counterpoint to a tendency to distribute holdings in as many sub-basins as possible (Cuno 1992:72, 91). In the example that Berque (1957:24–25) mapped, the families of the center show the greatest scattering of holdings around the village. Berque (1957:48) wrote of

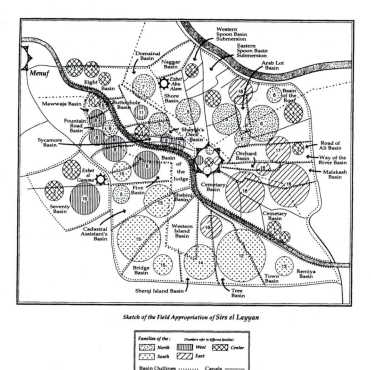

Sketch of the Field Appropriation of Sirs el Layyan

FIGURE 2   Based on Berque's (1957:24–25) study of the Delta village, Sirs el-Layyan. A tendency to distribute plots in different sub-basins exists in counterpoint to a tendency for families of the same clans from the same village "quarters" to cluster their holdings in adjacent plots and sub-basins. Hachure patterns indicate the village clans of the "quarters" which correspond to the cardinal directions and to the village center. The numbers refer to families (identified by Berque 1957:25). The plots of the families of the center show the widest distribution. Basin names are roughly translated from Arabic.

a dynamic competition between families and quarters that holds in check a tension favorable to village vitality.

The village was not just the cluster of houses, but included a surrounding agricultural territory with definite boundaries. The complexities of land tenure and landscape heterogeneities resulted in a variety of territorial "shapes" at the time of the first scale cadastral mapping in the last century. In the narrowest, southernmost parts of the valley below Aswan, village territories could take in the valley cross section between Nile and desert with a tendency for the main settlement to be located near the river (Figure 3(a); Lyons 1908:28).

To the north the valley widens in the Qena Bend, where the Nile river valley makes its greatest deviation from its general north-south course to swing as far as it will in Egypt toward the Red Sea, running nearly east-west at the bottom of the bend, where the famous site of Luxor and the Valley of the Kings is located, and at the top of the bend near the town of Qena (Figure 4(a)). In the Qena Bend (near Qus and Qift), there was a similar development of contiguous village territories, but the wider stretch of cultivation resulted in satellite hamlets near the alluvial-desert edge (Figure 3(b)). In the northern Qena Bend and the valley immediately north of it, "the lands of different villages interlace with each other in so remarkable a manner that it is difficult to believe that it is not due to some definite cause" (Figure 3(c); Lyons 1908:29). Farther north, as the Nile valley widens into Middle Egypt, "villages [and surrounding territories] line the bank and desert margin, while others are built in the middle of the plain where [the nucleus settlements] stand as islands during the inundation" (Figure 3(d); Lyons 1908:29).

The interlacing of villages' territories resulted from the land exchanges at the boundaries, but the propensity for scattered portfolios of land use could also have villages "possessing" plots in other villages, creating what Scott (1998) recently termed a "legibility" problem for the state as expressed by Lyons, who oversaw Egypt's first true cadastral mapping at the turn of this century and commented on "this confusing state of things" (Lyons 1908:95). "The resulting boundaries [of interlaced villages] are most inconvenient in their irregularity, but strong opposition was offered by the inhabitants to all proposals for simplifying them" (Lyons 1908:29). Villagers would also establish "colonial" housing near plots that were distant from the main territory. This may have created a mechanism of village "budding." Barclay offered a modern ethnographic example:

> People of nearby villages rented land to farm in [the village of] Kaum and the people of Kaum also rent and own land in other villages. Both renters from other villages and residents of Kaum itself sometimes erect mud houses near their cultivated land. As a result somewhat dispersed settlement pattern arises and carried on over the years leads to the appearance of clusters of houses which may eventually become hamlets and they, in turn, villages. (Barclay 1966:146)

We do not know for certain if villages played such roles and formed such patterns in ancient Egypt, but there is evidence that they probably did. Onomastica, Egyptian lists of nouns that essentially index their universe (sky, sun, star, Orion...god, goddess, spirit, king), include lists of settlements ordered south to north along the Nile Valley. These can be compared to town and nome lists from temples and other sources. The Onomasticon of Amenemope contains the longest list, with 80 place names for the Nile Valley and Delta (Gardiner 1947:40). But these are probably towns of a larger size class than villages, and "as to how much settlement was outside the towns, and of

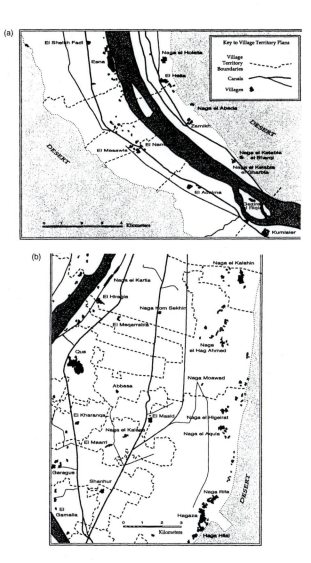

FIGURE 3   (a) Village territories in the narrow southernmost parts of the valley below Aswan, based on Lyons (1908:pl. xi). The territories take in the cross section of the valley from the Nile levee to the desert. (b) Village territories in the wider valley of the Qena Bend near Qus and Qift. Territories stretch out from the Nile levee across the flood plain, but the wider stretch of cultivation resulted in satellite hamlets near the alluvial-desert edge. Based on Lyons (1908:pl. xiv).

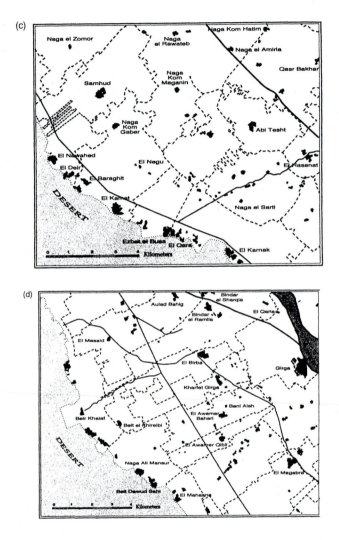

FIGURE 3   Continued. (c) Village territories in the northern Qena Bend and the valley immediately north of it interlace with each other. Based on Lyons (1908:pl. xiv). (d) Village territories just north of the Qena Bend where the Nile valley begins to widen into Middle Egypt. Villages and surrounding territories line the bank and desert margin, while others are in the middle of the plain where the nucleus settlements stand as islands during the inundation. Based on Lyons (1908:pl. xiii).

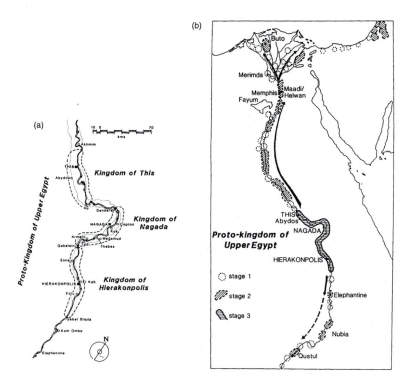

FIGURE 4   (a) Proto-Kingdoms of the Qena Bend. From Kemp (1989:34, Figure 8) who gives graphic expression to inferences of local rulers and proto-kingdoms emerging in the Qena Bend region at the end of the Predynastic Period. (b) Northward expansion of state-forming carriers of Nagada culture across Middle Egypt and the Delta. From Kemp (1989:45, Figure 13).

what kind, we have only a hazy outline" (Kemp 1989:311). In the Wilbour Papyrus, a cadastral survey of about 150 km in Middle Egypt in Year 4 of Ramses V (1142 B.C.), 416 settlement names are mentioned (Kemp 1989:311). "The nature of the place names is very much like that of modern Egypt. Some are proper names, but a large number are compounds in which the first element is descriptive. In modern Egypt the commonest are *Kom* (mound), *Bet* (house), *Ezbet* (originally a settlement for a landowner's peasants), *Naga* (a hamlet), and *Deir* (a Coptic Christian monastery).... Wilbour gives us *Iat* (mound), *At* (house), *Wehit* (hamlet), *Bekhen* (an official's villa), and *Sega* (tower). Altogether there are 141 of these places, subdivided as follows: 51 mounds, 37 houses, 29 hamlets, 17 villas, and 7 towers" (Kemp 1989:312). Whether villages included territories that exhibited patterns relative to the width of the flood plain, to land use, and other factors similar to those of recent centuries is also not certain, yet very possible or probable in light of historical hints. For example, in his tomb the Middle Kingdom nomarch, Khnumhotep II, states that in more than one generation of his line, the reigning king restored "that which a *niwt* (town or village) had taken from its neighbor, while he caused *niwt* to know its boundary with *niwt*, establishing the landmarks like the heavens, distinguishing their waters like that which was in the writings..." (Breasted 1906:283; Sethe 1935:27). Hassan (1993:560–563) cited al-Maqrizi (A.D. 1364–1442), who reported 956 villages in Upper Egypt and 1439 villages in the Delta at the time of the time of the Ikhshids (A.D. 934–968), and Russell (1966) who reports 2,261 villages in the 1400s in Upper Egypt and the Delta. "It is thus unlikely that the number of villages in Upper Egypt during Pharaonic times was greater than 956–1,439"(Hassan 1993:560).

In the pharaonic period local mayors were responsible for the tax obligations of their towns and villages as they were in the seventeenth to nineteenth centuries A.D. (van den Boorn 1988:243). What we know of ancient Egyptian mayors fits in many ways the profile of the shaykhs and umdas just prior to modernization.

> Ancient Egyptian mayors are an interesting group. In earlier periods they had been all-powerful locally, commonly holding the office of chief priest in the town's temple as well. To some extent they lay outside the regular bureaucratic systems, and did not possess a hierarchy of their own officials. Their power must have lain in the respect and influence they commanded by virtue of local landownership and family ties and a network of patronage and obligation. Although they had no bureaucracy of their own, they were normally responsible for seeing that local taxes were collected and delivered to the vizier, the king's chief representative. They presumably acted as a buffer between the external demands of the state and the well-being of the local community of which they were the symbolic head. (Kemp 1989:219)

3.3 TOWNS

The location of most of the important towns can be fixed through textual and topographic sources (O'Connor 1972:683). The spacing of towns presents a general, but not a rigid, regularity based on river distance which may reflect their "utilitarian character" (O'Connor 1972:688–689). Using a variety of sources, Butzer (1976:57–80) compiled a table of 217 ancient settlements "of reasonable size" for the Nile Valley from the First Cataract to just south of Cairo; 57 percent of these could be accurately located, while others could be placed in their south-north sequence and on the east or west side of the flood plain. Butzer counted 138 of these settlements as large villages, the others as towns or small "cities"; for which 29 mayors ($h3ty-c$) are attested (all but 9 of these were nome centers), and temples are known or likely for 113 of these settlements. Using an insight from central place studies that "median bifurcation ratios of at least 2:1 and 3:1 will be present between successive settlement hierarchies" (Butzer 1976:72), Butzer predicted a total of 178 small centers and 1,125 large villages for the pharaonic period.

3.3.1 **Illahun.** Egyptologists consider the Middle Kingdom's Twelfth Dynasty a time when centralized planning and bureaucratic control were at their height. The town at Illahun belongs to a class of "pyramid towns," settlements attached to royal pyramid complexes since the Old Kingdom (Helck 1957; Stadelmann 1981b, 1985), whose focus was the valley and upper temples attached to the pyramids. As a member of this class, we should expect the ground plan to evidence a premeditated, unified design. The rigid orthogonal layout shows this to be the case, and as such, we should expect the pattern to offer compelling insight into the way the "state," i.e., the royal house, organized people and production for a state enterprize.

The footprint of this town, named *Hetep Senwosret*, "Senwosret is at Peace," excavated by Petrie in 1889, is one of the basic documents for the study of the history of Egyptian urbanism (Petrie 1891; Petrie et al. 1923; Kemp 1989:149–157). The houses and other elements are packed densely into a walled enclosure 384 × 335 m (12.86 ha) with one entrance through a two-meter-wide gateway on the east (Figure 1). There must have been other entrances in the missing east part of the town. A thick wall divides the town into a larger eastern district and a narrower western part. Rows of small houses fill at least two thirds of the western enclosure, laid out in double back-to-back rows broken by a north-south street at the east end. Small houses also fill the area south of the large houses in the eastern part of town, making a total of about 220 small houses, a ratio of about 20:1 with the large houses. It is very possible that the one-third or more missing part of the town was also filled with small houses, so that the ratio of small to large houses may have been significantly higher (Kemp 1989:155). A row of six, possibly seven, of the large houses, each 42 × 60 m = 2,520 m², fill the north side of the larger part of the town. Another three large houses line the opposite side of the town's widest street running east-west. The house at the west end of the north row is surrounded by an extra thick wall. It was built on a rock outcrop with a stairway to the higher terrace. Stadelmann (1985:239) suggested that this is the king's own residence in his pyramid town. Below and south of this acropolis a small structure in the middle of an open area might have been the town shrine in a gathering place.

As mentioned, the large houses consist of a core house surrounded by small structures all tightly fitted within a rectangular compound which probably contained modular household industries. Granaries, typical of the Middle Kingdom, which Kemp recognized in the corner of the ground plan of the large Illahun houses, were also found in the Middle Kingdom forts in Lower Nubia

(Kemp 1986, 1989:177–178). Using figures from the forts for the heights of the granaries and caloric values for emmer and barley, Kemp estimated that collectively the large household granaries could have stored enough grain to feed annually 5,000–9,000 people. Assuming only half the original number of small houses is preserved in the ground plan, and 6 people per small house, we obtain an estimated population of about 3,000 (Kemp 1989:155). The conclusion is that the inhabitants of the small dwellings were the brewers, cooks, sandal makers, and other workers in the large households. In return for their labor they were fed by the large Illahun houses.

Why organize a "state" pyramid town around several large households, each a redistribution center, instead of one central granary? In the Old Kingdom we see several manifestations of a tendency to accomplish colossal tasks by replicating modular household structures and operations as many times as needed, rather than to radically reconfigure for mass production (although a trend in that direction can be seen over the long course of ancient Egyptian civilization). Our recent excavations at the Giza Plateau offer evidence that even the labor for the gigantic pyramids of the early Old Kingdom was provisioned by modular replication of basic household modes of production (Lehner 1992, 1994, 1996; Hawass and Lehner 1997). Kemp (1989:157) concluded from the Illahun pyramid town that "this team- or gang-organization of dependent population seems to have been common in ancient Egypt." But it was the "household that provided the model and the social vehicle where none other yet existed."

3.3.2 Amarna. Kemp's insight into the functioning of the Twelfth Dynasty urban estates was prompted in part from his familiarity with urban estates at Amarna, the short-lived new city of pharaoh Akhenaten in Middle Egypt, dating some 550 years after the town of Illahun. Occupying some 400 ha, much of the city plan has been retrieved. Like Illahun, it is a major document for the study of ancient Egyptian urbanism, now at the peak of empire, at the upper end of the settlement size scale, and a "capital," representing the footprint of the state where it stepped down for little more than a decade.

A central "downtown" area is composed by large temples, temple magazines, bakeries, and other production facilities, the king's official house and ceremonial palace, a kind of royal chapel, a records office, and a military post (Kemp 1989:271–294). The central city was flanked by northern and southern suburbs composed of neighborhoods that included both large walled urban estates and surrounding smaller houses. The neighborhoods and the interiors of each of the urban estates are more loosely organized than at Illahun, and whereas at Illahun there appear to have been two classes of people based on house size, at Amarna house sizes show a more even gradient. However, the large houses still reflect the pattern of a core residence surrounded by granaries, animal byres, wells, kitchens, weaving facilities, pottery manufacture and other workshops (Kemp 1989:296–309).

With its central "downtown" for official acts, records, and law enforcement, a central roadway, and its suburbs, Amarna has many intimations of urban modernity. Yet a kind of fractal pattern is reflected in two ways. Just as the central city was a focus of storage and production around the official residence and temples, flanked by the suburbs, so each large house compound in those suburbs enclosed a central residence, an adjacent religious shrine, granaries and production facilities, and large houses were flanked by smaller houses, "the overwhelming impression is of a series of joined villages" (Kemp 1989:294). And just as the state, that is, the royal house, from its capital, controlled land held far and wide throughout the territory, so, as Kemp has argued, each large Amarna household was also a farm center whose holdings may have included land adjacent to the new capital set aside for it, but probably also pre-Amarna holdings in home town areas and portfolios of scattered land rights. Each household was, in this sense, a kind of patrimonial "state in miniature," making the Amarna suburbs an aggregate of "small economic centres" (Kemp 1972:675) clustered around the economic nucleus of the central city.

> A proportion of officials at Amarna had links with more distant estates and houses in their home provinces. The more successful officials were, therefore, institutions in miniature. Their households also, to varying degrees, engaged in manufacture. In foodstuffs and goods, private estates had surpluses to dispose of, through gifts and also through sales, the latter sometimes delegated to the "traders." (Kemp 1989:316)

The large houses in the preplanned or newly designed settlements of Illahun and Amarna imply the existence of similar large households of notables and officials in the towns that are known from historical sources over very long periods of Egyptian history, such as the traditional nome centers. That these households must also have functioned as the home base of estates with portfolios of rights to scattered land is indicated by historical and archaeological sources like the Wilbour Papyrus (O'Connor 1972) and the cemeteries of certain towns (Kemp 1989:312).

3.3.3 Temple.

Town and temple must be considered together in ancient Egypt, for the temple was the nucleus of the town "cell," and, along with provincial notables, whose main residences were located in towns, the temples were agents of local control. Kemp points out that the Egyptians considered their temples quite literally as houses of the gods who were present in the forms of their statues. "In a sense, the gods were given the status of landed nobility" (Kemp 1972:658, 1989:190), and the New Kingdom temples were economically organized as a large household estate whose assets could include "animal herds, fishing and fowling rights, flax fields to provide the raw material from which linen garments were manufactured in temple workshops, vegetable beds, vineyards, and beehives." New Kingdom temples also controlled or owned cattle herds, rights to mineral resources, boats and merchant fleets (Kemp 1989:191–197). These assets imply a broad personnel of dependents or commissioned employees, such as the professional traders (*shuty*) who cycled material between households large and small. "The professional overlap between temple and private household is itself revealing as to the essentially common economic nature of both" (Kemp 1989:257).

Like the large, so-called "private" houses, temples were nodes for storage and distribution of surplus grain and a wide variety of other commodities. Kemp has estimated that the Ramesseum, the Mortuary Temple of Ramses II, in western Thebes, could have stored enough grain to feed 3,400 families, or between 17,00 to 20,000 people, for a year on the average rations for a workman's family. Kemp (1989:195) concludes, "major temples were the reserve banks of the time." In effect, they were to the town or settlement around them like the large Illahun or Amarna houses, each a reserve bank and redistributive center on a smaller scale.

In the Wilbour Papyrus (Gardiner 1948), a land register in the reign of Ramses V (1142 B.C.), New Kingdom temples appear to have been clearing houses and controllers for local land parcels that were tied to complex intersecting webs of portfolios of land use and rights. This included local land in the portfolio of the royal house (Eyre 1994b:119–121), but the cultivation and usufruct rights of local land were also held by a surprisingly broad range of people: priests, scribes, soldiers, stablemasters, the Vizier himself, also herdsmen and small farmers (O'Connor 1972:691–693; Kemp 1989:191, 311). The administration of claims to local land was in addition to the temples' management of their own land portfolios. Sometimes one temple rented to or from another, adding to the complexities of land tenure. In the Late Period at least some priesthoods were organized along kinship lines which Lloyd (1983:305) took as a hint of the "exploitation of kinship as a major integrating mechanism in the social, economic, and political life of the country."

Collectively the temples were to the overall Egyptian state what the large Illahun houses were to the town. When, for example, the New Kingdom state set out to colonize Nubia, it did so by replicating the basic town-temple unit of the Egyptian homeland. Kemp (1972:667) observed that "temples appear to have been the dominant physical feature of all Egyptian town sites of any importance in Nubia" and he pointed to "the advantages of making a temple economy the basic unit for the administration and exploitation of Nubia. . .it provided a ready-made self-sufficient unit integrated within the fabric of the Egyptian state. . . ."

3.4   LAND PORTFOLIOS

Put the evidence together, and we have the outline for the private sector of a highly complex pattern of landholding in which a 'farm' was not a single discrete parcel of agricultural land, but a whole series

of scattered plots held in more than one way: either owned outright or
rented from a temple or from some other landowner. (Kemp 1989:310)

In Egypt of the pharaonic periods, as in Egypt of the Islamic and Ottoman
periods, it may be overly simplistic to speak of land ownership. "The control
and use of the land was the important thing" (Cuno 1992:18, 82). For much
of the last two millennia (A.D.), the land was "state fiscal land." After the
Muslim conquest, Islamic jurists theorized that conquered land "belonged to
the Muslim community as a whole. . .thus it was immobilized like a charitable
endowment" (Cuno 1992:22). In theory, even the peasants who cultivated the
land in the proximity of their domiciles were receiving usufruct by state permission (Cuno 1992:36). In ancient Egypt, to the extent that all land was the
territory of a divine king, a similar concept was available. In actual practice,
traditionally held peasant land could be inherited, sold, rented, or pawned
(Cuno 1992:82–83). Land was, therefore, treated as though it were owned.

In ancient Egypt, land portfolios, and hints of complex webs of interconnected, embedded, hierarchical land tenure are widely attested in the textual
record of periods of unity. One of the most repeated and elaborated scenes in
Old Kingdom tomb chapels and pyramid temples is the long train of offering
bearers, each a personification of a village (*niwt*), estate (*hwt*), or nome, bringing produce to the center of the extended household (*pr ḏt*, literally "House of
Eternity") and, by extension, to the tomb, a focus of any large household for
the benefit and otherworldly endurance of deceased householders. Many of the
villages and estates that belonged to pyramid complexes and large tombs can
be plotted geographically as least as to the nome in which they occur. They
were spread throughout the country, but tended to be located mainly in the
broad valley of Middle Egypt and the Delta (Helck 1957:104; Jacquet-Gordon
1962:104–108; Kemp 1983:89–92, Figure 2.2). This was clearly a time, commensurate with pyramid building in the narrow valley just below the Delta
apex, of internal colonization, attested by titles like "Overseer of New Towns."

In the New Kingdom, Wilbour Papyrus land holdings were designated
by a hieroglyph of an arm with a down-turned hand. The word is *rmnyt*,
which Gardiner (1941, 1948) translated "domain" noting that it designated
assemblages of fields literally "under the control of a single arm," but which
were by no means contiguous. "Land portfolios" seems the most germane
translation. In ancient Egypt, as in other premodern societies (Scott 1998:39)
and particularly those based on flood recession agriculture (Park 1992, 1993),
an archipelago of land holdings of different quality spread throughout the
country was probably insurance against risk of floods that were too high
or too low, or microvariations in soils that could be redistributed annually
(Park 1992:95). Hekanakht's documents show, at a moderate scale of farming,
diffused land holdings. None of the fields mentioned, probably in the north
near Heracleopolis by the entrance to the Fayum oasis (Allen n.d.), were at his
home in a place called Nebesit (K. Baer 1963:3). In addition to the northern
holdings he enjoyed rights to land near Abydos, hundred of miles south of

Heracleopolis, as a perquisite of his being a funerary priest in Thebes (Allen n.d.).

3.5 BASINS

Great basins, *hawd*, or hod in Arabic, caught and retained the waters of the annual Nile inundation and formed a patchlike pattern (Figure 5) that comprised the broadest and most basic infrastructure of Egyptian civilization until the early twentieth century A.D. These considerable tracts of land were defined by longitudinal dykes running parallel to the river and desert edge, and by transverse dykes that ran east-west. In northern Egypt the dikes "divided the Delta into basins and served as roads throughout the year" (Cuno 1992:52). These are the great basins described by Willcocks (1889) in his hydrological survey of Egypt near the turn of the century. The basins described by Lyons (1908), who was in charge of the cadastral mapping of Egypt, are smaller units, also called *hawds*, within village territories (Figure 6(a)). Often defined by levees like the large basins, these sub-basins were tracts of land of the same quality, or nearly uniform crop yields, used as land units of given tax rates (Lyons 1908:322).

An old assumption that ancient Egypt was irrigated by a whole network of perennially flooded canals inspired a theory that civilization developed because of the need to supervise and control this vast network (Wittfogel 1957). These ideas do not fit the premodern operation of the Egyptian flood plain (Butzer 1976). By eroding its bed and depositing sand and silt along its banks, the Nile in Egypt created a convex flood plain that one historian compared to the back of a leaf with the raised spines as the Nile and its levees (Richards 1982:14). The highest valley land is close to the river; the lowest valley land is next to the desert. In between, a series of basins stepped downstream from south to north, dropping a total of 85 m from Aswan to the Mediterranean.

It has been generally considered that basin irrigation in ancient Egypt was essentially the same as in the last century (Schenkel 1973:775). A more detailed investigation must address the question of how soon and how far the system was developed at any given period in antiquity. In the nineteenth and early twentieth centuries, Upper Egypt was comprised of 136 great basins. As mapped by British engineers (Willcocks 1889:pl. 12) they look like great cells comprising the plant stalk of the Nile Valley (Figure 5). The basins held water for six to eight weeks each year and varied in shape and size according to differences in the width of land between river and desert. Each great basin had its own indigenous Arabic name. Delgawi Basin, at the tail end of the Sohagia Canal in Middle Egypt, was the largest, covering 201.6 km^2. The smallest was the Maasara Basin in Giza, covering 2.1 km^2. The average size of all the great basins was 37.8 m^2.

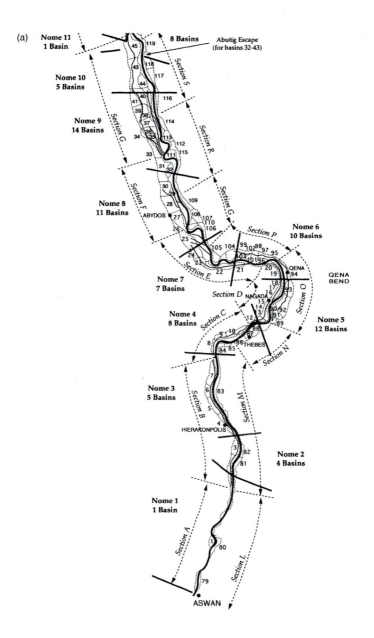

FIGURE 5   (a) Map of southern Upper Egypt and the Qena Bend region with great basins as mapped at the end of the nineteenth century A.D. (Willcocks 1889:pl. xii) and ancient nome boundaries based on Baines and Malek (1984:14). The number of nineteenth-century basins per ancient nome is indicated. Dashed lines and letters mark irrigation sections defined by escapes (drains) of basins systems.

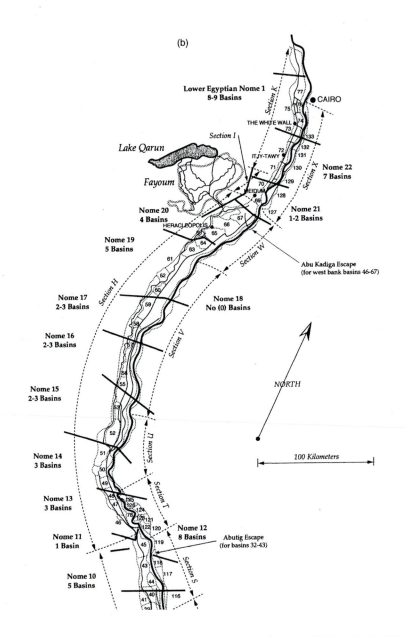

FIGURE 5 Continued. (b) Map of northern Upper Egypt which includes Middle Egypt and the narrow valley north of the Fayum entrance with great basins of the nineteenth century A.D. and ancient nome boundaries. Based on Willcocks (1889:pl. xii) and Baines and Malek (1984:14).

(c)

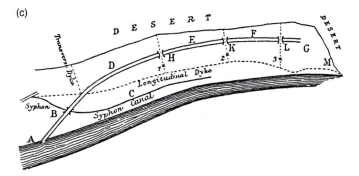

FIGURE 5 Continued. (c) Schematic sketch of a basin system from Willcocks (1889:44). A: head of feeder canal; B: syphon canal; C: highland along river; D, E, F, G: basins; H, K, L: regulators; M: desert escape.

3.5.1 Basin Systems.

Flood recession irrigation of the last century involved independent *basin systems*, consisting of rarely one but usually several basins, stepped down from south to north, watered by a single feeder canal with its head in a breach of the Nile bank (Figure 5(c)). The feeder canals swung out beyond the river levee and then turned to flow roughly parallel to the Nile, crossing the transverse dikes that separated one basin from the next lower one to the north. During the peak of the flood, the Nile Valley was a virtual lake with an average depth of 1.5 m. The villages situated within the basins were "so many small islands, between which communication is kept up by boats or by the dikes" (Willcocks 1889:44).

Two types of "escapes" drained flood waters from a basin system (Willcocks 1889:37–38, 45–57, passim). The water could escape into another basin system down the line. This was particularly characteristic of the west side of the valley for almost all of Middle Egypt where the basins were much larger than in the southern area of the Qena Bend (Willcocks 1889:48). Some of the largest basins of the Middle Egyptian series were located just in front of the entrance of the Fayum oasis (Figure 5(b), numbers 65–67) and immediately above the narrow stretch of valley, only 6 to 8 km wide, from the Fayum entrance to the Delta apex. In the last century the Koshesha Basin (Figure 5(b), number 67), 168 km^2 in area, was the last of the interlinked series of Middle Egyptian basin systems. At the peak of each flood season, Willcocks tells us, the Koshesha Basin retained so much water that it would "hang over Lower Egypt like a dark cloud during the later half of October." In the second kind of escape, a rocky spur of desert thrusts forward to close off a basin system and to force the water back into the Nile channel (Figure 5(c)). All the escapes

FIGURE 6   (a) Example of village boundaries, sub-basins, and plot patterns. Based on Lyons (1908:pl. xvi). (b) Plot patterns and water channels. Irregular plots follow silted-up water channel. Long striplike plots are oriented with narrow ends toward water channel when it carries water year round.

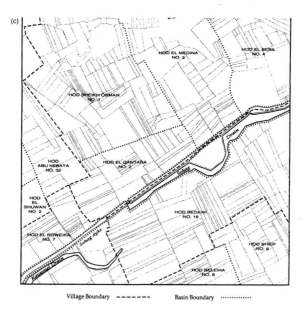

FIGURE 6   Continued. (c) Plot patterns in basin land. Plots tend to be long strips, but the narrow ends are not oriented to a water channel that flows only at the beginning or end of the flood season. Based on Lyons (1908:pl. viii).

on the east side of the valley from Elephantine to opposite Abydos are desert escapes, while six of eight escapes on the west bank of the same stretch are also desert escapes (Willcocks 1889:48, 57–69, Table 16)

3.5.2 Sub-basins.   The great basins were divided into sub-basins by the inhabitants of towns and villages (Willcocks 1889:37; Lyons 1908:64–66, 322–323). From the Arab, Ottoman, and modern periods, the sub-basins divided village territories. Each was given its own name, such as "the town basin," "the seventy," "the five," "the tree," "the road of the fountain," "the sycamore," "the way of the river" (Figure 2; Berque 1957:24–25). The sizes of the sub-basins were quite variable until the late nineteenth century. Then, in a classic example of what Scott (1998) calls a "state simplification" to impose "fiscal legibility" on a complex local situation, the government of 1892 divided village territories, an average of 2,000 feddans (840 ha) into more arbitrary *hawds* of 50 to 100 feddans (21–42 ha), sticking to natural boundaries where possible (Lyons 1908:65, 323).

3.5.3 Plot Patterns.   The sub-basins were further divided into individual plots which were marked off by boundary stones "stuck into the ground at intervals of six feet or more" (Blackman 1927:169). Plots patterns could vary but they tended, in recent centuries at least, to be long rectangular strips, with ratios of length to breadth as much as 300:1 or 400:1 as shown in Figure 6(a) (Lyons 1908:31). Plots were divided, by inheritance for example, along their length, resulting in thinner and thinner strips. Long strips allowed a narrow-end frontage onto a canal or small waterway like that in Figure 6(b) if it furnished water year round. In the broad basin lands, plot patterns were more irregular, and were not oriented to watercourses if they only delivered or drained water at the beginning and end of the inundation like that in Figure 6(c). Basin plots were submerged during most of the inundation season but still tended to be long strips so that each strip shared any microvariations along the length of the plot. In the village territories of southern Upper Egypt the plots were laid across the valley section perpendicular to desert and river (Figure 3(a)). Each strip shared in every "foot and finger of the land that the father has bequeathed" (Ammar 1954:24). In broader areas, like the great Fayum Basin and the Nile Delta, the plot patterns, like village territories, are less striplike and even more irregular in shape than in the Upper Egyptian basin lands (Lyons 1908:31).

3.5.4 Evidence of a Pharaonic Basin System. There are not many obvious textual references to basins and flood management in pharaonic Egypt, perhaps because local control left few administrative documents about the subject (Butzer 1976:43; Eyre 1987:18, 1994a:74). The pharaonic Egyptians must have tamed and regulated the natural, wild Nile Valley in stages over the 3,000 years of their civilization, but the flooding of the normal basin land in Upper Egypt was probably well regulated by the Middle Kingdom, Twelfth Dynasty (Eyre 1994a:75, 78, 80). Such a system may be evidenced by Eighteenth Dynasty references to the canals that seasonally channeled flood waters to the basins as "armatures of water" (Eyre 1994a:74–75). It is probably the basins that are identified by land names like "The Scribes Pallete of Khons" and "The Stable of the Milk Can of Amon" in leases of the Late Period (Hughes 1952; Malinine 1953), similar to basin names in the last century (K. Baer 1962:40, n.98). A general ancient Egyptian term for both tracts of land and bodies of water, perhaps best translated, "basin," is š, written with the hieroglyph of a rectangular basin. Egypt's great agricultural basins did double duty as land tracts and lakes, and this term, š, is used in contexts that suggest it was equivalent to the Arabic word, hawd, for these large units (Sauneron 1959; Yoyotte 1959; Berlandini 1979; Eyre 1994a:68–69). In one of Egypt's oldest annals, the Palermo Stone, inscribed in the Fifth Dynasty, certain years during the Archaic Period are especially remembered for the planning, measuring, and opening of large basins (š), with names like "Thrones of the Gods," "Friends of the Gods," and "Libation of the Gods." I would suggest that these are references to the formalization of large flood basins, rather than to royal funerary enclosures (Stadelmann 1981a:159–163). Similarly, in the Eighteenth Dynasty, the pharaoh Amenhotep III issued scarabs commemorating the making of a basin, š, measuring 71 ha, for his queen, Tiy, near her home town of Akhmim. The king navigated the basin on a royal yacht, to celebrate the festival, "Opening of the Basins" (*wb3 š*). This festival is also known from other sources (Yoyotte 1959:30–31) and probably refers to the filling of basins through the feeder canals or to the discharge of water through the escapes. In the Egyptian classic story of Sinuhe, he says that as a royal gift, "an upper *š*, ('basin') was made for me, fields were in it, and a garden in the right place" (Lichtheim 1975:233 who translates *š* as "funerary domain"). Similarly, in the tomb of the Twelfth Dynasty official Hapdjefay, it is stated, "See, I have endowed you with fields, with people, with flocks, with basins (*š*)..."(Eyre 1994a:66–67). In the Old Kingdom Tomb of Two Brothers, a scene of cutting timber, herding goats, picking fruits in orchards, vineyards, vegetable gardens, and a papyrus marsh are labelled in the framing text as taking place in the *šd(w)t* (plot of land) and *š* ([sub]-basin) of the estate (Eyre 1994a:61, Figure 1).

3.5.5 Perennial Irrigation. In addition to the development of the basin lands in pharaonic times, gardens and orchards were cultivated on the levees and other high ground that needed to be artificially watered (Eyre 1994a). The river levees could be watered by "siphon" canals that split from the Nile channel and ran along the levee, rather than breaking through it to the lower basins (Willcocks 1889) as shown in Figure (5). Such canals had to be excavated deep enough to conduct the water, and far enough to gain on the very gradual northward slope of the levees. Because levee canals were harder to create and maintain than regularizing the basins, they were slower to develop in the course of ancient Egyptian history. The alternative for watering high ground was some kind of water lifting. In the Old Kingdom this was done with water pots slung from shoulder poles, and probably skins, which limited water lifting to small amounts normally for small garden plots (Kemp 1989:12–13) (except for massive desert projects like pyramid building). It was only in the New Kingdom that the Egyptians began to use the *shaduf*, a simple counter-weighted pole on a bracket (Butzer 1976:43–46). The animal-drawn water wheel was introduced in the Ptolemaic (332–30 normalfontB.C.) or Persian Periods (525–332 normalfontB.C.), and the Archimedean screw (a wooden cylinder with an internal helix and a crank-turned axis) came later (Hurst 1952:44). True perennial irrigation was not extensively introduced until the nineteenth century A.D. (Butzer 1976:43).

3.6 NOMES

From the First Cataract to the apex of the Delta, the Nile Valley was organized, Lego-like and linearly, into 22 *nomes* (Figure 5(a)–(b)). The nome boundaries were fixed by river length (including bends) and natural boundaries (Helck 1974:200, 1975:34–44; Janssen 1978:225). The surrounding territory was organized as field complexes (*3ht*), villages (*niwt*), domains or estates (*hwt*) and household properties (*pr*) (Helck 1974:49). Each nome had a distinct

name, icon and a principal town that functioned as a capital city. The nome
was like a miniature state; conversely, the state, according to Helck (1974:199–
200) began like a nome around the Upper Egyptian town of This (or Thinis,
modern Abydos; [Figure 4(a)]), home to the first dynasty of pharaohs; its
surrounding territory became Upper Egyptian Nome 8 (Figure 5(a)). These
pharaohs moved their main residence, "the White Wall," north to where the
Nile Valley met the Delta, an area that became Upper Egyptian Nome 22
and Lower Egyptian 1 (Figure 5(b)). Helck (1974) believed the nomes were
an artifice imposed by the early pharaohs, but it is likely that they were
the formalization of administrative order on natural social and topographical
boundaries.

Nome leaders were called $h3tj$-^{c}, literally "foremost" or "chief," the word
later used as "mayor," $hq3$-$sp3t$, "nome ruler," $s\check{s}mt3$, "leader of the land,"
and, in the early periods, $^c\underline{d}mr$, literally, "canal cutter" (Helck 1974:51). The
first occurrences of the hieroglyph for nome accompanying different nome
icons, are attested from the Dynasty 3 reign of Djoser, builder of the Step
Pyramid, and then from a list of estates organized by nomes in the valley temple of Sneferu's Bent Pyramid in Dynasty 4. The nomes appear, therefore, to
have been systemized administratively during this period in the context of an
agricultural expansion commensurate with the building of giant pyramids in
the early Old Kingdom (Helck 1974:199–200). The processes of setting up or
establishing the Upper Egyptian nomes in the Archaic Period and Old Kingdom must have involved precisely the "creation of the relatively disciplined
landscape and water regime" (Eyre 1994a:80) by means of dikes and levees
that defined basins and controlled the flood waters. The Upper Egyptian sequence was complete from Nome 1 of Elephantine on the First Cataract to
Nome 22 in the valley just below the Delta apex. Nome administrators were
now called imj-r, "overseers." In Dynasty 6 they were known as hri-tp ^{c}3,
"Great Chief of a Nome" and they acted as chief priest of the town temple.
By the Middle Kingdom a "land council" ($qnbt$ n ww) is attested for nomes
as well as a "district scribe." By the New Kingdom a "commander of villages"
($tswwhjjt$) is attested for nome administration. The set of 20 Lower Egyptian
nomes, beginning with L. E. Nome 1 of Memphis, and taking in the Delta,
was only completed in late antiquity (Helck 1974).

The nome administration, through the local town and temple, appears to
have brokered the collection of harvest tax on behalf of distant temples, the
royal house, and anyone who had claim to shares of land within nome territory. New Kingdom documents dealing with collection of "tax," "rent," or
"shares" (Eyre 1994b:127) at harvest reveal a complicated system in which the
nome centers appear to play an intermediate role between local cultivators,
controllers of cultivators, and collectors from temples at Thebes (Gardiner
1941, 1948). In a system where large households, including other temples and
the royal house, possessed portfolios of scattered land, or rights to shares from
the harvest, the land was located within various nome territories (Gardiner
1948:25). For example, in tax records we find for the great Karnak Temple of

Amun, entries like "Apportioning Domain (or Portfolio, *rmnyt*) of the House of Amun, King of the Gods, [in the] domain (or Portfolio, *rmnyt*) of the Tract (or nome territory) of Hardai," the capital of Upper Egyptian Nome 17 (Gardiner 1941:51). This is a record of shares of the Karnak temple, part of its extensive portfolio, within Nome 17. The matter is complicated by the fact that the local nome temple, in addition to the administrative portfolio defined by its territory, could itself hold rights to land in other nomes. As Gardiner (1948:19) noted, "a larger *rmnyt* may thus comprise several subordinate *rmnyt*."

The set of 22 Upper Egyptian nomes and (later) 20 Lower Egyptian nomes are such neat synchronic sets, they seem a more imposed, centrally controlled, and static order than they actually were over the long haul of ancient Egyptian history. Nome capitals waxed and waned in influence and existence. Nome administrative units and boundaries were constantly changing in number and areal coverage, sometimes splitting into smaller units (Gardiner 1948:54–55; Helck 1974:56, 58). From his study of the Wilbour Papyrus, Gardiner concluded that Nomes 18, 19, and 21 were ineffectual in Ramssid times, since their centers are not mentioned in a cadastral survey that spanned the territory of traditional Upper Egyptian nomes 17–22 (Gardiner 1948:54). On a smaller scale, a similar degree of household and settlement fluidity may be indicated by the fact that Gardiner had difficulty finding many of the place names in the Wilbour survey in other sources. For example, in an inscription from the reign of Sheshonk I, dating some 207 years, or about 7 generations, later than the Wilbour cadastre and mentioning thirty towns and villages in Nome 20 which was covered by the Wilbour survey, Gardiner (1948:36) found "not half a dozen place names in common"; names of certain forts and temples occurred in both documents. Villages could multiply and disappear in short time scales as they did in the seventeenth to nineteenth centuries A.D.

3.7 TWO LANDS

At the largest scale, that of nation-state, Egypt's principal parts were the Nile Valley and Delta, known as the "Two Lands" in ancient times. The pharaoh is cited as Lord of the Two Lands numerous times, he wore the double crown combining the crowns of Upper and Lower Egypt, the iconography of the throne was the double Nile god or Horus and Set tying the Upper Egyptian lotus stalk and the Lower Egyptian papyrus stalks around the lung and windpipe hieroglyph topped by the royal name cartouche. Butzer's analysis of ancient site and settlement distributions, compiled through archaeological and historical sources, indicates that the highest population densities were in the north, below the Delta apex to the Fayum oasis entrance, and in the south from the Qena Bend to the First Cataract. Both are zones of constricted valley; "density was an inverse function of floodplain width" (Butzer 1976:101). Middle Egypt and the Delta were less-densely populated zones of land development and internal colonization well into dynastic times (Kees 1961:185 ff.;

Jacquet-Gordon 1962; O'Connor 1972; Helck 1974:49–51; Kemp 1983:90–91; Malek and Forman 1986:65ff; Butzer 1976:100). For long periods, the seven most southerly nomes comprised a unified Upper Egypt which was called "The Head of the South" which, by the Middle Kingdom, included Nome 8 of Abydos/This and later Nome 9 (Helck 1974:55–58).

4 PROCESSES

4.1 MECHANISMS OF HOUSEHOLD EXPANSION AND CONTRACTION

> My mother gave me a chicken, the chicken bought me a goose, the goose bought me a small goat, the goat bought me a sheep, the sheep bought me a small donkey, the donkey bought me a cow, and the cow bought me a *kirat* (one twenty-fourth a feddan of land). (Ammar 1954:22)

This children's song from an Upper Egyptian village reflects the fact that, even at the smallest scale, Egyptian householders are not satisfied when subsistence needs are met. They attempt to maximize profit, invest in land, and "add to one's inheritance" (Ammar 1954:22). Evidence available to Egyptologists indicates this is no less true for the ancient Egyptian farming household. If a case can be made that, true to Weber's vision, the Egyptian state emerged from and operated as an extended household of households, the search for the mechanisms of the rise and resurrection of the Egyptian state should involve the *mechanisms of household expansion*.

Throughout Egyptian history down to the nineteenth century A.D. households expanded by: feeding people (i.e., acting as patriarch); burying people (acting as son and heir, e.g., a nomarch ". . . buried every man of this nome who had no son, in cloth from the property of my estate" [Eyre 1987:33]); owning or having access to boats (the organization of a boat was the archetype for the organization of any body of men; Eyre 1987:11); buying land with people and livestock (Bakir 1952:8; Eyre 1987:34–35); patronage and influence peddling; resolving disputes; renting out property (land, trees, cattle, houses, shops, tanneries, boats, bakeries, oil presses); becoming an official with land usufruct rights-of-office; receiving royal gifts of land, livestock, people, precious metal; organizing and maintaining irrigation dikes, levees, and water-lifting devices; levying troops from dependant households as work gangs or militia; attacking towns and irrigation works; and seizing people and cattle for ransom. The use of estate and household resources for infrastructures—such as those of basin irrigation—that spanned several villages or the better part of a nome, increased dependence of all its users on the household.

The letters and accounts of Hekanakht show us some of these mechanisms in operation for a medium to small farmer. As Kemp (1989:240) pointed out, the documents "display a strong urge to maximize family income by means of shrewd deals with neighbors and others, with no reference to an outside system of authority." Hekanakht's deals included extending and collecting on grain loans, for which there could be a 100-percent return (K. Baer 1962:45); selling oil; using excess grain, linen, clothes, oil, and copper to pay for seasonal land rentals (K. Baer 1963:3, 9); raising bulls; serving as a priest in the cult of a high official, perhaps in return for additional land rights (Allen n.d.); and, primarily, speculating on the annual, seasonal wave of the Nile inundation, building up "substantial capital reserves" (K. Baer 1963:12).

The other side of the same processes involved mechanisms of household fragmentation and contraction. Hekanakht's accounts and letters indicate that one year he extended his household close to the critical threshold of outstanding loans and land rentals that its members could handle and still feed themselves (K. Baer 1963:11–12). His loans to others raises the question of what happened if a borrower defaulted. We can easily imagine that "a debtor who had to borrow at or after the harvest in March would be in no position to repay in grain, a winter crop, during the following inundation" (K. Baer 1963:10). Default on loans and rentals had the consequence of a household becoming the dependency of a more viable household. The well-known claims in the texts of substantial tombs that the owner fed the hungry, clothed the needy, and gave boats to the boatless reflects the reverse side of dependency. Transfer of dependency is explicit in documents of "self sale" known from Ramesside and later periods, where the subject, as a result of debt and basic need, bound himself or herself to a master "forever" along with present and future children, grain, land and other property (Bakir 1952:74–86). Within extended families and households a rule that was documented ethnographically in Egyptian villages in this century was that dependency upon a household is accompanied by transfer of landed property; for example, "a widowed sister lives with her married brother if she transfers to him her property of land or at least allows him to till it" (Ammar 1954:42). Household contraction can, therefore, be understood in a denotative sense of contract, not only to reduce in size, but, as in Latin *contractus*, "to draw together, bind."

4.2 RATES AND RENTS

Although Egyptian civilization is large, long-lived, and complex, certain bounded features and historical data on economic rates and ratios may make it amenable to study by computational agent-based modeling approaches. On the larger scale, the areas of the Nile Valley and Delta have remained relatively constant at 12,000–13,000 km^2 and 22,000 km^2, respectively (Abu al-Izz 1971:130). Butzer (1976:82) estimated that in Upper Egypt since dynastic times "the area of cultivable flood plain has remained basically similar, except from the perspective of technology." He gave reasonable estimates for changes in population density and total population from 4000 normalfontB.C. to 150 normalfontB.C. (Butzer 1976:83). For more recent periods there are values for cultivable land per kilometer of valley length for the various districts

TABLE 1   Rates and Values for Ancient Egypt

Tax rate	1/10 (1 $\underline{h}3r$ per 10 $\underline{h}3r$)	(K. Baer 1962:33, 45)
	10% of yield	(Bowman 1986:77)
Land Rent Rate	1/3 to 1/2 yield	(K. Baer 1962:34)
	30–60% of yield	(Bowman 1986:77)
Hekanakhte	5 $\underline{h}3r$ per aroura	(K. Baer 1963:9)
Yield	10 $\underline{h}3r$ per aroura	(K. Baer 1962:30)
	= 32.1 bushels/acre	
	Lower Egypt:	(Willcocks 1889:253)
	30 bushels/acre	
	Upper Egypt:	
	40 bushels/acre	
Seed	1/8 to 1/10 yield	(K. Baer 1962:31)
Cultivator per Field		
Pharaonic Period	1:20 aroura (1:5.47 ha)	(Allen n.d.:79)
Islamic Period	1:5 to 6 feddans	(Cuno 1992:67)
	(1:2.1 to 2.52 ha)	
Sustaining Area		
5-person household	3 to 10 feddans	(G. Baer 1962:76)
	(1.26 to 4.2 ha)	
Per person	2,500 to 8,400 m^2	
Loan interest	100%	(K. Baer 1962:45)

1 aroura = 2,735 m^2	1 $\underline{h}3r$ = 16 (N.K.) hekat	1 hekat = 4.78 liters
1 feddan = 4,200.83 m^2		1 bushel = 35.239 liters
1 ha = 10,000 m^2		
1 acre = 4,048.58 m^2		

which can be used to estimate cultivable area per ancient nome (Wilson 1955). The margin of the Nile flood volume from disastrously low to high is known (2.29 m; Willcocks 1889:326). The chaotic behavior of Nile flood variability has been demonstrated by Mandelbrot and Wallis (1968, 1969). For the late nineteenth century A.D., Willcocks (1889) published values for Nile discharge per season; water discharge per province; timing of filling and discharge basin by basin; optimal water volume per basin, lengths of Summer canals, flood canals, basin and Nile banks; water loss by evaporation; and number of corvée workers for Nile flood protection. On the local scale, textual sources give economic values for various periods. Table 1 is a preliminary set.

4.3   LOCAL CONTROL

In the last several centuries control over Egyptian labor and infrastructure was largely local, centered on the village, administered by village shaykhs or *umdas* (mayors) who were in effect the agents of both the central government, or the *multazims* (absentee tax farmers), and the village peasants. The power of these shaykh-of-shaykhs operated through other local notables, principally subsidiary shaykhs of the village-tillage quarters (Cuno 1992:92–95). In Upper Egypt they were in charge of annual land reallocations to their subordinate clan members and dependents. Under their roles as "shaykh of cultivation" (*shaykh al-zira'a*) (Cuno 1992:91), they supervised sowing, planting, harvest, and transport of produce. They oversaw postinundation land surveys in the village territory and assessed the land for taxation. They had their own armed forces (*ghafirs*) and were responsible for village security. They judged disputes and made arrests, conscripted for corvée and the state military. For a time during the beginning of this century they were responsible for the registry of births and census taking. The power of the shaykhs waned through the middle of this century (G. Baer 1969:37–46).

For ancient Egypt, the list of mechanisms by which households could expand their property and influence signals the local control of many aspects of life. There was local trade. Old Kingdom tomb scenes show markets for trade of the most basic structures and services of everyday life: food and drink, especially vegetables, fruits and fish, and oil; head rests, spindle whorls, cloth, fish hooks, simple jewelry, possibly leather work, staves, sandals, fans, and seals (Wild 1966:pl. 174); manicuring and barbering (like local markets in Egypt today) (Helck 1975:425–426; Moussa and Altenmüller 1977; Hodash and Berlev 1980). Local markets on the riverbanks are known from scenes in New Kingdom tombs. Male and female vendors sit in booths and trade fish, loaves, vegetables, fish hooks, sandals, and cloth for grain and, in one case, wine from ships possibly from as far away as Syria and the Aegean. Weights and balances are known archaeologically, and exchange was according to a system of values with reference to metal in units called *deben* (Kemp 1989:248–255). It is very possible that the scenes depict periodic local markets, like those centered in larger villages and towns in the seventeenth to nineteenth centuries A.D. (Cuno 1992:49–55). Officials maintained their own fleets. Kemp (1989:242–242, Figure 81) pointed out that in the elaborate set of wooden models found in the Eleventh Dynasty tomb of Meketre, models of four traveling boats, two kitchen tenders, four yachts, one sporting boat, and two fishing boats probably represent this official's personal fleet. Houses large and small, including temples, retained professional itinerant messengers (K. Baer 1963:9) and traders that visited markets all along the Nile and possibly abroad (Kemp 1989:257). In the Byzantine period, large estates could control their own standards of weights and measures (Hardy 1931:73–75), leading to a "confused condition" that was, nonetheless understood locally. As early as Dynasty 11, the relatively small house of Hekanakht could insist on using its own grain measure to collect on loans (K. Baer 1963:10). "The politics of measurement," and local vs. national standards, were general to premodern and early modern states (Scott 1998:28).

Large estate holders could levy troops and militia, particularly before the advent of a truly professional army in the New Kingdom. A revealing insight into an early "state" military operation against Asiatic Bedouin at the height of the Old Kingdom is the biography of Weni, a man who rose from lowly office to lead an army for pharaoh composed of natives of both halves of the Delta, seven Nubian tribes, Libyans and "...counts, royal seal-bearers, sole companions of the palace, chieftains and mayors of towns of Upper and Lower Egypt, companions, scout-leaders, chief priests of Upper and Lower Egypt, and chief district officials at the head of the troops of Upper and Lower Egypt, from the villages and towns that they governed, and from the Nubians of those foreign lands" (Lichtheim 1973:20). This is a "fractal" army, each troop an armature of the head of its own "house" just as the whole army acted as an ad hoc armature of pharaoh, the greatest house. "Chiefs" and "mayors" conscripted for this military force, just as the shaykhs and umdas conscripted in the Islamic Period. Eyre (1987:19) noted that "the administrators of landed property controlled their own levies, the foreigners were led by their own officials.... Through all this material, the local responsibility for registration and recruitment of work forces is clear."

Basic production, craft and industry, including metallurgy, weaving, baking, and brewing were organized around core houses surrounded by modular granaries, bakeries, breweries, butcheries, and wood shops along the lines of the patterns discussed for Illahun and Amarna. Prior to the New Kingdom, pottery, for the most part, was "not the product of a large-scale industry with wide distribution" (Arnold 1976:22, n. 65; Holthoer 1977:27–28; Eyre 1987:27).

The survey and appraisal of land for taxation, and its collection, is perhaps the aspect of administration that we would least expect to have been left to local control. Eyre (1987:23) speaks of the "impracticality of the collection of small endowments due on estates scattered through the country;" shares were collected according to the "concept of patronage." Local control of tax or apportionments needed local influence and patronage. Local control of taxation was a general feature of premodern states where the complexity of local production rendered community economics fiscally illegible to the state. "For its part, the state had neither the administrative tools nor the information to penetrate to this level" (Scott 1998:37–38). Although territory-wide cadastral surveys have always been a means of reasserting state control (Cuno 1992:21; Scott 1998), and although we have historical outlines for ideal annual state land surveys and assessment procedures in the Islamic Period (Frantz-Murphy 1986), in actual practice survey and appraisal for taxation continually slipped back to the local village notables. One weakness was the time lag between one "official nationwide survey by officials of the central government" and the next, often measured in decades (Frantz-Murphy 1986:56). Meanwhile, the local notables had to carry out their own form of annual survey to keep up with the kaleidoscope of land changes and transactions. Scott (1998:35) points out that cadastral maps and land registers "freeze a living process" in which land boundaries, tenure, and use is constantly changing. Therefore it was the "local notables who reported areal assessments to officials of the central government" (Frantz-Murphy 1986:55). In recent centuries,

The villages also preserved their own land records, keeping track of the inheritance and exchange of plots, information that was available to the *multazims* (tax farmers) but not the central authorities. In some villages a register was kept, and in others this knowledge was preserved by notary witnesses. These records, preserved in oral and written form, were used by the shaykhs in distributing the tax demand of the village. (Cuno 1992:64)

"Village notables," also called "notable persons," and "principle men" in the Greek Papyri and Arabic sources, were none other than the large landowners, the village headmen, or the shaykhs (Frantz-Murphy 1986:66, 70). This reflects an Egyptian tendency, older than the Arab conquest, to delegate, or leave intact, local responsibility for assessment and taxation. Local responsibility for taxation was assumed by the provincial "Great Houses" or large estates in the sixth century A.D. (Bagnall 1993:159–160); by local communities and church bodies in the fourth century A.D., and by provincial town councils and villages in the third century A.D. (Bowman 1986:70–71, 87–88).

In New Kingdom Egypt, the Legal Text of Mose (Gardiner 1905; Gaballa 1977) likewise highlights local control of land tenure and its tax obligations. In a case that went through as many as five lawsuits over control of, or rights to, disputed land in the Village of Neshi, the plaintive Mose, as descendant of Neshi, sought to overturn the judgment of the Qenbet, "council" or court of magistrates of Memphis. This was the "local board empowered to deal with the disputed estate" (Gardiner 1905:35) at the level of the nome, because Memphis was the capital of the nome in which the disputed land was located. The case eventually moved to the higher Great Qenbet over which the Vizier presided, at the national level. Mose took his appeal directly to the "notables of the village" (*rmṯw ꜥꜣw n pꜣ dmjt*) (Gardiner 1905:33–36; Allam 1989:111). Texts from other pharaonic periods attest to such notables as the "great men" (*rmṯw ꜥꜣy*), or "mighty men" (*rmṯw ḏry*) of a locality.

The notables represented a local board which could be addressed by the authorities in order to assist with the settlement of disputed matters in a given locality. It emerges from Mose's appeal that this board could equally be approached by individuals to bring about investigations and presumably to decide over conflicts in their locality... the local notables could generally act as a council (*qnbt*) authorized to decide current affairs in their locality as well as to judge on conflicts arising therein. (Allam 1989:111)

The local control by large households of many facets of ancient Egyptian life can be set against those indications that, even at the height of the New Kingdom, central government was, to a degree, ad hoc and reactive. According to Kemp:

The working of the Egyptian administration at its various periods are reasonably apparent, but they seem not to be the product of a abstract concept of administration elegantly applied across the broad spectrum of activities. Far from it. The system ran in channels of authority. Within any one channel the procedures could be remarkably effective (though not efficient) in achieving a given target, such as quarry, transport, erect a colossus of a particular size. This is where bureaucratic talents flourished. But we will look in vain for evidence of conscious integration of the individual parts into a general scheme of management. (Kemp 1989:235)

Government in Egypt was by royal decree, the system of administration was the sum of these decrees, and the resulting overlaps and confusions of responsibility were tackled by fresh decrees in response to specific complaints. (Kemp 1989:238)

4.4 THE NILE FLOOD WAVE: BASIN OPERATIONS

The operations of flood recession agriculture in ancient Egypt were decentralized and locally controlled. "Dynastic irrigation was naturally compartmentalized, so that a centralized administration was neither practical nor purposeful" (Butzer 1976:43, 51; Eyre 1987:18). Yet, "neither was the isolated work of an individual or a family or even one village community involved, because one system of irrigation might extend over the territory of several villages, while the basins had to be surrounded by dykes, and canals had to be dug to conduct the flood water to the basins" (Bakir 1952:2).

How did the people of households, villages, and field complexes communicate and collaborate across a great basin system, an average stretch of 40 to 60 kilometers (Willcocks 1889:45, 327)? In the last century, as the river began to swell in late summer, the heads of the feeder canals, which swung out from the Nile to run down through a stepped series of basins, were closed by an earthen dam. In Upper Egypt this blocking was cut around August 12–15, allowing the red muddy waters to pour down the feeder canal, at first with great velocity, carrying its slime to the basins. Filling could take as long as 40 days (Willcocks 1889:45). As the farther basins filled, the velocity of water gradually decreased until the tail-end basin was filled to within 30 cm of capacity (Figure 5(c)). Then all the openings of the transverse dykes were closed in sequence, starting from the tail-end and progressing to the head basin. Communication was required across the system to know optimal timing and to coordinate closing of the dikes. Coordination was also required for "wave-filling" a single large basin, that is, letting in the water in installments, so that it did not immediately collect against the far northern dike, leaving the southern head land bare, owing to the northward slope of the land. "The result of this is that a wave travels down the basin covering the high land at the upper end and yet not exceeding the proper limit at the lower end"

(Hurst 1952:40–41). The filling of the basins ended around September 22 in Upper Egypt. Then the heads of the feeder canals would be closed again to the Nile. During an average flood, the water would stand in the basins for 40 days simmering under the hot sun and depositing fresh silty slime, while the water in the Nile channel slowly fell.

The discharge of the waters, which began in the southerly basins around October 1, was a delicate operation that needed as much coordination across a basin system as the flooding. The head basin was full, and the tail-end basins were filled to within 30 cm of capacity. Each basin system had a tail-end "escape" that allowed the waters to be drained (Figure 5(c)). This escape was opened first, followed by the successive opening of the regulators, or temporary breaches, in each transverse dike back to the head basin. At first, the waters poured from the head basin into the next one down with greater force than through the regulators at the tail end of the series, so that the head basin was the first to be empty. The result was that the end basins filled to capacity just before they were drained. As the water slowed, this late filling-to-capacity allowed the tail-end basins to receive more of the water and fresh silt deposits. This subtle cascade is why the tail-end basins were kept not quite full until the end (Willcocks 1889:37, 44–46).

To coordinate basin system operations over tens of kilometers (in an era without electronic communications), the villages set up what Willcocks called "the corvée telegraph." During flood season the Nile banks were dotted at intervals of 50 to 70 m with lantern-lit temporary booths (Willcocks 1889:274, 1904:71) that sheltered watchmen who relayed messages. Such "water guards" may be attested in fourth century A.D. documents. Bagnall (1993:21, n.34) cites a "surety document for a man to serve as guard until the end of the watching of the waters and their release. The date is 20 August, near the height of the flood."

The most southern of the Upper Egyptian basins were dry normally by October 5, and the most northern by November 30. In ancient Egypt, sowing and growing comprised the season of *Peret*, "Coming Forth," followed by *Shemu*, "Harvest," and, beginning again in late Summer, *Akhet*, Inundation. The three seasons were divided into four months each for a twelve-month year.

4.5 SPECULATING ON THE NILE WAVE: MANAGING LAND PORTFOLIOS

In another flood recession agricultural regime, that of Pulaar-speaking people in the Senegal River basin, the heads of lineages reallocate lands to members after each flood (Park 1992). Such annual reallocations were made in some villages by the shaykhs in the eighteenth and nineteenth centuries A.D. (G. Baer 1969:22; Richards 1982:36–37), but in ancient Egypt there is more evidence for reallocation by land "leases" with annual terms. Historical documents from the pharaonic periods hint at speculations on land rented from postharvest to early flood (late Spring to early Fall) to be sown in various crops—flax, emmer, barley, wheat—when the waters receded in late Fall. "The greatest single concentration of dates on which the land leases were drawn up is to be found in the latter part of August and the beginning of September, but a very large part of them are scattered in date all the way from the end of June into December" (Hughes 1952:74). In dynastic times, land leases were normally for one year, flood to flood. In the third through the fifth centuries A.D. leases were not just for land: "While the water stood in the fields, owners and tenants drew up leases of land, laborers entered into work contracts, and owners of animals made agreements for their short-term lease by farmers who needed them for plowing" (Bagnall 1993:220).

Bagnall points out for Egypt of late antiquity that the market in land leases was far more complex than just the urban rich's leasing to the peasant poor. "Metropolitans owned land and were both lessors and lessees to villagers." Whereas "the bulk of the land was probably farmed directly by the families that owned it" (Bagnall 1993:121, 149), small landowners leased additional plots when needed for subsistence or desired for profitable expansion, but prosperous landowners could likewise use their wealth for leases, loans, and capital investments in fields owned by others great and small. Villages leased to and from other villages in the portfolio pattern, even for short-term land holding. "Though one would expect such transactions to involve closely neighboring villages, it was not always so. . . . Such activity could also cross nome boundaries" (Bagnall 1993:139). Medium-sized estates in the third through the sixth centuries A.D. operated their portfolios through agents, not unlike the "controllers" or "administrators" of ancient Egyptian land documents (Eyre 1994b:119–120). The agents rented to middlemen at the local village level, and the middle men could themselves participate in the cultivation of the leased plots, but they could also sublease them to other peasants, or the plots could be worked by hirelings (Bagnall 1993:150).

In pharaonic Egypt annual land reallocation was at least in part effected through a complex rental market, wherein the large and small households speculated and gambled on the quality of the flood, perhaps also on the changes to the microvariations of the flood plain (Park 1992:95). We are given a literary window onto the annual gamble on the flood wave in Hekanakht's documents. Letters I–II may have been written within a month of each other during the inundation, early Akhet (James 1962; K. Baer 1963), probably in August or early September (James 1962:3–4), "the season when land leases were normally arranged" (K. Baer 1963:9, n. 71) (there is a possibility that the letters were written early post-harvest according to Allen, n.d.). The letters express the anxious fretting of the head of the household about risk-management decisions that must be made in his absence near the crest of the flood wave: "You should find land, 10 arouras of land (to be planted) with emmer and 10 arouras with barley, which must be [good] land [of Kh]epeshit. Don't go down (i.e. 'rent') the land of (just) anybody, but ask Hau the Younger; and if you find that he has none, then you should go before [Heru]-nefer and he will put you on well-watered land of Khepeshit" (K. Baer 1963:4). This letter (Letter I, vs. 3–14) was written after a lean year. Hekanakht reduces the rations for his household members by about half according to Klaus Baer (1963:5, 7, n.49). The wheeling and dealing in land is glimpsed again in Letter I, vs. 10–12:

> Now as for all the affairs of my estate ($\underline{d}3tt$) and all the affairs of my farm ($\check{s}$) in _____ [followed by lacunae where there had been a place name?], I had planted them with flax - don't let anybody go down onto it (to rent it). And as for anybody who will talk to you, you shall go on account of him upon it [-----]. And you shall sow the farm with northern barley. Don't sow emmer there. But if it turns out to be a high inundation, you shall sow it with emmer. (K. Baer 1963:6)

A cultivator could wait to "roll the dice" of field and crop choice until there was some hint of the height of the inundation. In Letter II, vs. 4–5 Hekanakht asks, "But is the inundation ve[ry high]? Now [our fo]od is fixed for us in accordance with the inundation. So be patient each one of you. I have managed to keep you alive until today" (K. Baer 1963:7). After the waters receded, and field and plot boundaries were reestablished, quick action was required of individual cultivator-households to sow their respective plots in early Peret ("Coming Forth'"—Winter) in order to capitalize on land commitments made in pre-flood season. So, in Letter I, vs. 6, Hekanakht writes "now if my field is reached by the inundation" even Sneferu, presumably his youngest son, "should cultivate." The gamble involved in annual budgeting and planning is evident. There was "a question in Hekanakht's mind whether the threatened low Nile, which actually did materialize (II.4) would permit the irrigation of his fields at all" (K. Baer 1963:5).

In spite of the risk involved, renting land was nevertheless advantageous for small to medium farmers whose own family could work the land, but who could not afford to gamble an entire year's investment of time and labor on small fixed holdings that, as with some of Hekanakht's fields, might not be watered by the inundation, or whose soils might change from year to year. Rental rates, before the Saite Period (Twenty-sixth Dynasty, 664–525 normalfontB.C.), seem to have been fixed, defined by broad categories of land (K. Baer 1962:41), which meant greater profit from a good harvest. In his letters Hekanakht prompts his family "to rent land up to the limit of their ability to farm it, but no further..." Klaus Baer (1962, 1963:8, 16) concluded: "Purchase of land was, in general, not advisable for persons of Hekanakht's status, and I suspect that most of the land they owned was obtained either by inheritance or by gift." Without the means to own widely scattered land as risk management, the answer for a medium to small household was to rent.

On the other hand, "...it was advantageous for a landowner who could not farm the land himself to let it out rather than to farm it with hired help" (K. Baer 1963:8). Wealthier families could own extensive land that was widely scattered to disburse risk; dependant households or renters did the field labor. In the growth of property and dependent population of households there must have been a critical threshold which enabled a transition from renting to owning (K. Baer 1963:15).

5 SCHEMATA

> The model of the segmentary lineage structure is thus not a model which the actors operate in their actual political processes. It is merely a representation of the enduring form of their society, or, as it has often been expressed, a kind of ideology.... Instead of mistaking this ideology for actuality, it seems to be much more fruitful to inquire about its role and to investigate why the actors hold it when in numerous cases it is obviously at odds with their actual political processes. (Holy 1996:85)

What is said about the model of the segmentary lineage in the minds of actors in tribal societies and in the minds of the British social anthropologists who studied them might be applied to the model of pharaonic authority and centralized control of society in the minds of the ancient Egyptians and the Egyptologists who study them. If we hypothesize that the pharaoh's power was embedded in, and emergent from, the fabric of Egyptian society, and that the most basic facets of the economy were locally controlled, we have to ask why their representation of the enduring form of their society, or ideological model, focused on pharaonic absolutism. In CAS studies, ideological models, and "customs, traditions, myths, laws, institutions and so forth" are *schemata* that function as "prescriptions for collective behavior" (Gell-Mann 1994:20).

5.1 THE SOCIETY OF SELF, SELF AND SOCIETY

Pharaonic absolutism must be understood in the context of the isomorphism in ancient Egyptian worldview between self and society. Egyptian texts suggest that each person was seen as an assemblage of parts developing through transformations, *kheperu*, in life and death. Each part was considered a complete entity in itself (Lloyd 1989:117–120). For example, in the Eighteenth Dynasty tomb of Amenemhet in the Theban necropolis, each and every aspect of Amenemhet and his passage through life and death is individualized as a "god":

> For his *ka*, for his stela belonging to this tomb which is in the necropolis, for his *sha* (fate), for his *aha* (lifetime), for his *Meskhenet* (birth place), for his *Renenet* (upbringing), for his *Khnum* (fashioning). May these gods come to him to have control of them, be rich with them, be triumphant with them.... [For] his [*ba*], for his *akh*, for his *khat* (corpse), for his *shut* (shadow), and for all his *kheperu* (transformations). May these gods cause him to have superabundance of these

(offerings) that he should be joined with them, that he should eat of them, and drink of them like the ancestors forever. (Davies and Gardiner 1915; Lloyd 1989:118)

The ba and ka were the most important members of this "complex composite of many parts." Postmortem reunion of the ba with the ka was effected by the burial ritual, a reunion that created the final transformation of the deceased as an akh, a "glorified" spirit in full control of all faculties in the afterlife sphere of ghosts and gods. Ka and ba also bound together the complex composite of the Egyptian body politic.

Ka was an undifferentiated life force related to kindred and ancestors, shared by the entire Egyptian community, transferable through the family, clan, and lineage (Bell 1994). The upraised arms of the ka hieroglyph actually represent, in Egyptian artistic convention, an embrace which the Egyptians believed transferred vital force between two people, or between gods and king. A father could say of the birth of a child, "my *ka* repeats itself." Conversely an Egyptian could say, "my *ka* is my father." Ka is collective—for example, texts speak of the ka of the Lower Egyptians and the king as its source. The kas of common people were their ancestors. At death one's ka went to rest, subsumed back into its generic folds, a return to commonality. For everyone, this life force extended back through numberless generations to the Creator sun god who transferred his ka to the gods, who, in turn, transferred their kas to the king. The king was the life force, the ka, of his officials and people—the "living *kas*" (Kaplony 1980). He gives them nourishment. Ka was probably related to *kau*, a term for "food" or "sustenance" (Allen 1988a). The enormous pyramids towering above the smaller tombs of noblemen and officials make sense in the context of this Egyptian belief that the ka is tied to continuity in a kinship and social sense. Ka was the metaphysical correlate of the Egyptian social hierarchy of embedded households, the greatest house being that of pharaoh, who was the "ka of the living."

If the ka is generic life force, what Victor Turner (1969) might call *communitas*, the ba, is, in his terms, structure and status—a person's individual renown, one's distinctive manifestation, the impression made on others (Allen 1988a). The bas of gods were their manifestations in natural forces—stars, inanimate objects, even other gods. A ba of Shu, god of the air, was wind. Cities like Buto, Hierakonpolis, and Heliopolis had bas, as did inanimate objects like temple pylons, threshing floors, doors, and sacred books. The bas of the king were the manifestations of his power—for example, an armed military expedition that he might send to defeat his enemies (Zabkar 1968, 1973). In the early periods, such a ba of the king as an armed expedition was in reality an ad hoc composition of the ongoing soldalities along the Nile valley, as we have seen in Weni's fractal army of the Sixth Dynasty. The people, as his family, give the king his mighty manifestations of power such as pyramids (many of which have ba-names) and expeditions. His legitimacy rested in part on his reciprocal role of providing nourishment, life force.

Similar reciprocity governed the heads and dependents of households down the social scale. The economic reality of the communal ka, structured by status, ba, was the annual shares of harvest, which we can hardly distinguish as "tax" or "rent." "Post-harvest distributions through ties of dependence" and rights to shares (Eyre 1994b:123) was the material reality behind the transferability of "life force" and food sustenance. The distribution operated from the bottom up through a hierarchy of embedded households, each a domain of patronage and influence at its respective scale, focused in times of national unity by the symbolic program of the pharaonic Great Tradition, whose icons and monuments withstood time, giving us a view from the top down.

5.2 ORDER ON THE EDGE OF CHAOS

The Egyptians conceived their social and cosmic order as continuously threatened by chaos (Assmann 1989:65). A prime royal imperative was the maintenance of social, political, and cosmic order, *maat*, over chaos, *isfet*, and formlessness, reflecting an anxiety deeply embedded in Egyptian worldview from the earliest times (Asselberghs 1961). Control of chaos was symbolized on outer temple walls by apotropaic scenes of the king hunting wild animals, subduing the traditional nomadic tribes on Egypt's border, or balancing opposing forces (Kemp 1989:46–53). Fear of formlessness might be understandable in a society whose life depended on the appointments and apportionments of the land immediately after the recession of the flood waters that masked this order for six to eight weeks every year, rendering it formless. But the Egyptians were also inclined to see the threat of disorder inherent in themselves through *isfet*, "wrong-doing," "falsehood" (Assmann 1989:59).

In the beginning, the ordered world was chthonically "self-generated" by the creator Sun god, Atum (Allen 1988b). Like all of us, the Egyptians tended to "assume centralized control where it doesn't exist" (Resnick 1994:4), and they thought it was necessary to impose centralized control to keep the web of social and cosmic relations in balance. Life is dependent on order. It is hard to conceive that order can generate and persist by itself. The Egyptians, like most people, imagined that order must "be imposed from outside and constantly to be defended against *isfet*, a natural tendency towards chaos, disintegration, and death which is innate in man, society, and nature" (Assmann 1989:65). The annihilation of *isfet* and the realization of *maat* were achieved by satisfying the gods—which meant the king extending his patronage over the temple households—and by judging men. Judgment was not "between the righteous and the criminal, the good and the bad" as we might expect, rather "judgment is always between the *weak and the strong*, the miserable and the powerful, *the poor and the rich*...by this judgment the poor, weak, and miserable are to be rescued 'from the hand of' the strong, rich, and powerful" (Assmann 1989:60, emphasis mine). This was believed to be necessary because of the Egyptians' "negative anthropology" where "when three men travel on a road, two are found, for the greater number kills the lesser." Ancient Egypt's "pessimistic literature...is notorious for its strong centralistic, absolutistic, and perhaps even oppressive tendencies, thus confirming the link between 'negative anthropology' and 'absolutism'" (Assmann 1989:61).

The imagined imposition of order was personified by pharaoh, who could indeed override all other decisions, act as catalyst through social and economic initiatives, try to keep track of the Egyptians through centrally located officials, and exercise swift punishment on occasion. But the real operation of ancient Egyptian society involved processes too complex for absolute control. "No administration system is capable of representing *any* social community except through a heroic and greatly schematized process of abstraction and simplification...a human community is far too complicated and variable to easily yield its secrets to bureaucratic formulae" (Scott 1998:22). Pharaoh could not actively ensure the proper division of every field, the equity of each harvest distribution, loan payment, house, land, or cattle sale, or the uniformity of bread pots and beer jars, the timing of filling and discharging the flood basins. Authority was not so much delegated, as emergent, through the nome, village, and household apparatus, focused on the perception of protection at the pinnacle of patronage. The king's presence, and occasional edict or use of coercion, over complex networks ensured that the wealthy and powerful would refrain from "predatory affairs" and from unconscionably "living off the land" (Kemp 1989:236–237) in their spheres of influence. As son of the sun god, and the incarnation of Horus, the last of the lineage of gods who ruled as kings, pharaoh, like the other gods in their temple households throughout the provinces, was above personal gain, a necessity in that, "stable self-regulating maintenance of rules (i.e., legitimacy) hinges on contending actors' conviction that judges and rules are not motivated by self-interest" (Padgett and Ansell 1993:1260).

6   RISE AND RESURRECTION OF THE STATE

The Egyptian state emerged three times during its 3,000-year history—at the end of the formative Late Predynastic (3000 normalfontB.C.), and at the end of the First (2061 normalfontB.C.) and Second (1550 normalfontB.C.) Intermediate Periods. A revival of national unity, the Saite Period (664–525 normalfontB.C.) followed the Third Intermediate Period (Lloyd 1983). The designation, intermediate period, derives from the fact that the textual and monumental record indicates a collapse of what we view as the normative state of ancient Egypt. When the pharaonic kingdom collapsed, it broke into northern and southern parts and then into aggregates of nomes, constituent nomes, and city states (Kemp 1983:177–178). Following the segmentation of both the First and Second Intermediate Periods, lasting more than one or two centuries, respectively, when the Egyptian state resurrected itself it did so from the southerly part of Upper Egypt that brackets the Qena Bend (Figure 5(a)).

This pattern poses a question: why, before exogenous forces from the Near East and Mediterranean drew Egypt's center inexorably into the Delta, was the Qena Bend the traditional homeland and retreat of pharaohs? What were the conditions in this stretch of river valley that allowed for the emergence and reemergence of a greater Egyptian kingdom?

6.1   LOCAL RULERS IN THE FORMATIVE PERIOD

Pharaonic culture developed out of Naqada culture, named after an important predynastic site located on the Qena Bend north of Luxor (Figure 4(a)). Naqada culture originated in, and spread from, southern Upper Egypt. By the Gerzean or Naqada II phase of the predynastic period (3400–3200 normalfontB.C.), Naqada culture spread from the Qena Bend area throughout the whole of the Egyptian Nile Valley. The oldest known domesticated donkey bone dates to the Gerzean. This pack animal's capacity for carrying loads overland 15 to 20 km in a single day (Hassan 1988) may have been critical in transporting the grain harvest over wider local territories and in exploiting distant sources of copper. There are hints of a major advance in river travel. A salient feature of the Gerzean is a variety of jars made out of desert marl clays with red painted designs that feature multioared boats with plumes, cabins, and insignia that have been construed as the earliest territorial symbols and the precursor to hieroglyphic writing.

Closer to unification, in the Naqada III period, from representational art and from distinctively large tombs of comparable size at Hierakonpolis, Naqada, and Abydos we infer a time of conflict between small principalities. These are the tombs and representations of local rulers in the Qena Bend region. Kemp (1989:34, Figure 8) gave visual expression to these hints of emergent polities by mapping into the Qena Bend area the contiguous territories of the "kingdoms" of Hierakonpolis (comprising later Nomes 1–3), Nagada (Nomes 4–5) and This (Figure 4(a); Nomes 7–8). In Kemp's view, these were amalgamated into the "Proto-Kingdom of Upper Egypt" (Kemp 1989:45, Figure 13). By the end of the Naqada III period, kings of "Dynasty 0" had turned their attention to the Delta, where recent excavations confirm that an endemic Maadi-Buto culture was overtaken by late Naqada forms which soon extended like an armature from the Qena Bend as far north as southern Palestine (Figure 4(b)).

6.2   LOCAL RULERS AND THE FIRST INTERMEDIATE PERIOD

During the politically fragmented First Intermediate Period, literary and archaeological evidence reveals the dynamics of state formation. There is evidence of conflict, drought, and famine, but since the unified kingdom eventually reemerged from the conditions of this time, social and economic order must have persisted at some scale that held the potential for the reemergence of the Great Tradition of divine kingship over a unified Two Lands.

Tomb biographies of this period are literary windows onto events and aspirations of the heads of large households that controlled the nomes. One of the best examples is the text of Ankhtifi's tomb at Moalla (Vandier 1950) on the northern frontier of Nome 3 of Hierakonpolis, which had been the Late Predynastic capital more than 800 years earlier (Figure 4(a)). Ankhtifi was "Great Chief," "Chief Priest," and "Chief of a Nome" of the Nomes of Edfu and Hierakonpolis. He says that "Horus brought me" to straighten out Nome 2 of Edfu after "the House of Khuu," another important nomarch family, had collapsed. "I found the House of Khuu inundated like a marsh, abandoned by the one who belonged to it, in the grip of a rebel, under the control of a wretch. I made a man embrace the slayer of his father, the slayer of his brother, so as to reestablish the Nome of Edfu" (Lichtheim 1973:85). Ankhtifi says he fed and supplied grain to the provinces and to Upper Egypt. To the extent that his boasts reflect real circumstances, he was proactively filling a "network disjuncture within the elite" (Padgett and Ansell 1993:1259). With his arbitration and judgment between opponents, Ankhtifi also casts himself as both judge and boss, a "contradiction in state building or any organization" (Padgett and Ansell 1993:1260) resolved by the perception that the ruler is above self-interest. Other nome and town leaders may very well have perceived Ankhtifi as motivated by self-interest. They say in their biographies (Lichtheim 1988:21–38) that they fed the needy, provided boats to the boatless, and increased their livestock and grain, thus fulfilling the moral obligation of a ruler at any scale. Ankhtifi further informs us that he led with bravery "when it was necessary to join the three provinces together" (Grimal 1994:142), a reference to the amalgamation of Nomes 1, 2, and 3. Kemp (1989:239) points out that "Ankhtifi, having seized lands, was, for a short time, in effect ruling a miniature state." These voices of local rulers, like Ankhtifi, speak to us of processes that must have been very similar to those that led to the kingdoms of Hierakonpolis, Naqada, and This, in the formative Late Predynastic, albeit now at a higher level of complexity and sophistication, including literacy.

The first "rise of the state" in Egypt is theorized to have involved the emergence of a "proto-kingdom of Upper Egypt" (Kemp 1989:34, 45), just prior to unification with the north. In the First Intermediate Period, we have literary glimpses of the transition from nomarchy to protomonarchy, led by the House of Intef. In both north and south, large households and nomarchies that had been left autonomous with the fragmentation of the Egyptian kingdom began to reamalgamate in an inexorable formation of larger polities from local politics. Dynasties 9 and 10 were comprised of a line of 18 kings in the north, known in contemporary sources as the "House of Kheti" after the first of their line. They emerged from Heracleopolis Magna in the twentieth Upper Egyptian nome at the entrance of the Nile tributary, Bahr Youssef, into the Fayum Basin (Figure 5(b)). In the south the House of Intef at Thebes became strong enough to resurrect the united kingdom under Dynasty 11. Early in the period an Intef was Chief Priest of the local temple and Nomarch ("Great

Chief of the Scepter Nome"), although he called himself "Keeper of the Door of the South." Either this man, or a successor (Schenkel 1965:66), was called Intef the Great (son of Ikuy), later regarded as founder of the line to follow. The expansion of the House of Intef's pretence to patronage over all of the Qena Bend region may be signalled in the formulaic name: "Intef the Great, Great Chief of Upper Egypt" (Hayes 1953:149). Next came a Mentuhotep the Great, then Intef I, who, as the rival of Ankhtifi, may have forcibly taken the three amalgamated southernmost nomes. He declared himself King of Upper and Lower Egypt and took the Horus name (to signify himself as the divine incarnation of the falcon god of kingship, Horus), *Seher-tawy*, "Pacifier of the Two Lands." Under Intef II civil war broke out with the contemporary ruler of Heracleopolis in the north, Kheti III of Dynasty 10 (Grimal 1994:143). The Middle Egyptian nomes formed alliances with one or the other of the two houses.

The Intefs built long, low courtyard tombs in the low desert plain called el-Tarif at Thebes, just north of the entrance to the Valley of the Kings. Complete conquest of northern Egypt came under the fourth king of the Theban Dynasty, named Mentuhotep ("the god Montu is satisfied") Nebhepet-Re ("Lord of the Steering Oar of Re"). In the memory of later Egyptians, he was on par with Menes (Hor-Aha), the first king of Dynasty 1 who united Egypt. Like Menes, Mentuhotep hailed from the Qena Bend, united Upper and Lower Egypt, and began a tomb and temple spatially removed from the old cemetery and of an order of magnitude larger than any of the nomarchs or Intefs. Once again the cloak of royalty fell upon local rulers and hierarchies.

6.3   CEMETERY RECORD OF THEBAN HOUSEHOLDS: SECOND INTERMEDIATE PERIOD

The Middle Kingdom, Dynasties 11–12, waned as rulers of foreign origin, the Hyksos, rose in the north. After Dynasty 13 lost the northern capital district, the Egyptian Residence retreated to Upper Egypt where, for 75 years kings held the first eight nomes, from Elephantine to Cusae, while Lower Nubia came under the control of the Nubian rulers of Kerma (Grimal 1994:187). With some ambiguity, the ancient sources lead us to believe there was a continuous line of rule from Dynasty 13 to 17 for which Manetho lists 15 kings (Kemp 1983:159). The kingdom had again contracted to its point of beginning, the old homeland centered on the Qena Bend. These Thebans were well aware that their aspirations to resurrect the Egyptian state represented a historical cycle. Three Dynasty 17 kings took the name Intef (V–VII), as had one of their Dynasty 13 predecessors (Dodson 1994:33). They placed their tombs, topped by small brick pyramids, in the cliff-side plain called Dra Abu el-Naga, continuing a north-to-south series with the tombs of the Intefs I–III of Dynasty 11 in the adjacent el-Tarif plain.

The first systematic archaeological investigation of the Dra Abu el-Naga by Daniel Polz (1992, 1993, 1995a) has revealed a cemetery of household tomb complexes with great social diversification. These large shaft tombs, within a courtyard entered by a brick pylon, had a rear offering chapel that, in at least one case, contained a central niche, probably for a stela of the head of the household to which each tomb belonged. Rather than exhibiting a wide separation between "elite" and "commoners," the tombs contained:

> as many as 20 to 25 burials. Great variety in the quality of burials and burial equipment was evident. On the one hand there were 'rich' burials in painted wooden anthropoid coffins with inlaid bronze eyes, accompanied by a number of superbly manufactured and polished stone vessels, or canopic jars with stoppers in the form of human heads, plus other valuable grave goods. On the other hand [in the same tomb] there were 'poor' burials, some even sharing a single poor-quality wooden coffin, with grave goods consisting of only a couple of pottery storage jars. Other individuals, mostly children, were not buried in coffins but merely wrapped in mats or linen. (Polz 1995a:7)

Polz estimates that some 17,000 people were buried in this cemetery of Theban households, dominated by the pyramid tombs of the kings along the hillside. The burial of people of various economic status within a single large tomb enclosure reflects the inclusion of Egypt's various social classes or economic strata within any one of these large Theban households. We might at least keep in mind that Egyptian villages of the last several centuries were ruled by an "elite," that is, the shaykhs who also functioned as petty officials. But the shaykhs and their communities—villages, quarters, clans, and extended household associations—were formed along kinship lines. While shaykhs' families tended to intermarry, and although shaykhs could sometimes be abusive, or in collusion with the abuses of central authorities (Cuno 1992), this "elite" was not segregated from the peasant "commoners." Rather the rural notables were integrated with their subjects, with whom they were kin related. Even though we cannot transfer uncritically the community, clan, and kin organization from the last few centuries back to Dynasty 17, the Theban cemetery record does suggest a similar degree of community integration.

Our notion of social stratification, so automatic and integral to our vision and definition of complex society, is not appropriate for ancient Egypt. Social stratification "implies a hierarchy of pansocietal, horizontal layers" and "a large number of social scientists think this is a 'natural' way of viewing societies" (Fallers 1973:5). However,

> Inequality, especially in a human community of any substantial degree of sociocultural complexity, cannot easily be captured by grand dichotomies or typologies—*homo hierarchicus* versus *homo aequalis* for example—or by images such as the stratigraphic one or by the idea of a "fundamental structure" of status class. This is so because inequality... is inherent in sociocultural differentiation in all its dimensions:

sex, age, descent, occupation, religion, ethnicity, and even—on a wider scale—nation. (Fallers 1973:27)

Complex inequalities, and the co-occurrence of various levels of social status within a household, were reflected in the embedding of rights to land, including those who labored in the fields, within portfolios of larger more *inclusive*, rather than exclusive, households. This gave greater adaptability to premodern states than broad and separate social strata. Scott (1998:34–35) points out that "customary systems of tenure...should not be romanticized; they are usually riven with inequalities based on gender, status, and lineage. But because they are strongly local, particular, and adaptable, their plasticity can be the source of microadjustments that lead to shifts in prevailing practice."

6.4 REEMERGENCE OF THE GREATEST HOUSEHOLD: THE NEW KINGDOM

The last kings of Dynasty 17 began the campaign against the Hyksos and defeated them between 1575 and 1530 normalfontB.C. The victor, Ahmose I, founded Dynasty 18, the 250-year line of the Thutmossids and Amenhoteps that ruled Egypt during its golden age of greatest empire. It was the third time that southerners from the Qena Bend conquered the north to unite the Egyptian kingdom, albeit this time the north had been in the hands of people regarded as foreign by the Egyptians.

Ahmose I's reunification by conquest entailed the reweaving of the pan-territorial land portfolio networks of households and estates. One of his officers, Ahmose son of Ebana, relates in his tomb texts that during the campaigns of conquest the king granted him land and people, first in his home town, El-Kab, opposite Hierakonpolis (Figures 5(a) and 4(a)). With the addition of "five persons to augment his household, Ahmose belongs to the same context as Hekanakht. Master of a family farm, his household would be able to function as an independent rural economic unit, and to work the land in the absence of their lord..." (Eyre 1994b:114). By the end of his career, Ahmose son of Ebana held extensive land in different towns. "One must visualize a distancing between Ahmose and his nuclear family, at el-Kab or in the capital, and the extension of his 'house' into distant estates that provided him wealth" (Eyre 1994b:115). Ahmose son of Ebana was, no doubt, one of many in the king's retinue to receive such grants. Another was Neshi whose lands, centered on the Village of Neshi, were in dispute among his heirs some 300 years later (see above). Networks of estates and land portfolios, combined with local control of the most basic infrastructures, helped bind together the Two Lands under pharaoh:

The grants Ahmose made during the wars of reunification probably set the pattern for the feudal provision of wealth and for the military regime of the New Kingdom. Plots at home and estates in conquered territories were doubtless intended to patronize a class of colonist citizen farmers; to secure the country politically, and provide for the military, as well as to reward. However, the underlying policies relating land, service, and personnel are familiar from all periods. (Eyre 1994b:115)[6]

Not long after the New Kingdom was inaugurated by Ahmose I's defeat of the Hyksos, the size of the royal tomb once again increased by an order of magnitude over those of any large householder. It was removed far from the Theban cemeteries behind a curtain of cliffs to the Valley of the Kings where elaborately decorated, deep rock-cut tombs housed the mummies of the kings of Dynasties 18–20 who presided over the classic pharaonic culture of popular imagination.

6.5 BASIN ESCAPES AND HISTORICAL PATTERNS

Over the centuries the Nile altered its course through parts of Egypt, with an eastward shift from the area of pharaonic Memphis (Giddy 1994; Jeffreys and Tavares 1994) through Middle Egypt (Butzer 1976:33–36). According to Butzer (1976:17, 33–36) in ancient times the natural flood-plain basins would have been two to three times larger than the diked great basins of the nineteenth century A.D., but he based this estimate on the valley sector in southern Middle Egypt, just north of the Qena Bend where "meander location as well as amplitude and wave length have been subject to repeated change," and "the axis of the Nile ran far west of its present course between Akhmim and Cairo.... Relatively minor modifications are apparent in the constricted valley farther south" (Butzer 1976:35). While the local boundaries between basins, particularly those north of the Qena Bend, changed over time, the broad geomorphological configurations of the Nile Valley, such as high desert margins and *relative* valley width, probably changed very little.

As practiced in the last century (Willcocks 1889:37, 44–47) basin irrigation required social coordination over an area about the length of an Upper Egyptian nome. Butzer (1976:102–103) suggested that the nomes originated in the natural basins. The oldest nomes (Helck 1974), and the first proto-kingdoms that amalgamated in the Late Predynastic to become the Egyptian "state" (Kemp 1989:34), encompass the area of the Qena Bend, between the important sites of Abydos in the north and Hierakonpolis in the south (Figure 4(a)). One of the oldest hieroglyphic titles for a nome leader is *Adj Mer*, "He Who Cuts the Canal" (Helck 1954, 1974:51), presumably referring to opening the head of a feeder canal which might be the water supply for a series of basins about the length of the early Upper Egyptian nomes, although, in the last century, one system could have more than one feeder canal. The suggested

---

[6]I forgo the discussion here of the difference between feudal and patrimonial models, and the more appropriateness of the latter to ancient Egyptian society.

role of an ancient nome leader can be compared to that of the village shaykh, and the representative of central authority in the early nineteenth century:

> At the annual crest of the Nile the *qa'immaqam* (Turkish agent) of a village was to gather the shaykhs at the head of their peasants, to break the dikes and flood each basin in succession, "so that not a *qirat* (twenty-fourth of a feddan) remains unwatered." After its drainage, he and the shaykhs would inspect the land and designate the areas to be planted with the crops assigned to the village. (Cuno 1992:142)

Butzer (1976:103) argued that the Egyptian state arose first in the area of the Qena Bend because the smaller basins in this constricted part of the Nile Valley made them easier to organize and control, especially on the eastern side of the valley "where the basins did not require transverse dikes and where the basins filled and emptied like clockwork under natural conditions." Hurst (1952:39–40) recognized the advantages of the small east-bank southern basins in suggesting that basin irrigation began in this area when the Egyptians embanked small embayments. Smaller basins required less water to fill than large ones "since the country has a mean slope of about 1/10,800, the mean depth of water needed to cover a large basin some 15 or 20 kilometers long is much greater than that needed for a small basin some 5 kilometers long." Smaller upstream basins were more easily covered by water in low flood years. The communication required for the sequential filling and discharge operations would have been easier across the smaller basin systems.

A certain threshold of basin size and valley width may have been optimal for village territories. The narrowness of the valley in the Qena Bend and the stretch to the south allowed village territories in this region to cover the entire flood plain between river and desert in recent centuries (Figure 3(a)–(b)). This gave these territories the advantage of the variability of land and flood coverage in the convex cross section of the flood plain (Lyons 1908:27–30). On a smaller scale, taking advantage of land variability across the flood plain was the reason for long thin plots. In the narrow Aswan province during this century, inherited plots were divided in strips along their entire length between the Nile and the railway, "'from the sea to the mountain' as the villagers put it...to share in every 'foot and finger' of the land that the father has bequeathed" (Ammar 1954:24). In the narrow valley of southern Upper Egypt, the desert and the river offered secure natural borders on the west and east for village territories, while, on the north and south, series of contiguous village territories were enclosed by rocky promontories that thrust forward toward the river. A single independent basin system with its own "desert escape" (Figure 5(c)) could be enclosed within these bays of cultivable land. These advantages did not obtain to villages lying in the middle of the largest great basins north of the Qena Bend in Middle Egypt (Butzer 1976:102–103). Other villages could lie between these "island" villages and the river channel or desert (Figure 3(c)–(d); Lyons 1908:29).

Simple upstream-downstream rules also gave advantage to the Qena Bend region. Power derived from the fact that water from an upper basin system could help or threaten a lower basin system (Willcocks 1889:49). Hurst (1952:60–61) relates how, during a low flood year, a large village near the head of a canal banked off the canal where it crossed the boundary to a smaller village on its tail end. Although they lacked water, the shaykhs of the lower village were afraid to cut the banks and a higher authority had to intervene. Willcocks indicated this kind of practice could be widespread:

> The first regulators on the canals, when the regulators are less than 15 kilometers from the head, should be kept open the whole time of the [low] flood. By shutting these regulators, a few hundred extra acres are irrigated in the first basins at the expense of thousands of acres lower down. The loss of velocity, and consequently of discharge, is disastrous. More land is left unirrigated owing to the injudicious closing of these first regulators than can ever be conceived. (Willcocks 1889:332)

Not only for filling, but also for discharge, the upstream basins had advantage. During low flood "the landowners in the well-filled basins, where there is a chance of sowing broadcast, were anxious that the discharge should be delayed till the 10th October, while the landowners in the dry basins, depending for their supply on the discharge water, and those in the badly filled basins, where ploughing will generally have to be resorted to, are anxious that the discharge should begin as early as possible after the Salib, that is, after the 25th September" (Willcocks 1889).

Upstream-downstream rules must have been important in ancient periods. What Bagnall observed for the Fayum in late antiquity also applied to the Nile Valley at this and other periods:

> At the communal level, Fayum villages had a complex interdependence, growing out of the unique hydrological character of the area. Canal water, on its way from the Nile to Lake Moeris, passed by some villages before others. Those villages furthest along the canal network were dependent upon the competence of dike and canal maintenance at the earlier villages and the good will—or at least the absence of malevolence—of their neighbors. (Bagnall 1993:141)

The flip side of water sharing in low floods, is the threat from upper basins during high floods. Eyre (1994a:79) points out, "the destructive force of a very high Nile came not from the depth of the inundation, but from the massive surge of water when a dike broke." Willcocks witnessed just such a break during an unusually high flood in 1887:

The terror reigning over the whole country during a very high flood like 1887 is striking to anyone seeing a flood for the first time. On the settlement of a culvert in the Nile bank near Mit el Kholi, and the consequent first rush of water through the bank, the author witnessed a scene which must be common in Egypt on the occurrence of a serious breach, but which fortunately was rare in 1887. The news that the Nile bank had breached spread fast through the village. The villagers rushed out to the banks with their children, their cattle, and everything that they possessed. The confusion was indescribable. A very narrow bank covered with children, poultry, and household furniture. The women assembled around the local shaykh's tomb, beating their breasts, kissing the tomb, and uttering loud shrieks. And every five minutes a gang of men running into the crowd and carrying off something to close the breach. The men meanwhile were not in the least confused, but in a steady business-like manner were working at the breach and closed it in half an hour. (Willcocks 1889:187–188)

We can imagine appeals to the deity of the local temple in pharaonic times. Article 33 of the civil code stated "the proprietor who irrigates his land by means of machinery or of canals cannot compel the lower lands to receive water from his estate," while the native tribunal canal codes of the nineteenth century stated that "he who, by breaching the banks, or in any other manner, shall have caused mechanically an inundation, will be, according to the gravity of the offense, condemned to hard labor for a certain time or for life" (Willcocks 1889:292).

In addition to the upstream advantages and critical size threshold of the Qena Bend basins, the "desert escapes" (Willcocks 1889:37–38, 45–57, passim) of southern Upper Egypt must have been an important factor in the expansions of the state from the Qena Bend area. The systems of very large basins on the east bank of the broad valley of Middle Egypt drained one into another all the way to the large Koshesha Basin (number 67) at the entrance to the Fayum and just above the narrow bottle neck of valley from here to the Delta apex, the traditional capital zone. Through most of Middle Egypt only two main escapes, at the Abutig and Abu Kadiga (Figure 5(b)), drained back into the Nile channel (Willcocks 1889:48). The Nile has probably moved eastward across the Middle Egypt through ancient times, and its earlier division of the valley floor may have made for smaller diked basins than in the last century. On the other hand, if the natural basins were two or three times larger in this area, there may have been, as in the last century, very large basins near the entrance to the Fayum. If they held inundation water backed up from broad Middle Egyptian basins, interlinked by escapes from one basin system to the next then, like the Koshesha Basin, they would "hang over Lower Egypt like a dark cloud during the later half of October" (Willcocks 1889:79). Capital settlements may have been located within easy distance of this area to regulate this flood reservoir, in addition to having proximity to the Delta. In the

Archaic Period the principal northern residence, called "The White Wall," was at a choke point, then as narrow as 3 km, near Saqqara, at the northern end of the capital corridor (Jeffreys and Tavares 1994). The first residence of the Fourth Dynasty pharaoh Sneferu, under whose reign the Middle Egyptian nomes may have been consolidated (Helck 1974), was probably at the foot of his first giant pyramid at Meidum, just north of the place of the Koshesha Basin (Figure 5(b)). Soon royal residences moved back to the plain below Saqqara. Here settlement migrated and expanded east and south, following the sequence of Old Kingdom pyramids built on the high western desert, eventually developing into the capital Memphis (Giddy 1994). Just southwest of the Koshesha Basin, the House of Kheti established a residence and northern capital, Heracleopolis, in Dynasties 9–10 of the First Intermediate Period. Amenemhet I, the founder of Dynasty 12, brought the Middle Kingdom administration north to his new capital Ity-tawi ("Seizing the Two Lands"), located just north of Meidum, at the southern end of the narrow neck of Nile Valley just below the umbra of the Delta. The enormous reservoir of flood water in the area of the Koshesha Basin (Figure 5(b), number 67), recycled through the interlinked basin systems of Middle Egypt, may be what allowed later Twelfth Dynasty pharaohs to divert it through the Hawara Channel into the Fayum Basin for additional development and internal colonization.

Southern Upper Egypt had no interlinked basins "hanging over" it to the south. Rather, the valley narrows to practically nothing at Elephantine and the First Cataract (modern Aswan, Figure 5[a]), above which the flood plain of Lower Nubia was far narrower than in Egypt. In the last century the basin systems of Upper Egypt, from the Qena Bend southward, had mostly "desert escapes" which would not have changed since ancient times. The basins were small and manageable. Desert promontories framed small cradles of flood recession agriculture, possibly organized as basin systems, that could nourish the growth of large households and associations of villages. The flood-regimen independence enjoyed within the alluvial bays must have an important factor in the rise and resurrection of the Egyptian state from the area of the Qena Bend.

When the map of the Upper Egyptian nomes (Baines and Malek 1984:14) is overlaid on a map of the nineteenth-century A.D. basins (Willcocks 1889: pl. xii), the spacing of the escapes from Aswan to Asyut (southern Upper Egypt) approximates the intervals between ancient nome borders. The escapes defined "cycles of irrigation," indicated by dashed lines in Figure 5(a). The number of basins for each of Nomes 3 through 12 is greater than in the more northerly nomes of Middle Egypt, rendering the southerly nomes more patchlike. While we must keep in mind that ancient settlements may have been destroyed or obscured by the Nile's changing course (Butzer 1976:36), there is evidence to suggest that Middle Egypt, like the Delta, was a less densely populated zone of land development and internal colonization well throughout dynastic times. The highest population densities, as Butzer argued, were in the north, below the Delta apex, and in the south from the Qena Bend to the

First Cataract (Butzer 1976:102–103). The Middle Egyptian nomes were still being established, which probably involved the development of basin systems, at the beginning of the Old Kingdom (Helck 1974:199–202).

7 ANCIENT EGYPT AND CAS METAPHORS AND ANALOGIES

This outline has drawn freely from premodern structures spanning nearly five millennia. To introduce analogies with concepts from CAS studies, I have selected, emphasized, or supposed generalities over dramatic and profound changes in religion, ideology, and technology. Detailed examination of different periods is required to test the general applicability of this outline. Another challenge is to see what changes over time were truly systemic, altering the nature of the overall system, and to track the ways in which the system evolved to increasing complexity.

7.1 FRACTAL FEATURES AND MODULARITY

There are a number of ways in which the Egyptian Nile Valley system was characterized by "spatial scale-free structure" (Bak 1994:479), or by "patterns that repeat their general features over a wide range of scales" (Smolin 1997:169). At the bottom of the scale and arguably applicable to many of the ancient Near Eastern societies (Schloen 1995), a fractal pattern is described by the Patrimonial Household Model (PHM):

> Familiar household relations, born of personal ties of kinship and master-slave association, provided the 'local rules' for all social inter-action—rules that themselves emerged out of social interaction generated within the smallest viable social unit, namely the household. The applications of these rules to other social settings served to integrate many disparate households into a social whole consisting of a "fractal" hierarchy of households within households, not through the imposition of an overall structure from above, but through the on-going operation of a simple set of local rules for social interaction. (Schloen 1995:23)

Modular patterns can be recognized in the archaeological record of towns, cities, cemeteries, temples, and palaces, where Egyptian society's most basic production was centered on core houses surrounded by granaries, bakeries, breweries, butcheries, wood shops. Even at the peak of unification, when the ancient Egyptian state undertook large-scale enterprises, it organized people and produce in a series of large urban or rural estates, i.e., households, on which the occupants of smaller houses depended. The suggestion is that the planned modularity in a town like Illahun was a formalization of unplanned, natural, social modularity. Amarna shows a combination of "self organization and planning," "two complementary procedures which become effective in the development of all settlements, though to different degrees" (Schaur 1991:215). The accounts and letters of the moderately wealthy farmer, Hekanakht, in Dynasty 11 (James 1962; K. Baer 1963; Allen n.d.) designate monthly "rations" for household members; in this and other respects, "repeating on a tiny scale the precise system of ration distribution so familiar from [state] administrative texts" (Kemp 1989:240). Hekanakht certainly did not pattern family and household after the Egyptian state. Rather, the Egyptian state emerged from, was conceived as, and operated like an extended patrimonial household that could and did grow to gargantuan proportions (Bendix 1962:334), the word "pharaoh" deriving, in fact, from the Egyptian term, "Great House." At all times, there was a little bit of state in each and every "cell" of the Egyptian social system.

Households were nodes of scattered land holdings; they held portfolios of land-use rights. As a function of the hierarchical nesting of households, there were portfolios within portfolios: "a larger *rmnyt* [portfolio] might thus comprise several subordinate *rmnyt*" (Gardiner 1948:19). For example, the holdings of the great Karnak Temple of Amun contained the portfolios of each of the smaller temples (literally, "houses") and shrines that, like Lego-pieces, comprised the large temple (Gardiner 1941). Amun's portfolio was administered through provincial nome temples, whose portfolios included the Amun Temple's as well as the land holdings of other households, and each portfolio included shares and rights to the produce of the land held by controllers, cultivators, and the local peasants who actually did the labor.

If village organization in ancient Egypt corresponded to that of more recent centuries, then settlements and territories exhibited a similar pattern at several scales. The village was like a nome in miniature with its surrounding territory (Figures 3(a)–(d)) and, sometimes, portfolios of land plots held in other village territories (Lyons 1908:28, 95). Just as the villages were probably distributed throughout the territory of the nome with its capital town, so hamlets and small groups of houses (*ezbets*) were scattered about the territory of the main village. The village of recent centuries was a patrimonial state in miniature. Each of its clans, focused in different village "quarters," were governed by a shaykh. There could be 8 to 10, and as many as 20, shaykhs per village before the mid-nineteenth century (Cuno 1992:89), the whole ruled by a shaykh-of-shaykhs. Each *shiyakha* (shaykhdom) had its own agricultural domain within the village territory (Figure 2). The nome was like a state in miniature, with its surrounding territory of field complexes (*3ht*), domains or estates (*hw.t*), household properties (*pr*) and village territories (Helck 1974:49). The nome towns were to the capital or residence city as the villages were to the central nome town.

7.2 HOUSEHOLDS AND INCREASING RETURNS

The concepts of "increasing returns" and "lock-in" (Arthur 1989), may be applicable to the mechanisms of expansion and contraction evident for ancient households. The idea of increasing returns is that slight advantages due to chance or historical circumstances can, in unpredictable ways, lead to weighted advantages for the increase of products, technologies, or firms. The concept may not apply to "parts of the economy that are resource-based," like agriculture, when there are "limited amounts of fertile land" (Arthur 1990:93). However, through much of ancient Egyptian history land was plentiful, productive, and cheap; it was labor that was in short supply (K. Baer 1962). If all households were maximizers and the Egyptian economy was dominated by diminishing returns, or if households were not maximizing and the economy was one of centrally controlled redistribution, ancient Egyptian society might lack the structure, pattern, and the cycles of unity and fragmentation so evident in the long view of history. Small effects that gave initial advantages that became magnified through positive feedback could be found in the chaotic variability of the annual Nile flood (Mandelbrot and Wallis 1968, 1969), the speculation in the land rental market, and profits or losses at harvest time. Increasing returns—"them that has gets" (Waldrop 1992:17–18, 34–36)—could have amplified small choices which were made during inundation and sowing as part of risk management of random deviations in flood height and soil variations (Park 1992), but the reverse must have been true for subcritical households. If, after taking a loan, the following harvest was poor, a household would fall into greater debt or dependency; 'them that hasn't, gets worse.' The default or bankruptcy of one household must have lent to the increase of another which subsumed its resources (rights to land use, people, animals) when it took on its obligations (paying tax, rent, loans, and feeding its members). Such processes are suggested in biographies, especially during the First Intermediate Period, like that of Ankhtifi where he takes over the adjacent nome from the House Khuu, and other texts that speak of feeding and providing for the less fortunate.

Lock-in refers to nearly exclusive dominance by a firm or product in a market or domain whether or not the firm or product is the optimal fit (which may be unknowable) for given criteria. The ancient Egyptian state rose and was resurrected when one of the large households achieved lock-in in the Qena Bend region, like the House of Intef at the end of the First Intermediate Period. The next move was north across the broad valley of Middle Egypt to take the narrow neck of Nile Valley just below the Delta apex, a choke point, a "Gateway to the Delta," and the capital zone for unified rule over the Two Lands (Figure 4(b)). Lock-in of the ruling house was ideologically absolute, albeit inclusive rather than exclusive of other households.

7.3 PATCHES: MONARCHS, NOMARCHS, VILLAGES, AND BASINS

> But what, if anything, characterizes the optimum patch-size distribution? The edge of chaos; large patches freeze into poor compromises. When an intermediate optimum patch size exists, it is typically very close to a transition between the ordered and the chaotic regime. (Kauffman 1995:262)

In the First Intermediate Period Egyptologists see the nomes operating as "states in miniature" (Kemp 1989:239), each with a "self rule" garnering "resources primarily for local consumption" (Lichtheim 1988:21). Competition between small principalities for land, livestock, and suzerainty over people in the First Intermediate Period was probably similar in ways to Qena Bend conditions in the Late Predynastic (Figure 4(a)), when the state first emerged. I suggest an analogy with patch procedures in which effective control and fitness of a macrostructure is achieved by its division into smaller, self-similar, competing patches, each patch "climbing toward a fitness peak in its own landscape" while linked to its neighbors (Kauffman 1995).[7] The formative and intermediate periods may have provided conditions "on the edge of chaos" for the entire Egyptian CAS to move toward more optimal fitness peaks. Analogy is made to the phases of increased random molecular activity in physical systems at high temperatures, such as the annealing of iron in cycles of heating, cooling, and hammering. Extending the analogy to ancient Egypt over the millennia, we might recognize a level of abstraction where it could be said that through order bursts and cycles of fragmentation the pharaonic system was "annealing" itself (Kauffman 1995:251), particularly in the crucible of the Qena Bend region where the southern nomes were comprised of basins that were optimally sized for the viability of larger household firms protected within desert bays—the seed beds of statehood. Larger interlinked basins may have made the Middle Egyptian Nile Valley a patch onto itself.

The great basins comprised a set of patches within that of the nomes (Figures 5(a)–(b)). A linked series such as formed a basin system in the last century system would have filled a nome territory and certainly required cooperation between villages, resulting in village complexes. A competitive patch procedure (Kauffman 1995:245–271) might not have been played out at the scale of a basin system, which required cooperation among villages along the extent of its territory for filling and draining operations in order to derive optimal benefit from the flood wave; but it could have been played out between basin systems or nomes, as it did in the First Intermediate Period, especially by communities of the Qena Bend area that enjoyed irrigation autonomy by virtue of the desert escapes. Each great basin was organized into a smaller set of patches—the named and numbered sub-basins that comprised village territories, divided in turn between sometimes competitive (Berque 1957:48)

---

[7]Kauffman, of course, refers to the abstract fitness landscapes.

village quarters and clans (Figures 6(a) and 2). These optimized the benefits of the annual Nile flood for the greater basin and basin system. Willcocks (1889:330–331) observed that to economize water, enhance siltation, and for efficiency of discharge it is better to subdivide a large basin into smaller units. Looping a certain metaphor for abstract fitness back to a real landscape, we ask if "couplings between landscapes," and the competition between subdivisions could have effected the coevolution of the Egyptian Nile Valley system to an "ordered regime near the phase transition between order and chaos," to "the complex regime... optimal for the coordination of complex tasks..." (Kauffman 1994:109, 120).

7.4 CAS CYCLES: ORDER BURSTS, NETWORKS, AND PHASE TRANSITIONS

> The cadastral map is very much like a still photograph of the current in a river. It represents the parcels of land as they were arranged and owned at the moment that the survey was conducted. But the current is always moving, and in periods of major social upheaval and growth, a cadastral survey may freeze a scene of great turbulence. (Scott 1998:46)

We might think about long-lived dynasties and kingdoms, and the cycles of order and fragmentation of the ancient Egyptian state, in terms of the concept of "critical systems." Critical systems maintain themselves in stable configurations far from equilibrium if they are open systems with a steady flow of energy at a critical range (e.g., the Nile flood) required for self-organization (Bak 1994:479); if they are characterized by processes that cycle materials comprising the system (e.g., itinerant traders, local markets, portfolios of land ownership, usufruct, rental); and if the rates of these processes are determined by feedback mechanisms to keep the processes in relative balance (Smolin 1997:124).

Historical texts, like those of Ahmose son of Ebana, the associate of Ahmose I, founder of the New Kingdom, show the royal house in the role of catalyst, reestablishing portfolios of land rights that interlaced communities and territories from Upper to Lower Egypt. The interconnectedness of land portfolios, embedding of households, and rights to shares makes taxation look like "a tangle of individual systems of revenue collection, by which institutions and groups of officials quite literally lived off the land" (Kemp 1989:237). Ancient Egypt is not alone among premodern states in having "variable and unsystematic... absolutist taxation" (Scott 1998:23). In pharaonic tax records (Gardiner 1941), the flurry of traffic to collect harvest shares resembles a "scramble of 'wires' and logic" (Kauffman 1994:103). Yet such scrambles were probably most extensive and complex during periods of greatest political unity. Analogous to other CAS, it may have been this very "scramble" that held together a "very powerful 'antichaotic order.'"

Community markets may have cycled material culture in overlappping local networks. Such markets are indicated by tomb scenes in the pharaonic period (see above under 4.3 Local Control). They took place in the provincial towns of late antiquity (Bowman 1986:107; Bagnall 1993:85–88). In recent centuries there were periodic markets in villages, serving areas with radii in the range of 10 to 15 km (Cuno 1992:53). During times of unity such overlapping local networks may have formed cumulative links across the national territory, and from this linkage the typological conformity of material culture may have emerged. Ancient Egyptian pottery, for example, shows greatest regional variation during times of political fragmentation (Bourriau 1981). In the New Kingdom professional traders operated over broader national and even international regions, creating wider networks between houses great and small, and cycling material culture among the components of Egyptian society and its relations abroad (Kemp 1989:244, 257–259). We might look for possible feedback mechanisms that helped maintain Egypt as a critical system, with multilayered networks, local control of infrastructure, and webs of patronage.

Great dynasties and kingdoms that endured for centuries were "stable configurations" yet "far from equilibrium" because the entire system was tethered to the vagaries of the annual inundation, chaotic in the mathematical sense (Mandelbrot and Wallis 1968, 1969; Park 1992). We can, therefore, relate the periods of Egyptian stability to the metaphor of order ever poised near the edge of chaos, and hypothesize that slight that changes in the fortunes of households tied to the properties of the Nile inundation could amplify into dramatic transitions and realignments, which is in fact what we see over the long haul of ancient Egyptian history. Large-scale breakdown of the system occurred in great cycles, but the local control of infrastructure allowed the larger polity to recompose itself from its basic building blocks after the segmentation of the intermediate periods. Thus ancient Egypt may illustrate similarities to the unfolding of other complex adaptive systems which exist in "stable configurations, far from equilibrium, 'on the chaos-order axis' in a critical state near the 'edge of chaos'" (Kauffman 1994).

Critical systems undergo "phase transitions." The concept of phase transition may apply to changing alignments and networks of households, land portfolios, and harvest apportionments in cycles of breakdown and unity. Dramatic change occurs in critical systems during phase transitions, but the result of change is not a different system or infrastructure, but a different phase of the same infrastructure. Critical systems in phase transitions are characterized by fractals, patterns that are repeated at different scales. In a phase transition, there is "an enormous separation between a tiny fundamental scale and a much larger scale at which interesting phenomena are observed" (Smolin 1997:172). Nothing happens to the elementary structures at the fundamental scale when a phase transition takes place, rather there is a rearrangement of their positions and relations. To the extent that ancient Egypt conformed to the patrimonial household model, there was an enormous separation, yet a kind of fractal similarity, between the fundamental scale of a basic family and household and the state as the "great house." The metaphor of a critical system in phase transition would predict that during times of change toward political fragmentation or unity a rearrangement of household alliances and land portfolios at various scales would take place, from the state as the household of households—the dynastic lineage, to the nomes, towns, great estates, and villages. In fact we see evidence of the rise and diminution in status and prominence, or outright disappearance, of all these aggregates in the Egyptian historical and archaeological records. The metaphor also predicts "temporal scale-free behavior" (Bak 1994:470), so that the rise and collapse of the royal house at the beginning and end of dynasties and kingdoms would involve mechanisms of household expansion and contraction that were operative at smaller scales in the household hierarchy at all times.

We cannot see phase transitions in single snapshots of ancient times given by individual historical documents, such as the cadastral survey in the Wilbour Papyrus (Gardiner 1948). But Klaus Baer sensed something like a phase transition in land portfolios between the Old Kingdom and First Intermediate Period. Large estates with extensive panregional land portfolios are well attested in the tombs of Old Kingdom noblemen and officials. Baer (1963:13) noted that "it was not the practice of the Egyptians to entail estates, and in the course of several generations a large estate would normally be divided and subdivided among the children of successive heirs." Ironically, the need to endow a postmortem cult for the head of the "House of Eternity," as estates were called, by giving land to ka-servants (mortuary priests) and by division through inheritance, may have been common mechanisms which fractured the estate, yet led to the increase of other, smaller households. Such small-scale mechanisms were always operative over long time intervals, but they did not affect many large estates all at once in short time intervals. On the other hand, there could be dramatic changes on a larger political or territorial scale, but over a shorter, relatively sudden time scale, such as a political/patronage crisis by the lack of an heir to the throne after a long reign, that is, the collapse of a dynasty; hostilities between nomes; or north-south civil war. Land portfolios spanning the Two Lands were not possible if the webs of patronage were snapped and open hostilities reigned. Massive transport shocks and network disruptions would have quickly fractured many large estates, resulting in realignments of households and reconfigured land portfolios at several scales. After large-scale disruption, numerous small households would expand their holdings, first at the local level, as the claims of distant households were severed. Baer pointed to the "frequent mention of the acquisition of land in the biographies of the First Intermediate Period.... The evidence indicates rather vaguely that individual land holdings during the First Intermediate Period were somewhat smaller than those usual among the officials of the Old Kingdom..." (K. Baer 1963:14). He related these changes to the relatively small but increasing land holdings of Hekanakht, our example of a moderately wealthy farmer who lived in the early Middle Kingdom, when the state was reascendant. It may have been a time when many new portfolios were being formed, as in the case of Ahmose son of Ebana at the end of the Second Intermediate Period. In an intermediate-period phase-transition analogy, new household configurations characteristic of both phases—centralized patrimonial state and smaller dependent households—would be expected at all scales. To paraphrase a prediction: What happens is a rearrangement of the dependencies, land tenure rights, and obligations of the smallest families and households. This rearrangement took place over the whole of society, which is many orders of magnitude larger than the individual households.

8 CONCLUSION

In the 1960s a "New Archaeology" arose that sought to explain broad cultural processes in an evolutionary framework. Emile Durkheim and Karl Marx had far more influence than Max Weber on the body of archaeological theory that followed. The "organic analogy," the idea that "societies constituted integrated systems, whose institutions were interrelated like the parts of a living organism" in equilibrium (Trigger 1989:246; Harris 1968:469, 515), was widely assumed in structural-functionalist and Marxist approaches. A "superorganic" focus is inherently top-down, so much research was designed along a "highly aggregate perspective" (Epstein and Axtell 1996:16) on centrally important variables such as environment, demographics, climate, trade, and warfare—all symptomatic of a centralized mindset (Resnick 1994).

Ironically, the top-down focus on societies as systems may actually hinder the application of complex adaptive system metaphors to social complexity (to say nothing of CAS studies applied to organisms). This is because the Durkheimian-Marxist organic analogy obscured or de-emphasized the agency-structure linkage that is at the heart of Weber's interpretive understanding of social action (Kalberg 1994).

> Individuals act, for Weber, not social organisms or collectivities. Nor can social reality be adequately explained if persons are viewed as merely responding to scientific laws, the "social facts" of Durkheim, evolutionary forces, or the putative necessity for societies to fulfill certain functions. (Kalberg 1994:25)

When we reify social systems and subsystems we obscure the basic agents and the relationships between them that generate complex societies. Similarly, if we reify different "stages" of social complexity, we will have a hard time seeing how one "stage" led to another. However, if the same or similar principles of social order characterize society at all points along the continuum from centralization to fragmentation, the two poles being different phases of that order, then CAS theory and agent-based modeling offer ways of investigating the emergence of complexity through the particulars of the "local" or micro-scopic scale where we find the rules that generated the macroscopic, global order in its various cycles and phases. The CAS paradigm, therefore, has po-tential for integrating archaeological theory about culture complexity and the generation of civilizations, with Egyptology which, by virtue of its command of basic skills of 3,000 years of language, art, and history of a highly literate civilization, controls the ethnographic content of three millennia of Egyptian civilization.

When we look for the "rules" of the ancient, or, more generally, premodern Egyptian states in the details of the textual and archaeological record, they do correspond well with some of the most basic concepts underlying current theoretical models of archaic states and early social complexity. The lack of fit is not just an "etic"-"emic" issue. It is not the case that the ancient Egyp-tian system worked according to these models whether or not the supposedly analytic terms of the models can in any meaningful way be translated into ancient Egypt language. Some of these terms are so far from the texture of the empirical record that they obfuscate as much as elucidate.

First, we need to think more about the contrast "simple vs. complex" im-plicit the very use of the term "social complexity." Scott (1998) may provide an irony for archaeological theory's preoccupation with the idea, "complex so-cieties" by showing that in many ways premodern societies are more complex than modern ones. Consider land tenure. Portfolios of widely scattered land held by single households; portfolios of land usufruct rights embedded within larger portfolios of land usufruct rights; households embedded within house-holds by ties of dependency; land held in shares by several people and insti-tutions; village territories interlacing in intricate irregular patterns; cadastral surveys compiled as verbal descriptions of plots or narrative "maps"; values for standards of measurement varying from one community to another; local control of land survey and assessment for taxation by each village—all makes for a far more complex system than "modern freehold [land] tenure that is mediated through the state" (Scott 1998:35).

Or, consider the picture provided by the few letters and accounts of Hekanakht, our moderately wealthy Middle Kingdom farmer. From year to year, he could change the plots he farmed, renting to and from others, paying in cloth and oil, raising and trading bulls, saving scraps of wood, extending and collecting loans, transactions that, changing seasonally, could only have been accounted and surveyed locally, within locally well-known land areas with locally familiar names. It is hard to conceive of pharaoh's centralized bureaucracy doing a better job than the premodern state of more recent cen-turies in keeping track of the yearly deals of tens of thousands of Hekanakhts.

States exercise control through simplifications in the way they see their domain. Only by simplifying can they exist as the phase, or the state, of systems that are locally so complex as to be "illegible" to the state, yet un-derstood by members of the local community. When they intervene, states plant trees and houses in rows, rank and file, but in premodern societies state intervention could only be selective. Without modern communication and transportation technology, control over the entire Egyptian territory had to be disbursed through provincial towns, temples, villages, and households. With modern technology, state control is still, to some extent, disbursed, but people and products can be numbered, counted, and bar-coded; states can be more invasive and pervasive, imprinting simple orthogonal grids across vast landscapes to be farmed or covered by cities in place of self-organized complex systems of tillage plots and village paths.

Egyptologists sometimes try to fit evidence of ancient Nile Valley polities to models of states borrowed from general archaeological theory. When this happens it sometimes seems that the facts of ancient society go out of focus in favor of the theory. Class stratification is a basic idea in archaeological theory about early "complex society." Class is supposed to have superseded kin. Discussing Nubia, O'Connor (1991:145) cites Johnson and Earle (1987:270): "In a state, stratification is based on class, society being divided into rulers and landowners on the one hand, and producers and commoners on the other." But this class dichotomy does not fit well with the picture given by the Wilbour Papyrus of land tenure in the late New Kingdom at the height of statehood. On land theoretically owned, or at least accounted for, by gods—that is, their "houses" or temples—small plots were held by a variety of people. The plots could be inherited and transferred, so that the holders "position was, or else closely resembled, that of private owners" (Gardiner 1948:75). Plot holders included a royal prince, the Vizier, the Overseer of the Treasury, the high priests of Thebes and Heliopolis, native Egyptian and foreign military personnel, scribes, physicians, priests, stablemasters, soldiers, potters, coppersmiths, weavers, embalmers, "cultivators" cultivating for themselves, herdsmen, beekeepers, fishermen and people with the title most often translated as "slave" (Gardiner 1948:75–84, 197; O'Connor 1972:693–695). Fallers (1973:9) points out that the "stratigraphic conception of society" only appeared in the eighteenth century A.D. Nowadays class stratification may be a natural way for social scientists to view societies, but if one considers carefully the records available to Egyptologists, inequality among people of various superordinate and subordinate relationships may be found within any given household or temple at various size scales. Where should we place the literate farmer Hekanakht, or the men of his household, including his sons, who worked the land themselves (as Hekanakht probably did for his father)—with the "elite" or the "commoners"? If we misconstrue the basic agents, and reify classes and stages of our artifice, modeling traditional societies and archaic states becomes more problematic.

There is extensive literature on any one of the topics of ancient Egyptian land and water management, society, and economy and, of course, on theory of early states. Needless to say, the sources used in this paper are a small sample. One recent and lengthy work is David Warburton's *State and Economy in Ancient Egypt* (1997) which was unavailable to me when I wrote the body of this paper. While still assessing his Keynesian approach to New Kingdom economy, and his conclusion that it was a "precapitalist market economy," I note his view of how Egyptologists' assumed or implicit models of pharaonic Egypt (e.g., Pharaoh's absolute control by an invasive and pervasive central bureaucracy) are passed by way of secondary (or "popular") literature into anthropological theory about the development of early states, and how this comes back to haunt Egyptology, in that Egyptologists can be possessed to give the models priority over their own empirical domain. In the context of discussing the treatment of ancient Egypt in Service (1975), Warburton writes that "Egyptologists have been unconsciously evolving interpretations [of state development] since the birth of their science" in "published popular form" whence political historians, economists, and anthropologists borrow the interpretations "in discussions about the emergence of states and civilizations." When Egyptologists look to non-Egyptologist social theorists for models, "it is these theories which return to us as received truth. This places the fundamental basis upon which the discourse takes place at risk of being amateur at best, for our own theories return to us in an unrecognizable form..." (Warburton 1997:47).

Here I have tried to construct a preliminary outline of the most basic parts and processes of the ancient Egyptian system, looking at it explicitly through the lens of the Patrimonial Household Model (PHM) derived from Max Weber and David Schloen (1995). This approach does not assume a priori the applicability of concepts like social stratification, redistributive economy, private vs. public, a social dichotomy of elite vs. commoners, or even state and economy. Like the models comprised of these concepts, the PHM is a simplification. Much more investigation into the records of ancient Egypt is required to check the heuristic value of the PHM, or whether facts go out of focus through the lens of this model. Seeing how ancient Egypt operated through the agency of the household, at various scales, offers a view that is more compatible with analogies and metaphors borrowed from studies of CAS in other fields. The *complexity* in ancient Egypt lay not in centralized decision making, which in itself was not all that complex, but in the connections between people and households. Ancient Egypt lasted as a unique cultural system for three thousand years not because it was held together forcibly by pharaoh. The PHM brings into relief the local complexities that really generated ancient Egyptian civilization in all its phases, cycles, and evolution, and that underlay state simplifications and ideologies. The household provides a lens through which we can see the ancient Egyptian record in terms of the CAS paradigm.

ACKNOWLEDGMENTS

David Koch, The Ann and Robert H. Lurie Family Foundation, Jon Jerde, and Bruce Ludwig provided the support that made this work possible. I wish to thank them and Matthew McCauley for introducing me to many of the concepts and studies of complex systems and for supporting my participation in this workshop. I thank David Schloen for introducing me to the Patrimonial Household Model and McGuire Gibson for reading drafts of this essay.

REFERENCES

Abu al-Izz, M. S.
1971 The Landforms of Egypt. Cairo: American University in Cairo.

Allam, Shafik
1989 Some Remarks on the Trial of Mose. The Journal of Egyptian Archaeology 75:103–112.

Allen, James P.
1988a Funerary Texts and Their Meaning. *In* Mummies and Magic: The Funerary Arts of Ancient Egypt. Sue D'Auria, Peter Lacovara, and Catherine. H. Roehrig, eds. Pp. 38–49. Boston: Museum of Fine Arts.
1988b Genesis in Egypt: The Philosophy of Ancient Egyptian Creation Accounts. Yale Egyptological Studies, 2. New Haven, CT: Dept. of Near Eastern Languages and Civilizations.
n.d. The Heqa-nakht Papers, unpublished MS.

Ammar, Hamed
1954 Growing Up in an Egyptian Village: Silwa Province of Aswan. London: Routledge & Paul.

Arnold, Dorthea
1976 Wandbild und Scherbenbefund. Zur Topfertechnik der alten Ägypter vom Beginn der pharaonischen Zeit bis du den Hyksos. Mitteilungen des Deutschen Archäologischen Instituts, Abteilung Kairo 32:1–34.

Arthur, W. Brian
1989 Competing Technologies, Increasing Returns, and Lock-in by Historical Events. Economic Journal 99:116–131.
1990 Positive Feedback in the Economy. Scientific American, February, 262.2:92–99.

Asselberghs, H.
1961 Chaos en Beheersing: Documenten uit aeneolithisch Egypte. Leiden: E. J. Brill.

Assmann, Jan
1989 State and Religion in the New Kingdom. *In* Religion and Philosophy in Ancient Egypt. Yale Egyptological Studies, 3. William Kelly Simpson, ed. Pp. 55–88. New Haven, CT: Dept. of Near Eastern Languages and Civilizations.

Baer, Gabriel
1962 A History of Landownership in Modern Egypt: 1800–1950. London: Oxford University Press.

1969 Studies in the Social History of Modern Egypt. Chicago, IL: University of Chicago Press.

Baer, Klaus
1962 The Low Price of Land in Ancient Egypt. Journal of the American Research Center in Egypt 1:25–45.
1963 An Eleventh Dynasty Farmer's Letters to His Family. Journal of the American Oriental Society 83:1–19.

Bagnall, Roger S.
1993 Egypt in Late Antiquity. Princeton, NJ: Princeton University Press.

Baines, John, and Jaromír Málek
1984 Atlas of Ancient Egypt. Oxford: Phaedon.

Bak, Per
1994 Self-Organized Criticality: A Holistic View of Nature. *In* Complexity: Metaphors, Models, and Reality. George A. Cowan, David Pines, and David Meltzer, eds. Pp. 477–496. Santa Fe Institute Studies in the Sciences of Complexity Vol. XIX. Reading, MA: Addison-Wesley.

Bakir, Abd al-Mohsen
1952 Slavery in Pharaonic Egypt. Supplément aux Annales du Service des Antiquités de l'Egypte. Cairo: IFAO.

Bakker, J. I. Hans
1995 [1988] Patrimonialism, Involution, and the Agrarian Question in Java: A Weberian Analysis of Class Relations and Servile Labour. *In* State and Society: The Emergence and Development of Social Hierarchy and Political Centralization. John Gledhill, Barbara Bender, and Mogens Trolle Larsen, eds. Pp. 279–301. London: Routledge.

Barclay, Harold B.
1966 Study of an Egyptian Village Community. Studies in Islam, July–October 3.3-4:143–166, 201–226.

Bell, Lanny
1994 Mythology and Iconography of Divine Kingship in Ancient Egypt. Paper presented at Daley College, March 25.

Bendix, Reinhard
1962 Max Weber: An Intellectual Portrait. New York: Doubleday.

Berlandini, Jocelyn
1979 La Pyramide "Ruinée" de Sakkara-Nord et le roi Ikauohor-Menkaouhor. Revue d'Égyptologie 31:3–28.

Berque, Jacques
1957 Histoire Sociale d'un village égyptien au Xxe siécle. Paris: Mouton.

Blackman, Winifred S.
1927 The Fellahin of Upper Egypt. London: George G. Harrap.

Bourriau, Janine
  1981 Umm el-Ga'ab. Pottery from the Nile Valley Before the Arab Conquest. Cambridge, UK: Cambridge University Press.

Bowman, Alan K.
  1986 Egypt After the Pharaohs. Berkeley, CA: University of California Press.

Breasted, J. H.
  1906 Ancient Records of Egypt I. Chicago, IL: University of Chicago Press.

Butzer, Karl
  1976 Early Hydraulic Civilization in Egypt: A Study in Cultural Ecology. Chicago, IL: University of Chicago Press.

Cowan, George A., David Pines, and David Meltzer, eds.
  1994 Complexity: Metaphors, Models, and Reality. Santa Fe Institute Studies in the Sciences of Complexity Vol. XIX. Reading, MA: Addison-Wesley.

Cuno, Kenneth
  1992 The Pasha's Peasants: Land, Society, and Economy in Lower Egypt 1740–1858. Cambridge, UK: Cambridge University Press.

Davies, N. de Garis, and A. H. Gardiner
  1915 The Tomb of Amenemhet. Theban Tomb Series I. London: Egypt Exploration Fund.

Dodson, Aidan
  1994 From Dahshur to Dra Abu el-Naga: The Decline and Fall of the Royal Pyramid. KMT 5.3:25–39.

Durkheim, Emile
  1964 [1893] Division of Labor in Society. New York: Free Press.

Epstein, Joshua M., and Robert Axtell
  1996 Growing Artificial Societies: Social Science from the Bottom Up. Washington, DC: Brookings Institution and Cambridge, MA: MIT Press.

Eyre, Christopher J.
  1987 Work and the Organization of Work in the Old Kingdom. In Labor in the Ancient Near East. American Oriental Series, 68. M. A. Powell, ed. Pp. 167–223. New Haven, CT: American Oriental Society.
  1994a The Water Regime for Orchards and Plantations in Pharaonic Egypt. The Journal of Egyptian Archaeology 80:57–80.
  1994b Feudal Tenure and Absentee Landlords. In Grund und Boden in Altägypten. Shafik Allam, ed. Pp.107–133. Tübingen: Gulde.

Fallers, Lloyd
  1973 Inequality: Social Stratification Reconsidered. Chicago, IL: University of Chicago Press.

Frantz-Murphy, Gladys
  1986 The Agrarian Administration of Egypt from the Arabs to the Ottomans. Cairo: IFAO.

Gaballa, G. A.
1977 The Memphite Tomb of Mose. Warminster: Aris & Phillips Ltd.

Gardiner, Alan H.
1905 The Inscription of Mes: A Contribution to the Study of Egyptian Judicial Procedure. Leipzig: J. C. Hinrichs'sche Buchhandlung.
1941 Ramesside Texts Relating to the Taxation and Transport of Corn. The Journal of Egyptian Archaeology 27:19–73.
1947 Ancient Egyptian Onomastica.Oxford: Oxford University Press.
1948 The Wilbour Papyrus, Vol. II: Commentary. Oxford: Oxford University Press.

Gelb, Ignace J.
1979 Household and Family in Early Mesopotamia. In State and Temple Economy in the Ancient Near East. I. E. Lipinski, ed. Pp. 1–97. Leuven: Dept. Oriëntalistiek.

Gell-Mann, Murray
1994 Complex Adaptive Systems. In Complexity: Metaphors, Models, and Reality. George A. Cowan, David Pines, and David Meltzer, eds. Pp. 17–64. Santa Fe Institute Studies in the Sciences of Complexity Vol. XIX. Reading, MA: Addison-Wesley.

Giddy, Lisa
1994 Memphis and Saqqara During the Late Old Kingdom: Some Topographical Considerations. In Hommages à Jean Leclant. Pp. 189–200. Bibliothéque d'Étude 106/1. Catherine Berger, Giséle Clerc, and Nicolas Grimal, eds. Cairo: IFAO.

Goedicke, Hans
1984 Studies in the Hekanakhte Papers. Baltimore, MD: Halgo.

Grimal, Nicolas
1994 A History of Ancient Egypt. Ian Shaw, trans. Oxford: Blackwell.

Hardy, E. R.
1931 The Large Estates of Byzantine Egypt. New York: Columbia University Press.

Harris, M.
1968 The Rise of Anthropological Theory. New York: Thomas Y. Crowell.

Hassan, Fekri
1988 The Predynastic of Egypt. Journal of World Prehistory 2.2:135–185.
1993 Town and Village in Ancient Egypt: Ecology, Society, and Urbanization. In The Archaeology of Africa. Thurstan Shaw, Paul Sinclair, Bassey Andah, and Alex Okpoko, eds. Pp. 551–569. London and New York: Routledge.

Hawass, Zahi, and Mark Lehner
1997 Builders of the Pyramids. Archaeology 50.1:31–38.

Hayes, W. C.
1953 The Scepter of Egypt I. From the Earliest Times to the End of the Middle Kingdom. New York: Abrams.

Helck, Wolfgang
1954 Untersuchungen zu den Beamtiteln des Ägyptischen Alten Reiches. Gluckstadt: J. J. Augustin.
1957 Bemerkungen zu den Pyramidenstädten im Alten Reich. Mitteilungen des Deutschen Archäologischen Instituts, Abteilung Kairo 15:91–111.
1974 Die altägyptischen Gaue. Beihefte zum Tübinger Atlas des Vorderen Orients, Reihe B (Geisteswissenschaften) Nr. 5. Wiesbaden: L. Reichert.
1975 Wirtschaftgeschichte des alten Ägypten im 3. und 2. Jahrtausends vor Chr. Handbuch der Orientalistik 1.5. Leiden: E. J. Brill.

Hodash, S. I., and O. D. Berlev
1980 A Market Scene in the Mastaba of D̠3d̠3-m-ᶜn⌣h (Tp-m-ᶜnh). Altorientalische Forschungen 7:31–49.

Holmes, Diane L.
1993 Rise of the Nile Delta. Nature 363:402–403.

Holthoer, R.
1977 New Kingdom Pharaonic Sites: The Pottery. The Scandinavian Joint Expedition to Sudanese Nubia, vol. 5(1). Stockholm: Esselte Studium.

Holy, Ladislav
1996 Anthropological Perspectives on Kinship. London: Pluto Press.

Hughes, George R.
1952 Saite Demotic Land Leases. Studies in Ancient Oriental Civilization 28. Chicago, IL: University of Chicago Press.

Hurst, H. E.
1952 The Nile, a General Account of the River and the Utilization of Its Waters. London: Constable.

Jacquet-Gordon, Helen
1962 Les nomes des domains funéraires sous l'Ancien Empire égyptien. Bibliothéque d'Étude 34. Cairo: IFAO.

James, T. G. H.
1962 The Hekanakhte Papers and Other Early Middle Kingdom Documents. The Metropolitan Museum of Art Egyptian Expedition 19. New York: MMA.

Janssen, Jac
1978 The Early State in Ancient Egypt. In The Early State. J. M. Claessen and Peter Skalník, eds. Pp. 213–234. The Hague: Mouton.

Jeffreys, David, and Ana Tavares
1994 The Historic Landscape of Early Dynastic Memphis. Mitteilungen des Deutschen Archäologisches Instituts, Abteilung Kairo 50:143–173.

Johnson, A. W., and T. Earle
1987 The Evolution of Human Societies. Stanford, CA: Stanford University Press.

Kalberg, Stephen
1994 Max Weber's Comparative-Historical Sociology. Chicago, IL: University of Chicago Press.

Kaplony, Peter
1980 Ka. *In* Lexikon der Ägyptologie. III. Wolfgang Helck and Eberhard Otto, eds. Pp. 275–282 Wiesbaden: Harrassowitz.

Kauffman, Stuart
1994 Whispers from Carnot: The Origins of Order and Principles of Adaptation in Complex Nonequilibrium Systems. *In* Complexity: Metaphors, Models, and Reality. George A. Cowan, David Pines, and David Meltzer, eds. Pp. 83–160. Santa Fe Institute Studies in the Sciences of Complexity Vol. XIX. Reading, MA: Addison-Wesley.
1995 At Home in the Universe: The Search for the Laws of Self-Organization and Complexity. Oxford: Oxford University Press.

Kees, Hermann
1961 Ancient Egypt: A Cultural Topography. London: Faber & Faber.

Kemp, Barry J.
1972 Temple and Town in Ancient Egypt. *In* Man, Settlement, and Urbanism. Peter J. Ucko, Ruth Tringham, and G. W. Dimbleby, eds. Pp. 657–680. Cambridge, MA: Schenkman.
1983 Old Kingdom, Middle Kingdom, and Second Intermediate Period. *In* Ancient Egypt: A Social History. Bruce Trigger, Barry J. Kemp, David O'Conner, and Alan Lloyd, eds. Pp. 71–182. Cambridge: UK: Cambridge University Press.
1986 Large Middle Kingdom Granary Buildings (and the Archaeology of Administration). Zeitschrift für Ägyptische Sprache und Altertumskunde 113:120–136.
1989 Ancient Egypt: Anatomy of a Civilization. London: Routledge.

Leahy, Anthony
1985 The Libyan Period in Egypt: An Essay in Interpretation. Libyan Studies 16:51–65.

Lehner, M.
1992 Giza. *In* The Oriental Institute 1990–1991 Annual Report. William M. Sumner, ed. Pp. 19–22. Chicago: Oriental Institute.
1994 Giza. *In* The Oriental Institute 1990–1991 Annual Report. William M. Sumner, ed. Pp. 26–30.Chicago: Oriental Institute.
1996 Giza. *In* The Oriental Institute 1995–1996 Annual Report. W. M. Sumner, ed. Pp. 54–61. Chicago: Oriental Institute.

Lewin, Roger, Teresa Parker, and Birute Reine
1998 Complexity and the Organization: Beyond the Metaphor. Complexity 3(4):36–40.

Lichtheim, M.
1973 Ancient Egyptian Literature, Volume I: The Old and Middle Kingdoms. Berkeley, CA: University of California.
1988 Ancient Egyptian Autobiographies Chiefly of the Middle Kingdom: A Study and an Anthology. Orbis Biblicus et Orientalis 84. Göttingen: Vandenhoeck & Ruprecht.

Lloyd, A.
1983 The Late Period. *In* Ancient Egypt: A Social History. Bruce Trigger, Barry J. Kemp, David O'Conner and Alan Lloyd, eds. Pp. 279–348. Cambridge, UK: Cambridge University Press.
1989 Psychology and Society in the Ancient Egyptian Cult of the Dead. *In* Religion and Philosophy in Ancient Egypt. Yale Egyptological Studies, 3. William Kelly Simpson, ed. Pp. 117–133. New Haven, CT: Dept. of Near Eastern Languages and Civilizations.

Lyons, H. G.
1908 The Cadastral Survey of Egypt: 1892–1907. Cairo: National Printing Dept.

Malek, Jaromir, and Werner Forman
1986 In the Shadow of the Pyramids: Egypt During the Old Kingdom. London: Orbis.

Malinine, Michel
1953 Choix de Textes Juridiques en Hiératique "Anormal" et en Démotique (xxv–xxvii Dynasties). Paris: Bibliothéque de l'École des Hautes Études.

Mandelbrot, B. B., and J. R. Wallis
1968 Noah, Joseph, and Operational Hydrology. Water Resources Research 4(5):909–918.
1969 Some Long-term Properties of Geophysical Records. Water Resources Research 5(2):321–340.

Morowitz, Harold
1998 Metaphysics, Metaphor, Meta-metaphor, and Magic. Complexity 3(4):19–20.

Moussa, Ahmed, and Hartwig Altenmüller
1977 Das Grab des Nianchchnum und Chnumhotep. Mainz am Rhein: Philipp von Zabern.

O'Connor, David
1972 The Geography of Settlement in Egypt. *In* Man, Settlement, and Urbanism. Peter J. Ucko, Ruth Tringham, and G. W. Dimbleby, eds. Pp. 681–698. Cambridge, MA: Schenkman.

1991 Early States Along the Nubian Nile. In, Egypt and Africa: Nubia from Prehistory to Islam. W,V. Davies, ed. Pp. 145–165. London: British Museum Press.

Padgett, John F., and Christopher K. Ansell
1993 Robust Action and the Rise of the Medici, 1400–1434. American Journal of Sociology 98:1259–1319.

Park, Thomas K.
1992 Early Trends Toward Class Stratification: Chaos, Common Property, and Flood Recession Agriculture. American Anthropologist 94:90–117.

Park, Thomas K., ed.
1993 Risk and Tenure in Arid Lands: The Political Ecology of Development in the Senegal River Basin. Tucson, AZ: University of Arizona Press.

Petrie, William Matthew Flinders
1891 Illahun, Kahun, and Gurob. London: D. Nutt.

Petrie, William Matthew Flinders, Guy Brunton, and Margaret A. Murray
1923 Lahun II. London: B. Quoritch.

Polz, Daniel
1992 Bericht über die 1. Grabungskampagne in der Nekropole von Dra' Abu el-Naga/Theban-West. Mitteilungen des Deutschen Archäologischen Instituts, Abteilung Kairo 48:109–130.
1993 Bericht über die 2. und 3. Grabungskampagne in der Nekropole von Dra' Abu el-Naga/Theban-West. Mitteilungen des Deutschen Archäologischen Instituts, Abteilung Kairo 49:227–238.
1995a Excavations in Dra Abu el-Naga. Egyptian Archaeology 7:6–8.
1995b Bericht über die 4. und 5. Grabungskampagne in der Nekropole von Dra' Abu el-Naga/Theban-West. Mitteilungen des Deutschen Archäologischen Instituts, Abteilung Kairo 51:207–225.

Resnick, Mitchel
1994 Turtles, Termites, and Traffic Jams: Explorations in Massively Parallel Worlds. Cambridge, MA: MIT Press.

Richards, Alan
1982 Egypt's Agricultural Development, 1800–1980: Technical and Social Change. Boulder, CO: Westview.

Ritner, Robert
1990 The End of the Libyan Anarchy in Egypt: P. Rylands IX. cols. 11–12. Enchoria 17:101–108.

Russell, J. C.
1966 The Population of Medieval Egypt. Journal of the American Research Center in Egypt 5:69–82.

Sauneron, S.
1959 L'inscription: Pétosiris, 48. Kêmi: Revue de Philologie et d'Archéologie 15:34–35.

Schaur, Eda
1991 Non-planned Settlements: Characteristic Features, Path System, Surface Subdivision. Stuttgart: Karl Krämer.

Schenkel, Wolfgang
1965 Memphis, Herakleopolis, Theben; die Epigraphischen Zeugnisse der 7.–11. Dynastie Agyptens. Ägyptologische Abhandlungen 12. Weisbaden: Harrassowitz.
1973 Be- und Entwässerung. Lexikon der Ägyptologie I: Wolfgang Helck and Eberhard Otto, eds. Pp. 775–782. Wiesbaden: Harrassowitz.

Schloen, David
1995 The Patrimonial Household Model and the Kingdom of Ugarit. Ph.D. dissertation, Harvard University.

Scott, James C.
1998 Seeing Like a State. New Haven, CT: Yale University Press.

Service, Elman R.
1975 Origins of the State and Civilization. New York: W.W. Norton.

Sethe, Kurt
1935 Historisch-biographische Urkunden des Mittleren Reiches I. Leipzig: J. C. Hinrichs'sche.

Smolin, Lee
1997 The Life of the Cosmos. Oxford: Oxford University Press.

Southhall, A.
1988 The Segmentary State in Africa and Asia. Comparative Studies in Society and History 30:52–82.

Stadelmann, R.
1981a Die ⌣HNTIW-S, der Königsbezirk Š N PR' und die Namen der Grabanlagen der Frühzeit. Bulletin de l'Institut Française d'Archéologie Orientale 81:155–264.
1981b La Ville de Pyramide a l'Ancien Empire. Revue d'Égyptologie 33:67–77.
1985 Die Ägyptischen Pyramiden. Mainz: Philipp von Zabern.

Stanley, D. J., and A. G. Warne
1993a Nile Delta: Recent Geological Evolution and Human Impact. Science, April 30, 260:628–634.
1993b Sea Level and Initiation of Predynastic Culture in the Nile Delta. Nature, June 3, 363:435–438.

Stein, B.
1977 The Segmentary State in South Indian History. In Realm and Region in Traditional India. R. G. Fox, ed. Pp. 3–51. New Delhi: Vikas.

Trigger, B. G.
1989 A History of Archaeological Thought. Cambridge, UK: Cambridge University Press.

Turner, Victor.
    1969 The Ritual Process. New York: Aldine.

Vandier, Jacques
    1950 Mo'alla: la Tombe d'Ankhtifi et la Tombe de Sébekhotep. Bibliothéque d'Étude 18. Cairo: IFAO.

Waldrop, M. Mitchell.
    1992 Complexity: The Emerging Science at the Edge of Order and Chaos. New York: Simon and Shuster.

Warburton, David A.
    1997 State and Economy in Ancient Egypt: Fiscal Vocabulary of the New Kingdom. Orbis Biblicus et Orientalis 151. Fribourg: University Press.

Weber, Max
    1988 [1909] The Agrarian Sociology of Ancient Civilizations. R. I. Frank, trans. London: Verso.
    1978 [1956] Economy and Society: An Outline of Interpretive Sociology. Guenther Roth and Claus Wittich, eds. Berkeley, CA: University of California.

Wendorf, Fred, Angela E. Close, Romauld Schild, Krystyna Wasylikowa, Rupert A. Housley, Jack R. Harlan, and Halina Krolik
    1992 Saharan Exploitation of Plants 8,000 normalfontB.P. Nature, October 22,
    359:721–723.

Wild, Henri
    1966 Le Tombeau de Ti, Fascicle III, La Chapelle (deuxieme partie). Cairo: IFAO.

Willcocks, William
    1889 Egyptian Irrigation. London: Spon Ltd.

Wilson, Edward O.
    1998 Consilience: The Unity of Knowledge. New York: Alfred A. Knopf.

Wilson, John
    1955 Buto and Hierakonpolis in the Geography of Egypt. Journal of Near Eastern Studies 14.4:209–236.

Winlock, H. E.
    1955 Models of Daily Life in Ancient Egypt. Cambridge, MA: Harvard University.

Wittfogel, Karl
    1957 Oriental Despotism: A Comparative Study of Total Power. New Haven, CT: Yale University Press.

Yoyotte, Jean
    1959 Le bassin de Djâroukha.Kêmi: Revue de Philologie et d'Archéologie 15:23–33.

Zabkar, Louis V.

1968 A Study of the Ba Concept in Ancient Egyptian Texts. Studies in Ancient Oriental Civilizations 34. Chicago: Oriental Institute.

1973 Ba. *In* Lexikon der Ägyptologie. I. Wolfgang Helck and Eberhard Otto, eds. Pp. 588–590. Wiesbaden: Harrassowitz.

Modeling Sociality: The View from Europe

Nigel Gilbert

Social science research based on computer simulation, much of it using multiagent, multilevel models, has grown dramatically in Europe since the early 1990s. This growth has been inspired by the recent upsurge of work within computer science on distributed artificial intelligence, autonomous agents, and object-oriented systems, developing the metaphor between agents and people/social actors.

This chapter reviews some recent and influential European examples of the multiagent simulation of social phenomena. One common thread running through what is otherwise a very heterogeneous collection of studies is the description and exploration of a small number of generalized "logics" or "abstract social processes." It has been possible to investigate these through the construction of "artificial societies," and it is this methodological discovery that partly accounts for the current energy and excitement in the field of computational social simulation.

However, the assumption of a simple correspondence between agents and social actors needs to be applied with some care if it is to be useful in understanding human societies. The same epistemological puzzles and problems that sociologists have struggled over during the last hundred years can recur in trying to understand soci-

Dynamics in Human and Primate Societies, edited by T. Kohler and G. Gumerman, Oxford University Press, 1999.

eties through computer simulations. Some of these problems will be described, again with reference to current European studies.

While the use of simulation as a methodological tool is a commonplace in the natural sciences and engineering (e.g., Shannon 1975; Zeigler 1976), it still strikes many people as remarkable that one could use simulation in the social sciences. The very idea of modeling the obvious complexity, unpredictability, and autonomy of humans and their societies using computer simulation is considered by some social scientists as absurd.[1] They suggest that if simulation of social phenomena could ever be possible, it would have to involve such simplification that nothing of value could be learned. Clearly, the whole enterprise is just an excuse for playing around with computers.

While I do not agree with this view, there is a real question at the heart of many social scientists' skepticism. Is simulation a valuable tool for doing social science? If so, how could it contribute to the theoretical development of social science disciplines? In this chapter I shall try to answer this question with respect to sociology in particular. I shall focus mainly on the development of social science simulation in Europe, where there is now a widespread but reasonably cohesive community working in this area. There would be little value in merely summarizing the rather large number of studies using simulation that have been carried out or which are now in progress in Europe; collections of recent papers can be found in Conte et al. (1997), Gilbert and Conte (1995), Gilbert and Doran (1994), Hegselmann et al. (1996), Troitzsch et al. (1996). I shall, therefore, propose a particular methodological view of the role of simulation and illustrate this with a sprinkling of examples of recent research. One difficulty with my brief to review European simulation research is that ideas and the researchers themselves are no respecters of national boundaries. While there is perhaps a loose "invisible college" within Europe, it includes US citizens and others from around the world and is eager to incorporate researchers from outside Europe as quickly as possible. This must be borne in mind when considering my choice of examples.

1 HISTORY

Computer simulation in sociology had a difficult birth (Troitzsch 1997). Although there are isolated earlier examples, the first developments in social science computer simulation coincided with the first use of computers in university research in the early sixties. Almost all of the work was American, and the majority of it consisted of either discrete event simulations or simulations based on system dynamics. The former models the passage of units (for example, police cars) through queues and processes in order to predict typical

---

[1]For example, consider the debate about simulating the development of scientific knowledge summarized in Ahrweiler and Wörmann (1998).

throughput (Kolesar and Walker 1975). The latter makes use of large systems of difference equations to plot the trajectories of variables over time, for example, the world economy (e.g., the Club of Rome studies: Meadows et al. 1972; Meadows 1992). The Club of Rome simulations, in particular, made a major impact but also gave simulation a bad name as it became clear that the results depended very heavily on the specific quantitative assumptions made about the model parameters, and these assumptions were backed by rather little evidence.

This early work also suffered in another respect: it was focused on prediction, while sociology is, as a discipline, almost entirely preoccupied with understanding and explanation. This is partly due to skepticism about the possibility of making social predictions, founded both on the inherent difficulty of doing so (arguments about the indeterminacy of specific outcomes from chaotic systems are intuitively obvious to social theorists) and also the possibility, peculiar to social and economic forecasting, that the forecast itself will affect the outcome. I shall return to this point later in the chapter.

One approach which did blossom, impelled by policy concerns, is rather misleadingly called "microsimulation" (Orcutt et al. 1986; Harding 1996). This is a very specific technique, yet until recently was the only form of simulation that had any widespread recognition within European sociology. Microsimulation is based on a large random sample of a population of individuals, households or firms. Each unit is "aged" using a set of transition probabilities which determines the chance that the unit will undergo some change during the passage of a year (e.g., women within a certain age range would have a specific probability of giving birth to a child). After every unit has been aged by one year, the process is repeated for the next year, thus advancing the sample through simulated time. Aggregate statistics can be calculated and used as estimates of the future characteristics of the population. Microsimulation has become "big business" in some parts of the world (particularly Germany, Australia, and Canada) where its results have been influential in devising policy for state pension arrangements, graduate taxes, and so on.

Microsimulation has some problems that are instructive when compared with other approaches to simulation. First, it has no pretensions to explanation whatsoever: it is simply a means of predicting future fiscal distributions. Second, it treats each unit (individual, household or firm) individually: there is no attempt to model interactions between units. Third, the motivations or intentions of the units are disregarded: each unit develops from year to year only in response to the throw of the dice represented by a random number generator.

Apart from microsimulation, little was heard about simulation during the 1980s, in marked contrast to the situation in the natural sciences where simulation is now a basic methodological tool. However, in the early 1990s the situation changed radically, mainly as a result of the development of multi-agent models that offered the promise of simulating both autonomous individuals and the interactions between them. In Europe, an influential small workshop was held in 1992 in Guildford, UK (the proceedings were published as Gilbert and Doran 1994). This was the first of a series, with workshops then held in Siena, Italy (Gilbert and Conte 1995); Boca Raton, Florida; and Cortona, Italy. In the autumn of 1997, the first international conference on Computer Simulation and the Social Sciences took place (Conte et al. 1997), with a second due in Paris in 1999. The UK Economic and Social Research Council has supported a "Centre for Research on Simulation in the Social Sciences" (CRESS) to promote the use of computer simulation through training activities, review articles (to be published in a special issue of the American Behavioral Scientist in 1999), and a Web site (http://www.soc.surrey.ac.uk/research/simsoc/simsoc.html). Similar activities are developing elsewhere, for example: the Programme for Social Simulation at the Italian IP-CNR in Rome, http://pscs2.irmkant.rm.cnr.it/users/rosaria/; the SOCIONICS framework, http://www.tu-harburg.de/tbg/SPP/Start_SPp.html; and some European Union social science research projects that are using simulation as an integral part of their work. In spring 1998, an electronic journal was started in order to bring work in the area to a wider audience: the *Journal of Artificial Societies and Social Simulation,* http://www.soc.surrey.ac.uk/JASSS/.

2   REAL MECHANISMS

A theme that has informed much recent work in Europe is the idea of investigating artificial societies (a term which seems to have been invented more or less simultaneously and independently on both sides of the Atlantic by Epstein and Axtell [1996] and Gilbert and Conte [1995]). Typically, what is meant by an artificial society is a system of computer-based agents operating within a simulated environment (Doran 1997). The agents are able to perceive features of their local environment and messages from other agents (communicated through the environment), to process these perceptions (either reactively or in a goal-seeking way) and to act on the environment, including communicating with other agents. Thus, artificial societies are usually implemented within a multiagent system architecture (O'Hare and Jennings 1996).

However, the significance of the idea of an artificial society does not come from its possible implementation but from the methodological approach which it implies. An artificial society is one which has been constructed by the social scientist in order to allow computational experimentation. Artificial societies include societies as they could be and thus allow the exploration of a space of possible societies. The assumption is that there are some "laws" which apply to all societies within this space, and the task of the theorist is to identify these laws.

Thus the interest in artificial societies depends on the idea that it is possible to develop abstract theories of multiple agent systems, irrespective of whether they are implemented in a computer or are composed of biological life forms. In particular, by working in the computational domain, we are able to undertake controlled experiments that would be unethical or practically impossible on human societies. If one can formulate and test abstract social theories using computational multiple agent systems, one can then hope to transfer these to human social systems (Doran this volume).

There are some important methodological implications resulting from this approach. First, it suggests (*contra* the earlier simulation research such as system dynamics and microsimulation) that a simulation model should not start by attempting to mimic the observed social world as closely as possible. A simulation model is interesting in so much as it illuminates and or tests a social theory, not because it correctly reproduces any specific aspects of the world. This methodological precept is illustrated in many of the following examples, which share the characteristic that they are not founded on models of the "real world." Second, this approach is based on a particular epistemology: realism. According to the realist position, social scientists should be concerned with uncovering the properties of the real causal mechanisms that operate in the world. The primary focus of realist science is on the mechanisms that are thought to underlie and generate the data which are observed. Realist epistemology is a natural progenitor of computational simulations. It is a short step from developing *theoretical* models of mechanisms to developing *computational* models of mechanisms. It is also the case that simulation provides an appealing way of both formalizing and exploring realist theoretical models.

Realism is, however, a rather uncommon position in contemporary sociology, although it is enjoying a small-scale revival (e.g., Archer 1995). It directs our attention to what I have called "abstract social processes," social processes that have emergent effects when carried out by any collection of interacting agents, whether computational or human (Gilbert forthcoming; see Kontopoulos [1993] for the similar idea of "logics of social structure"). One way of regarding recent European simulation research is as an endeavor to identify and understand such abstract social processes. The following section provides some examples of what these might look like and illustrates them with thumbnail summaries of related simulation-based work.

3   SOME ABSTRACT SOCIAL PROCESSES

For each proposed abstract social process, I provide a definition, a description of its emergent features, and some examples.

3.1   HIERARCHICAL CONTROL

The process: Agents differentiate themselves through a division of labor which coordinate the actions of the rest.

The consequence: is a hierarchy, with the "managers" above the "workers." The managers are likely to acquire additional status, resources, etc. by virtue of their greater than average control. Once formed, the hierarchy is self-maintaining, since those at the bottom are restricted to local information, while those at the top have access to more global, "strategic" information that gives them an advantage.

There may be several levels to the hierarchy. The social advantage of hierarchical control (i.e., the advantage for the society as a whole) is that communication paths are much reduced (each agent communicates only with its "manager," instead of with the other $N - 1$ agents). As the number of agents increases, the number of communication paths increases only as $O(N)$, rather than $O(N^2)$. This leads to more effective communal efforts. The disadvantage of hierarchical control is that because control flows from the top of the hierarchy, local autonomy is necessarily reduced, and the structure as a whole may react too slowly to changes in its environment.

Egidi and Marengo (1995) have experimented with an "accountants model" in which the overall task is to count a large number of dollar bills. This task may be subdivided among N accountants, each of whom is located in a hierarchy at level p and can count up to k bills in a given time interval. Egidi and Marengo construct a classifier system that changes the hierarchy in order to optimize the organizational structure. They consider two versions. In one, there is just a single classifier that represents the all powerful chief executive who redesigns the whole organization in an attempt to optimize the division of labor of all the accountants (the boundedly rational centralized coordination mechanism). In the other, each accountant is represented by a classifier (the decentralized mechanism). In this version, all the accountants are able to move autonomously throughout the structure of the organization to optimize their own local performance.

In simulations in which the accountants counted their bills without error, the centralized mechanism was found to be more efficient, but if the accountants were prone to mistakes (and had to stop and recount after making an error) the decentralized system was more efficient. Such local control over a macrostructure, such as a hierarchical organization, also has been found more effective in circumstances of noise and complex constraint by Kauffman (1995) in his discussion of "patches." It aligns with some classic findings of organizational sociology, such as Burns and Stalker's (1961) distinction between mechanical (i.e., "bureaucratic") organizations, which are more efficient in static environments, and organic organizations (rather similar to the current fashion for delayered, flexible, team-based structures), which were found to be more effective in circumstances where the environment changes rapidly.

A somewhat different approach to hierarchy is found in the EOS experiments, which began with the problem of accounting for the emergence of social complexity in southwest France in the Upper Paleolithic period (Doran et al. 1994; Doran and Palmer 1995). The central issue was to examine competing archaeological theories about the change that occurred in this period from small-scale, family-based, nonhierarchical societies to larger societies differentiated by status and role. The simulation involved an environment through which agents with planning and communication abilities were able to move in search of resources, some of which required collective action to harvest. It has been found that flexibility in agents' commitment to particular hierarchies promoted the survival of the community. Again, it seems that local flexibility of decision making in changing circumstances carries with it an advantage at the level of the whole community.

3.2 SELECTION BY SIMILARITY

The process: An agent's interactions are biased toward those agents that are similar in some way to itself. The reason for the bias may be due to proximity (possibly resulting in positive feedback if those with whom the agent interacts are induced to stay in the locality), a need to learn from those who are most similar to oneself (and therefore most likely to provide a good example) or just a preference for associating with those like oneself. Agents' choices tend to be reciprocal and self-reinforcing.

The consequence: is segregation of the agents into clusters or neighborhoods, in which those in the cluster are more like each other than those outside. Once established, the clusters are resistant to external disturbances, such as "invasion" by other agents.

The most famous example of such clustering is Schelling's (1971) segregation or "tipping" model. Two recent examples are Nowak and Latané's (1993) model of dynamic social impact and my work with Chattoe on economic stratification through imitation (Chattoe and Gilbert 1997).

In Latané's theory of dynamic social impact, social impact is defined quite generally as a change in a person's subjective feelings, motives, emotions or beliefs as a result of the actions of other individuals. In an early paper, Latané (1981) proposed that social impact is proportional to the product of the number of people influencing an individual, their strength (the amount of status, persuasiveness, attractiveness, etc.), and their immediacy (e.g., their closeness in space or time to the person being influenced). Subsequently, this relationship has been shown to hold in a wide variety of situations.

Nowak and Latané (1993) have used a cellular automata model to explore the reciprocal effects of social impact within interacting populations. In one experiment, each agent is given attitudes to three different and independent binary issues, with the attitudes distributed among the individuals at random in the proportion 60:40 for those for and against each of the three issues, with no correlation between an individual's attitudes. As the simulation runs, individuals influence their neighbors, and their neighbors, in turn, influence them. If for a particular individual the sum of the influences in one direction exceeds the sum of the influences in the other, that agent changes its attitude.

Rather than being overwhelmed by the combined influence of the majority view, the minority survives, although with a reduced percentage of adherents. While individuals continually change their affiliation as a result of social impact, overall a minority of more or less constant size remains. Furthermore, the distribution of attitudes changes from the initial random pattern to being spatially clustered. That is, individuals with similar attitudes are grouped together, influencing each other to stay in line. It is the clustering that protects the minorities from extinction, because it is only the individuals on the edges of clusters that are exposed strongly to the other attitude. Although changes of attitude on the three attributes are modeled as being entirely independent at the individual level, the three attributes become correlated at the level of the population. This is because as the simulation proceeds, clusters of like-minded individuals develop. These clusters are different for each of the three attributes, but because a person in one cluster is somewhat more likely than random chance to be in another cluster (or vice versa), at the population level there will apparently be a correlation between the attitudes.

The features of the simulation that are essential for the development of clusters are: the individuals must be located in social space so that they have more influence on near neighbors than on distant strangers, attitudes must be on a discrete rather than a continuous scale (this introduces nonlinearity into the system), and the distribution of strengths in the population must not be uniform (the strong individuals protect the borders of minority clusters).

While Nowak and Latané's work models changing individual attitudes, Chattoe and Gilbert (1997) have been concerned with behavior. They are interested in understanding the processes by which people learn to budget, that is, decide how much of their income they should allocate to categories such as rent, food, leisure, travel, and so on. They have suggested that this learning could involve both individualistic calculation (based for example on a projection of likely expenditures) and social imitation of others' budgeting strategies. They have experimented with a simulation consisting of 50 agents, each receiving a regular, fixed income of an amount drawn from a uniform random distribution. Each agent decides on its pattern of spending according to a decision rule, which it evolves using a genetic algorithm on the basis of its "preferences," its experience, and its calculations of predicted income and expenditure. At the same time, unless an agent is able to satisfy all its desires through purchases, its preferences are modified by imitating the behavior of other agents who had similar expenditure patterns. The results of the simulation show that agents drift into having similar sets of preferences. At the level of the whole population, the agents can be seen to have evolved a number of "lifestyles," patterns of spending which are effective and affordable given a certain broad range of income. Because these lifestyle patterns are differentiated according to the agents' incomes, the clustering appears to have the effect of stratifying the agents into classes from poor to rich.

Chattoe and Gilbert (1997) conclude that in unstable or uncertain environments, social learning, which has the advantage of pooling many agents' separately acquired experiences, is more important than individual learning. Because agents select which others to imitate and these may reciprocate, differences between agents can become accentuated, moving the agents into separate groups or clusters. Thus the agents, although uniformly distributed over a range of income, may eventually become segregated in terms of their purchasing behavior through the process of selection by similarity.

3.3 COMPARATIVE ADVANTAGE

The process: In a competitive situation, one agent acquires a small advantage over others, and this advantage gives that agent access to better resources which can then be used to acquire still greater advantage.

The consequence: is a distribution of resources that is very unequal and which the richer agents can use to maintain their advantage.

An interesting example is Windrum and Birchenhall's (1998) model of the process of distributing research funds within the scientific community. They model a number of "research units" that are competing to acquire resources from a "research council" (e.g., the National Science Foundation in the U.S.). The units attempt to understand their "world," represented by a nonlinear function whose form is not known to the simulated agents. In order to maximize their funding, the units need to have a successful track record in developing theories (or "mental models" as Windrum and Birchenhall call them) to describe the world. In carrying out their science (i.e., exploring the shape of the function), the units formulate theories and generate data with which to test these theories. The data are used to improve the units' mental models using a procedure based on a genetic algorithm. If they are successful in finding a reasonable approximation to the function representing the world, they are more likely to receive funds from the research council on the next round.

There is a degree of positive feedback in the award of funds: high-quality research requires access to high-quality inputs, which in turn requires the ability to raise money to pay for these, and this is assisted by a track record of having previously performed high-quality work. On the other hand, good work done some time ago is less persuasive than more recent work, so the positive feedback is moderated by a discount rate which de-emphasizes older results. Nevertheless, in one typical run they report that after 80 rounds of simulated research funding, four research groups start to receive all the grants and rival researchers never again get a grant. These four groups are then able to dictate the research agenda completely, a situation which calls to mind the fact noted by Windrum and Birchenhall that half the federal science funding has gone to 33 of the 2000 U.S. higher education institutions in recent years, and more than half of U.K. science funding goes to 13 of the 100 institutions in the U.K.

Such processes of positive feedback have also been described by Arthur (1989) as "lock-in," the well-known examples being the dominance of VHS video tapes after a competitive struggle with the Beta format, and the supremacy of Microsoft operating systems. Merton (1968) named this phenomenon the Matthew Effect after the verse in the Gospel According to Saint Matthew (Matt. 12:13):

> For whosoever hath, to him shall be given and he shall have more abundance: but whosoever hath not, from him shall be taken away even that he hath.

It has been claimed that similar processes are responsible for the stability of scientific paradigms, raising a question about how paradigm shifts and "lock-outs" could ever arise. Frenken and Verbart (1998) introduce the idea of a paradigm life-cycle, arguing that a paradigm's problem-solving capacity follows a logistic curve and that converts to a paradigm are influenced primarily by the decision-making behavior of others among their own "generation" and not by the "old guard." Thus even after lock-in, there are opportunities for alternatives to arise as the paradigm matures. Some such abstract process would need to be considered for almost all instances of positive-feedback-induced lock-in if long-term change is to be modeled. Similar ideas are applied to the development of specialties in the scientific community by Gilbert (1997).

3.4 ADAPTATION AND COEVOLUTION

The process: An agent's actions change as a consequence of changes to the agent's strategy. These changes result from the adaptation of the strategy in the light of its previous success. The adaptation may be due to some type of learning (e.g., as in the training of neural networks), a process analogous to biological evolution, or a combination of these. Because agents are acting and learning in an environment affected by the actions of other agents, which are also adapting, the trajectory of adaptation may show coevolution.

The consequence: is that agents adopt patterns of activity which are path dependent. These patterns may never reach a stable equilibrium.

One example of the evolution of strategies has already been described in Chattoe and Gilbert's (1997) simulation of budgetary decision making. Another example is the work of Parisi and colleagues (Parisi et al. 1995, Pedone and Parisi 1997), which starts from the puzzle of explaining the evolution of altruistic behavior (see also Tooby and Cosmides 1997).

Evolutionary theory seems to predict that individuals will behave "selfishly" i.e., act according to their individual interest, because they will thus maximize their chances of reproduction. Altruistic behavior, which increases the chances of other agents and reduces the altruist's, would tend to disappear. Nevertheless, altruistic behavior is sometimes found, in both animal and human populations. Kin selection theory provides an explanation for the preservation of altruism toward one's own kin (altruism is preserved if the behavior increases the reproductive chances of one's kin who also carry one's own genes). Pedone and Parisi (1997) demonstrate this in a simulation in which the agents are modeled by neural networks with input units encoding the relationship of the potential receiver (sibling or nonsibling) and output units encoding the decision to be altruistic or not. The development of the population of these networks is simulated using a genetic algorithm that evolves the neural networks' weights. It is found that the networks adapt over many generations to discriminate between kin and nonkin and give to the former but not the latter.

While this solution to the problem of altruism has been known for some time for kin-directed altruism (Axelrod and Hamilton 1982), not all human altruism is between genetically related kin. Parisi et al. show that the critical factor for the maintenance of altruism is that agents are constrained to behave in a similar way. In kin-directed altruism, this is done through sharing genes, but other ways can be imagined that would apply to human groups who share a common culture, for example, the imposition of normative sanctions (Castelfranchi et al. 1998).

3.5 SECOND-ORDER EMERGENCE

The process: An oddity about the abstract social processes mentioned so far is that although one might describe them as social processes, with the implication that they are to be found in societies, there is little about them to restrict their application to human societies or, indeed, to societies of any kind. Clearly, for example, all living organisms are subject to adaptation and one can readily think of examples of the process of comparative advantage in chemical reactions. The fact that these processes seem to be very general indeed is perhaps not surprising. However, there seems to be something missing. One does not have to be anthropocentric to believe that humans are distinctively different in their capabilities from molecules, or even from ants. The abstract social processes considered above do not capture this difference.

The characteristic that most obviously differentiates humans and human societies from aggregations of molecules or from ants and ant societies, is that humans interact by means of language. Although some insects and higher mammals can be considered to possess the rudiments of a very simple language (perhaps better considered as a message distribution system than a language), humans have a well-developed linguistic capability and, in particular, are able to form concepts, that is, develop abstract generalizations from particular events and features. (The evolution of this language capacity has been studied by means of simulation: see, for example, Hurford et al. [1997] and Steels [1997].)

One of the major objectives of the approach being reviewed here is to generate, through simulation, emergent phenomena and thus to understand and explain the observable macrolevel characteristics of societies. As humans, and social scientists, we are able to observe these macrolevel characteristics and describe them through language (Gilbert 1995). For example, we might describe western societies as capitalist. "Capitalism" is a macrolevel description, not immediately observable from microlevel attributes of individual members of society. The very notion of society is a concept that describes a macrolevel phenomenon. Thus, one of the important features of human language is that it allows us to conceptualize macrolevel phenomena, to discuss them, and even to change them. A large proportion of human discourse seems to be concerned with macrolevel or emergent phenomena. Consider, for example, even the simple hunter-gatherer who talks about her family, a collective which emerges from individual actions that are biased toward particular kin and away from other kin and from nonkin.

However, the abstract social processes described above are indifferent to this human capacity to conceptualize, recognize, and react to emergent phenomena. These abstract social processes explain certain kinds of emergence, but they do not recognize that in human societies, the consequence may be that microlevel actions can change as a result of agents' recognition of and reasoning about macrolevel phenomena. For example, recognizing that a state is a democracy, a citizen may feel impelled to vote, even though from the point of view of rational choice, voting is a cost, not a benefit, and even though the agent may also realize that its individual vote counts for nothing. Moreover, the conceptualization of certain emergent phenomena in terms of language may itself have major significance: consider the impact of Marx's description of relations of production as "capitalism" for the subsequent history of the world.

Luc Steels (1995:90), quoting Baas, terms this "second order emergence," defined as: the situation in which "the system (i.e., the individual) is able to detect, amplify, and build upon emergent behavior." Theories of abstract social processes (where "social" refers to human societies) need to be able to handle the consequences of second order emergence.

4 CONCLUSION

In this chapter, I have used the excuse of reviewing European simulation research to explore a theoretical idea: that we should be trying to generalize social simulation research in order to pull out the commonalties, by identifying basic "abstract social processes." This methodological strategy has respectable antecedents in the physical and biological sciences and even within the field of complexity theory. It must be admitted, however, that it is an unusual and perhaps unpopular strategy within sociology which, at least in most of Europe, is not much enamored of approaches that strive for universal generalizations.

One reason for this is that sociology is rightly reluctant to copy the methods of the natural science, believing that its subject matter requires methods appropriate to the discipline. This is not the place to revisit what has been a long and sometimes tedious debate about the unity of the sciences, but it should be recognized that human societies do have special characteristics not found in the physical world. I have mentioned one when discussing second order emergence. Another feature of sociology that is important to recognize is the role of interpretation. Indeed, a substantial part of sociology is founded on some variety of interpretativism, taking as its goal the aim of explaining social life in terms of members' shared interpretative frameworks (Halfpenny 1997).

Members of society have a range of interpretative frameworks that can be deployed flexibly to make sense of others' actions, that is to make their actions accountable. These interpretative frameworks are shared resources that are developed and negotiated in the course of interaction, not private mental states which cause actions. Thus interpretativism moves away from a mechanistic causal analysis of action toward the idea that meanings are constitutive of action, not independent antecedents of them: meanings and concepts describing both the physical and the social world are said to be socially constructed by members of society.

Although it may seem that such a social constructivist approach is antithetical to simulation, all that is required is that the simulation should model the social processes of negotiation, interaction, and social construction posited by the approach. While some of the simulations mentioned above include elements of this, I know of no thorough-going social constructionist simulations in the literature. If simulation is to have a significant impact within sociology, it will have to develop in this direction. Otherwise, it is likely to be doomed to play a role no more important than, for example, sociobiology (the attempt to explain sociological issues solely in biological terms).

This remains the most significant challenge for using simulation to explain small-scale societies through agent-based modeling.

ACKNOWLEDGMENTS

This chapter emerges from interaction with Edmund Chattoe (many thanks), and its preparation was assisted by support from the Economic and Social Research Council and the European Union.

REFERENCES

Ahrweiler, Petra, and Stefan Wörmann
    1998 Computer Simulations in Science and Technology Studies. *In* Computer Simulations in Science and Technology Studies. P. Ahrweiler and N. Gilbert, eds. Berlin: Springer.
Archer, Margaret
    1995 Realist Social Theory: The Morphogenetic Approach. Cambridge, UK: Cambridge University Press.

Arthur, W. Brian
  1989 Competing Technologies, Increasing Returns and Lock-In by Historical Events. Economic Journal 99:116–131.

Axelrod, Robert, and W. D. Hamilton
  1982 The Evolution of Cooperation. Science 211:1390–1396.

Burns, Tom, and G. M. Stalker
  1961 The Management of Innovation. London: Tavistock.

Castelfranchi, Cristiano, Rosaria Conte, and Mario Paolucci
  1998 Normative Reputation and the Costs of Compliance. Journal of Artificial Societies and Social Simulation 1(3): http://www.soc.surrey.ac.uk/JASSS/1/3/3.html.

Chattoe, Edmund, and Nigel Gilbert
  1997 A Simulation of Adaptation Mechanisms in Budgetary Decisionmaking. In Simulating Social Phenomena. R. Conte, R. Hegselmann, and P. Terna, eds. Pp. 401–418. Berlin: Springer.

Conte, Rosaria, Rainer Hegselmann, and Pietro Terna, eds.
  1997 Simulating Social Phenomena. Berlin: Springer.

Doran, Jim
  1997 Foreknowledge in Artificial Societies. In Simulating Social Phenomena. R. Conte, R. Hegselmann, and P. Terna, eds. Pp. 457–470. Berlin: Springer.

Doran, Jim, and Mike Palmer
  1995 The EOS Project: Integrating Two Models of Palaeolithic Social Change. In Artificial Societies. N. Gilbert and R. Conte, eds. Pp. 103–125. London: UCL Press.

Doran, Jim, Mike Palmer, Nigel Gilbert, and Paul Mellars
  1994 The EOS Project: Modelling Upper Paleolithic Social Change. In Simulating Societies: The Computer Simulation of Social Phenomena. N. Gilbert and J. Doran, eds. Pp. 195–222. London: UCL Press.

Egidi, Massimo, and Luigi Marengo
  1995 Division of Labour and Social Coordination Modes: A Simple Simulation Model. In Artificial Societies: The Computer Simulation of Social Life. N. Gilbert and R. Conte, eds. Pp. 40–58. London: UCL Press.

Epstein, Joshua M., and Robert Axtell
  1996 Growing Artificial Societies: Social Science from the Bottom Up. Washington, DC: The Brookings Institution and Cambridge, MA: MIT Press.

Frenken, Koen, and Okke Verbart
  1998 Simulating Paradigm Shifts Using a Lock-In Model. In Computer Simulations in Science and Technology Studies. P. Ahrweiler and N. Gilbert, eds. Berlin: Springer.

Gilbert, Nigel
 1995 Emergence in Social Simulation. *In* Artificial Societies: The Computer Simulation of Social Life. N. Gilbert and R. Conte, eds. Pp. 144–156. London: UCL Press.
 1997 A Simulation of the Structure of Academic Science. Sociological Research Online 2(2): http://www.socresonline.org.uk/socresonline/2/1/3.html.
 Forthcoming Models, Processes and Algorithms: Towards a Simulation Toolkit. *In* Social Science Simulation: Parameter Estimation and Sensitivity Analysis. R. Suleiman, K. Troitzsch, U. Mueller, and N. Gilbert eds. Berlin: Physica.

Gilbert, Nigel, and Rosaria Conte, eds.
 1995 Artificial Societies: The Computer Simulation of Social Life. London: UCL Press.

Gilbert, Nigel, and Jim Doran, eds.
 1994 Simulating Societies: The Computer Simulation of Social Phenomena. London: UCL Press.

Halfpenny, Peter
 1997 Situating Simulation in Sociology. Sociological Research Online 2(3): http://www.soresonline.org.uk/socresonline/2/3/9.html.

Harding, Ann
 1996 Microsimulation and Public Policy. Contributions to Economic Analysis. Volume 232. Amsterdam: Elsevier North Holland.

Hegselmann, Rainer, Ulrich Mueller, and Klaus G. Troitzsch, eds.
 1996 Modelling and Simulation in the Social Sciences from the Philosophy of Science Point of View. Dordrecht: Kluwer.

Hurford, James, C. Knight, and Michael Studdert-Kennedy, eds.
 1997 Evolution of Human Language. Edinburgh: Edinburgh University Press.

Kauffman, Stuart
 1995 At Home in the Universe. Oxford: Oxford University Press.

Kolesar, Peter, and Warren Walker
 1975 A Simulation Model of Police Patrol Operations. Santa Monica, CA: RAND.

Kontopoulos, Kyriakos M.
 1993 The Logics of Social Structure. Cambridge, UK: Cambridge University Press.

Latané, Bibb
 1981 The Psychology of Social Impact. American Psychologist 36:343–356.

Meadows, Donella H.
 1992 Beyond the Limits: Global Collapse or a Sustainable Future. London: Earthscan.

Meadows, Dennis, Donella Meadows, Erich Zahn, and Peter Milling
1972 The Limits to Growth. London: Earth Island.

Merton, Robert K.
1968 The Matthew Effect in Science. Science 159(3810):56–63.

Nowak, Andrzej, and Bibb Latané
1993 Simulating the Emergence of Social Order from Individual Behaviour.
In Simulating Societies: The Computer Simulation of Social Phenomena.
N. Gilbert and J. Doran, eds. Pp. 63–84. London: UCL Press.

O'Hare, Greg, and Nick Jennings, eds.
1996 Foundations of Distributed Artificial Intelligence. London: John Wiley & Sons.

Orcutt, Guy H., Joachim Merz, and Hermann Quinke, eds.
1986 Microanalytic Simulation to Support Social and Financial Policy.
Amsterdam: North Holland.

Parisi, Domenico, Federico Cecconi, and Antonio Cerini
1995 Kin-Directed Altruism and Attachment Behaviour in an Evolving
Population of Neural Networks. *In* Artificial Societies. N. Gilbert and
R. Conte, eds. Pp. 238–251. London: UCL Press.

Pedone, Roberto, and Domenico Parisi
1997 In What Kind of Social Groups Can "Altruistic" Behaviours Evolve?
In Simulating Social Phenomena. R. Conte, R. Hegselmann, and P.
Terna, eds. Pp. 195–202. Berlin: Springer.

Schelling, Thomas C.
1971 Dynamic Models of Segregation. Journal of Mathematical Sociology
1:143–186.

Shannon, Robert E.
1975 Systems Simulation: The Art and Science. Englewood Cliffs, NJ:
Prentice-Hall.

Steels, Luc
1995 The Artificial Life Roots of Artificial Intelligence. *In* Artificial Life:
An Overview. C. Langton, ed. Cambridge, MA: MIT Press.
1997 The Synthetic Modeling of Language Origins. Evolution of Communication 1(1):1–34.

Tooby, John, and Leda Cosmides
1997 Friendship and the Banker's Paradox: Other Pathways to the Evolution of Adaptations for Altruism. *In* Evolution of Social Behaviour
Patterns in Primates and Man. W. G. Runciman, J. M. Smith, and R.
I. M. Dunbar, eds. Oxford: Oxford University Press.

Troitzsch, Klaus G.
1997 Social Science Simulation: Origins, Prospects, Purposes. *In* Simulating Social Phenomena. R. Conte, R. Hegselmann, and P. Terna, eds.
Pp. 41–54. Berlin: Springer.

Troitzsch, Klaus G., Ulrich Mueller, Nigel Gilbert, and Jim Doran
   1996 Social Science Microsimulation. Berlin: Springer.

Windrum, Paul, and Chris Birchenhall
   1998 Developing Simulation Models with Policy Relevance: The Implications of Recent UK Reforms for Emergent Scientific Disciplines. *In* Computer Simulations in Science and Technology Studies. P. Ahrweiler and N. Gilbert, eds. Berlin: Springer.

Zeigler, Bernard P.
   1976 Theory of Modeling and Simulation. New York: Wiley.

Agent-Based Modeling of Small-Scale Societies: State of the Art and Future Prospects

Henry T. Wright

1 THE HUMAN TOTALITY

The thematic social sciences—economics, political science, psychology, and so on—often privilege that aspect of human action on which they focus. Can we fruitfully understand change in human affairs from the perspectives of these disciplines? Philosophers have (for millennia), and anthropologists and geographers (for little more than a century) have said "no," and have attempted to view human phenomena as a totality. Anthropology, a holistic discipline, at its best integrates human biology, cultural anthropology or ethnology, psychological anthropology, linguistics, and archaeology. But the task is daunting, and has led often to elegant, but very specific case studies. However, new theoretical approaches to nonlinear and adaptive systems and to modeling such approaches give hope that rigorous general formulations are possible.

The Culture Group of the Santa Fe Institute focuses on long-term stability and transformation in cultural developments. In December 1997, with the support of the Wenner-Gren Foundation for Anthropological Research, a diversity of researchers gathered in Santa Fe to assess the progress of this working group and to chart future directions. We had many fruitful exchanges, ranging from general theoretical problems of cultural change and its explanation to the specifics of modeling actual cultural processes. The touchstones

Dynamics in Human and Primate Societies, edited by T. Kohler and
G. Gumerman, Oxford University Press, 1999. **373**

of the discussions were breakthroughs in the modeling of small-community networks in southwestern North America, but new developments in other theoretical and empirical areas also proved important in pointing toward future efforts. This volume presents the much discussed and revised papers from the Santa Fe meeting.

The conference began, as does this volume, with overviews of the state of the art of modeling. George Gumerman, in his preface, touches on the roots of modeling whole social and cultural systems in North America, threads of inquiry which are picked up in many chapters of this volume. Tim Kohler, in his elegant introduction argues the advantages of agent-based modeling as the resolution of several outstanding problems in traditional social science. Nigel Gilbert then provides rich insight into recent work in Europe, little known to many North American social scientists outside the modeling community. In much of this work, theoretical principles are investigated in the context of "artificial societies," paralleling those developed by Epstein and Axtell (1996) and Axelrod (1997). The work through which Gilbert guides us deals with important sociological issues and merits wider dissemination and further work. Examples of studies of the effectiveness of hierarchies, the formation of groups, the problem of resource allocation, coevolution and the problem of altruism, and the emergence and impact of reflective cultural understandings are introduced. Gilbert's final plea for an actor-based modeling approach to processes of interaction, negotiation, and social construction will, we are certain, find willing advocates.

2 BACK TO THE BASICS: MODELING NONHUMAN PRIMATE SOCIETIES

Some workshop participants are working on nonhuman primate foraging, but their work has clear relevance to human foraging as well. For primate societies, the theoretical issues of representing the nonlinear relations between group decisions about foraging for resources and individual decisions about relations with other individuals are cogently discussed in the first section of the chapter by René te Boekhorst and Charlotte Hemelrijk (Zurich). They use variants of MIRROR worlds as a platform for modeling behaviors similar to those of chimpanzees and orang-utans. Using minimal rules of immediate perception and action, these models generate behaviors often taken to indicate cognized evaluation of social histories and the outcomes of possible action. Though these models of "artificial apes" are intended primarily to point to problems with extant perspectives and to areas for new research, they do have consequences that are testable with the primates and comparative studies of primate organization. If these consequences are sustained, these models will present a challenge to proponents of cognitive and functional approaches.

For their impressive modeling of forager strategies in environments with different types of resource "patch" size and spacing types, paralleling environments such as savanna, gallery forest, and mixed environments, John Pepper and Barbara Smuts (Michigan) use a Swarm platform. This enables them to deal with a focal issue in evolutionary ecology, that of individual versus group selection, and the relation of kin selection to other forms of group selection. Their model represents foraging activities and the consequences of such foraging for different kinds of "altruistic" traits. In particular, they investigate selection for foragers' self-restraint in the use of plants (which involved some deficits to some restrained individuals, defined as "weak altruism"), and for forager's use of alarm calls (which involved consistent deficits to all alarm givers, defined as "strong altruism"). The results are often surprising, not the least because they show that patchy resource distributions can be a context in which traits beneficial to groups but not to individuals can be favored, even in the absence of kin selection. The model as it stands focuses only on foraging of stationary plant foods, and not on scavenging and hunting and issues of developing communication systems could be added in future phases of development. Also, the model at present does not represent predation of the foragers by other animals. Nonetheless, though deliberately highly simplified, Pepper and Smut's results have relevance to phenomena ranging from the virulence of viruses, to the feeding strategies of fish, to the depredations of modern fishing fleets.

The theoretical problem of generating simple systems of meaning and communication in the adaptive contexts faced by nonhuman primate foragers, was presented by Brian Skyrms (Cal Tech). Skyrms proposes to model primate communication as a sender-receiver games with Nash equilibria. In this context, he shows how more complex language communication functions might be generated from simpler calls, given only the logical connectors "or" and "not," with a simple selective model. The next step would be to embed Skyrms' insights in an extant foraging model, such as those which are the bases of the two chapters discussed above. It would be instructive to see what kind of "languages" primate agents might be able to generate under different interactive rules and different environmental structures.

3 MODELING HUMAN FORAGERS

Those modeling specific foraging and food processing behaviors among human foragers have several decades of experience, and they have used a variety of approaches. An influential early effort was that of Hans Martin Wobst (1972) who modeled the types of networks which arose when gendered agents in a uniform communication space sought mates according to different types of alliance rules. The model established the minimal population sizes needed to sustain various systems and other interesting limits, but it made no attempt to represent the full range of forager activities and generated few testable implications. The first effort to represent foraging activities on a realistic landscape and to generate a tool distribution which could be tested with the observed archaeological distribution of tools discarded on the landscape was the modeling of foragers in the Reese River Valley of Utah by David Hurst Thomas (1972). These early efforts were not pursued in part because of limitations in both hardware and programming platforms, and in part because of the inability of these early models to deal with emergent phenomena. It is only recently that efforts to evolve foraging groups in a more dynamic manner have succeeded. The Oaxaca modeling project of Kent Flannery (Michigan) and Robert Reynolds (Wayne) (1989) presented in the book *Guila Naquitz* details the plant-gathering activities of one group of virtual early Holocene foragers in central Oaxaca in southern Mexico, during successive wet seasons. The input data was derived by Flannery through his decade-long study of modern Zapotec wild plant collectors by Flannery. The model was the first by anthropologists that used a full "agent-based" perspective in a simulation of an actual environment, thus generating empirically testable implications. At the Santa Fe gathering, Reynolds expanded on this work, discussing how he represents cultural knowledge, building on programmed learning models and on John Holland's concept of genetic algorithms. He described the "cultural algorithms," representing codified knowledge, a kind of "schemata" in Murray Gell-Mann's (1994) terms, which could encode selected plant knowledge. Through the success or failure of agents' actions based on such knowledge, new strategies could be generated over time. Under specified adaptive circumstances, their model can even generate emergent patterns of plant manipulation leading toward domestication, well beyond normal forager repertoires.

In this volume, Mark Lake (University College, London) illustrates such an approach with a modeling of Mesolithic hunter-gatherers in early Holocene Scotland, using the MAGICAL software written in C++. This model allows representation of resource spaces and series of conceptual spaces in the multiple layers of a Geographical Information System, each conceptual space associated with a specific actor, who makes decisions in terms of simple rules called into action by an "event scheduler" and the information in his particular conceptual space and forages across the simulated resource landscapes, leaving discarded stone tools where various activities are performed. A comparison of the tool distributions predicted by a series of runs of this model, realized in terms of foraging for hazelnuts on the Hebridean island of Islay, with observed stone tool distributions recorded by Steven Mithen and Lake in the Southern Hebrides Mesolithic Project (Mithen and Lake 1996) revealed a limited fit. However, other simulations with other resources or combinations of resources, will be needed to fully explore the utility of the model.

In the future, it is certain that foragers will be the object of increasingly sophisticated modeling efforts. There is a rich ethnographic record of both forager lifeways and archaeological site formation for Southern Africa (Yellen 1977; Lee 1993), central Australia (Meggitt 1962; Gould 1980; Myers 1986), and the North American Arctic (Balik 1970; Binford 1978). However, much of the long and diverse archaeological record of foragers is represented by the attenuated evidence of stone tools and bones, and if we are to have any human understanding of the 99% of proto-cultural and cultural evolution in which foragers predominated, model-building will be essential.

4 MODELING SMALL AUTONOMOUS FARMING COMMUNITIES

The North American Southwest provides a unique arena for developing and evaluating models of small-scale societies. Over the last century, the peoples of living native communities of the Southwest have taught anthropologists about many aspect of their lives in this beautiful, varied, and often difficult land. Archaeologists, geoarchaeologists, paleoethnobotanists, dendrochronologists, and many other scientists have constructed the most precise chronological sequences, environmental reconstructions, and cultural understandings available for any prehistoric peoples anywhere. We know that between A.D. 200 and 1500, the ancestral Pueblo peoples took up more varied and often more intensive horticulture and more effective long-term food storage techniques, developed larger settlements and created more elaborate ceremonial systems. However, they periodically faced crises, abandoning large areas of the Southwest. Explicating growth, transformation, and crisis is a challenge to theorists and model-builders. The construction of model cultures is proving to be an increasingly fruitful vehicle for representing the complicated interrelations between many variables. In the previous year's meeting of the Culture Group, earlier versions of two models of the settlement systems of Puebloan ancestors had provided promising representations of settlement distributions and changes during the growth phase, but had failed to show expected responses to environmental crises. However, this year we learned that changes in agricultural variables suggested by several of participants in the 1996 SFI Culture Group meeting, had produced responses to environmental change within the range of the archaeologically documented responses.

A model in which the agents are households which can grow, fission, make adaptive choices about production and storage, make choices to move, and, in the worst circumstances, fail, should generate the periodic aggregation to larger communities followed by abandonment that archaeologists can document in Puebloan prehistory. A team of anthropologists George Gumerman and Jeff Dean (Arizona) with model-builders Josh Epstein, Rob Axtell, and Miles Parker (Brookings Institution), Stephen McCarroll, a neurophysiologist (University of California at San Francisco), and Alan Swedlund, an anthropological demographer (UMass, Amherst), has designed such an artificial world, usign the Brookings Sugarscape platform. It represents households in the relatively small Long House Valley in Northeastern Arizona from A.D. 400 to 1400. The households respond to known annual rainfall and potential garden productivity, documented by dendroclimatology and geomorphology, resulting in settlement trajectories recorded in time-sequence graphs and in maps comparable to those produced by archaeological survey. The presentation in this volume begins with a most instructive detailing of the complicated procedures and compromises that must be undertaken to evaluate soil responses to changing moisture and possible maize productivities on these soils. This is particularly difficult to do for Long House Valley because it has not been a focus of agriculture—either Puebloan or European—in recent centuries, and there are no local productivity studies that might be used as proxies for past production. This problem, however, is pragmatically resolved, and the second part of the presentation discusses the results, showing impressive broad parallels between the simulated and actual patterns of the utilization of types of land, changing ratios of large to small settlements, and pattern of population change, including a marked decline in the late thirteenth century. As one expects with a baseline model, there are interesting divergences as well. First, the predicted population in general is higher than that which archaeology documents in Long House Valley. Some adjustment of model parameters representing production, storage and consumption or some additional subsystems better representing social decisions about child raising may be warranted. Second, the model generates an early phase of aggregation into larger settlements during the 11th centuries, when in fact settlements remain relatively small. Since aggregation engenders conflicts and social mechanisms for conflict resolution within and between communities must evolve, it is not surprising that aggregation did not arise the first time in which agricultural circumstance might have made it advantageous. Third, even in the dire environmental circumstances of the late thirteenth century, the model households, unlike the archaeologically documented households, do not leave Long House Valley. Since the existence of large settlements and higher order clusters of settlements assures us that larger social groupings did exist, it is possible that at some point the valley could not support such large aggregations and complete abandonment was the only option. Though it was not the intent of the baseline "Artificial Anasazi" simulation to deal with social and symbolic issues, its results provide a clear challenge to future modeling efforts.

What, however, would be the trajectory of adaptation in a larger and less homogenous geographical space? The team of Tim Kohler (WSU) and Carla Van West (Statistical Research Inc.) has been developing a model of adaptive choices by households in the Mesa Verde region of southwestern Colorado from A.D. 900 to 1300. They have represented this system with a Swarm-based model designed by Eric Carr and Jim Kresl (WSU) with the help of Chris Langton (SFI and Swarm Corp.) which represents household decision making in a manner similar to that of the Brookings model, also resulting in a sequence of both maps and time-series graphs. By choice, their model represents household demography and the cultivation of maize and beans in great detail, and has not yet dealt with other aspects of production such as collected and hunted wild foods or with other aspects of social life such as kinship, broader alliances, and warfare. In their presentation in this volume, they provide both an overview of previous work and an update on recent accomplishments. First, they explicate how they built detailed representations of the landforms and the soil and water resources of the landscape on which their virtual early Puebloans live. Second, the object structure, the parameters, and some key variables of the model are laid out in succinct tabular form. Finally, the results of recent runs with a variety of parameters are presented. The most striking and important results are that—whereas previous runs of the model with more generous crop productivities and no consideration of water accessibility had departed far from the known population trajectories and patterns of site location—those current runs with lower productivities (which one would expect with prehistoric maize varieties) and more stringent water requirements show impressive parallels to known trajectories and patterns. It is the case that neither the process of settlement aggregation (of great interest to anthropologists in the southwest) and the general abandonment of the region in the late thirteenth century (of great interest to everyone who lives in this semi-arid region) are replicated by the model, but, as with the Long House Valley simulation, this is to be expected with a baseline construction which focuses on household population and food production. One of the strengths of those approaches is that they serve as null models that point fairly precisely to what additional behaviors need to be introduced to achieve results similar to those seen in the world. In this case, the team next proposes to introduce reciprocal exchange and a paleo-hydrological reconstruction into the model to see if this will lead to settlement aggregation.

The models developed for the Southwest and evaluated with the rich data of Puebloan life will be useful in understanding similar developments in other areas of the world. For example, archaeologists and dendrochronologists in the lake district of southern Germany, Switzerland, and adjacent France (Gregg 1988; Schweingruber 1988; Whittle 1996) are building as rich a record of village societies of the fourth and third millennia normalfontB.C. as that from the Southwest, amenable to the same approaches. These communities, however, have the added resource of the lakes and of domestic animals, whose interactions with plant cultivation and with the broader natural environment, present new challenges to agent-based modeling. In another area of the world, 40 years of detailed anthropological research in highland New Guinea, both western (Pospisil 1958, 1963; Hieder 1970) and eastern (Rappaport 1968; Strathern 1971; Weissner 1998) have built a very detailed (albeit temporally shorter) record which can be modeled in the same terms used for southwestern communities. These New Guinea cases have detailed information on warfare, and will be particularly useful in testing ideas about the role of competition within networks of farming villages. Also, new work has just begun on the modeling of household decision making in the early Holocene environments of the first farming villages in the hills of the Levant during the ninth and eight millennia normalfontB.C., work which will no doubt profit from some of the approaches developed in mesoamerica and the American Southwest.

Do we model farming communities which are parts of larger, more complex socio-political entities in ways similar to those used for village networks? We are fortunate to have an overview of the successful effort to use a modeling approach to understand agricultural decision making in the traditional kingdoms of Bali by John Stephen Lansing (Arizona). The development of stable strategies and regional patterns was investigated in "Priests and Programmers," (1991) his challenging treatment with James Kremer (USC), of the self-management of irrigation systems on the Indonesian island of Bali, using a model with a LISP-based programming language. Lansing's chapter in this volume provides a useful retrospective on his Balinese study, and also summarizes recently collected data from the actual deliberations of Balinese rice-growing cooperatives, which shows that the factors of water cost and pests are indeed taken into account in the way implied by the model. Those who argue that models and artificial societies cannot or need not be tested with empirical work might profitably give this careful attention. Lansing's chapter ends with a discussion of other areas—for example, Central Asian regions where nomadic pastoralists have long flourished—where both scholars and planners could profitably use a similar approach.

5 MODELING INCREASING SOCIAL AND POLITICAL COMPLEXITY

Other workshop participants are working on more complex cultural developments. In considering the problems of evolving socio-political hierarchy, the workshop was fortunate to benefit from Jim Doran's (Essex, UK) years of experience in the modeling of "artificial societies." After a brief overview of the history of both agent-based modeling and agent-based artificial societies (to which he has made signal contribution), and a brief sketch of the use of the EOS model to represent hunter-gatherer societies, Doran turns to innovations that will be needed if we are to model "trajectories to complexity." In particular, he outlines the ways in which the newly developed SCENARIO-3 model represents both collective beliefs and misbeliefs and the emotional dynamics that would bring such (mis-) beliefs into play in social action, creating patterns similar to coalitions, "cults," and ideologies of rank. Finally, Doran turns to methodological problems with artificial societies, including the biases introduced by extant programming technology, by our own cultural preconceptions, and by our concepts of "agents," "causality," and "time." He urges us to question the ultimate objectives of modeling, and to consider using models to generate "sets of all trajectories" or "world histories" and look at the properties of these sets, rather than seek to replicate a single trajectory that happened to occur.

As our experience with simpler autonomous communities of foragers and farmers shows, we are able to question assumptions about hierarchical societies, and to generate new approaches, in the context of specific modeling efforts. A study of the marriage strategies of chiefs in the Tongan archipelago by Cathy Small (Northern Arizona) is a challenging example. Tongan chiefdoms evolved over three millennia in an extensive central Pacific archipelago centered on the larger raised coral island of Tongatapu. Small, working with a C^+ language, was able to represent in the "TongaSim" model, the interaction of up to fifty chiefly lineages, each member of which acquires a rank status based upon the status of their parents, their ability, and support from other allied kin groups. This status is important in chiefly marriage, and the status of the couple is a primary contribution to the status of their children. Wealth in the form of tribute from people of lower rank does not affect status, but it does enter into the calculus of marriage and thus the future status of children. By iterating the model, beginning with ten lineages with identical initial states, under different marriage restrictions, Small is able to generate the effects of these rules on the range of status variation, measured in various ways, and on the stability of chiefly rank, showing that some proposals by anthropologists about the stability engendered by chiefly marriage alliances are robust under many conditions, while other proposals account for the ethnographic data only under very specific conditions. Perhaps most importantly, "TongaSim" is able to generate emergent patterns of class structure from a context of ranked lineages, a process which must have occurred as Polynesian chiefdoms evolved, but which has not hitherto fore been satisfactorily explicated. It must be emphasized, that at present "TongaSim" is a baseline model for considering the effects of chiefly marriage in social change. Small is now working to embed this model in a representation of Tongan geographical space, one which will allow chiefly marriage and status changes to be linked to conflict and warfare. Such an expanded model will no doubt generate new and surprising results.

An effort to directly confront the role of conflict in the formation of more differentiated cultural systems is presented by Robert Reynolds (Wayne). Reynolds is concerned with the specific case of the trajectory toward complex chiefdoms and the first states in the Valley of Oaxaca in southern Mexico, the object of much important research recently summarized by Joyce Marcus and Kent Flannery (1994). Reynolds wishes to model processes of social violence that have not existed for more than two millennia, so there is no modern Oaxacan analog which might indicate the rules by which these ancient wars were planned and fought. So Reynolds first task is to construct such rules. He begins this effort with a consideration of cross-cultural variations in warfare in chiefdoms, and then turns to the inductive analysis of archaeological settlement pattern evidence from Oaxaca to establish a possible decision sequence for settlement location in the prestate and early state periods in the Valley of Oaxaca. His next step will be to embed the indicated decision making process for the early periods in a framework which experiments with possible evolutionary choices and develop more effective decision making for offense and defense. The results will be of great interest to theorists interested in state origins.

Our final formal presentation at the 1997 "Culture Group" meeting in Santa Fe, and the final chapter in this volume, was by Mark Lehner (Chicago, AERA Inc.), an Egyptologist very active in new research on Egyptian civilization during the third millennium normalfontB.C. Giving us some sense of the richness of extant knowledge of Old and Middle Kingdom lifeways, Lehner makes a plea for complexity-based perspectives, but warns of the dangers of moving too fast into the modeling of complex cultural phenomena such as the entire Nile Valley in the Pyramid Age. Instead, he outlines an approach to modeling a single subsystem, a portion of a "nome" or province.

Without doubt, modeling trajectories toward more complex cultural systems is not yet as developed as the modeling of the trajectories of small scale societies. This is attributable in part to sheer scale—to the number of variables and actors involved—in such systems. It is also the case, that in contrast to the great range of well-studied smaller primate, forager, and village societies which allow more control of individual historical contingencies, there are relatively few "civilizations" that modelers might use as target cases, and each is the object of a vast and seemingly arcane scholarly apparatus. Nonetheless, progress is being made with both the construction of "artificial complex societies" and the specific modeling Old and New World examples. Following Doran's counsel, assumptions about the constitution of actors and cultural logics must be constantly questioned. It is also important to not only continue to work on the specific modeling of elements in Mesoamerican and Egyptian developments, but to begin work on the well-documented Andean, Mesopotamian, and Far Eastern developments. The potential of modeling the building blocks of the early civilizations for which we often have complementary textual and archaeological data—the Egyptian nome, the Mesopotamian city (Wright 1969; Adams 1981), the Italian city state (Ansell and Padgett 1993) the Chinese province (Skinner 1977), the Aztec city-state (Hodge 1984)—will undoubtedly be recognized and pursued actively in the coming decade, laying the foundations for the study of the broader cycles as networks of smaller states are integrated into regional states and transregional empires only to break down into smaller polities (Fienman and Marcus 1998).

6   FRUITFUL DIRECTIONS IN THEORY BUILDING

Beyond the specifics of models and case studies, there are several general areas of endeavor that must be addressed.

- First, on the theoretical plane, we must have better ways to represent cultural knowledge in such a way that simulated actors can revise this knowledge and evolve new classifications and strategies. Lake's "knowledge sets," Doran's "belief systems," and Reynolds' "cultural algorithms" represent promising avenues, but they are only beginnings.
- Second, on a purely practical plane, we must make the results of modeling efforts more widely available. Book length publication with summaries of codes and graphical and tabular presentation of many simulations are planned. We must also make available more detailed presentations—the

actual code in which working models are written, and the examples of repeated runs under different conditions—so that other researchers can build on extant work. This raises practical problems but these may be overcome with dissemination via the Web and other means.

- Third, on the pedagogical plane, we must provide both intellectual and material support for students with the ability to carry these endeavors in new directions.

Our meeting ended with a wide-ranging discussion of what the Culture Group should do to nurture the promising initiatives generated during our workshop. While there is much interest in Swarm as a platform for future efforts—particularly as it grows to incorporate new capacities for representing such symbolic elements as "individual knowledge sets," "cultural algorithms," and "(mis-) belief"—there was also discussion of the value of continuing to model with a diversity of platforms. It was also generally agreed that a key challenge will be to learn to "grow" more complex systems from the simpler ones which had been a primary focus in this workshop. This, however, should not be the focus only of archeologists in the Culture Group. Primatologists such as te Boekhorst, Hemelrijk, Pepper, and Smuts; linguists and philosophers such as Skyrms; computer scientists such as Doran and Reynolds sociologists such as Gilbert; and cultural anthropologists such as Lansing and Small are making vital contributions to the understanding of concepts, including "culture" itself, as well as to the specifics of both simpler and more complex case studies. What the eventual results of these various efforts at agent-based modeling will be is unknown. Recognizing the complexity of the human career, we can surely agree that the Culture Group members—as well as the Santa Fe Institute community as a whole—have an obligation to contribute to the building of modes of responding to future global changes, not simply in the natural environment, but in the total human environment.

REFERENCES

Adams, Robert McCormick
    1981 Heartland of Cities. Chicago, IL: University of Chicago.

Ansell, Christopher K. and John F. Padgett
    1993 Robust Action and the Rise of the Medici, 1400–1434. American Journal of Sociology 98:1259–1319.

Axelrod, Robert
    1997 The Complexity of Cooperation: Agent-Based Models of Competition and Collaboration. Princeton, NJ: Princeton University Press.

Balikçi, Asen
    1970 The Netsilik Eskimo. Garden City, NY: Natural History Press.

Binford, Lewis
1978 Nunamiut Ethnoarchaeology. New York: Academic Press

Epstein, Joshua, and Robert Axtell
1996 Growing Artificial Ssocieties: Social Science from the Bottom Up. Washington, DC: Brookings Institution Press and Cambridge, MA: MIT Press.

Feinman, Gary M., and Joyce Marcus
1998 Archaic States. Santa Fe, NM: School of American Research.

Flannery, Kent V.
1986 Archaic Foraging and Early Agriculture in Oaxaca, Mexico. Kent V. Flannery, ed. Orlando, FL: Academic Press.

Gell-Mann, Murray
1994 The Quark and the Jaguar: Adventures in the Simple and the Complex. New York: W. H. Freeman.

Gould, Richard A.
1980 Living Archaeology. Cambridge, UK; New York: Cambridge University Press.

Gregg, Susan A.
1988 Foragers and Farmers: Population Interaction and Agricultural Expansion in Prehistoric Europe. Chicago, IL: University of Chicago Press.

Hieder, Karl G.
1970 The Dugum Dani: A Papuan Culture in the Highlands of West New Guinea. Chicago: Aldine.

Hodge, Mary G.
1984 Aztec City States. Ann Arbor: Museum of Anthropology, University of Michigan.

Lansing, John Stephen
1991 Priests and Programmers: Technologies of Power in the Engineered Landscape of Bali. Princeton, NJ: Princeton University Press.

Lee, Richard B.
1993 The Dobe Ju/'hoansi. Fort Worth, TX: Harcourt Brace College.

Marcus, Joyce, and Kent Flannery
1994 Zapotec Civilization. Orlando, FL: Academic Press.

Meggitt, Mervyn J.
1962 Desert People. A Study of the Walbiri Aborigines of Central Australia. Sydney: Angus and Robertson

Mithen, Steven J., and Mark W. Lake
1996 The Southern Hebrides Mesolithic Project: Reconstructing Mesolithic Settlement in Western Scotland. In The Early Prehistory of Scotland. T. Pollard and A. Morrison, eds. Pp. 123–151. Edinburgh: Edinburgh University Press.

Myers, Fred R.
    1986 Pintupi Country, Pintupi Self: Sentiment, Place, and Politics Among Western Desert Aborigines. Washington, DC: Smithsonian Institution Press; Canberra: Australian Institute of Aboriginal Studies.

Pospisil, Leopold
    1958 Kapauku Papuans and Their Law. New Haven, CT: Department of Anthropology, Yale University.
    1963 Kapauku Papuan Economy. New Haven, CT: Department of Anthropology: Yale University.

Rappaport, Roy A.
    1968 Pigs for the Ancestors; Ritual in the Ecology of a New Guinea People. New Haven, CT: Yale University Press.

Reynolds, Robert
    1987 Archaic Foraging and Early Agriculture in Oaxaca, Mexico. Kent V. Flannery, ed. Orlando, FL: Academic Press.

Schweingruber, Fritz Hans
    1988 Tree Rings: Basics and Applications of Dendrochronology. Dordrecht; Boston: D. Reidel.

Skinner, G. William
    1977 The City in Late Imperial China. Stanford, CA: Stanford University Press.

Strathern, Andrew
    1971 The Rope of Moka: Big Men and Ceremonial Exchange in Mount Hagen, New Guinea. Cambridge, UK: Cambridge University Press.

Thomas, David H.
    1972 A Computer Simulation Model of Great Basin Shoshonean Subsistence and Settlement Patterns. In Models in Archaeology. David Clarke, ed. London: Methuen.

Weissner, Pauline J.
    1998 Historical Vines. Bloomington: University of Indiana.

Whittle, A. W. R.
    1996 Europe in the Neolithic: The Creation of New Worlds. Cambridge, NY: Cambridge University Press.

Wobst, H. Martin
    1972 Boundary Conditions for Paleolithic Social Systems. A Simulation Approach. American Antiquity 39(2):147–178.

Wright, Henry T.
    1969 The Administration of Rural Production in an Early Mesopotamian Town. Ann Arbor: Museum of Anthropology, University of Michigan.

Yellen, John
    1977 Archaeological Approaches to the Present: Models for Reconstructing the Past. New York: Academic Press.

Index

A

abstract social processes, 359, 366
  examples of, 359–366
adaptation, 7, 8
  evolving, 8
  trajectory of, 378
  See also coadaptation
adaptation and coevolution models,
    364–365
  learning in, 364
adaptive agents, 208, 214, 216
adaptive dynamics, 87
adaptive landscapes, 220
agency, 109, 208
agent design, 93
  anthropomorphic beliefs, 94
  beliefs, 94–95
  egocentric vs. sociocentric, 101
  genotypes, 111, 126–129
  in MAGICAL software, 110–114
  memes, 100
  subagents, 102
agent-based artificial societies, 89–91,
    102
  abilities of, 91

advantages of, 98
cultural preconceptions in, 99–100
EOS project, 91, 92, 360, 380
hunter-gatherer project, 92–93
methodological problems, 98–102
role of emotions in, 95–98
SCENARIO-3, 95, 380
agent-based modeling, 1, 2, 9–11, 13,
    14, 48, 52, 71, 89–90, 102, 139,
    179, 180, 225, 383
  advantages of, 48, 69, 201–202, 374
  agent design in, 110
  of ancient Egyptian society, 276
  challenges to, 379
  emergence in, 69
  usefulness of, 12
  vs. agent-based artificial societies,
    98
  vs. equation-based modeling, 69–71
  See also abstract social processes
agent-based models. *See* adaptation
    and coevolution models; Artifici-
    al Anasazi model; Bali model;
    comparative advantage models;
    computer simulations; hierarchi-